City of Heavenly Tranquility

JASPER BECKER

City of Heavenly Tranquility
Beijing in the History of China

OXFORD
UNIVERSITY PRESS

2008

OXFORD
UNIVERSITY PRESS

Oxford University Press, Inc., publishes works that further
Oxford University's objective of excellence
in research, scholarship, and education.

Oxford   New York
Auckland   Cape Town   Dar es Salaam   Hong Kong   Karachi
Kuala Lumpur   Madrid   Melbourne   Mexico City   Nairobi
New Delhi   Shanghai   Taipei   Toronto
With offices in
Argentina   Austria   Brazil   Chile   Czech Republic   France   Greece
Guatemala   Hungary   Italy   Japan   Poland   Portugal   Singapore
South Korea   Switzerland   Thailand   Turkey   Ukraine   Vietnam

Published by Oxford University Press, Inc.
198 Madison Avenue, New York, New York 10016

www.oup.com

Oxford is a registered trademark of Oxford University Press

Library of Congress Cataloging-in-Publication Data
Becker, Jasper.
City of heavenly tranquility : Beijing in the history of China / Jasper Becker.
p. cm.
Includes bibliographical references and index.
ISBN 978-0-19-530997-3
1. Beijing (China)—History.   2. China—History.
3. Beijing (China)—Description and travel.   I. Title.
DS795.3.B43 1998
951'.156—dc22   2008004249

1 3 5 7 9 8 6 4 2

Printed in the United States of America
on acid-free paper

Contents

List of Illustrations   vii
Acknowledgements   ix
Maps   x

Introduction   1

1 In Xanadu   15

2 The Emperor of Perpetual Happiness   33

3 Madness in the Forbidden City   45

4 On the Wild Wall   61

5 The Ming Tombs   71

6 In the Garden of Perfect Brightness   80

7 The Broken Bowl Tea House   96

8 The Last Sanctuary of the Unknown and
Marvellous   109

9 The Last Manchus   127

10 In Search of the Golden Flower   148

11 Mao and Beijing   162

12 History in Stone   183

13 The Strange Death of Lao She   196

14 The Red Maid's Tale   219

15 The Last Playboy of Beijing   236

16 The Protectress of Flowers   255

17 Radiant City of the Future   276

CONTENTS

18 Destroy!   301
19 The Eternal Present   314

    Bibliography   327
    Sources and Notes   334
    Index   345

List of Illustrations

1a. The doors of a traditional courtyard home marked for demolition (courtesy of Li Jiang Shu)

1b. Demolished hutong, 2006 (courtesy of Li Jiang Shu)

2a. The city gate at Xuanwumen before it was torn down (courtesy of Li Jiang Shu)

2b. The old city wall and gate at Xizhimen (courtesy of Li Jiang Shu)

3a. Emperor Wan Li's tomb at Ding Ling (reproduced by permission of Panda Books)

3b. The site of the tomb at Ding Ling at the time of its excavation (reproduced by permission of Panda Books)

4a. The Bell Tower and Drum Tower in the 1950s (courtesy of Li Jiang Shu)

4b. Old Beijing city wall (courtesy of Li Jiang Shu)

5. Cai Jinhua, the Golden Flower concubine (courtesy of Li Jiang Shu)

6. The Fragrant Concubine, Xiang Fei, as painted by Castiglione (courtesy of Li Jiang Shu)

7a. The home of Cai Jinhua, as it appears today (photograph by Li Jiang Shu)

7b. Xiang Fei's tower (courtesy of Li Jiang Shu)

8. Wang Shixiang (courtesy of Wang Shixiang)

9. Sun Yaoting, the last living eunuch of China (courtesy of Virginia Stibbs Anami)

10. Liang Sicheng and Lin Huiyin on the Temple of Heaven, 1936 (reproduced by permission of the University of Pennsylvania Press)

11. Liang Sicheng as a member of the United Nations Board of Design, with Le Corbusier and Oscar Niemeyer, New York, 1947 (courtesy of the United Nations)

12. Liang Sicheng's proposal to make Beijing's city walls and gates into a continuous public park (reproduced by permission of the University of Pennsylvania Press)

13. A market in Beijing in the late nineteenth century (courtesy of Li Jiang Shu)

14. *Shifting to Fight in North Shaanxi* by Shi Lu (reproduced by kind permission of Mrs Min Lisheng)

15. The Chinese Central Television building (courtesy of Charles Pope)

Acknowledgements

I wish to thank Andy Roche, T. C. Tang, Antoaneta Becker, Gail Pirkis, Wang Zhenru, Dmitri Napara, Hong Ying and Orville Schell, and the Society of Authors for a grant.

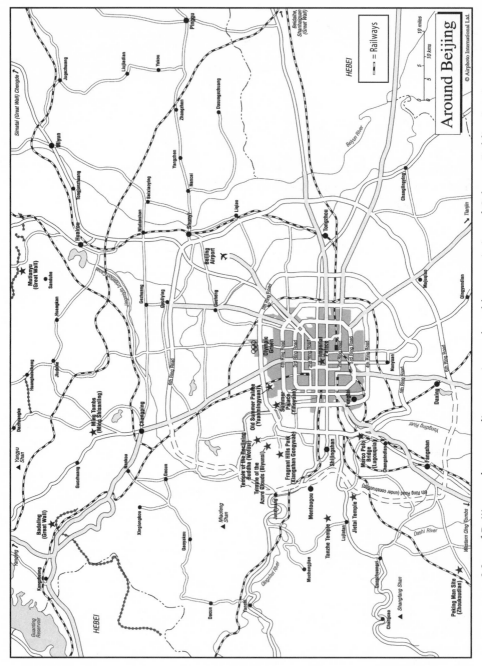

Map of Beijing and surrounding area (reproduced by permission of Odyssey Publications)

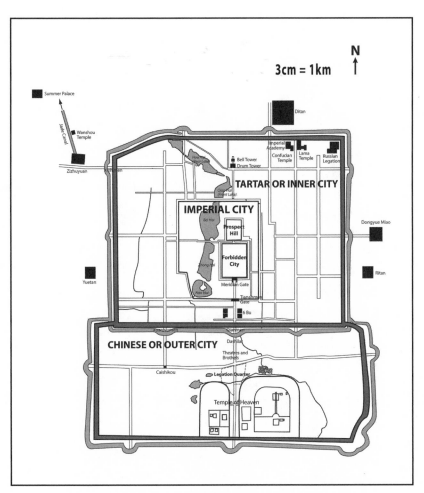

The four cities of Beijing in the Ming and Qing dynasties
(map by ZhuYu)

Introduction

The sales agent had a brisk, confident air, a pageboy haircut, and a demure matching skirt and jacket ensemble. She carried an executive leather case containing a sheaf of gold and purple folders with publicity brochures neatly tucked inside. Sunshine had chosen her own English name, she explained, because she thought it made a good impression.

'This outstanding property', began Sunshine Xiao in a loud and commanding voice, 'is an advanced, modern high-quality project which offers European royal elegance . . . In 1999 it was chosen as one of the ten landmark buildings that comprise Beijing's Central Standard Index and in 2000 it was also awarded the first Beijing "Best Property Honour" . . . We call this development the Middle Sea Purple Gold Garden. It contains the most luxurious waterside apartments in western Beijing. A world-famous international architect designed it with the motto "The harmony of man with nature".'

I moved over to a large plate-glass window and down below could see the white marble of the Grand Canal, built in the Yuan dynasty some eight hundred years ago, and fed by water piped from the ancient Jade Spring. Many emperors, reclining in a dragon barge, en route to the Summer Palace, had come this way. A little further along stood the red walls of the Wanshou Temple, or Longevity Temple, built in the sixteenth century by a powerful eunuch during the reign of the Ming emperor Wan Li. It became a favourite stopping place for the great Qing emperor Qianlong (1711–99), a prolific poet. In one of the 20,000 verses he composed during his sixty-year reign, he describes stopping at the lock for a few moments one year, and noting the green fragrant crops growing on either side of the canal, before celebrating the sixtieth birthday of his revered mother, a devout Buddhist, in the temple.

Beijing was once full of corners like this where you could at once find traces from more than a thousand years of history all jumbled together. A few years earlier, there were no high-rises, but intimate courtyard houses, built in the Ming dynasty and occupied by families whose ancestors had manned the lock with its dragonhead water-spouts in earlier dynasties. They had erected a small shrine to burn joss sticks and call on the protection of the Dragon King who controls all waters. Now the courtyard houses had been bulldozed and the last rubble was being cleared away. The canal had been cleaned up, widened and straightened out. In just ten years, starting in 1997, millions of Beijingers were relocated and scenes like this became everyday sights. You passed by a well-loved spot to find the houses and people gone, and a fenced-off construction site with workers scattered about a gigantic hole in the ground, the foundation pit for the mega-construction that would be ready a year later.

'From here you can see the Summer Palace and the Fragrant Hills,' Sunshine Xiao explained after she came and stood next to me at the window. That day the city was blanketed in whitish smog that reached up to the twentieth floor. For a week the low monsoon clouds of July had trapped the dust and the exhaust from the millions of cars, creating a thick haze. 'The serene natural beauty and historical back-ground has won praise all around the city,' she continued, undaunted. The rumble from the traffic was muted by the thick double windows, but above the low hum of the air conditioners, which made the sticky temperatures bearable, piped classical music was playing.

'Vivaldi?' I asked.

'If you look from the master bedroom, you can see why this is called the royal residence of Silicon Valley,' she pressed on, and led me up the circular stairs past a bathroom with a black-and-white marble jacuzzi set into the floor. The master bedroom had a handsome teak bed, a modern version of a medieval four-poster. Waking up, one would see through the bedroom window an assortment of square tower blocks that made up the Zhongguancun high-technology park.

'Nearby are shopping malls at Chengxiang, Shuanguan, and Dang-dai which offer a leisurely shopping experience. And also Beijing

University, Qinghua University, numerous renowned high schools with cultural surroundings that are best for children's growth,' she said. After we walked around the two smaller bedrooms, inspected the kitchen, the maid's alcove and the downstairs toilet, she gave a garbled explanation of the decor: 'The whole design fully exudes a modern European style. We have boldly adopted the European three stages of architectural influence: neo-classical columns, French windows with light green double-decked glass and high-class sprayed aluminum alloy frames. The walls are made with bricks that imitate marble.'

Heavy brocade curtains in purple cascaded down to the floor. Fussily gilded rococo chairs stood ordered round a dark-polished dining table. The coffee table was made of glass that had been tinted ocean blue and rimmed with bronze; it stood on a white pile carpet. A curvy chaise longue stood opposite two stiff eighteenth-century chairs with curved wooden legs that ended in talons and balls. On the walls hung some familiar prints in large frames – Constable's *Hay Wain*, Giacometti's *Women of Venice* – and on another wall, above a fake fireplace, was a Rubens, or so I assumed from the fleshy, half-naked women.

'I like it, especially the fake fireplace. This is real luxury,' I said politely.

'Later, I will show you the landscaped garden, the vast lawn, the children's playground, the European fountains, the stylish sculptures, the beautiful flowers, and the underground car park,' she said.

'Is there a club house, satellite TV?'

'Ownership of a penthouse duplex automatically entitles you to membership of the prestigious private club where there is everything you need to relax your body and soul – indoor swimming pool, tennis court, golf simulators, sauna, gym, karaoke room and café,' she finished. 'Oh, we also provide twenty-four-hour security.'

'How much is it?' She nodded and we sat opposite each other on two rococo chairs. Sunshine pulled a large calculator from her leather briefcase and punched out some figures. At 16,000 yuan per square metre, a duplex penthouse with a high ceiling cost 3.2 million yuan or US$ 400,000. The original residents had been made to accept compensation of a mere 2,000 yuan per square metre. Sunshine told me that the developers could help arrange a 60 per cent mortgage from the China Agricultural Development Bank.

'And who are the developers, exactly?'

Sunshine said the site was owned by China Overseas Holdings Ltd., a Hong Kong company, and showed me an organization chart. It revealed very little.

'I heard the main investor is a Singaporean businessman, is that right?'

Sunshine looked uncertain, and a small frown creased her fine arched eyebrows. 'Hong Kong, I think.'

'I heard that he set up the project and got the land with the help of a powerful Chinese partner,' I said, mentioning the name of a 'princeling', the son of a senior leader on the Communist Party's Standing Committee, the most powerful political body in the country.

Sunshine laughed the way Chinese do when they are nervous or frightened. 'This project has always enjoyed the highest support from the authorities. We are nearly sold out so you must decide soon.'

Then we went down in the lift and stood in the lobby for a moment. 'And what was here before this was built?' Sunshine looked non-plussed again and said, 'I don't think there was anything here before. I don't remember anyone living here before.'

When the developers had arrived the two hundred or so families had put up a spirited resistance led by Mr Zhao, a thin intense man with a bony head. When the bulldozers arrived to demolish Zhao's house, he sat on the roof wearing a cotton-padded coat covered in Mao badges. 'He just sat there like a madman singing these songs from the Cultural Revolution. When the bulldozers came to his house, he just stood on the roof and refused to come down,' said Carl Crook, an Englishman who had built himself a fine house nearby made from traditional grey bricks, the only Chinese-style house left. Zhao's ances-tors had arrived in Beijing in the 1630s and he had a record of their lives going back eleven generations. One ancestor had joined the court by becoming a eunuch, although he was by then already 17. His elder brother had found a job as a lock-keeper. The eunuch amassed enough wealth to build a family temple, the Dou Mu Gong, but that and the cemetery, including the eunuch's tomb and those of generations of his ancestors, had been buried, destroyed by the builders of the Middle

Sea Purple Gold Garden. The cemetery now lay beneath a newly widened road and, in place of the courtyard house, a rock garden had been laid out to prettify the apartment block. Zhao still possessed title deeds stamped by the seal of the Emperor Tianqi (r. 1621–7), but that counted for nothing when the residents took their case to the courts. The low compensation paid out to them meant that they could no longer afford to live inside the city. They had scattered to new developments built in distant satellite cities, far from Beijing. One day I tracked Zhao and his family down and found them living in a village of migrant workers near the Jade Fountain.

I never made an offer for the apartment, foolishly, perhaps, because prices soon tripled. The apartments sold quickly, mostly to newcomers from the provinces who had made good in the boom or to wealthy overseas Chinese. The rebuilding of Beijing certainly spawned corruption on a grand scale but the historical fabric of China's greatest city, capital to five dynasties, was torn up not just in search of quick profits. The Chinese had set out to substitute replicas of Western culture for their great cultural heritage, leaving the only traditional house left in this neighbourhood belonging to a foreigner. Why did this happen? How did the rich and storied past of a great city – and an ancient civilization – disappear almost overnight?

This book sets out, first, to tell the history of this ancient, magical city, to reveal what made Beijing so delightfully unique and then to explore why the city was devastated in the name of modernity. The story of Beijing is therefore about China's drive to become modern, international – to Westernize, if you like, the greatest non-Western civilization in history. The modernization project began in the final decades of imperial China in the late nineteenth century. Many intellectuals wanted to jettison everything, even uniquely Chinese inventions like written characters and chopsticks, in order to 'save' China. People adopted Western customs for every stage of life, from childhood to marriage and even death. Most readers know something of the Cultural Revolution (1966–76), the most extreme phase of this rejection of the Chinese inheritance when Red Guards ran riot, destroying anything that smacked of the 'old society'. Yet the desire to remake China was not abandoned by Mao's successors. On the contrary, by bulldozing the old capital Chinese leaders feel they are fulfilling a long-standing goal. The architectural destruction of Beijing was accelerated by a decision taken in the summer of 1997 by a handful of China's top leaders, without any public debate. To be fair, the Chinese are not alone in East Asia in wishing to destroy their heritage like this; other Confucian nations like Korea and Vietnam share the same desire. At times the modernization project is a story of benevolent change, but it is also a tale of absolute leaders who have not hesitated to use extreme violence to tear up Chinese culture by its roots.

The book is also about the lives of people like Mr Zhao, who bravely resisted this change, who thought it was not necessary for China to discard everything in the pursuit of modernization. It opens with the story of the Mongols, followed by an account of the struggle of the Manchus and other minorities to preserve their identity. Later chapters tell the stories of painters, writers, historians, architects and collectors who risked everything to salvage something from this apocalypse: Liang Sicheng who battled to protect Beijing's architecture, another about Madame Sun who tried to keep the traditions of Peking Opera alive, or Wang Shixiang who rescued the tradition of Chinese furniture-making.

The foundations of Chinese history run deeper in Beijing than almost anywhere. Beijing has been a capital of China since the ninth century and it was massively rebuilt by the Ming dynasty in the fourteenth and early fifteenth centuries. By 1949 it had survived almost unscathed for five centuries. At a time when London, Paris or Rome boasted only a few hundred thousand inhabitants, Beijing had a million, secured behind magnificent walls that enclosed 25 square miles. For many centuries it was the pivot of empires that were larger and more populous than even the European colonial empires created in the nineteenth century. This was the home of the Son of Heaven, to whom the peoples of Asia came to deliver tribute and homage, century after century. Its importance to the history of Asia is unique.

Beijing was not just an administrative centre but a military headquarters, protected by the Ming Great Wall, the single largest fortification ever built by man. It was a great religious centre, the largest in Asia, filled with thousands of temples where a bewildering number of deities were once worshipped. Over the centuries more than twenty-four emperors assembled in their palaces a magnificent collection of art, the richest in Asia. Beijing attracted the best artisans, scholars, calligraphers, writers and painters, and it still does. The Chinese like to say that they are the heirs to five thousand years of civilization, and Beijing's art and architecture represent some of the best of a grand tradition. Asia has preserved other beautiful cities: Kyoto in Japan, Hue in Vietnam, the ruins of Angkor Wat in Cambodia or Borobudur in Indonesia, but only Beijing encompasses so many different cultures, religions and races. China has other ancient cities like Xi'an and until recently had hundreds of other walled cities, but in Beijing the two great strands of Asian history are united: the settled urban civilization, steeped in Confucianism, and the wilder world of the Huns, the Mongols, the Manchus and other nomadic peoples who roamed the steppes of Asia, living in felt tents.

As a foreigner, I felt privileged to be able to live here. In 1985 when I first arrived China had been largely closed to the outside world for thirty-five years. Since 1949 only a small number of foreigners, mostly diplomats and a few fellow travellers, had been granted residency rights. Beijing had become an unknown city. The most recent history of the city had been written in the 1930s, on the eve of the Japanese occupation, and Beijing, its rulers and its citizens seemed mysterious and remote. They lived behind high walls and any contact was fraught with danger and suspicion. It was hard to understand what had happened in the recent past, when Chairman Mao Zedong lived half-mad, surrounded by his books, on an island in Zhongnanhai, next to the Forbidden City. It was not much easier trying to interpret the political manoeuvrings of his successors as they tried to move China into a new age. Some Beijingers were energized by the prospect of change but the city itself seemed steeped in a hopeless lethargy. Although the city was dirty and neglected, it fired my imagination. This dusty old curiosity shop was filled with cobwebbed trapdoors that could open and drop you into another age. And it was coming alive again after a long sleep. The army moved out of the palaces and temples it had occupied since the 1960s, allowing everyone to visit places that had been hidden or forbidden. Beijingers could be seen again singing old opera arias, walking their caged songbirds, gawking at temple fairs and sampling traditional dishes from street peddlers. And what stories people began to tell of the strange and often terrifying events they had witnessed!

Beijing seemed eternal. Armies had marched in and trooped out: British, French, German, Japanese, Boxers, warlords, Nationalists, Communists, Red Guards and, in 1989, the People's Liberation Army tanks. They all had had their entrances and exits but none had really dared change Beijing itself. A glittering cast of khans, emperors, concubines, eunuchs, imperialists, generals, kings, seers, poets and thinkers of every sort had had their moment and then departed. Their stories added to the pool of memory, briefly stirring the surface waters, then settling to the bottom like autumn leaves. This rich sediment had nourished a tolerant, unhurried, cultured people with a knowing humorous smile.

Mao (1893–1976) had always intended to destroy old Beijing and tear down its city walls but his rule was too chaotic and he died before realizing this goal of creating a new capital for the new China. Beijing began to change rapidly some twenty years later. The destructive haste was justified when Beijing won the right to host the 2008 Summer Olympics. China will have spent US$ 40 billion on preparing for this event, while Athens spent just US$ 12 billion to host the 2004 Games. By contrast, in 2006 the central government spent just US$ 560 million on health care for the 900 million rural Chinese, the vast majority of whom have annual incomes of less than US$ 360, far below the US$ 2 a day international benchmark for poverty set by the World Bank. I doubt if there is another example in history of an ancient capital being destroyed and rebuilt so thoroughly and in such a short space of time. Even Baron Haussmann left 40 per cent of nineteenth-century Paris untouched, but Beijing will be left with less than 5 per cent of its buildings. Out of the 25 square miles of largely Ming buildings that had survived into the 1950s, just three have been kept. If one subtracts the sizeable grounds of the Forbidden City, just twenty-five historical areas have been left as isolated pockets in a new city that sprawls over 50 square miles. In 1980 there were still 6,100 old streets, known as hutongs, but only a few hundred have been preserved, plus a handful of temples and courtyard houses. Only one of the forty-four princely palaces, or *wangfu*, will be saved in its entirety.

Setting to one side the Olympic Games bill, the rebuilding of Beijing must count as one of the greatest building projects ever undertaken and the cost probably exceeds US$ 200 billion. The government has shipped in millions of peasant labourers who have worked round the clock on seven thousand building sites. It summarily evicted some three million of its inhabitants, destroying communities that had lived in one place for hundreds of years. The state ruthlessly trampled over existing planning regulations, tore up ancient property rights and overturned all earlier urban development plans, which were designed to preserve the old city, the *Gu Du*. It is true that Beijing needed to build a new infrastructure and to rehouse millions of people, but it would have been quite feasible to spare the historic centre of Beijing and build a modern city around it.

Imagine the outcry if, in less than a decade, London underwent a similar transformation. If the West End, Notting Hill, Knightsbridge, Holland Park and the City of London were to be levelled and replaced by giant residential and commercial blocks. If every landmark – Oxford Street, Piccadilly, Pall Mall, Regent Street, Covent Garden, the courtyards of the Temple, the alleys of Soho – were to disappear at once. Imagine the outcry if in less than a decade New York underwent a similar transformation. If Wall Street, Central Park, Greenwich Village, SoHo, the Bronx, the Upper East Side were to be levelled and replaced by giant new residential towers and commercial office blocks. If every landmark – Times Square, Madison Square Gardens, Radio City – were to disappear at once. Consider also the political context in which the fate of old Beijing was sealed. It started in earnest eight years after the uprising of 1989, when the Tiananmen Democracy Movement brought over a million Beijingers into the streets. President Jiang Zemin had no popular mandate to rule, let alone to order Beijing's demolition. He had arrived from Shanghai in 1989, entering the city in secret in an unmarked car, after Zhao Ziyang, secretary general of the Communist Party, had been illegally ousted by a cabal of retired party veterans who also sent in tanks to crush the student-led protests of 1989. Jiang Zemin stayed in power only by ruthlessly crushing dissent, sometimes by withdrawing liberties adopted in the 1980s and by instituting a 'strike hard' crackdown on crime in which an estimated ten thousand people were executed every year after only summary trials. In this pervasive climate of fear, no one dared oppose the party's will, even when that will included ordering the destruction of old Beijing.

The 1989 protests came close to ringing down the curtain on Chinese Communist Party rule, just as democracy protests in Eastern Europe brought down the Soviet empire. For three heady months the city was gripped by feelings of freedom the likes of which I had never imagined possible. One evening I heard live rock and roll music on the streets and turned around to see a grinning group of students with drums and guitars, on a flat-bed Liberation truck, driving around the city for the hell of it. On the seventieth anniversary of the May Fourth demonstrations of 1919, over a million people took to the streets. Like those earlier modernizing movements, this rebellion was led by students from the top universities, like Qinghua, and supported by their professors. It seemed that the country could wrest power from the dictators who had controlled China's fate since the 1920s. People hoped that the protests would lead to political liberalization and the restoration of normal civic freedoms.

Deng Xiaoping and the other elderly ex-generals who still ran the army feared the party would be swept from power. Deng ordered in the People's Liberation Army, which became the only army in recent history to carry out a full-scale military assault on Beijing. Like a flash of lightning at night, the raid briefly exposed the real nature of the Communist Party's grip on Beijing. Suddenly one could see how much of the city belonged to the secret police and the military. One became aware of all the unmarked and unnamed compounds guarded by soldiers with rifles and bayonets: the shops, hospitals and apartments reserved for the party or the security forces; the disguised entrances to the network of tunnels and bunkers; the CCTV cameras and the army of human informers that kept the population under surveillance.

Since 1949 the party leaders had lived in their capital like guerrilla fighters who worked at night in the shadows, still fearful and distrustful of the residents. The assault against peaceful protesters on Tiananmen Square provoked a reckless rage from Beijing's citizens that astonished me and even the rulers. For the first time, the population was determined to resist the occupier, something they had never dared against the Japanese, the warlords or the eight foreign armies who in

1900 entered the city to relieve the besieged foreign legations. The People's Liberation Army attacked the city from four directions and people came out of their shabby tenements and hutongs to fight the tanks with whatever came to hand. Ordinary citizens stood defiantly in their vests on the overpasses of the second ring road where the great city gates had once stood. When night fell the darkness was lit up by tracer bullets, exploding artillery shells and flames from burning buses and tanks. At the entrance to the Nationalities Hotel, built by the Soviets in the 1950s, people came out, seized weapons from the soldiers and beat them to death. All over the city I saw abandoned and burning Armoured Personnel Carriers (APCs). Along the western approach, a whole convoy of dozens of tanks, trucks and APCs was stopped and somehow defeated. Elsewhere people strung the bodies of dead soldiers from pedestrian crossings. Thousands of people died before the People's Liberation Army established martial law across the city.

In some ways the destruction of old Beijing and the eviction of its residents can be considered a collective punishment visited on a population that had dared to rebel. As Bertolt Brecht famously wrote after the 1953 uprising in East Berlin: 'The people had failed the government, it was necessary for the government to dissolve the people and elect a new people.' After 1998 the original population was exiled from the centre and dispersed to satellite towns around Beijing. As the city was rebuilt, the bulldozers demolished the physical memories of earlier protests, such as the Democracy Wall in Xidan, where after Chairman Mao's death thousands of citizens put up long, impassioned posters demanding change and the restoration of their political and civil rights; the prison where Democracy Wall Movement activists were imprisoned; all the places associated with the Cultural Revolution, like the headquarters of the Cultural Revolution in Beijing (now a department store), buildings associated with the Republican government, and institutions like China's first parliament are largely gone.

In the new Beijing, the state only protected sites that served to bolster its own self-justifying version of history. So this book is not just about Beijing and the fate of Chinese culture, but is also an attempt to give an account of Chinese history, a history that is even now being rewritten. Even as they were destroying Beijing's past, the authorities boasted of how they were spending US$ 800 million on preserving its traditional culture. This was conservation only in the sense that the British Museum preserves such dead cultures as the Assyrians or ancient Egyptians. Beijing was China's history set in stone. Once Beijing was gone, the hundred and fifty or so newly established museums meant that the state could change the presentation of history to the people whenever it wished. When family or community links to historical sites were obliterated, the state created a monopoly over China's historical memory. In this way the recent past changed all the time. National leaders whose faces and words had been everywhere would suddenly vanish as if they had never existed. It was not just ordinary citizens who would be picked up on the streets and disappear; leaders of the Communist Party in the 1980s, like Hu Yaobang or Zhao Ziyang, could disappear just as suddenly. Even Mao's slogans, which were painted in red on walls all over the city for thirty years, all but vanished. Still in place, however, are his mausoleum on Tiananmen Square and the portrait hanging over the Gate of Heavenly Peace. In a city where the past is constantly changing, only the grandeur of a glorious new modern China is clothed in certainty.

The destruction was not limited to the capital. Across the country hundreds of historic cities, towns and villages have been torn down in the greatest act of historical vandalism in Chinese history. Only a handful of ancient cities have survived, like Pingyao in Shanxi province, Lijiang in Yunnan and the 'watertowns' around Suzhou. In these tourist centres, the original inhabitants were either forced out or inspired to do so through profit, and their houses rebuilt or altered. When the authorities want to make money from tourism, they have constructed new 'historic' buildings or temples from scratch. Most of Beijing's US$ 800 million in conservation funds has gone to building a new city gate at Yongdingmen and a new Ming street at Liuli Chang, the old antiques centre.

This architectural destruction is only the terminal phase of the Cultural Revolution, which started when the modernization project began at the turn of the last century. The Nationalist Party (KMT) had begun to destroy temples and turn them into schools well before the Communists came to power. After 1949, every aspect of traditional culture was outlawed and in Mao's Cultural Revolution a violent effort was made to confiscate or destroy photographs, books, furniture, porcelain, jewellery and anything else that anchored people in their history. So when local governments set about earning money from tourism in places like Pingyao, they had to institute a desperate search to find authentic pieces to fill the newly restored old houses.

Some brave individuals in China have had the courage to resist this whirlwind of destruction, but they have usually stood alone without support from the outside world. Prestigious architects and historians have not spoken out, let alone organized an international preservation campaign like the one that saved Venice when it was threatened by floods. Rather, the architectural world has applauded the destruction and competed to win contracts to design new urban developments and experiment with daring designs. Many of the world's leading media companies have aided and abetted the state's efforts to suppress the memory of events like Tiananmen through the censorship of books, newspapers and websites. The speed and secrecy with which the destruction of old Beijing proceeded prevented anyone from organizing a successful resistance. The impotence of the few Chinese who raised their voices in the face of overwhelming force is not just a loss for China but for the whole world. The huge collections of Chinese art gathered by the world's great museums, and the high prices now paid by collectors of Chinese art, all testify to the veneration accorded to the sophisticated achievements of Chinese culture and their rarity. Sadly, the destruction of China's architectural legacy has been allowed to take place, out of a mixture of greed and misplaced deference to an expanding economic giant. This book first takes the reader through the history of Beijing, and later introduces a sample of the individuals, races and places whose richness and culture gave the city its extraordinary charm and fascination.

I

In Xanadu

Tiananmen Square is bare of the elegant cafés that grace St Mark's in Venice, where idlers sip coffee or feed the busy flocks of tame pigeons. The vast totalitarian space, surrounded by its endless circling traffic, is staked out by watchful secret police who discourage dawdlers from staying too long.

When Marco Polo arrived from Venice with his two uncles sometime after 1272, he must have stood here and felt a sense of awe and wonder. A journey of 5,000 miles that began outside the Doge's Palace had finished at the forbidding entrance to the Great Khan's palace. An embassy from Europe's great maritime trading power had reached the capital of Khublai Khan, perhaps the wealthiest and most powerful ruler who ever lived. Somewhere round about where Mao's mausoleum now squats, the Italian merchants would have been made welcome at one of the buildings that housed the six government boards or ministries that administered an empire stretching across all the land from the Yellow Sea to the Persian Gulf and Baltic and the Black Sea coasts.

The young Venetian's account of his travels established Beijing in the consciousness of the West for the first time. And he arrived here at the very time when Beijing first became a great city. Khublai Khan had enlarged the already huge Mongol empire by conquering some sixty to eighty million Chinese. Marco Polo arrived in Beijing when, for the first time, it was in a sense the capital of all China and thereafter became a place of great importance in the history of China. So for both reasons it is right to begin a history of the city at this point even though it was already a place of significance during the two dynasties that preceded the Mongol Yuan dynasty (AD 1279–1368).

Although Tiananmen has changed so much, Marco Polo would have recognized many aspects of today's city: the chequerboard layout of the streets, the great imperial palace with its lakes and gardens where the Mongols pitched their white felt tents, the astronomical tower at the eastern end, the bell tower to the north sounding out the hours, the Muslim quarter with its ancient mosque, the extravagant consumption by the powerful and the troops who mount a nervous surveillance over the populace.

Khublai Khan, whom Marco Polo describes in great detail, gave him employment in his empire and by some accounts made him an official responsible for the salt monopoly in the important city of Yangzhou at the southern end of the Grand Canal. Some now question whether Marco Polo really ever travelled to China, as no record of his employment in Yangzhou has ever been found. Yet, as I discovered when I retraced his journey from Beijing, or Khanbalik as it then was, to its sister city on the steppes, Shangdu, or Xanadu as we now call it, the travels seem to have been recorded with great accuracy. The struggle between the warrior horsemen of the Asian steppes and the settled civilization of the Chinese is one of history's greatest epic struggles. China's stubborn resistance lasted thousands of years but the past has been so successfully rewritten that most Chinese are no longer consciously aware of the role Beijing played in their history. It is a reminder that the Chinese were not supreme throughout history, as they claim was the case before the defeats in the Opium Wars of the mid-nineteenth century. Just as Moscow started out as the place where the Russians paid their taxes to the Mongols, Beijing owes its origins to the place where the Chinese came to deliver their tribute to their uncivilized neighbours. It was a terminus at the junction of two worlds, where a finger of the vast north China plain points north and meets a southerly extension of that great belt of rich grasslands that stretches as far west as the Carpathian Mountains. Unlike most other great cities in the world, it is not served by a river or a seaport. Instead, for over a thousand years the wealth of China's Yangtze delta was shipped up along a 1,552-mile-long man-made canal, the Grand Canal, specially built to deliver this treasure.

The medieval Russians spoke of their Mongol overlords as Tartars, the name given by horrified Europeans to all the predatory and violent nomad tribes of Central Asia who supposedly came from Tartarus, the Latin name for hell. Westerners continued to refer to the Manchu quarter of Beijing as the Tartar City right down to the 1940s. The Chinese, too, lived in terror of these 'tartars'. Chinese dynastic histories invariably speak of them as inferior barbarians whose rulers humbly offered tribute and strove to learn from a superior culture. Contemporary Chinese students also learn from school textbooks that the Khitans, the first to turn Beijing into a walled city, learned agriculture, metalworking, weaving, literacy and political organization from the Han Chinese. It is true that the Chinese created a settled, urban, literate civilization and farmed irrigated land. This required a stratified social organization to raise taxes and mobilize large numbers of peasants to build and maintain flood controls and irrigation works. By contrast, the 'barbarians' came from a pastoral nomadic culture. They lived in felt tents and hunted or raised horses, sheep, goats, cattle and camels. For most of the year they lived in small independent groups and tended to unite in loose federations under a great khan, who was often elected. Textbooks list the dynasties of Mongols, Jurchens, Khitans and other barbaric tribes as if they were no different from those of any other Chinese dynasty. Although this is misleading, the 'barbarian' khans who ruled from Beijing for such a large part of its history did bridge the two cultures by establishing and living in Chinese-style cities.

As the following four chapters explain, Beijing is also the creation of the very Chinese Ming dynasty, especially one emperor, Yong Le (1360–1424), who in 1421 moved the court and the bulk of the empire's military resources from Nanjing to the north as a strategy of forward defence. Yong Le bridged the two cultures by mastering the art of mobile warfare, but he also built Beijing's mighty battlements, which came down only in the 1950s and 1960s. He created the great city, which remained largely intact until the 1990s, and a grand necropolis for himself and his dynasty, the Ming tombs, whose secrets have only recently come to light. And it was Emperor Yong Le who constructed at vast cost the Great Wall, the gigantic system of fortifications designed to protect Beijing, which visitors are taken to see in the hills outside the city, and which were still being enlarged two hundred years after his death. The Great Wall ultimately failed the

Ming dynasty when in 1644 the Manchu armies rode through its gates without a shot and established a new dynasty, the Qing, which lasted until 1911. The stones of Beijing therefore tell a story of greatness, of courage and resistance, but also of defeat and humiliation.

Beijing first became a city of importance in AD 936 under the rule of a northern tribe, the Khitans, who established the Liao dynasty (907–1125). The Khitans have all but been forgotten even in China, but they were once sufficiently well known for the Russians to call the Chinese *kitaitsy*, a name that remains to this very day. The Khitans were Buddhists who built many temples and monasteries in a city with a circumference of 12 miles and walls 30 feet high with eight gates. The most poignant reminder of their rule in Beijing is Tianning Temple, the Temple of Heavenly Tranquillity, which somehow survived into the twentieth century as a gramophone factory. The graceful but rather sad pagoda, stripped of its bells, stands forlornly behind barbed wire next to a brick chimney, like a good fairy beside a witch. The Khitans became wealthy by controlling the international trade routes across Asia and by forcing the Chinese Song empire to the south to trade on very unequal terms. Following a Khitan invasion in 1004, the Song emperor Zhenzong was forced to acknowledge the Khitan's offer to pay 'tribute', which in reality meant that it was the Chinese Song dynasty that had to deliver vast amounts of silk and silver bullion every year to the Khitans.

How the nomad tribes, inferior in numbers, technology and culture to the Chinese, ever succeeded in dominating them, is hard to grasp. Yet a band of horsemen in armour, sometimes not more than a few thousand strong, regularly defeated a huge army of Chinese foot soldiers. The Mongol army numbered around 100,000 and the whole nation around 7 million. Only part of this force was able to overrun first the Jurchen empire with 40 million people, then the Song empire with 70 million. By a quirk of nature, the Chinese struggled to create an effective cavalry force because Chinese soil lacks selenium, a mineral essential to the breeding of sturdy horses. They could only import their mounts from the steppes, something the nomads often agreed to, safe in the knowledge that the buyer must soon come back looking for replacements. It was as if, during the early twentieth century, one side always had a monopoly of tanks. Often the Chinese sat tight in their great walled cities, granaries filled with food, hoping to last out a siege.

In earlier times nomad kingdoms rarely sought to conquer China. The pastoral tribes on the grasslands preferred to inflict punitive raids to force Chinese rulers to agree to supply trade goods at cheap prices that could be shipped along the Silk Route. They rarely had any desire to pick up the onerous burden of governing and collecting taxes from all those peasants. As with two giant corporations doing business, it seems to have been easier for each side to deal with a single monopoly partner. From the beginning of the first millennium there was a long period of stability lasting four hundred years when China's Han dynasty (206 BC–AD 220) coincided with the empire of the Huns on the steppes. When one side collapsed in disunity, the other side often fell apart as well. Chinese dynasties succumbed to domestic conflicts, like disputes over succession or revolts by the normally docile peasantry against excessive taxes. Nomad states, often loose confederations of independent peoples, easily fractured when tribes competed to divide up the profits from trade. If one federation of tribes became dissatisfied with its share, it would stage raids into China, breaking the terms of trade. If there was civil war, then either taxes could not be gathered or the international trade was disrupted. A Chinese leader who sought to usurp power often engaged mounted nomad mercenaries to defeat his opponents. The Tang dynasty (seventh to tenth centuries AD) based in Xi'an relied heavily on such nomad troops, often Uighurs and other Turkish peoples, to win and maintain power. Under the Tang, the influence of nomads was so strong that the Chinese came to adopt many barbarian customs, from sitting in chairs to wearing trousers, and many of its emperors are suspected of having more foreign than Chinese blood.

By the tenth century AD, strategists of the Song dynasty had to calculate whether to wage a costly war or give in to the demands made by the Khitans and various nomad states on its periphery. Under the guise of offering tribute, the Western Xia dynasty, another border kingdom founded by ethnic Tibetans around the Yellow River, in what is now Inner Mongolia, had begun pressing the Song to deliver 130,000 rolls of silk, 50,000 ounces of silver and 20,000 pounds of tea each year. Learning of this, the Khitans then raised their demands and wanted 300,000 rolls of silk and 200,000 ounces of silver each year. In the mid-tenth century the Song elected to mount an attack against the Khitans in Beijing but were defeated by the Khitan empress Xiao Rui-ji, who staged a heroic defence. According to legend, she saw her six sons die in a great battle and later built them a shrine near Tangshan outside Beijing. The Song then tried another strategy of 'using barbarians to control barbarians' by entering into an alliance with another tribe in the far north called the Jurchens, ancestors of the Manchus. Together they launched a coordinated attack on the Khitans. Finally, Jurchen forces stormed through the Nankou Pass, north of Beijing, and captured the city in 1125.

After their defeat, the Khitans vanish from the history books, but some years after the collapse of the Soviet Union, when I was travelling in the Russian Far East, I discovered what had happened to them. I was doing a story on the Gulag and the town of Magadan, headquarters of a network of slave camps, where I came across Anna Khabarova, leader of the Association of Small Peoples and Ethnic Groups of the North. A short, slightly stocky woman, Anna sat in one of those Soviet-style government offices with wooden panelling, like a barrister's chambers, behind a big desk. She said she was an Evenk, a tribe of reindeer breeders who were now in a sad state, but their ancestors were Khitans. There were some 29,000 Evenks left in the world, many scattered over Siberia but some 10,000 in northern China, and 4,000 in Mongolia. Sunk in apathy and alcohol, they had by the end of the Soviet Union even forgotten how to hunt or fish.

'They don't know how to look after the reindeer herds any more or how to live in the Taiga, they just drink vodka,' she said. 'Even the language has been forgotten.'

Anna claimed that after their defeat the Khitans had scattered and some had fled into the remote forests and steppes of the far north. There they stayed until the last memories of their former glory had dimmed. 'And to think that we once ruled all of China,' she said with a sigh.

The Jurchen army did not stop after overrunning the Khitan empire, but went on to invade the Song empire, too. In 1126, they sacked the capital at Kaifeng on the Yellow River and captured the Emperor

Huizong. Although lamentable as a strategist, Huizong is a rather interesting figure. Famed as an art collector and calligrapher, he styled himself Master of Learning and of the Way and was proud of his collection of 6,000 paintings. Until his death nine years later, the Jurchens kept Huizong a prisoner in Beijing at a temple, the Fayuan Si, which can still be visited today. Victorious, the Jurchens fought their way south as far as Hangzhou, as Southern Song's leaders quarrelled among themselves, unable to decide whether to fight the invaders or buy them off. One general, Yue Fei, was so determined to fight that on his back he had a tattoo with the motto 'loyal to the last'. He was opposed by the Song prime minister, Qin Gui, who executed the loyal general and paid off the Jurchens under a peace treaty. Yue Fei has gone down in history as a national hero whose image can be found in many temples in China placed next to statues of Guandi, the God of War. His tomb in Hangzhou remains a place of pilgrimage and his loyalty is celebrated at the annual Lantern Festival. Qin Gui is remembered as a villain and a traitor.

The Khitans established the Jin (Gold) dynasty, enlarged Beijing and extended the Grand Canal so that the barges bringing the riches from the south could reach Tongxian (formerly Tongzhou), just 10 miles east of Beijing. They also tried to solve the city's water shortage by collecting and channelling it from small intermittent rivers like the Luguo, Yongding or Wenyu that flow out of the limestone Western Hills. And by channelling water from the Jade Spring near the Summer Palace, the Jurchens also irrigated fields at what is now Haidian, the university district. To store the water they created a series of artificial lakes inside and around the Forbidden City. (Another lake is now the Diaoyutai ('fishing platform'), where visiting heads of state often stay. It gets its name from the story that the Jin emperor Zhangzong (r. 1190–1209) used to fish there.) Soon it was the turn of the Jin dynasty to suffer attacks from another power emerging on the steppes, the Mongols. Genghis Khan had begun by conquering other states on the frontiers of China like the Western Xia, then turned his attention to the Jurchens. At first the Jurchens held him off at the Nankou Pass in the Western Hills, but eventually the Mongols stormed through, laying waste to Beijing in 1215. Genghis Khan's attention then switched westwards and he died in 1227 before conquering Song

China. Before his death, he split the already vast empire between his four sons, Ogodei, Chagadai, Jochi and Tolui. His grandson Khublai Khan moved to Beijing in 1267 and by 1272 declared it the capital of the Mongol empire, of which he had become the supreme khan. The Mongols hunted down the Jurchen emperor, tracked him south and finally killed him near present-day Hong Kong. The rest of the Jurchens fled north, and three centuries later they returned although they now called themselves Manchus. Khublai Khan then attacked the Southern Song empire, whose great walled cities fell one after another. The Mongol invasion of the Middle East had provided them with new technology, siege machines like trebuchets, powerful enough to hurl missiles and destroy the mud-wall defences of the Chinese.

The Mongols were the first invaders to conquer the whole of China and then try to govern it. The empire founded by Genghis Khan was expanded by his sons and especially his grandsons, in particular Khublai Khan, until it covered most of Asia – except Japan – and all of China. Khublai Khan became the first to monopolize both the goods made by the industrious Chinese and the routes to all the markets in Europe, South Asia and the Middle East. The Mongol occupation of Beijing lasted around a century until 1368, and this was the time when the city became first known in the West. Marco Polo's name is so closely linked with China's that it is easy to forget he actually came to trade with, and then work for, the Mongols; China did not then exist as a nation. He described Beijing as a closely watched and patrolled city, kept under a tight curfew, and it may be imagined as a sort of United Nations administered territory, like Sarajevo, with a colourful medley of well-paid outsiders like Marco Polo who lorded it over the resentful locals. Khublai Khan brought many Persians, Turks, Central Asians and Arabs, whom Marco Polo lumped together as Saracens; one of them, called Ahmad, seems to have been 'mayor' of Beijing for twenty years. In his *Travels*, Marco Polo gives a breathless description of a city full of beautiful palaces, temples and broad avenues. In some areas, Beijing's street plan has not changed since the thirteenth century. The name for the narrow streets in Beijing, 'hutongs', comes from the Mongolian word for a well. Some state temples still date from Mongol times. Khublai Khan built the first temples of Grain and Soil, which still exist at the south-west corner of the Forbidden City complex. There he carried out the ancient rites for the agricultural year as a way of commanding the obedience of the Chinese. A large stretch of Khublai Khan's original city wall has survived, lost among rows of decrepit housing blocks in a neglected public park. What was the north side of the city wall now lies beyond the second ring road in Hepingli district. When I first saw it, it had lost its dignity, a shapeless mound with trees protruding, fronted by a green, malodorous moat that was cleaned up only after 2002. The Yuan dynasty Temple of the Ancestors, the Tai Miao, survived for eight hundred years until the last traces were lost in the late 1990s, when the site was destroyed to make way for a six-lane highway.

Khublai Khan ordered a Chinese engineer, Guo Shoujing, to extend the canal from Tongxian right into Beijing so that barges could travel directly into the city. Guo built twenty-four locks and Khublai Khan was so delighted with what he saw when returning from a hunting trip that he called it Tonghui He, 'the graceful link'. The Tonghui He still exists and was until recently a forgotten and rather smelly sewage canal running past factories which one glimpsed from trains coming into Beijing railway station, though it is now being cleaned up again. When it reached the old city walls, where the second ring road now runs, it continued until a place called Jishuitan, or 'collect-water-pool', where it met a small river, the Chang He. Near Jishuitan stands a seldom visited temple perched on a small hill, which has an exhibition devoted to Guo Shoujing's technical achievements. Without such a great engineering feat, a city like Beijing, without a river running through it, could never have become China's capital.

The excavation of the Grand Canal had begun five hundred years earlier when the Chinese Sui dynasty (AD 581–618) set out to conquer north-east China and Korea. Some 5.5 million men dug a canal linking the Qiantang, Yangtze, Huai and Yellow rivers. Shipment by canal was preferred because ships travelling up the coast might easily fall victim to pirates, and the Japanese were especially notorious. The Grand Canal started at Hangzhou, which Marco Polo described as the greatest and richest city in the world. It had 1.5 million inhabitants while his native Venice had just 100,000. He described how the Mongols press-ganged teams of peasants to pull barges mostly filled with corn and rice, and when after forty days they arrived in Beijing they were noisily greeted with gongs and drums. Two and a half million workers were conscripted to shorten the Grand Canal from 1,550 miles to 1,100 miles by cutting a new section between the Yangtze and Yellow rivers. The Jesuit priest Matteo Ricci (1552–1610), writing in the later part of the Ming dynasty, left this description of travelling up the canal from Nanjing:

Each year the southern provinces provide the King with everything needed or wanted to live well in the unfertile Province of [Peking] . . . all of which must arrive on a fixed day, otherwise those who are paid to transport them are subject to a heavy fine.

The boats called cavaliers are commanded by palace eunuchs, and they always travel rapidly, in fleets of eight or ten. The canal is navigable only during the summer season, when the water is high, perhaps due to the melting of the snow in the mountains . . . During the hot summer season much of the food stuffs . . . would spoil before reaching [Peking]; so they are kept in ice, to preserve them. The ice gradually melts, and so great stores of it are kept at certain stops, and the boats are liberally supplied with enough of it to keep their cargoes fresh until arrival.[1]

Under the Manchus (1644–1911) about 100,000 peasants pulled the 11,000 or so barges each year. When Lord Macartney led his English trade delegation in the eighteenth century, they travelled to Beijing by canal barge. On arrival they noticed a series of 'immense magazines of rice' near the Forbidden City. Beijing relied on the 'grain tribute' from the south until 1900, by which time railways and maritime trade combined to render the canal obsolete; Tianjin and its port became the great entrepôt and industrial centre of the region. In Beijing, one can still find alleyways called *miliang ku* – rice warehouse, or *ciqi ku* – porcelain warehouse. There are also *lumi cang hutong*, meaning salary grain warehouse, *haiyun cang*, sea cargo storeroom hutong, or *nanmencang*, south gate granary, and *dongmencang*, east gate granary. The names of many streets can be traced back to Mongol times and a few dozen Ming warehouses – fortress-like buildings of grey brick, with a short ventilation tower on top like the pit of a coal mine – survived until very recently.

Once safely delivered to Beijing, the tea, silk, porcelain, gold and silver could be strapped onto the backs of camels. Caravans filed out of the walled city, crossing a stone bridge, now called Marco Polo Bridge, towards the Nankou Pass. Then they plodded uphill, past Badaling and the Great Wall, until they reached Kalgan (now renamed Zhangjiakou). Kalgan is a Mongol word that means 'The Gate' and it was once a great bazaar and the gateway to the steppes. From Kalgan the caravans would proceed step after patient step for a further six months across endless grasslands to reach Lake Baikal. From there they might cross the Urals and reach Moscow's Chinatown, the *Khitaiski gorod*, or they would wend south-westwards along another part of the Silk Route towards Central Asia and the markets of Europe. The camel caravans disappeared only when the Peking–Kalgan railway opened in 1909. It was the first railway in China built entirely with Chinese funds. The track climbs steep gradients, passes through numerous tunnels and under the Great Wall itself.

With the rebuilding of Beijing its Mongol heritage past seems invisible but it once had a sister city, Shangdu (meaning upper capital), where the past is very visible. Its existence has been almost forgotten in China, which gives the Mongol dynasty little of the importance reserved for the later Han Chinese Ming dynasty (1368–1644). Shangdu, known to us as Xanadu thanks to the English poet Samuel Taylor Coleridge, is where the Mongol khans spent their summers. Before the weather turned hot and humid, the Mongol emperors would take the road from the North China plains through the Nankou Pass and climb some 6,000 feet up to Kalgan on the Mongolian steppe, where it was cool and fresh. When he became old and corpulent, Khublai Khan would make the journey sitting on a pavilion built across the backs of four elephants, followed by courtiers in silken robes and troops wearing fur and armour. The ruins of Xanadu now lie inside a top-security military region in Inner Mongolia and it required a special official chop (or stamp) on a permit for me to be allowed to visit the site. It took years of trying before the permit came through. When the day arrived, I set off with James Pringle, a colleague from *The Times*, and other friends in a small bus for the journey to Blue Sky Banner Township. The trip was given an added interest by some new discoveries: no contemporary portrait of Genghis Khan exists, but some Chinese archaeologists had found near Xanadu statues of what may be Mongolian khans. If they had found his image, it would be a remarkable discovery.

We followed the same route that Khublai Khan's elephants would have taken, heading out of the city north-west towards the Nankou Pass, China's equivalent of the Khyber Pass. Every invader – the Khitans, Jurchens, Mongols and Manchus – has had to ride through or around this gateway to attack China. Genghis Khan tried in vain to storm his way through it several times. A century ago travellers reported that Kalgan still had a memorial dedicated to the memory of Genghis Khan's brother, Khabaut Kassar, who fell during one such attempt. A motorway now climbs up the steep limestone gorge along-side a small stream that tinkles down the pass, which caused the Chinese to call this the Tanqin Xia, or Lute Gorge. There is also an older, smaller road that has a special charm in the autumn when the peasants spread their corn across it to dry before being threshed. The old road passes by an archway called Yuntai, or Cloud Terrace, that has phrases from Buddhist scriptures recorded in different orthographies: Chinese, Sanskrit, Tibetan, Uighur, Mongolian and Tangut. The latter derives from the name of the ethnic Tibetans who founded the Western Xia dynasty in the eleventh century. The archway was built in 1345 by the last of the Mongol Yuan dynasty emperors when their empire stretched from Poland to Korea. It stands as mute witness to the cosmopolitan character of *Pax Mongolica*, which had covered so much of the world.

In many periods, the Nankou Pass has been heavily guarded. The road passes the Guan Kou fortress, rebuilt from scratch in the 1990s as a tourist attraction, and the Juyong Guan, once known as the First Fortress in the World, due to its importance. At the top of the defile it reaches Badaling, some 2,000 feet above sea level. The Great Wall once had sturdy iron gates controlling the way into or out of China. A century ago this was the uttermost limit of the Chinese world and these fort-resses were built as part of the massive line of Great Wall fortifications and watchtowers. Juliet Bredon, who wrote a book about Beijing in the 1930s, said all Chinese who died beyond the Nankou Pass asked to be brought back and buried in China: 'Every Chinese dislikes to reside outside the Wall and if he can afford it, invariably provides that, should he die "beyond the mouth," his body should be brought back and buried within the pale. Lest the spirit lose its way, therefore, a cock is carried with the corpse, so that morning and evening his crowing may guide the soul to follow the mortal remains.'[2]

Whoever controlled this pass controlled the trade that went through it and had a lock on the most lucrative international trading concession in the world. Once past the Badaling fortifications, the modern traveller drives along a road that traverses a series of washed-out loess soil ravines. We drove along a dual carriageway dodging in and out of the hundreds of trucks bringing coal to Beijing from open pits in Inner Mongolia. As the road climbed steadily towards the Mongolian plateau, young girls stood by the roadside waving at the grimy drivers, hoping to entice them to stop and eat at restaurants hung with big red lanterns. Close to the road, standing forlornly in the fields, are round towers made of mud bricks, like beehives abandoned by some race of giant bees. These were once a marvel of medieval communications, beacon towers that enabled the Mongols to flash messages from Beijing to Xanadu in minutes. Kalgan itself is now a large, ugly city with a sizeable garrison, but, at nearly 6,000 feet above sea level, the air is pleasant. The steely grey clouds that blanket Beijing all summer are gone and the light makes the colours brighter and sharper. The old road to Xanadu is hard to find and we turned onto a rough gravel road that passed through impoverished villages where Chinese migrants settled in recent times hoping to eke out a living from stony and windswept fields. Then all at once we arrived on the steppe land and were bouncing along a grass track to the Blue Sky Banner Township. The air smelt richly of wild herbs. Skylarks and orioles tumbled and twittered under the azure sky. We drove into the small town with growing excitement as horsemen herded their cows along the central boulevard. The journey had taken nearly ten hours, but we were now close to the fabled Xanadu.

First, though, came a friendship banquet with the local party secretary and provincial foreign affairs office. We sat around a circular table exchanging small talk as the first round of drinks arrived together with the first course of cold dishes. Two Mongolian girls in flowing dresses and bright caps promptly entered bearing small glasses of aquavit. The toasts began. It was a Mongolian custom that each person seated had to make a small speech, or preferably sing a song, before the toast was downed. 'Marco Polo came here bringing friend-ship and trade,' began the local party secretary, a shortish man in a brown suit. He had a face reddened from the wind and sun, or perhaps too many banquets. Sitting stiffly on the other side were two men who had travelled all the way from Hohot, the capital of the Inner Mongolian Autonomous Region, to keep an eye on us.

'Foreign friends, let us drink to the spirit of Marco Polo and his great friendship with the Chinese people,' he said, swallowed the vodka, and smiled. His eyes disappeared into the folds of his skin. Mongols have broader faces than Chinese and a double fold of skin over their eyes.

'This is excellent drink,' I lied in response. Then, holding up a new and brimming glass, I launched into a little speech of my own: 'The French have Napoleon cognac, the Greeks have Metaxa brandy named after Alexander the Great and you have Genghis Khan vodka in honour of another great conqueror.'

'Hurrah!' grunted our host as his eyes vanished once again.

We downed the vodka again and turned up our glasses to show they were empty. Large chunks of roasted lamb began to appear on the table and I noticed the Chinese officials were smiling a little uncomfortably as the talk turned to Genghis Khan's exploits. A prov-incial foreign affairs office official, Mr Song, produced some lapel badges with Marco Polo's picture on them and began handing them round. He gave a short, formal speech about tourism and foreign investment, and we had another toast. The banquet was beginning to get quite merry when the two Mongolian maidens appeared holding silver bowls and carrying a beaker of fermented mare's milk. One of them stood stock-still and began to sing a long, slightly mournful incantation that rose and fell like a breeze bending the grass. She filled one of the bowls and presented it to James, who grasped it with both hands, raised it to his lips and downed the liquid in one go. 'As a member of a minority nationality myself,' he began, and his mild Scottish accent began to thicken perceptibly, 'I know how it feels to be part of a large country and to struggle to keep one's identity and customs in the face of indignities . . .'

As he talked, the table fell still. Our host looked on at James quite goggle-eyed and the two Chinese officials shuffled uncomfortably in their seats as they realized what the foreigner was saying. Any sign of Mongolian nationalism, let alone talk of independence or self-determination, was an absolute taboo. During the Cultural Revolution, Inner Mongolia had been broken up and divided between different provinces. Some 700,000 ethnic Mongolians had been persecuted and over 50,000 killed after being accused of belonging to the fictional Mongolian independence party, the Neiren Dang. Even thirty years later many Mongolians were still being arrested on suspicion of agitating for independence.

James pressed on regardless and there was a short silence when he finished. The evening broke up. The two Chinese officials excused themselves and retired to bed. James wanted to carry on and tour the township's discos and the party secretary felt he had no choice but to accompany his guests. At the Red Rose discothèque, anxious couples danced cheek to cheek under the strobe lights and at the next place, the Black Yak bar, there was a younger, more boisterous crowd. 'Let's go galloping across the steppes!' they sang. After a whole night's drinking, on top of the long drive, I went outside and threw up while the party secretary supported me sympathetically.

'I must sit down,' I mumbled. He nodded in a tolerant sort of way and we went on to find a patch of grass. It was midnight by now and the chilly but crisp night air helped clear my head. I looked up, surprised to see a blue sky ablaze and crowded with bright stars. The party secretary fished in his pockets, pulled out a small silver-and-amethyst snuff bottle and hospitably offered me a snort. Then he took one himself. 'They still think of us as savages, barbarians, you know,' he said abruptly, thinking about the banquet. 'They still say we plundered their cities and raped their women.' Despite more than half a century of propaganda celebrating the 'unity of the great multi-ethnic family in the new China', the past was not so easily forgotten by either the Mongols or the Han Chinese.

Next morning, in a state of high excitement, we drove down a new gravel road out to Xanadu. The square walls soon came into sight, standing as they had done for six centuries, in the midst of the green plain. There was nobody there and cashmere goats were grazing along the walls. Through the gates we glimpsed horses cropping grass inside what was still recognizable as a model rectangular Chinese city.

In his poem, Coleridge said it had 'twice five miles of fertile ground', and the walls indeed enclosed about five or six square miles. The town and palaces are aligned along a north-south axis and, as in Beijing, a second wall encloses an inner city and within this a third wall protects the inner palace. The outer wall once had gates at the four cardinal points. We climbed up the side of the South Gate and reached the remains of a watchtower. James pulled out a leather-bound copy of Coleridge's collected works, opened it at a well-thumbed page, and began solemnly to recite the verses. Of Alph the sacred river I could see no sign, though herds of long-maned horses did graze on marshy pastures watered by sinuous rills. Frogs croaked lustily in the moat that still girdled the battlements of fallen brick and mud. As far as we could see, there were no incense-bearing trees, nor any chasm, deep, romantic or otherwise, but the pleasure-dome had probably existed once. It would have been a traditional round Mongolian yurt covered in rare animal skins and assembled for the summer.

We laughed out loud at the sheer pleasure of being there. For a while, this was the centre of the world. For three months every year the Great Khan gathered around him a glittering court of some 50,000 Mongol chieftains, their wives and children, accompanied by Arabian astronomers and writers like Rashid Al-Din as well as Tibetan lamas, Persian dancers, Taoist sages, Nestorian Christians from Syria or Iraq, Kashmiri magicians and Chinese engineers, scholars and officials. Khublai Khan's yurt was reported to be very grand, so large it could hold a thousand feasting warriors at once. We decided it would have stood on some high ground just beyond the North Gate, which led directly out of the inner palace. Marco Polo wrote that Khublai Khan also had 'a huge palace of marble and other ornamental stones' at Xanadu and that 'its halls and chambers are all gilded, and the whole building is marvellously embellished'. There were marble slabs lying on the ground, delicately carved with flowers and dragons, some still held together by the original iron brackets. Pieces of fine porcelain tiles with a lustrous glaze of cobalt blue, ultramarine and green, which must have fallen from the roof, still littered the grass. Field mice whose ancestors must once have shared the munificence of Khublai Khan's table scampered about. Shards of brown pottery revealed where the palace's granary had probably once stood.

Few Mongols would have wanted to actually live or sleep in such a palace. Even in Beijing it is said they preferred to erect their yurts in the parks of the Forbidden City rather than sleep inside any building. They disdained the sedentary routines of administration, preferring to spend their time hunting in the parks created near Beijing. Or they would be away campaigning. Why then, one wonders, did Khublai Khan ever bother to build Xanadu or rebuild Beijing in the first place?

After the Mongol armies occupied Beijing, some of Khublai Khan's advisers proposed massacring everyone and turning their fields into pasture for the Mongol herds of sheep, goats and camels. In Chinese history, Khublai Khan's leniency is attributed to the persuasive voice of one man, Ye-lu-chu-cai, whom we know only by the transliteration of his name into Chinese monosyllables. He was not Chinese but a Khitan, an official of the recently defeated Jin dynasty. He persuaded the Mongol khans that it would be more profitable to tax the new Chinese subjects than to massacre them. For this good deed, he has long been venerated by Chinese, and his tomb near the Summer Palace was for centuries the site of annual devotions. To this day, Khublai Khan's clemency has made him a controversial figure among the Mongols. Some say they can never forgive him for conquering China and moving the capital from the original Mongol capital in Karakorum, far in the steppes, dooming the Mongols to be absorbed like raindrops into the vast sea of Chinese humanity. The Mongols cannot have numbered more than a few million and they ended up having to administer a vast territory with perhaps 110 million inhabitants. To win the loyalty of at least some Chinese, Khublai Khan deemed it necessary to appear as a traditional Chinese ruler, which may also be why he felt it necessary not only to rebuild and enlarge Beijing but to create a model Chinese city out in the steppes.

When Chinese archaeologists recently began to map and investigate the site, they discovered an ancestral temple some four miles away. Coleridge had written of 'ancestral voices prophesying war' in his poem and here was proof, for the first time, that there had been a temple built by Genghis Khan's descendants devoted to the worship of his ancestral spirit. They called on this spirit by offering libations of fermented milk taken from a herd of special white mares. We went to inspect the site and although there was little to see apart from stones and earthworks, the archaeologists had unearthed four head-less but life-size stone statues, seated on folding chairs and wearing Mongol riding boots and Chinese-style imperial dragon robes. Xanadu had been sacked by an army of Chinese peasants in 1368 and they pursued the last Mongol Yuan dynasty emperor, Toghon Timur, all the way here, but he escaped into the steppes. The Chinese destroyed the site and shrine but they never found where the Mongol khans were buried. If they had, they would have surely destroyed and desecrated them, a common practice throughout Chinese history. The Mongol khans were buried in great secrecy and to this day their tombs have never been discovered. They lie buried underground somewhere deep in the mountains of northern Mongolia.

For the next six centuries Xanadu lay forgotten and undisturbed by anyone apart from some Japanese archaeologists who came in the 1930s. After 1949 it became the property of the May First State Farm. Some two hundred poor herdsmen lived within the crumbling battlements, raising animals to supply the People's Liberation Army with meat. They looked poor and their grubby children peered at us from the homes made from mud and straw. They were all Mongols and complained meekly in their soft, sibilant-filled tongue that their wages had not been paid for months. Thanks to Coleridge, Khublai Khan lives in the Western imagination as an exotic, romantic figure, but to the Chinese, the Mongols were nothing but cruel and terrifying invaders who have at last been utterly subdued.

2

The Emperor of Perpetual Happiness

The only portrait we have of Emperor Yong Le, the colossus of Chinese history, shows a powerfully built man with a bull neck and a trailing black beard. The painter set out to show Yong Le seated poised and calm, wearing a plain robe and a black cloth cap, as a Confucian ruler should, but he also managed to convey that this man possessed a violent energy. In the late fourteeth century, Yong Le, whose real name was Zhu Di, arrived in Beijing as a 10-year-old boy to find an abandoned ruin. Weeds and brambles grew in the palaces where Khublai Khan had wintered, feasting with his followers. Outside the walls, the fields lay fallow and the villages were deserted. The grain shipments from the south had stopped and the last residents were starving; some reports said they had resorted to cannibalism. For twenty years Zhu Di ruled this distant border settlement as the Prince of Yan, adopting the city's original Khitan name, which means the City of Swallows. By the time he died in 1424, Yong Le had created a magnificent new city that would last almost unchanged for five hundred years and change the course of Chinese history.

His father, Zhu Yuanzhang, had declared himself the first emperor of the Ming dynasty in 1368 and for the next 276 years the Zhu family ruled over a prosperous and powerful empire. Nicknamed 'The Pig', both because of his features – a pug nose, thick lips and protruding lower jaw – and because his surname is a homonym for pig, Zhu led a rebellion in the Yangtze valley. Under the Mongols, the heavily taxed peasants had starved and so rose in rebellion in many parts of central China. After both Zhu Yuanzhang's parents died of hunger, he became a monk and then joined an underground millenarian sect called the Red Turbans. The rebels defeated the Mongols and expelled them from Beijing, and Zhu's followers defeated the other contenders for power. The Ming dynasty, meaning brightness or brilliance, would last until the invasion of the Manchus in 1644. Zhu Yuanzhang constructed a new and magnificent capital in the Yangtze valley, the economic and cultural heartland of China. In Nanjing – meaning the southern capital – one can still marvel at impressive sections of the 24-mile-long wall. Zhu Yuanzhang was an enigmatic and compelling figure who gave himself the reign title of Hong Wu, which means 'great military power'.

The semi-literate son of poor peasants emerged as a skilful military commander, an efficient administrator and a social visionary. Yet his court lived in constant fear of his paranoid rages and the horrifying purges that followed. Zhu Yuanzhang set out to create a rural utopia populated by smallholders who worked their own lands. The new bureaucracy he established was so small that it had just 8,000 poorly paid positions. These civil servants were forbidden to leave the walls of their respective towns even to gather taxes. Every village was to be a self-governing community with its own charter and its own committee of elders empowered to settle civil disputes. Each household had to have a copy of a book, *The Grand Monitions*, in which Zhu laid out his principles of sound government. In each community he ordered two pavilions to be built: one to commend the good deeds of local residents, another to reprove wrongdoers. On the pavilions of these community centres, the elders pasted up the good and the bad deeds of the villagers. Twice a year Zhu's subjects had to assemble to attend lectures, recite his precepts, hear new laws and witness how individuals were reprimanded for antisocial behaviour. It is no wonder that Chairman Mao is so often compared to Zhu. To guard against the ever-present threat from the steppes, Zhu Yuanzhang ordered his twenty-six sons to serve on the frontier and he relocated millions of soldier-farmers and their families to colonize borderlands, much as Mao would later do. Each family was entitled to 15 *mu* of land, about two and a half acres, to grow grain, two *mu* for garden plots, and a three-year tax holiday.

In the 1370s Zhu sent General Xu Da north to repair Beijing's walls and to turn it into a headquarters for border defence. Zhu Di, Zhu's fourth son, went with the general and so he grew up among soldiers and generals on active service. The future emperor would spend the next two decades in Beijing building up an army of five divisions – approximately 50,000 men – many of them recruited from the Mongols. His mother may have been the Empress Ma but could also have been a Korean woman who was a secondary consort. The son grew up tall and strong, a man of action, at ease leading troops, but his father passed the throne on to a 21-year-old grandson, a gentle and scholarly youth called Zhu Biao (Emperor Jianwen). When his father died, Zhu Di decided to grab power for himself. It took four years of heavy fighting before his forces, filled with skilful Mongol horsemen, could subdue the south. Most of the Ming armies supported Emperor Jianwen and regarded Zhu Di as a usurper. In July 1402, at the age of 42, he declared himself emperor, choosing the reign name Yong Le, meaning Perpetual Happiness. Then he moved decisively to destroy any other claimants, killing most of his father's family and their followers. The body of Jianwen, the legitimate heir, was never found. Yong Le's American biographer, Henry Tsai, described this purge as 'among the most brutal and barbarous political acts in Chinese history'.[1]

In the portrait now in Taiwan, Yong Le sports a raffishly waxed and curled moustache that gives him the air of a brigand chief; he also had such a sharp intellect that his contemporaries called him 'The Razor'. People both admired and feared his decisiveness. Once firmly established, he discarded his father's utopian system of government and reorganized the empire in such a way that he effectively started a new dynasty. His boldest move, to remove the capital from Nanjing to Beijing, stemmed from his belief that he must learn from the mistakes of the Song dynasty and commit the state's entire resources to a strategy of forward pre-emptive defence. To secure the empire against the Mongol threat, in the year 1421 he transferred its centre of gravity from the Yangtze delta 1,000 miles to the north. He rebuilt Beijing, turning it into a massive fortress, and moved about a million troops to construct and defend the Great Wall, a complex network with 700 miles of walls, watchtowers and fortresses. The new capital was protected by an additional belt of walled cities, towns, fortresses and camps. One of the largest was 160 miles away at Datong, where a huge garrison protected the western approaches. Around Beijing itself Yong Le stationed one-sixth of the empire's 493 guard units. Eventually a quarter of the Ming empire's military forces would be deployed in the Northern Metropolitan Area.

Yong Le justified his decision in various ways. 'The site is strong and secure, the mountains and rivers protect it well, the ten thousand nations lie on its four sides. It is a place favoured by sound reasons, by the mind of heaven and by exact divination,' he announced. It was situated to 'intimidate the outer regions and bring prosperity to the central regions'. His geomancers said it had a 'ruling air' and sat in the powerful embrace of a twisting dragon whose form was visible in the serrated peaks of mountain ranges along the boundary of the grasslands.[2] It was also a pragmatic calculation. Instead of paying the Mongols 'tribute', he poured the empire's tax revenues into creating these defences. The troops and the courts continued to depend on shipments of essential supplies, including grain, coming up the Grand Canal. Every year teams of peasants hauled 11,600 barges to Beijing, much as they had in the days of Khublai Khan. Even the timber, bricks, tiles and stones used to rebuild the city came from the south.

Yong Le personally led five campaigns deep into the steppes, reaching as far as Karakorum, but he realized that he could never finally defeat the Mongols. They remained the greatest military power on earth and descendants of Genghis Khan still ruled Persia, Russia and huge territories across Asia. In 1405 the great conqueror Tamerlane marched east from Samarkand at the head of 20,000 mounted warriors to attack the Ming empire, and might have succeeded had he not died en route. Tamerlane intended to join forces with various Mongol allies and emulate Khublai Khan's success. In the fifteenth and sixteenth centuries Mongol forces repeatedly broke through the Ming defences protecting Beijing. Another Mongol leader, the Altan Khan, came within sight of Beijing's Andingmen Gate in 1550. Yong Le's strategic thinking extended to commerce, and he tried to find alternatives to the trans-Asian land trade routes controlled by the Mongols. Between 1405 and 1411 he sent seven naval expeditions overseas, led by Admiral Zheng He, a Muslim eunuch from Yunnan province, who reached Africa and as far south as Madagascar. For the first time in history China was poised to become a seagoing nation but the initiative faltered after Yong Le's death in 1424; he died at the age of

64 while leading his fifth military campaign against the Mongols. He renamed his capital Beiping, meaning Northern Peace, in 1402, soon after winning power but another seventeen years would pass before he actually started to enlarge Beijing and build a new palace. When he formally transferred the court to the north, wealthy families from the Yangtze delta were forced to live as virtual hostages in a dusty, windblown city that was half construction site, half military encampment. The construction work lasted for thirty years. The palaces for imperial princesses were finished in 1428 and the fortifications only in 1438. In 1442, seventeen years after Yong Le's death, the new government ministry buildings opened, finally ensconcing the Ming administration in Beijing.

Construction of the outer walls and gates had started in 1419; the work took three years. The walls were 36 feet high, 56 feet wide, with a circumference of nearly 15 miles; 360 bulwarks jutted out at regular intervals. A Dutch visitor, Johan Nieuhof, observed how twelve horses could run abreast on top of the wall without hindering one another. When an embassy from the Persian monarch Shahrukh visited in 1422, his court historian Hafiz Abru left this account: 'All around the city wall . . . there were set up one hundred thousand bamboo poles . . . in the form of scaffoldings. Since it was still early dawn the gates had not yet been opened, the envoys were admitted to the city through the tower which was being constructed and made to alight at the gate of the Emperor's palace.' Inside he described the paved courtyards, latticed arcades, magnificent columns and floors of fine cut stone, such that 'If the master-craftsmen of these lands were only to see these things then they would believe and express their appreciation of the same'.[3] Multi-storeyed towers that served as guardhouses and forts crowned each of the nine gates. The largest loomed nine storeys high and in front of each was a semicircular space surrounded by a high wall that served as a parade ground. Beyond the walls, the moats surrounding the city were faced with stone. Eventually the wooden bridges spanning them were rebuilt with marble.

The titanic labour of construction was carried out by 200,000 workers, artisans and engineers, many of whom were convicts forced to wear a cangue, a heavy block of wood, around their neck. Many tried to escape, so their handcuffs were removed only while they were working: some were skilled artisans, press-ganged into military service and paid such low wages that they could barely feed their families. Some tried to escape by paying bribes. In modern parlance, Beijing could be described as the centre of a slave-labour colony and one Ming dynasty mandarin, Li Shimian (1374–1450), was thrown in jail after writing the emperor a memorial protesting at the conditions:

The costs have been staggering . . . The peasants, who were coerced to provide labour, were separated from their families and could not attend to their farming and silk production . . . At the same time, the demands on the populace by your bureaucrats increased day by day. Last year when they said they needed green and blue paint, hundreds of thousands of people were ordered to find this material . . . But since the beginning, even the carpenters and masons have used your name to force people to move out of their homes, creating a new army of homeless people. At present, a starving multitude in Shandong, Henan, Shanxi, and Shaanxi provinces eat nothing but tree bark, grass, and whatever crumbs they can find. Others, in desperation, are forced to sell wives and children for their own survival.[4]

After Yong Le died his eldest son and heir, the Emperor Hongxi, was determined to move the capital back to the Yangtze and only his own premature death in 1425 prevented him from doing so. The senior officials who ran the empire were equally homesick for the luxuries and refinements of the south. Beijing seemed an alien exile. Mongol influence was so strong that Yong Le had issued regulations specifically outlawing Mongol customs and language. He even had to order its residents to give up their Mongol gowns and wear proper Chinese clothing. It was a long time before visitors to Beijing felt that life there could match the refinements enjoyed by the wealthy classes in the Yangtze delta. A Korean official, Ch'oe P'u (1454–1504), on his way home after surviving a shipwreck in the south, described why Beijing fell so far short of elegant cities like Suzhou or Hangzhou:

Barbarian chieftains had built their capitals there one after another, and all their customs were customs acquired from the northern barbarians. Now Great Ming has washed off the old dirt and made those who buttoned their coats on the left [that is, like Mongols or Tibetans] take the ways of hat and gown. That can be seen in the splendour of the court ceremonial. But in the streets, they revere the Taoist gods and the Buddha, not Confucius. They work at business, not farming. Their clothing is short and tight, and men and women dress the same. Their food and drink are rancid. The high and the low use the same implements. There are still habits that have not been obliterated and that is regrettable. The mountains, moreover, are bare and the rivers filthy. Sand and dirt rise up from the ground and dust fills the sky. The five grains are not abundant. In that setting, the numbers of people, the profusion of buildings, and the richness of the markets do not, I am afraid, come close to those of Suzhou and Hangzhou. Everything needed in the city comes from Nanking, Suzhou or Hangzhou.[5]

A century later the Jesuit Matteo Ricci was still complaining that for all the splendour of the palace, 'Very few streets are covered with brick or stone and those are always filthy with dust or mud. And because it rains so infrequently, the whole place is usually dust ridden.' In the heat of the summer, Beijing stank and one Chinese writer wrote of returning from riding through the streets with his 'nostrils as black as coal mines'. Then as now, Beijingers covered their heads with a veil or mouth mask to keep out the dust. In the sixteenth century this gave an anonymity which some welcomed because it enabled them to avoid all the polite ritual of greeting acquaintances on the street.

Gradually the court settled down and Beijing's martial atmosphere gave way to a more urbane and cosmopolitan character. Out of the military imperium emerged a grand emporium. Beijing grew from an encampment of 50,000 troops to a bustling metropolis of between 800,000 and a million inhabitants. The soldiers and press-ganged artisans who had somehow escaped from their military service opened up shops and restaurants in a warren of streets south of the palace. The streets and alleyways of the Xuanwumen district preserved the names of their ancient trades, such as Old Clothes Lane, Straw Hat Lane, Hemp Rope Lane, Stone Stele Lane, Horsepost Lane, the Millers Lane, the Curtain Lane, the Manure Warehouses, Stone Warehouses, Beef Lane and Felt Cloth Lane, until the 1990s. In the western quarter (Xicheng), you could until recently also find Red Mat Lane, Beancurd Alley, Gold Foil Lane, Hairpin Lane, Tea Delicacies Lane, Wu's Rug Market and Whip Lane. Many of those families who started these trades and services under the Ming would remain where they had begun right down to the twentieth century. There was the Huang family of veterinarians, the Yao family of potters, or the Xu family in Shashou Lane, whose dish of steamed pig-heads made them rich when they became purveyors to the court. In 1999 a young entrepreneur in Beijing set about reviving a taste for steamed pig-head at his restaurant at Jinsanyuan and tried to lodge a patent for the Xu family recipe.

In Beijing there were many markets, such as one that opened before dawn south of the Daming Gate at the southern end of what is now Tiananmen Square. Here traders and artisans stood with placards advertising their skills or merchandise, much as one can still see in other parts of China today. Near the Palace some shops had signs 30 feet long, chased with gilt and colour, or bordered with spotted bamboo; some were carved with a golden ox, white rams, or black mules to signify their trademark or brand. The inhabitants could buy cotton clothes of various grades, light and heavy silk cloth, brocade fabrics, sheepskin robes, leather trousers, fur-lined jackets, felt socks for the winter and embroidered shoes for indoor life. Scholars could shop for fine writing papers: housewives for oil paper for doors and windows, copper and iron pots, cinnabar lacquerware, delicate enamels and elegant bowls and teacups. In 1433 alone the court shipped more than 400,000 pieces of the finest white-and-blue porcelain from Jingdezhen in the Yangtze valley. There was so much left over that the surplus was sold on the markets. Up along the Grand Canal came spices, medicinal herbs, liquors, lychees, longans, walnuts, dates, crabs, tangerines, pickled fish, aubergines, pears, peaches, olives, tea, wild fowl, pork, mutton, venison and vegetables as well as woven mats, bamboo furniture, soup, glue, combs and straw baskets. Eventually Beijing's markets and bazaars became so impressive that visitors remarked how crabs and fish were sold cheaper than in the Yangtze delta where they had been caught.

Beijing's biggest rice market was Dongjiangmishi at East River Rice Alley, which is where the Legation Quarter would be built in the nineteenth century. State subsidies kept rice prices low; the rice was hoarded in official granaries at Tongzhou and in warehouses inside the city, which were demolished only in the last few years. Many hutong names still recall their original function in the Ming, like Haiyun (Sea Transport) Warehouse Hutong; or the North Gate and

South Gate Depositories Hutong, or the Yongding Gate Warehouse Hutong. Bing Jiao Hutong – Ice Corner Hutong – preserved the name of the warehouse that was used to store ice sold in the summer.

In the old Yuan dynasty imperial hunting parks to the south, peasants developed an ingenious method of market gardening, which enabled them to supply the court all year round. They built greenhouses heated by fires in pits dug beneath the carefully tended seed beds. The plain around Beijing became covered with dykes, channels and earthworks so it began to resemble the wet, verdant fields of the Yangtze delta. Even in the bitter cold the greenhouses produced spinach, celery, radishes, cucumbers and other vegetables. And every day hundreds of carts entered the city bringing fresh flowers, not available again until the 1990s. Poorer Beijingers survived all winter on a type of cabbage which was introduced from the south in the fifteenth century, dubbed 'arrow shafts' because of its elongated shape. It remains a staple part of the diet today. Indeed, fifteenth-century Beijingers probably ate a more varied diet than sixteenth-century Europeans and certainly enjoyed a richer and fresher diet than Beijingers in the 1950s or even the 1980s.

The greatest and most extravagant bazaar in the empire was the Lantern Bazaar, at a crossroads called Dengshikou. A ceremonial gateway with three arches and yellow tiles marked the spot until the 1960s (today it has been replaced by a branch of Kentucky Fried Chicken). The fair opened on the eighth day of the first month and closed on the seventeenth, and it stayed open all night. To enjoy it, great officials, nobles and court favourites would reserve for them-selves a spot in one of the elaborately decorated pavilions that lined the Lantern Bazaar for half a mile. One visitor in 1594, Hu Yonglin, recorded how they came to see

row upon row, tier upon tier of shining lanterns fashioned in the shapes of birds and beasts, insects and flowers [that] suffused the fairgrounds with a multi-coloured glow that obscured even the light of the moon. Lutes, drums, flutes and cymbals filled the night air with a melodious chatter as troupes of musicians played through the evenings. Below the lanterns, strollers thronged the lanes: above them those who could afford the price, which ran to several hundred ounces of silver for a single room, packed the nearby storied pavilions to the eaves.

Hu Yonglin was dazzled by what he could buy there:

Once I saw a lantern at the lantern fair that was completely fashioned from
eggshells: the lanterns proper, the lantern covers, the sashes, and the tassels
were all made from eggshells. In all I reckoned several thousand shells were
used. Each shell had four pairs of doors, and each door had fluted arches and
lattice windows resplendent with gilt and vert. It was extraordinary; but so
thin and fragile it was useless – no different from carved ice or painted butter
sculptures. The price was very high, but a eunuch carried it off for three
hundred ounces of silver.[6]

The decline of the Ming dynasty was marked by growing numbers
of poor and destitute on the streets. The late fifteenth century saw the
first poor-riots recorded in Beijing. In the winter the bodies of thousands of starved and frozen vagrants appeared on the streets. The
Ming even established poor-houses, such as the Yang-chi Yuan, a
public hostel run by the government which fed and clothed thousands
of orphans and widows. The poor had to register there so that on
imperial birthdays, weddings and other joyous occasions they could
receive special allowances of rice and cloth. By the early sixteenth
century, as government finances foundered, even the official clerks
and servant classes complained that their wages were not keeping pace
with the cost of living. These petty officials began to demand 'squeeze'
and levied so many fees and taxes that the city's commerce began to
collapse.

Today you can hardly find a statue or painting of emperor Yong Le
in all Beijing but the city he built survived almost unchanged into the
twentieth century. Beijing, the Forbidden City, the Great Wall, the
Ming tombs are all his work and survived largely intact for five
hundred years. In the 1930s, Juliet Bredon wrote in her book *Peking*:
'To him are due not only the splendid proportions of the Forbidden
City, with its handsome buildings and noble courtyards, but her finest
temples and stateliest bridges. In fact, with the exception of a few
repairs and some imitations by the earlier Manchus – who as is well
known, possessed no original architectural ideas – the plan of the city
has scarcely changed from his day to ours.'[7]

Until the turn of the twentieth century, the land around the walls was still being preserved as commons on which to pasture horses, sheep and goats. Xiao Qian, the son of a Mongol guard who served at Dongzhi Gate, recalled in his memoirs *Traveller without a Map* how as a child he herded a flock of goats on the fields beyond the moat at Andingmen Gate. 'While they grazed I would lean against a weeping willow and read.'[8] Yong Le's mighty walls and towers lasted largely intact until 1958, when Mao ordered them all to be torn down. The Dongbian Gate in the south-eastern corner survived and it now looms incongruously over a flyover on the second ring road. Looking over the top of the battlements, one can imagine the sight of Yong Le's troops parading at dawn, the officers' armour flashing beneath their white sable furs and silk embroidered gowns. A last stretch of the original Ming wall is still visible, preserved by accident. Workers at the Beijing railway station used it as a wall for the lean-to sheds they needed to store their equipment. The bricks have gradually been stolen by local residents, who built themselves ramshackle houses against it that stick to the vast bulk like limpets to a ship's sides. On top of the wall whole trees had taken root, but I have never managed to find a way through the maze of these hovels and climb onto it.

From Dengshikou, once the Lantern Bazaar, one can still stroll into the Dongsi mosque with its minaret that the Ming general Chen You built in 1447, or through Zhijia Jie (Zhi's Home Street), named after the powerful Ming dynasty official who once lived there, or sneak a peek past the guards at the entrance of the barracks of the East City Quarter barracks in Dongcheng to glimpse remnants of the Ming dynasty Jie Hua Temple. Nearby is the Gold Fish (Jinyu) Hutong, whose name evokes the Ming scholars who once came there to buy or sell the delicate fish they loved to cultivate, but these are some of the last remnants. The Longfu Temple, once famous for the markets at its temple fairs, has gone. On the site stand the Longfu department store and the Dongsi People's Bazaar. At Dongan Gate, where the court came to shop for jewellery, precious jades and other objets d'art at the *neishi*, or imperial bazaar, there is now a luxury shopping mall, the Sun Dongan Plaza, opened in 1992 by a Hong Kong developer. The Ming buildings that Yong Le's grand vision breathed into existence have gone, only a few of their names lingering on in a ghostly fashion, their origins forgotten. His greatest surviving architectural legacies are the Forbidden City, the Ming tombs and the Great Wall, which are described in detail in the following chapters.

3

Madness in the Forbidden City

When soldiers in the Drum Tower struck the thirteen giant kettle-drums to signal the third watch at 1 a.m., Beijing was still in darkness. The servants in the palace hurried to light candles and rouse manda-rins, eunuchs and generals to ready them in time for the morning audience. As the court officials hurried to put on their thick silk brocade gowns, dawn was still hours away but their secretaries were soon at work busy preparing paperwork; the reports, lists and mem-orials that were needed for the dawn audience with the emperor. This was part of the demanding routine which Emperor Yong Le established for his court and it continued with little alteration until the curtain fell on the Qing dynasty in 1911. Winter or summer, the court unfailingly rose in the middle of the night to be ready in time. Although the emperor rose last, the ritual spared no one and not even he dared alter it.

I get up at 4 a.m. every morning, put my clothes on, and meditate. At that time, when my head is clear and my spirit good, I ponder over all the matters from the four corners of the empire. I deliberate issues and make big as well as small decisions, and then send them out to appropriate ministries and agencies for execution.[1]

And this was only the first audience. There was another at noon and a third in the evening. Yong Le had taken power by the sword but he exercised it with the pen. He designed a system that would automati-cally regulate the actions of the eunuchs who worked inside the palace, the cautious scholar officials who administered bureaucracy from offices outside the gates and the generals who required huge sums to fund the elaborate defences. Yet without a strong, powerful figure like Yong Le at the centre, this machinery often broke down.

When the fourth watch sounded at 3 a.m., hundreds of officials would assemble outside the Meridian Gate (Wumen) to the Forbidden City. Courtiers and soldiers waited in shelters on either of the great gates facing Chang'an Jie, the Avenue of Eternal Peace, that protected them from inclement weather. Neither rain nor snow could interrupt the ceremony, but it was not until 1477 that the emperor approved a regulation permitting the officials to have servants carry an umbrella over them as they walked from the shelters to the open-air audience. Just as the kettledrums sounded the hour, the greatest officers of the land filed through the Meridian Gate and stopped in the Sea of Flagstones (Haimen) before the Hall of Supreme Harmony (Taihe Dian), where the emperor would appear, a remote, divine presence whom his subjects never saw in the flesh.

At the outer city gates, thousands of peasants and their carts loaded with produce waited for dawn to break, the signal for the guards to throw them open. Next to them stood low-ranking eunuchs whose job was to inspect the goods and levy taxes. No matter if a peasant brought just a basket of eggs, the eunuchs would demand one or two of them. The original Drum and Bell towers date back to Khublai Khan, and were still sounding the hours and marking the start of the nightly curfew well into the twentieth century, although under the Qing (1644–1911) the inspectors were agents of the imperial princes. By 5 a.m. a bustling crowd was already setting up stalls in Daming Market, south of what is now Tiananmen Square.

A sense of foreboding can still grip the visitor as he approaches the very centre of power, crossing the marble bridges over the Golden Water Canal, entering through the great red doors studded with giant nails and passing on into the dark tunnel under the Gate of Heavenly Peace. Ahead loom the great red walls of the Forbidden City and the Meridian Gate, which forms the true boundary between two worlds – the 'Great Within' and the empire without. For centuries, the Meridian Gate, rather than the Gate of Heavenly Peace (Tiananmen), was the most significant spot in the entire city. It is now a rather banal place, a parking lot where tourists congregate, pestered by postcard vendors, before buying tickets to enter the Forbidden City. Yet it was from the battlements above the Meridian Gate that imperial proclamations were made, and the emperor reviewed parades of prisoners of war. Every year when the emperor issued the imperial almanac and officials from the Board of Ceremonies lowered the document from the gate, attached to a dragon's head and suspended from a pole by a coloured cord, special emissaries bearing this lunar calendar dispersed on horseback as far as Vietnam and Korea. Even during the Korean War, American soldiers were astonished to meet Korean peasants asking them to obtain an imperial almanac in order to plan their harvests.

The visitor proceeds northwards from the Meridian Gate through a hierarchy of gates and towers designed to instil a sense of majesty. Yong Le's architect was a Vietnamese called Nguyen An who designed six major halls, all aligned along a south–north axis that linked the palaces and gates. By modern standards, the inner palace buildings seem neither large nor especially sophisticated but their elegant pro-portions, the huge space under the sky, gives them a power to inspire awe. The Sea of Flagstones appears greater than it actually is because the flat, low buildings on either side seem to amplify the scale. Until recently, the grass growing between the flagstones added to its remote, otherworldly feeling.

On the Sea of Flagstones, the court lined up in descending order of rank; the civil officials on the east and the military on the west. Two diagonal lines of square paving stones still mark the correct positions each should take. Each of the most powerful men stood on a spot that exactly marked his place in the hierarchy. Sewn on the silk robe of each man was a square patch about breast height that also marked his status. For the top rank, there were two cranes soaring above the clouds; the lowest rank wore a pair of quails pecking at the grass. The emperor sat on a high throne elevated in the centre of a vast and gloomy hall shrouded from sight by clouds of incense. The morning audience took place before the Hall of Supreme Harmony, which was the symbolic centre of the whole world. On his head, the emperor wore a hat like a mortar board, with a curtain of beads in front and behind because no one was permitted to raise their eyes and look directly upon him. It was even forbidden to breathe normally in his divine presence and those taking part had to shield their mouth with a piece of ivory. From his Dragon Throne, the emperor could look out, reassured that, in his world, each knew his place and rank.

The eunuchs cracked their whips and called for order. Then all assembled shouted out in unison, 'Ten thousand blessings to his Majesty.' Then they prostrated themselves nine times, knocking their heads on the flagstones in the ritual kowtow. Four imperial historians stood around taking a roll-call and noting down the names of those who coughed or spat, who stumbled or dropped the ceremonial tablets they carried raised against their chests. Then they recorded what business took place. The design of the Hall of Supreme Harmony is clever. The dimensions are amplified first by the three balustrades of marble on which it rests and then by the roof, the grandeur of which is bolstered by the complicated bracket system. Inside, pillars of bronze-coloured lacquer and others of a deep red support a coffered roof painted blue and green. While the dim hall itself feels disappointingly bereft of its former power, the great courtyard still possesses its magic. Standing directly beneath the wide sky in the presence of the emperor, it would not have been difficult to experience a sense of direct communication with heaven. The emperor sat here on the Dragon Throne as representative on earth of Shang Di, the Supreme Deity who lived at the apex of heaven, which the Chinese believe is marked by the Pole Star. (This is *ziwei* in Chinese, and as the character *zi* also means purple or violet, the Forbidden City is also called the Purple City.)

When the entire court was assembled, the various departments and ministries made their reports. At times, the emperor asked questions and gave oral instructions. The entire proceeding was completed before dawn, when the emperor returned to his work, sifting through documents selected by ten eunuchs at the Office of Transmission. The emperor sat in these great halls, a spider at the centre of a web of bureaucracy stretching across the vast empire. It was his task to generate a constant flow of commands to activate the different layers of his administration and to read the reports which flowed back. He read and marked with red ink an average of 400 memorials and petitions a day. In practice, one of his eunuchs had usually already drafted a response, which was then checked by a staff member of his inner council, the Grand Secretariat.

'After the audience with my officials, I never go straight to my private chambers,' Yong Le himself wrote. 'I read every memorial, and report from the four corners. Those concerning border emergencies, floods, and droughts require my immediate attention, and measures are quickly taken to resolve the problems. I generally put off matters of the Inner Court [affairs relating the Palace] until I've finished the matters of the Outer Court [affairs concerning the state].'[2]

At the midday audience, Yong Le approved promotions and awards after listening to the Ministry of Personnel and the views of the Bureau of Appointments and the Bureau of Records. He also read the reports filed by the secret police, headquartered in the Dong Chang, or Eastern Depot, inside the Forbidden City, who gathered reports on all incidents in the city, from such mundane matters as the price of rice to political rumours. Those suspected of dangerous political activities would, at his command, be tortured into making confessions. Yong Le also designated himself head of all organized religions. Under his patronage, Beijing became significant as a religious centre filled with a growing number of temples, monasteries and shrines. So in addition to the tedium of the court rituals, he also had to perform many kinds of state religious rituals.

'To his mind the three religions or schools of thought were not contradictory but only differed in function,' observes Henry Tsai. 'Yong Le in fact simultaneously donned a Confucian cap, a Daoist robe and Buddhist sandals.'[3] In his records, Yong Le tells his subjects that he is never at rest. 'Whenever I can find the time, I read history books and the classics so as to avoid idle living. I constantly remind myself that the world is so vast and state affairs so important that I cannot succumb to laziness and complacency for even a moment. Once one has succumbed to laziness and complacency, everything will become stagnant.'[4]

Even in his moments of leisure, he seemed busy. In the gardens and lakes of Zhongnanhai and Beihai Park he could have strolled idly among the trees and flowers but instead he retired to a simple thatched hut surrounded by a wicker fence. There he pretended to live as a simple Daoist hermit, to remind himself of the virtues of frugality. In fact he occupied a palace as large as any medieval city. With a total of 9,000 rooms, the Forbidden City has justly been described as the largest logistical base in the world. Its 700 acres encompassed factories, warehouses, workshops, kitchens, a pharmacy, libraries, armouries, numerous temples, theatres, libraries, treasuries, art galleries, printing presses, many offices and several schools.

After the Hall of Supreme Harmony, the visitor reaches another smaller hall, the Middle Hall of Harmony (Zhonghe Dian), where the emperors sat to prepare the messages to be read at the Temple of the Ancestors, and where each year Yong Le would inspect agricultural implements and samples of seed used in the rituals performed at the Temple of Agriculture. The next and third great hall of power is the Hall of Preserving Harmony (Bao He Dian), where the emperor would receive the scholars who had taken the top degrees in the civil service examinations. The emperor himself presided over these triennial examinations held in the same hall. Its successful graduates earned the highest honours and merited the most powerful positions. Behind the three great halls of state lies the Gate of Resplendent Brilliancy, entrance to the emperor's private quarters. The halls of state continue in a line down the centre; the Palace of Heavenly Purity, formerly the living quarters of four Ming emperors, and the Palace of Earthly Tranquillity, which in Ming times served as the residence of the empresses. Lastly, one reaches the imposing Gate of Divine Military Genius (the Shenwumen), out of which emperors would be carried upon their death. Later, the Qing emperors used the halls for different purposes. The Kangxi and Qianlong emperors gave audiences to the Grand Council of Ministers in the Palace of Heavenly Purity and held famous banquets to celebrate their respective sixtieth years on the throne. The Empress Dowager Cixi turned the smaller Hall of Vigorous Fertility, which once housed the Ming imperial seals, into her throne room.

If you spend too long wandering the Forbidden City it seems a claustrophobic maze. The walls are high and imprisoning. And beyond the walls, one knows one is trapped by still more. The buildings no longer seem magnificent but oppressive and wearying in their monotony. The system that Yong Le created turned an emperor into a prisoner of iron routine, forced to appear and disappear at intervals like the cuckoo in a cuckoo clock. No wonder many future emperors loved to collect the mechanical clocks brought from Europe. The endless and numbing cycle of audiences and state rituals slowly turned some emperors mad. Unlike Yong Le, few of his successors ever managed to escape the sedentary life to lead military campaigns against his enemies. Yong Le alone managed to fulfil both the Chinese and Mongol ideals in which a leader must be both an active warrior and a passive symbol. Yet sometimes even he had had enough, and in a flash of temper would suddenly demand the execution or beating of a hitherto trusted and loyal subordinate.

The twenty-four emperors who lived there must have found their private lives subject to intolerable controls. The living quarters for the emperor, his wives, concubines and eunuchs are smaller intimate courtyards, but it is clear that the palace was never really a home. It does not feel like an English country house whose charm derives from the accumulated effect of additions and alterations made by each succeeding generation according to their foibles or the fashions of the age. Rather, as he marches from hall to hall the visitor has the gnawing sensation that he is in a cold and lifeless shell shuffled off by some great creature. The British poet and critic William Empson described it as 'a biological device for ruling the world'; the American gentleman-scholar George Kates called it 'the hive of some rare species of insect'.[5] Guarded like a prisoner by thousands of soldiers, the emperor lived here as the only functioning male, surrounded by his eunuch drones and servicing his empresses, consorts and concubines. At the height of the Ming dynasty, the Forbidden City employed 20,000 eunuchs and 3,000 servant women. Beyond any other role, an emperor's primary function was reproductive; to ensure a smooth succession and hence the empire's political stability. As inheritance was based on primogeniture, it was of vital importance that no one could challenge the origin of the heir, or the state might be ruined by a civil war. Since no eunuch could produce heirs of his own, it followed that they could be trusted.

Although the next dynasty, the Qing, employed far fewer eunuchs, it still used them to monitor and regulate the emperor's sex life. The sexual opportunities of any emperor, surrounded from birth by eunuchs and hundreds of women devoted to his service, fires the imagination. One late Ming poet, Chen Chen, wrote of the opportunities in 'To the Hall of Heavenly Enlightenment':

Thousands of beauties locked in the palace
Waste their youth in bitterness.
As lions and dragons whirl in the shadowy light,
The emperor dallies with maidens the whole night.

Yet the reality was different. Although the palace maids are conventionally described as being like 'sculptured jade' or 'fully blossomed peach trees', parents were often anxious to marry their girls off as early as possible to prevent them being selected for the court. Part of the Forbidden City resembled a sort of nunnery filled with hundreds of plain or unwanted girls who ended up spending their lives in a physical and emotional prison without ever once sleeping with the emperor. Few Ming or Qing emperors enjoyed happy marriages or normal relationships of any kind. They had little privacy and could easily lose any sense of personal identity. Not for nothing did Red Guards rename the Forbidden City as 'The Palace of Blood and Tears'. While Yong Le had done exactly what he pleased and spent much of the year on military campaigns, his successors lived lives rigidly constrained by the rules he had established.

The Confucian scholars insisted that an emperor should play no role in military life, nor engage in martial exercises or in fact in any kind of spontaneous activity. Rather, he was required at all times to move solemnly and deliberately in the most uncomfortable clothing. He had to take part in frequent rituals, like that marking the start of the farming season. At the Altar of the Earth (now Ditan Park) the emperor would arrive in a procession and, after changing his robes and undertaking rites to purify himself, pretend to plough a field. Some two hundred farmers were called in to witness this event in which actors dressed up and pretended to be the deities of wind, clouds, thunder and rain. Two officials led an ox, two older farmers brought a plough, while other peasants carried farm implements and barrels of human faeces, the most common fertilizer. The emperor touched none of these. Instead, he marched around a field, holding a whip in his left hand, and in his right a ceremonial plough carved with a dragon painted in gold, and accompanied by two elders. This procession marched around the field three times, then the ruler retired to his tent to watch his courtiers, led by the minister of revenues, repeat the process. Seeding was performed by the prefect of Shuntian county and his staff. No sooner was the soil covered than actors in peasant clothing presented samples of the five principal grains to the emperor, to symbolize a good harvest. Then the sovereign was congratulated by all present.

Those brought up from birth in the court often tried to revolt against the stultifying life. Few were capable of living up to the standards set by Yong Le and sticking to the exhausting and tiresome routine. One emperor, the playboy Zhengde (1491–1521), tried to cut down the audiences to just one, which he wanted to hold at night, immediately followed by an amusing banquet. This proposal sank in a storm of opposition. The Emperor Jiajing (1507–67) escaped by devoting himself to Daoism and spent twenty years 'cultivating his mind in solitude'. He was obsessed by the search for the elixir of life and spent years collecting rare minerals to use in experiments. Jiajing believed that Daoist sexual practices could prolong his life, and he tried to extract the feminine essence by recruiting teenage girls; it is rumoured that he boiled down their private parts. After eighteen palace girls tried to strangle him as he slept, he refused to live in the Forbidden City and retreated to a villa in the palace grounds. Emperor Wan Li (1563–1620) also became a virtual recluse for twenty-five years and refused to attend any imperial audiences after the age of 25. His successor, the Emperor Tianqi (1605–27), grew up illiterate and preferred to spend much of his time working on carpentry. Even so, the efficiency with which the Ming empire was governed deeply impressed visitors. The Augustinian monk Juan Gonzalez de Mendoza, in his book *The great and mighty kingdom of China and the situation thereof*, published in 1585, judged 'this mightie kingdome is one of the best ruled and governed of any that is at this time known in all the world . . .' By the end of the sixteenth century a bureaucracy with 20,000 officials administered what was by far the world's most populous country, with an estimated 155 million people. The whole of Europe contained approximately 60 million people.

Those who came top in the civil service exams would join the Grand Secretariat of Advisers or work in one of the ministries established south of the Meridian Gate around a T-shaped courtyard called the Heavenly Streets (Tianjie). (This must have had the atmosphere of an

Oxford college where high-minded dons hurry back and forth across the quadrangles.) These officials were aided by clerks, recognizable by their black jackets with tight collars, who worked in the offices that lined the walls on both sides of the Meridian Gate. These ministry buildings survived until the 1950s, when they were demolished to create the vast empty space of Tiananmen Square. Also demolished were two gates exiting to the Avenue of Eternal Peace (Chang'an Jie) on the east and west and the storehouses for imperial carriages and processional regalia.

Court politics in many Chinese dynasties revolved around the rivalry between two competing groups, the eunuchs, who were usually Buddhists, and the mandarins, who worshipped Confucius. Yong Le employed both, but under Wan Li the mandarins lost out. During Wan Li's forty-seven-year reign, his private inclinations collided with the demands of these bureaucrats, provoking such a grave crisis that some believe it precipitated the downfall of the Ming dynasty. Wan Li reigned longer than any other Ming emperor, though he spent most of it fighting the imperial system. After Wan Li married the Empress Xiaoduan, he fell in love with a Lady Zheng, with whom he had a son he insisted should be named his heir. The court officials doggedly refused to agree: this was Wan Li's third son and it was contrary to the Confucian principles of primogeniture. When the mandarins refused to back down, Wan Li dismissed his Grand Secretary and henceforth refused to meet any of them. He stopped attending the obligatory daily lectures on Confucianism and punished the officials by refusing to make new promotions in the state bureaucracy. Effectively, he went on strike and thus paralysed the whole system. By the end of his reign, most bureaucratic posts had become vacant and thousands of documents had piled up unread. As he refused to meet his officials, all communications between the emperor and the outside world had to go through the quaintly named 'Office for Transmitting Letters'. This, like everything else, was run by the eunuchs, who by the time Wan Li died had multiplied to 100,000 men divided into forty-eight grades. The mandarins took this badly. Yong Le had granted senior officials certain privileges, such as the sole right to reprimand the emperor, specifically by writing personal memorials and depositing them at two pillars called Hua Biao (Flowery Signposts) that still stand before the Gate of Heavenly Peace. These pillars, which have dragons winding round them with two wings at the top and are crowned by lions with open mouths, are to remind emperors to walk in the path of virtue.

The Gate of Heavenly Peace continues to serve as the nearest thing China possesses to Speaker's Corner. After Mao's death in 1976, democracy activists posted petitions on the short-lived 'Democracy Wall' criticizing his policies. Then, during the 1989 pro-democracy protests, students and professors marched past the Hua Biao criticizing Deng Xiaoping. Students deliberately imitated the Ming scholars by kneeling down before top officials and handing over their memorials. Years after the 1989 Tiananmen protests had ended, I stood in front of the Hua Biao on some anniversary and witnessed a dissident (or possibly a madman) suddenly emerge from the tourists milling around and hurl political pamphlets in the air like confetti. As dozens of plain-clothes police sprang to life, one man jumped over the railings like an Olympic hurdler but was tackled by police who converged on him like a pack of forwards.

The most exemplary Ming official was an upright man called Hai Rui who dared reprimand not one but two emperors. His first memorial bluntly accused the Emperor Jiajing of being vain, cruel, selfish, suspicious and foolish. Hai Rui also complained of excessive taxation, widespread governmental corruption, exorbitant palace spending and rampant banditry. He ended his memorial by saying that 'all that is needed is a change of heart on Your Majesty's part'.[6]

Writing a memorial was one thing, surviving another. If the emperor was angered by the author, he would be arrested, beaten in front of the Meridian Gate with wooden clubs and his name struck off the civil service register. In the worst cases the victim died from his wounds. Not surprisingly, Jiajing, obsessed with Daoist elixirs, condemned Hai Rui to death by strangulation. Luckily the emperor suddenly died before the execution took place and Hai Rui was saved. Others might have stayed silent after such a gift from heaven, but not Hai Rui. He rose to become the censor-in-chief at Nanjing, from where he fired off further memorials to the new emperor, Wan Li. In 1586 he urged him to deal with corruption by reinstating the severe penalties that the Ming dynasty's founder, Zhu Yuanzhang (Emperor

Hongwa), had promulgated. This included skinning any official caught embezzling public funds, stuffing the skin with straw and exhibiting it in public. Given what we know of Wan Li and his attitude to annoying officials, his response seems reassuringly sensible: 'His suggestion for cruel punishments contradicts our sense of good government. Furthermore, he has made some personal criticisms of myself; the wording is silly and inept, so I have decided to ignore it.'

In the course of Wan Li's reign, however, many upright officials were arrested and killed in prison after enduring cruel torture, especially those who tried to stop the corruption practised by the eunuchs. One case concerned the most powerful eunuch, Wei Zhongxian (1568–1627), who was accused of poisoning Wan Li's most favoured son with a 'wonder-working pill'. He went on to rule through the weak and illiterate Emperor Tianqi. In collusion with the emperor's wet nurse, Wei Zhongxian tyrannized the court, murdering upright officials and exacting heavy taxes through a nationwide network of eunuch agents. Wei Zhongxian even began building shrines to himself across the country. The Ming had developed one of the most complex tax codes in history, but the effectiveness of the Ming bureaucratic machine broke down irreparably during Wan Li's reign. After his death in 1620, the dynasty managed to stagger on for just twenty-five more years. Even in the early fifteenth century, the state had struggled to gather enough taxes from the Yangtze to supply both the court and the half a million or so troops garrisoned in and around Beijing. Under Wan Li, state expenditure rose still higher. He was accused of being personally extravagant because he levied extra taxes to pay for his tomb. Extra expenditure was also needed to enlarge and extend the Great Wall's defences. When Wan Li boycotted the officials, the burden of levying taxes and organizing the empire's defences was shifted almost entirely into the hands of the eunuchs. Some became immensely wealthy and corrupt, but they left their imprint on Beijing in a remarkable way.

More eunuchs found employment in Chinese palaces than was the case in any other civilization. Eunuchs existed in ancient Assyria, Rome and Constantinople; in more recent centuries, Turkish sultans and Indian maharajahs have employed them to guard their harems, but they have rarely been entrusted with ministerial responsibilities.

Chinese rulers, always anxious about a civil war started by rival contenders for the succession, felt the eunuchs were more loyal than their relatives. One emperor praised them as 'creatures docile and loyal as gelded animals'. On the other hand, the rulers tried to keep even their children as far away as possible. Eunuchs had served in the palaces of Chinese emperors and kings from the eighth century BC onwards, but the Ming dynasty marked the height of their power and numbers. When Zhu Yuanzhang founded the Ming, he issued a decree that 'eunuchs must have nothing to do with politics', but Yong Le ignored this. He relied on them to staff his household within the Forbidden City and entrusted some with great tasks. Perhaps Yong Le believed that if he split his administration into two rival camps, it would make both easier to control.

Beijing became a city uniquely given over to this third sex who talked in high falsetto voices and walked about with a mincing gait. Often described as 'palace rats', they not only filled 'the great within' but also populated the city's mansions, monasteries, shrines and tombs. The majority ended up doing menial jobs, transporting goods, cleaning, or labouring in a workshop that served the palace. Inside the palace they tended to live little better than slaves, occupying small cells called 'menials' houses' attached to the sides of main buildings where their employers resided so that each of the myriad of courtyards in the Forbidden City had its own colony of eunuchs. Others were left to fend for themselves on the streets, often dying of hunger. Some sons of poor families were castrated but never managed to enter the palace gates. They joined the army or formed themselves into gangs and terrorized the markets and alleys, where they were known as 'shock troops'. Some eunuchs became so powerful that, like Renaissance cardinals, they built themselves palaces and bequeathed grand monastery complexes filled with magnificent works of art. In Peking Opera, eunuchs are invariably cast as scheming, manipulative and power-hungry villains. While the scholar-officials come across as pedantic prigs, obsessing about the rules, the eunuchs often show a certain panache. They splashed out on art while the officials kept the records and wrote the operas.

It was only natural that the mandarins felt contempt towards eunuchs, whose chief qualification was a willingness to submit to castration, while they had to pass very competitive examinations. In fact, some eunuchs attended a eunuch school within the palace grounds from an early age and received a thorough grounding in the Chinese classics. Once employed inside the court, they had an advantage over the mandarins since their influence could be exerted on many levels. They surrounded the young heir from his earliest days, interpreting their charge's wishes and manipulating his moods. Later they not only oversaw the flow of paperwork to him but also attended to the emperor and his family outside the regular daily audiences. A whispered word in the emperor's ear by a eunuch could destroy a brave general's reputation or ruin the career of an upright official. Still, success carried a price. No matter how rich or grand they became, they could never pass on their wealth or position. Some tried to escape their fate by 'marrying' palace women and adopting sons. Others patronized a nephew or some handsome junior eunuch to whom they could bequeath an inheritance. Mostly, they built themselves luxurious mansions, gripped by a flaunt-it-now, you-can't-take-it-with-you impulse. Others became devout Buddhists in the belief that through good deeds and many bequests to monasteries they would be reincarnated in the next life as whole men; the eunuchs endowed hundreds of temples and shrines in and around Beijing and established monasteries in the hills, which were maintained by revenues from gifted estates that produced oil, incense and other specialist products. These estates often supported communities of retired eunuchs who banded together in charitable associations.

In the hot summer months, powerful eunuchs escaped the monotonous court routine by staying in monasteries. Some temples were so closely associated with their eunuch patrons that a Chinese scholar, Lu Zhong (1436–94), observed that court officials often came to these retreats to conduct much of their business. Petitioners would gather at a temple associated with a certain eunuch in the hopes of catching an opportunity to plead their cases. Some eunuchs also built temples through subscription drives, including one of Beijing's most splendid, the Fahai Temple, built in the fifteenth century by a eunuch called Li Dong. He served the unfortunate Emperor Yingzong (1427–64), who was captured by the Mongols. The walls of the main hall are covered with elaborate frescoes of Buddhist luminaries and reflect the glories of earthly pomp as well as the splendours of heaven. The temple is now in the industrial Shijingshan district of western Beijing, where there are eunuch graveyards with tombs built on as grand a scale as that of the emperors they served.

Another of the few buildings to have survived from that era was built by a powerful eunuch called Wang Zhen. When the Mongols invaded in 1549, Wang Zhen urged Emperor Yingzong to lead a military expedition in person. On hearing of a minor defeat at the front, Wang Zhen panicked, beat a hasty retreat and forced the emperor to take a needless and dangerous detour to his hometown in Hebei province. There the Mongols attacked and massacred the unprepared Ming troops and captured the emperor. His brother then succeeded to the throne until Yingzong was released. For his misdeeds Wang Zhen and his relatives were executed and his lavish home became a Buddhist temple called Zhihua (Wisdom Attained) Temple. Only some of the original seven halls are left but it is still one of the largest and finest surviving examples of Ming architecture. It includes the Hall of Ten Thousand Buddhas, the walls of which have 9,000 niches, each housing a small statue of the Buddha. The ceiling and lattice windows, delicately gilded and painted, survive intact. The temple housed a group of monks who played in an orchestra during Buddhist ceremonies. Astonishingly, the musicians are still there today and have handed down the music through twenty-seven generations. The temple musicians are still able to play and sing pieces more than three hundred years old. Inside the temple archives, the monks have preserved scores dating back to 1694, which rely on an old form of Chinese musical notation. Much of the music, slow-moving and ceremonial, may date back to the Tang dynasty in the eighth century. The monks fell on hard times during the 1920s and 1930s and started to sell off some of the temple's possessions, especially its intricately carved wooden panels and roofs. An American connoisseur, Lawrence Sickman, acquired its octagonal cupola, now in the Nelson-Atkins Museum of Art in Missouri.

The Ming eunuchs' legacy has almost been forgotten; the eunuchs were blamed for the downfall of the Ming dynasty and belong to the shameful past. Most of the hundreds of temples, shrines, palaces, graveyards and monasteries they left behind inside the city and in the countryside are now being carelessly destroyed. As we shall see in Chapter 9, I was fortunate to meet the last surviving imperial eunuch before his death.

4

On the Wild Wall

Coming in to land at Beijing airport on a flight from Europe, you peek out of the window and see that the vast sandy expanse of the Gobi Desert has been left behind. Suddenly there is a brief glimpse of the Great Wall itself, riding crest after crest of green mountains and ragged escarpments, and you gasp as if some mythical creature, a unicorn or a phoenix, had appeared in view. So many Chinese tourist sights disappoint, never quite matching the image created by the mind's eye. The imaginary Cathay is always more exotic, more compelling than the bare temples and palaces the visitor trudges through, assaulted by the braying loudspeakers and hectoring megaphones of the tourist guides. The Great Wall alone exceeds any expectations. Even up close, as one hikes from one watchtower to the next, puffing and sweating, the sheer immensity and doggedness of this endeavour overwhelms the imagination. The wall hugs the steepest, most inaccessible crags with resolute bravado, then plunges precipitously and implacably down into every gully, rising again like a roller-coaster frozen in stone. Sometimes it descends, staggered like a staircase, and vanishes into rivers, lakes and reservoirs, only to emerge tireless on the other side. So steep is the descent that in places gravity alone has over time pulled huge stones out of position, casting them down in a tumble at the bottom. At some points the wall widens to the breadth of a paved road and at others it narrows to just a foothold, and as you edge along, nervously holding on to the parapet. That this is the world's greatest defensive engineering project – a venture that every year occupied the labour of one and a half million men for 230 years until 1644 – is beyond doubt.

Approached from the north, the wall often rears up 30 feet, a sheer

61

impenetrable cliff, marked by stout battlements and arrow slits. No waterspouts project on this side, only on the south, to deny invaders the least help. The few gateways allowing access onto the ramparts are only on the south side, and travellers have to walk miles to find one permitting them to cross under the wall and enter Hebei province. Tramping along the wall you notice, too, that the quality of the masonry and the engineering is not uniform. Where the masons were careless water has crept in and destroyed the mortar binding the outer stones, and the rubble filling the interior has spilled out. Where the commanding officer was strict, the wall has resolutely resisted the elements. During its construction, each province and district had to conscript craftsmen and soldiers and send them to build and man a particular sector. Sometimes they migrated with their families, settling in walled villages on the lee side of the wall. Their descendants are still there and from each village there is always a narrow trail up a valley leading to a tower which their forefathers had built and manned. Sometimes, from the top of such a tower, you can just make out the smudge of grey pollution obscuring Beijing, but sometimes there is nothing but limestone hills long shorn of their trees.

Even visitors too lazy to do more than take a cable car at Mutianyu to see the ribbon of grey wall snaking over the hills may feel first exhilarated, then exhausted simply thinking about the stupendous labour the wall required. How could the builders ever chisel and hammer such an uncountable number of stones or transport them up these precipices with the help of nothing more than donkeys and ponies, and then painstakingly fit them all together? The uncomfortable thought seeps in, along with wonderment, that there is something irrational about its excessive scale. It smacks of madness and obsession, a cold war that stretched from century to century, like the compulsive digging of missile silo after missile silo. The wall is magnificent, but so outsized it is abnormal, planned by a mind gripped by a dangerous megalomania. The vantage towers stretching to the horizon, where the soldiers kept their swords and halberds oiled in readiness, and where they stacked the beacon-kindling and the wolf-dung and kept it dry generation after generation, all bear silent witness to a tedious eternity of watching and waiting. As you stumble up the broken stairs or stop to rest by an abandoned fireplace inside a deserted guard-tower, you also wonder what would have happened if defeat had not brought this building to a halt; what further castellations and crenellations might have been added to heighten the natural drama of the scenery, had the train of history not come to a sudden stop?

Under Emperor Wan Li, the Ming dynasty started a fresh bout of determined wall-building to stretch the defences to Shanhaiguan, the last fortress before the wall plunges into the sea at the Gulf of Bohai. The building was still going on even as the Manchu armies crossed the wall, without a fight, on their way to Beijing. The watch-towers, the staircases and archways of white marble, the tablets recording the names of the commanders and their titles – now all stand as if they had been abandoned not centuries but mere decades ago. Gradually one feels a tug of bewilderment: how could such an impregnable fortification ever fail?

Voltaire, who praised the wall as a greater engineering feat than the Pyramids, also derided it as an effort 'as vain as it is immense'. In some respects he was wrong; it was never a medieval Maginot Line that failed. For many years it succeeded in preserving the Ming until the dynasty was overthrown from within. But perhaps Voltaire was right – in the end the Great Wall did not protect Yong Le's dynasty but ultimately destroyed it. Karl Marx was close to the mark when he said the Great Wall symbolized the stagnation of the whole Chinese social and economic system. Yong Le's gigantic public-works scheme had helped bankrupt his state. It required such heavy taxes that in the end even China's cowed peasantry rose up. The Chinese Communists hailed the chief rebel leader, Li Zicheng (1606–45), as a hero. In Cultural Revolution posters he is glorified in tinted polychrome colours leading the victorious peasant masses against the corrupt court. There is now a statue of him, astride his steed, in the middle of a municipal roundabout near the motorway to Badaling.

Yong Le's wall is often thought to be the same as that built by the first emperor of China, Qin Shi Huangdi in 220 BC. It is true that after he conquered the other Chinese states, Qin deployed the labour of defeated armies and peoples to build a great wall that still exists. Yet this was of mud, pounded together, like that of Khublai Khan around Beijing. Such walls require a tiled roof merely to save them from being washed away in the summer rains and were not so much defensive fortifications as boundary walls. Even by the time of the Yuan dynasty in the thirteenth century such walls had become technologically obsolete. Marco Polo famously never noticed the Great Wall. When Khublai Khan was mounting the invasion of southern China, his troops were thwarted for five years by the mud walls around the Yangtze valley stronghold of Xianyang. Khublai Khan then brought various foreign engineers from Persia (then under Mongol rule) who were capable of building the mangonels and catapults commonly used in crusader warfare. These siege engines could accurately lob huge missiles capable of demolishing stone castles and they quickly knocked down Xianyang's mud walls. After that, resistance across southern China collapsed. When Yong Le decided to throw a defensive network across the northern frontier lands and to enclose Beijing in a multi-layered belt of defences, he rejected the cheap option. Instead of pounding earth, he ordered walls constructed of huge slabs cemented together with a rubble of mud and stone inside. The fortifications, like the walls of Beijing, were fronted with solid grey bricks stout enough to resist bombardment. This was a novelty. Most of the earlier mud walls seemed intended to serve first as a boundary. Chinese cities are normally not planned with defence in mind but usually set on a plain near a river. Rarely does a fortress on a hill loom over a Chinese city, as in European cities like Prague or Edinburgh.

The use of siege engines against the Ming Great Wall would be difficult in this wild country of inaccessible peaks and crags. And there is not just one wall protecting Beijing but a double curtain with 700 miles of loops and spurs and many fortresses and watchtowers beyond the wall. Yong Le created a linked perimeter of major garrisons interspersed with innumerable forts and walled camps. The largest of these is the huge garrison settlement protecting the western approaches at Datong, 160 miles west of the capital. More fortresses guarded the soft underbelly of the southern defences. In addition, Yong Le kept seasoned troops around the capital to lead expeditionary campaigns against the Mongol hordes that he wanted to drive away to distant pastures in the far north or south. After his death, these forward positions beyond the wall were gradually abandoned because they were so costly to maintain and the nomads moved back closer, depriving defenders of vital early intelligence of their movements. Yong Le thought that by moving the court so close to the front line, he would force them to make defence a priority. Yet later this proximity undermined the authority of military commanders because the court intervened too often. Generals became pawns in convoluted power struggles between eunuchs and bureaucrats, and towards the end of the dynasty the eunuchs, ignorant of warfare, often meddled in tactical and strategic planning. In one such case in 1506 the supreme commander of the frontier forces, Yang Yiqing, fell victim to the devious eunuch Liu Qin, who asserted his power first by rejecting the general's petition for funds to repair and strengthen border defences and later by imprisoning Yang, successfully accusing him of wasting public funds.[1]

The Mongols often rode around the most heavily fortified defences. Sometimes the Ming failed to coordinate troops and combine them in large enough numbers to resist attacks. Often by the time the troops arrived the raiding horsemen had long gone. Officials at the Ming capital even became confused about the names of leading khans. As the Mongol incursions came closer and closer to the Ming capital, the court ordered counterattacks which led to disastrous defeats, including one in the fifteenth century when the Mongols captured Emperor Yingzong. Discipline declined too. Some military officers kept the soldiers' wages and grain for their own purposes and in one incident at Datong in 1553 officers staged an uprising when a new commander arrived to restore discipline. As the court became nervous about the threat of an ambitious general staging a *coup d'état*, some emperors preferred to concentrate a very large proportion of their forces close to the capital just to keep an eye on them. Many Ming troops were actually ethnic Mongols who often resorted to banditry, preying on the huge traffic in goods transported to Beijing from the south. In 1479 the eunuch Wang Zhi complained in a report of witnessing these bandits riding horses, blockading roads, wounding people and making off with their merchandise. 'These are largely Mongolian army officers and Mongolian officers-in-waiting,' he pointed out, describing how they seized merchandise, then secretly entered the garrisons.

When faced with apprehension, they gather together their cohort and resist capture and fight back to the point that those sent to apprehend them fear their savagery. [They] dare not go forward in pursuit of this kind of person. Their barbaric nature seems to remain unaltered. [They] are not susceptible to the rewards for doing good. If we do not make plans, will they not grow increasingly fierce and unbridled in [their] reckless actions?

Another report sent to the Minister of War in 1488 observed that Mongols in the Ming army 'appeared no different from Mongols of the steppe', as they were dressed in armour and helmets, carrying bows and arrows, and were mounted on horses. It insisted that without more generous rewards, no one would risk his life by confronting them. The area around Beijing became plagued with highwaymen known as 'whistling arrow bandits' (*xiangmazei* or *xiangma* in Chinese) from their habit of tying bells to their mounts and using whistling arrows to announce their presence before attacks. These bandits, well mounted and armoured, became confident enough to stage raids in broad daylight around the capital. Some of them hid out in the enormous Wenlan marshes south of the capital. By 1631 some thirty-six bandit armies with a combined strength of over 200,000 men were reckoned to be rampaging across north-western China. The Ming dynasty was also threatened from the north-east, where the Manchu leader Nurhachi (1559–1626) had consolidated the Manchu tribes. The Manchus were the descendants of the Jurchens, who had earlier set up the Jin dynasty. He rejected his vassal allegiance to the Chinese throne and ceased delivering tribute. In a sworn statement, he justified his actions by listing 'seven grievances against the Ming dynasty'. He argued that 'because the emperor of the southern dynasty [the Ming] inhabits the deep recesses of his palace, he is cheated and deceived by civil and military officials of the border regions and has created no policy to comfort the people'.[2]

By 1622 Nurhachi was powerful enough to have conquered the northern Liaodong province, Korea and Inner Mongolia, and to have established his own dynasty, the Gold or Jin dynasty based in Shenyang. Only one Chinese general, Yuan Chonghuan, succeeded in inflicting a defeat on Nurhachi and his forces, but he was accused of treason and executed in yet another court intrigue (see Chapter 18 for the story of how one family struggled to preserve his tomb in Beijing from the bulldozers). In response, Wan Li boosted defence spending and enlarged the Great Wall by linking up more and more watch-towers. A watchtower, which was usually 30 feet high and 120 feet in circumference, cost 65 ounces of silver. Wan Li built tens of thousands and they gradually became linked by curtain walls so that the Wall also became known as Wan Li's Wall.[3] This spending put an enormous strain on the economy because the north-eastern defences now required three times as much grain than before, which the transportation system struggled to deliver.

Over the course of the Ming dynasty much of the land around Beijing – once reserved for military colonies or camps – became transferred into the hands of the aristocracy. From the age of 16, 'Princes of the Blood' were automatically awarded large tracts of land, tax exempt. Eunuchs collected rent and fees from the tenants on these estates, which were themselves passed on to the next generation. In this manner, large quantities of good land became free of tax, eroding the local tax base and putting an ever greater tax burden on the rest of the community. Impoverished peasants began to flee rather than pay onerous taxes or face prosecution for failing to pay them. State tax revenues declined and eunuchs were blamed for diverting taxes into their own pockets. When their crops failed thousands of peasants joined outlaw bands. One was led by Zhang Xianzhong (1605–47), son of a petty merchant, who plundered and murdered wealthy officials and then founded a 'Great Shun State' in southern China. He took a cruel revenge on the scholar-official class, inviting them to serve his state and, when they arrived, killing them slowly by inflicting the death of a thousand cuts. He then announced fresh civil service examinations and when the candidates arrived, he murdered them too.[4]

Li Zicheng, who had started life as a post-station master in Mijie in Shanxi province, led another rebel army and tried to win popular support with a political programme that included land reform. A leaflet, *For the Calming and Pacification of the People*, laid out his case against the Ming:

The fatuous and self-indulgent emperor of the Ming dynasty is not humane. He spoiled his eunuchs, relied heavily on exam graduates, was greedy for taxes and levies, used harsh punishments, and could not save the people from calamities. Every day the army robbed the people of their wealth, raped their wives and daughters, and exploited everyone most harshly. Our army is made up of good peasants who have worked the fields for ten generations; we formed this humane and righteous army to rescue the people from destruction.[5]

In 1640, Li recruited an army in drought-stricken Henan province, known as the 'dashing bandits', and attacked Beijing. He managed to march through the massive Juyong Pass fortress after its officers and eunuchs surrendered without a fight, and he led his bandit armies in triumphal procession through the main gates of the capital on 25 April 1644. The most powerful Ming army, the Shanhaiguan garrison led by General Wu Sangui, did nothing. Some speculate that Li managed to enter the city without a fight because a plague had decimated most of its garrison. Or perhaps the court feared the Manchus more than the rebels. Certainly, General Wu was being courted by all sides after Li's men invested the capital. For reasons still hard to fathom, General Wu chose to throw his lot in with the Manchus despite the fact that Li held both his father and his favourite concubine hostage. It may have been a recourse to the Southern Song strategy of using the barbarians to defeat the barbarians. In May 1644 Li rode out of Beijing and fought General Wu in a battle near Shanhaiguan on the coast; the Manchu cavalry was unleashed and the peasant rebels were defeated. Li escaped, returned to Beijing where he cut off the head of Wu's father and placed it on the battlements of the city before fleeing. By early June Beijing was in Manchu hands.[6] Li Zicheng only occupied the capital for two months, leaving little trace (although once near the western entrance gate I stumbled by accident into Li's former quarters in the Forbidden City, a run-down courtyard and huge state hall, closed to visitors and overgrown with grass). Li's peasant troops had ransacked the city and tried to force the remaining officials and eunuchs to divulge their hidden treasures, but they left most of it undamaged.

Curiously, the Manchus used the slogan of 'Restoring [the] Ming Dynasty' when they called on the Ming Chinese remnant armies to join them in crushing the peasant rebels. Wu Sangui pursued Li Zicheng to Xi'an, killing him in 1645. Zhang Xianzhong was caught and executed about a year later. After the establishment of the Qing empire, Wu was rewarded with the title 'The Great General Who Pacifies the West' and given Sichuan and Guizhou provinces to rule as his personal fiefdom. He continued to lead his army in battles against pretenders to the Ming throne. The remaining Ming loyalists briefly established a second capital at Nanjing and the last Ming pretender was finally tracked down in Burma, brought to Yunnan and executed in 1662.

With peace imposed by the Manchus, the Great Wall was abandoned and forgotten, merging in popular memory with the wall of the first emperor, built in 210 BC. In 1793, George Staunton, a member of Lord Macartney's trade delegation to the Emperor Qianlong, passed the Great Wall through the Gubeikou fortress, heading north to the Qing summer palace in Chengde (formerly Jehol). Somewhat surprised, he and the others found it was not manned at all and the entire party became fascinated with calculating the wall's scale – some reckoned it had enough stone to equal all the dwelling houses in England and Scotland. They were surprised that their Manchu hosts looked at it with indifference, but it had become an obsolete symbol of resistance to their rule. The wall slipped further into myth after the Manchu dynasty began to decline, until Dr Sun Yat-sen, whose 1911 revolution overthrew the empire, elevated it to a national symbol because it had helped preserve the Chinese race from northern invaders. When the Japanese occupied Manchuria in the 1930s, the wall became a popular symbol of resistance against these new invaders from the north. Propaganda photographs showed Chinese troops marching and fighting on it. After 1949, the newly adopted national anthem, 'March of the Volunteers', called on all those who would not be slaves to build a new Great Wall. The Ming wall was turned into an icon of Chinese nationalism and a picture of it hung in the reception room of every government office. It lapsed in importance at the height of China's friendship with the Soviet Union but revived again when the two Communist giants fell out in 1969 and waged a brief border war. When the Chinese publicized it as a symbol of vigilance and unrelenting resistance to their northern neighbour, *Pravda*, the Soviet mouthpiece, then responded by cheekily suggesting that China ought to withdraw from Manchuria as the Great Wall marked its northern border.

In the 1970s, as the Chinese military prepared to resist an expected Soviet invasion, they placed tanks and artillery in caves hidden in valleys along the wall. Naturally, when China and America formed a loose alliance against the Soviet Union President Nixon was brought to stand on its battlements; it was a symbol of their joint stand against the Red Army to the north. 'This is a great wall and it had to be built by a great people,' Nixon said on his 1972 visit. An apocryphal version claims that he actually said, 'It sure is a great wall.' Ever since, every visiting statesman, hundreds of them by now, is taken to Badaling where he or she struggles to coin a flattering or wittier bon mot. Beyond Badaling one can tramp for hundreds and hundreds of miles along deserted ramparts, pushing through overgrown bushes that smell of wild lavender and thyme. The villages in its shadow are poor and the villagers talk of going to Beijing as if it were New York, although the section nearest to Beijing, at Huanghua Chen, lies just 35 miles north of Deshengmen Gate. Children run barefoot in the summer while their parents farm small patches of fields with a thin soil. They comb the steep hillsides for wild rhubarb, garlic, onions or medicinal roots. Sometimes you see a peasant striding downhill with a brace of wild pheasants over one shoulder and a homemade musket on the other. The women shyly offer for sale chestnuts, walnuts and dried mushrooms on a string. They make a milky drink that tastes of sweet almonds by gathering fallen apricots and crushing the kernels. On this Wild Wall you sometimes see no one but a distant shepherd and hear nothing more than the wind carrying tinkling bells from his herd of goats. The Wild Wall is a rare wilderness in China, serendipit-ously created along this ancient no man's land, just as the Iron Curtain in places became a nature reserve. At times there is a brief glimpse of a lynx or fox scouting for wild hares, or the shadow of an eagle falls across the worn stone as it hunts for lizards basking in the sun. Now the Great Wall guards nothing more than butterflies and wild apricot trees.

5

The Ming Tombs

A picnic at one of the Ming tombs used to be one of the pleasures of life in Beijing. Even when almost all of China was out of bounds, one could still drive there, an hour from the polluted city, and breathe the air. Rusting signs in English and Chinese still stand on paths just behind the walled and wooded burial mounds of tombs, warning foreigners not to proceed a step further without authorization. Far from Beijing's ugly pretensions to modernity, one felt a little freer and in such a haunt of ancient peace could savour an unchanging China fixed for ever in a romantic decay. Compared to the Great Wall or the Pyramids of the Pharaohs or the vaulted stone splendours of Gothic cathedrals, the Ming tombs look as modest as a country churchyard. Tourists who disembark from their coaches to see Yong Le's Chang Ling (*ling* means 'tomb') see bare halls and burial chambers as evocative as an empty bank vault. Official signs point out the extravagant cost compared to the income of the labouring classes, the proletarian lives sacrificed to fell rare *nanmu* trees and pull the trunks from the distant south. Only two tombs are open, those of Yong Le and Wan Li. The other nine had until recently been left as abandoned ruins, but were restored after 2002.

My favourite ruin was the tomb of the Emperor Zhengde, the foppish, youthful playboy who wanted to hold official audiences at night. The yellow tiles on his spirit tower had mostly fallen off, leaving the roof beams sticking out in a dishevelled manner. Inside the stone arch beneath the tower, a donkey was stabled and often found eating noisily from a pile of fresh hay. Grass grew between the marble slabs on the paths that led to bridges spanning streams which had run dry and were now planted with corn. Pines and cypress trees grew out of the tomb walls, thrusting aside the huge stones with commanding strength. In the walled forecourt where Zhengde's descendants came to kowtow, humble cabbage heads aligned in ranks like so many officials making their obsequies waited to be picked. We placed bottles of wine on the sacrificial altar, next to the stone urns and bowls arranged for the libations and offerings that had not been made for nearly a century. On a summer evening, blossoms drifted over from the local village's apple and peach orchards, and with swallows and magpies just above, one could not help wondering why Chinese people never came to share this beauty, but romantic decay is antithetical to the prevalent spirit of the modernization project. The wistful longing of Tang poetry, the elusive dreams of Taoist philosophy, the sketches of temples hidden in craggy forested peaks or the ink-wash strokes that cast solitary boats adrift in the rain belong to another China. In 2002 the Ming Tombs Special Zone Administrative Office decided they must be restored and now they look like new. Behind the tomb where Chongzhen, the last Ming emperor, is buried, the authorities built an artificial ski park where loudspeakers now blare out 1970s disco hits. Here Chinese utilitarianism overwhelms Western romanticism.

The entire valley with its thirteen Ming tombs will never again be made to look as it once did. It was burnt and ransacked twice, first by the Ming rebel leader Li Zicheng in 1644 and then by the invading Manchus. The desecration of ancestral graves was a frequent act of political revenge throughout Chinese history. The tombs of the Liao and the Jin dynasties had been destroyed by Emperor Wan Li because, in the face of the growing threat from the Manchus, he followed the advice of a geomancer. 'If the tombs of the Jin emperors in Fangshan are destroyed to dispel its magic luck, the army of the Ming will turn defeat into victory,' he was told. As the Manchus are descendants of the Jin, the geomancer persuaded Wan Li that, by destroying their ancestral tombs, he could destroy their ancestral magic. The tombs took two months to burn and all one can now see of them are a few broken stelae in a field south of Beijing. (The Mongol khans were wise enough to be buried in such utter secrecy that their tombs have never been found.) In revenge, the Manchu general Dorgon ordered his troops to destroy the Ming tombs and the troops took care to wreak the greatest ruin on Emperor Wan Li's tomb. Only one stela was left. At Yong Le's Chang Ling tomb, only the great Hall of Heavenly Favours survived the destruction. Before the advent of modern technology it was perhaps the largest building in China. Its beautiful roof was supported by sixty massive columns made of a dense tropical timber, the *nanmu* wood mentioned above, and inlaid with gold.

With the construction of the Ming tombs, Yong Le made Beijing China's grandest necropolis. It was one of the costliest and greatest of his projects, and he spent 8 million taels of silver on it, equal to two years' state revenues. He selected the site himself and sent a force of 400,000 troops and civilians to create a dynastic mausoleum covering 48 square miles. It was ringed by high walls and towers and was almost part of the Great Wall defences. For eighteen years they laboured to complete the magnificent approach, with its arches and a 'spirit way' lined with statues of animals, officials and generals. When a member of the imperial family died, the body would be brought out of the North Gate of the Forbidden City and taken to the Shou Huang Dian, a complex at the foot of Coal Hill. (It has since become the Beijing Children's Palace and talented children are sent there to be coached in dancing, singing, acting, painting and sport.) There the deceased would lie in state before rows of ancestral portraits, waiting for an auspicious day to be determined. In 1910, the Empress Dowager Cixi waited there a whole year before her body was taken to the Qing tombs in a vast cortège of weeping eunuchs, priests and lamas led by the Dalai Lama himself. The journey took more than a week.

In Beijing, ancestral worship also took place in ceremonies performed at the Tai Miao, Temple of the Ancestors, and this is perhaps the most sacred spot in the city. The Tai Miao is now inside the Beijing Working People's Cultural Park and lies at the south-east corner of the Forbidden City. One can still walk among the groves of wonderful cedars that Yong Le planted. It was the dynasty's family shrine, and Yong Le, who performed sacrifices there five times a year, built it as a replica of the original Ming ancestral temple in Nanjing. After every military victory prisoners were marched there for the approval of the ancestral spirits. Every ancestor had his own spirit tablet, a plain oblong piece of lacquered wood with his name carved in gold characters before which offerings were made. Even an Associate Prince or Duke, or an Associate Meritorious Minister, had such a tablet. Before each ceremony they were all brought into the hall, after which an official proceeded to slaughter red bullocks, black boars and white sheep. In front of the altar, wine was poured into jade cups, fruit piled onto bamboo baskets and dried grapes laid on porcelain. Other vessels held boiled grain, parched grain and glutinous millet. The ancestral spirits were offered dishes such as white flour cakes, hazelnut kernels, water chestnuts, crayfish, waterlily seeds, dates, dried venison, sea slugs, biscuits, leeks and tripe. Similar sacrifices were performed at the tomb of each emperor.

In 1531 the Ming also built another temple in the city, the Di Wang Miao, dedicated to the entire pantheon of all 188 Chinese emperors, including some who are entirely legendary. Each one had a tablet. (This temple remained in use until 1911, when it was turned into a girls' school and then a middle school.) Occasionally it happened that a dead emperor was, so to speak, dropped from the team. For instance, in the seventeenth century the great Qing emperor Kangxi evicted two of the last Ming emperors, Taichang and Tianqi, whose reigns immediately followed Wan Li, arguing that their performances in office were too shamefully inadequate to merit a place. It is hard now to grasp the importance of ancestor worship. Wan Li became emperor at 10, and at 18 he was already planning the construction of the vault of his tomb, the Ding Ling. The last trip he made out of Beijing was to inspect progress on it and he did not leave the city again until his death thirty years later. No matter what rank the deceased enjoyed, the Confucian dogma of filial piety, *xiao*, obliged a family to build lavish tombs and mount extremely costly funerals. Funerals were once one of Beijing's most colourful sights. George Kates was lucky enough to witness a warlord's send-off, one of the last great processions ever held in the city. It stretched for several miles and even the electric lines for trolleys had to be propped up to let it through. Men led the way bearing large banners reading 'Kai Dao' (Open the Road). The chief mourner, dressed in hemmed and bleached coarse white cloth, a long wand in his hand, was supported in his grief by attendants. Next came the catafalque, which was always borne by bearers in multiples of eight. For very grand personages there would be sixty-four bearers.

Every 10 feet the chief mourner knelt on a cushion and knocked his head on the ground three times. Temporary mat-sheds for serving tea lined the route. Monks marched along with 10-foot-long horns carried for them by little boys. Manchu aristocrats were accompanied on their journey by their camels, falcons and hunting dogs. Modern warlords were sent to the afterlife with paper models of foreign motor cars and radio cabinets, which were burnt.

The tradition of attacking hapless dead ancestors continued even during the Cultural Revolution amidst the most violent attack on tradition. Red Guards smashed up the tomb of the Jesuit Matteo Ricci, the first Catholic priest to spread the gospel in China. In 1900 the Boxer rebels had attacked it and indeed all the foreign graves they could find. Ironically, it was the opposition by the Catholic Church to ancestor worship that caused many of the troubles faced by such Jesuits in China. When the Vatican ignored the advice of the Jesuits and forbade Chinese Catholics to take part in ancestral worship, it led to a breach which did not heal for centuries. Ricci was the first Westerner admitted to the Forbidden City when he entered to fix one of the mechanical clocks he had gifted to Emperor Wan Li. The emperor requested that he stay near the Forbidden City to wind up the clocks, and Ricci was able to build on this imperial tolerance, although he never once saw Wan Li in the flesh during all the twenty years he spent there. His tomb, if not his remains, is now to be found in a former Catholic seminary which is now the municipality's Communist Party School, renamed the Beijing Administrative College. He lies behind a huge red spirit wall on which Deng Xiaoping's calligraphy urges the resident students of Marxism to 'Seek Truth From Facts'. Ricci's once bore a resemblance to an imperial tomb with a mound and a spirit avenue with stone sculpture, but is now less impressive, despite the restoration that began in 1984. It is surrounded by tall stelae, embellished with crosses and curling dragons, that record the names and lives in Latin and Chinese of Adam von Schall, Ferdinand Verbiest and sixty-two other foreign missionaries who ended their lives in China.

The legacy of the Ming dynasty continued to cast its shadow on a deputy mayor of Beijing in the 1950s called Wu Han, who was an expert on Ming history and wrote a detailed biography of Zhu

Yuanzhang, the dynasty's founder. It was he who had calculated that there were 100,000 eunuchs in Wan Li's reign and proposed opening Wan Li's tomb. Archaeologists hoped it would be as great a feat as Howard Carter's at the Valley of the Kings in Egypt. It would glorify China and at the same time demonstrate the extravagance and super-stition of the feudal past. Many imperial tombs had been robbed or ransacked in the past, but this would be the first scientific excavation. The obvious choice was Yong Le's tomb. He was the mightiest of all the Ming emperors, and archaeologists fully expected to find treasures surpassing Tutankhamun's. But had it been left untouched by robbers and rebels? Wu Han pushed for Wan Li's tomb, which had the attrac-tion that an excavation could answer a still burning question: had the emperor ensured that in death he would be united with his beloved Lady Zheng and buried with her? Or had the mandarins triumphed over the recalcitrant Wan Li and entombed him only with his acknowl-edged wives? The excavation was led by Professor Xia Nai and his 28-year-old assistant, Zhao Qichang. Everyone was nervous. The vaults had hidden entrances and booby traps, such as poisoned arrows or swords unleashed by hidden mechanisms, to stop tomb robbers. They quickly discovered, too, that the local peasants revered the emperors and were scared of disturbing their ancestral spirits. It would bring bad luck, they said, and they were proved right. Soon after the start of the digging an old woman began foaming at the mouth, apparently possessed by an evil spirit. Then lightning struck several of the excavators, almost killing them. The workforce were terrified. They insisted on sacrificing two live chickens to placate the ancestral sprits. Even the resolute men of science became uneasy. They knew about the mummy's curse. Many of the men – more than thirty, some said – who had helped Howard Carter open Tutankhamun's tomb had died in mysterious circumstances. Some believe they succumbed after inhaling deadly bacteria trapped in the Egyptian tombs: could that happen here in China? As the first bricks to the entrance were pulled open, 'a muffled puffing noise was heard as from a punctured rubber ball, and heavy black mist poured out of the opening. It was followed by a hoarse growling, similar to the snarling of wild beasts in the dark night . . .'[1] A black mist streamed out of the tomb with a strange rustling noise as the archaeologists, donning protective gas masks, entered the tomb. A massive slab blocked the white marble entrance door.

By sliding an L-shaped metal key between the door panels, they could push the slab back and open up the entrance to the tunnel leading to the vault itself. They found themselves in a huge rectangular structure made entirely of stone blocks with a vaulted stone ceiling. In the haze, they could see three white empty thrones. Stalactites had formed, which in the dim light looked like flying sabres, but they found no hidden traps. Inside the main vault they found a dais on which rested three lacquered coffins. The Emperor Wan Li lay next to his two unloved empresses, Xiaojing and Xiaoduan, all three of them dwarfed 'by the immense void of the lonely underground palace'.[2] It seems that even in death the officials had won and Wan Li was prevented from sharing the afterlife with Lady Zheng. In this dreary and desolate setting, Wan Li lay in his coffin, not a well-preserved mummy, but a grim skeleton. A yellowish-brown beard hung from his lips, and his right hand bent upwards, as if he was about to stroke it. His left hand still grasped a string of beads. The empress Xiaojing had been buried with Buddhist scriptures while Wan Li himself wore the plain robe of a Taoist priest underneath a legendary dragon robe; these could take ten years to stitch and this is the only one of its kind ever found. Two side chambers were empty and there was no sign of Lady Zheng. There was some treasure, but not much. On his skull, Wan Li wore a crown made entirely of fine gold thread woven into a gauze-like material and shaped like a bonnet with two wings. Another box contained a crown with wings of gold netting. The empresses were buried with pieces of jade, pins of gold and precious stones. Underneath the bodies were laid paper money, gold coins and small ingots so that they could pay their way in the afterlife.

Besides the coffins, the archaeologists found a few blue-and-white pots, twenty-six wooden boxes left in disorder, a jumble of costumes, rolls of silk and various household objects useful in the next life. This was not an Aladdin's cave of treasures but more like the prop room of a Peking Opera house. The silk brocades, however, were an astonishing find. The colours were still dazzling. In all, the tomb contained 200 bolts of cloth. Under a light-yellow brocade quilt, Empress Xiaojing had been laid to rest in a lined yellow satin jacket stitched with gold thread and embroidered with a hundred boys in playful scenes. Lower down, she wore a red satin skirt over padded trousers of yellow satin. Empress Xiaoduan lay dressed in a brilliant jacket embroidered with dragons. Apart from these finds, the excavation was a disappointment, and worse was to follow. The Communist tomb-raiders had indeed awoken a malign spirit that quickly destroyed the lives of everyone connected to the excavation. Even as the team marvelled over their finds, the cold hand of a new despot reached out to grasp them. Professor Xia fell victim to one of Chairman Mao's purges, during which a million intellectuals were arrested in the Anti-Rightist Movement, and he disappeared from sight until 1972. Days after the tomb was opened to the public, his assistant, Zhao Qichang, was detained and sent to labour in the countryside; he would not return to archaeological work for another two decades. The report of their research was not published until 1989, three decades after the tomb's opening.

In 1959, the curators of the Ding Ling museum replaced the original coffins with plaster casts; they threw the originals over the walls of the tomb into a gully, and peasants in the village of Yu Ling retrieved them. One couple made two trunks from the wood. One day they came home to find their four children missing. After a search they found four pairs of shoes by the trunk and opened the lid. Inside, they found the children pressed together, dead. They had been playing when the lid fell on them, locking them in, and had suffocated. There was blood around their fingernails and scratches on the thick wood.

Then in 1966, as the museum staff became embroiled in the Cultural Revolution, they split into different factions. The radicals of the 'Fight-for-Truth' team resolved to extend Mao's campaign against the 'Four Olds' (which amounted to anything from the past) and destroy the museum and all its relics, which by definition were all symbols of feudalism. In the museum courtyard, the Red Guards shouted 'Down with Wan Li, chieftain of the landlord class' as they heaped the three skeletons, together with their portraits, onto a bonfire. All that remained were a few strands of hair and a fistful of imperial molars. The other treasures found in the tombs were also lost, including the hundreds of wooden statues of court officials, palace maids and horses, meant to serve the dead in the afterlife. After the statues had been dipped in wax to preserve them they quickly shrank into deformed shapes, the dazzling colours of the beautiful brocades faded and, exposed to air, were eaten up by black spots. The thick silk embroidery turned brittle, then shrank and puckered into a formless mass.

Wu Han lost his life in 1969 after being dragged before a crowd of Red Guards at the Workers' Stadium screaming for his death. Inspired by the courage of the upright Ming official, Hai Rui, who had dared criticize two emperors, Wu Han had composed an opera that was a veiled attack on Mao and his policies. He composed it during the Great Leap Forward famine (1958–62) in which 30 million starved to death. Four years later, the Cultural Revolution was started with a piece of criticism attacking the opera. Mao took his revenge and his mummified corpse still lies in a huge tomb in the centre of Beijing. No one has yet dared to desecrate it.

6

In the Garden of Perfect Brightness

The silence spread like a dark tide across the broad expanse of polished wood that separated me from Professor Li Jinling of the Chinese Forestry Research Institute. We sat on opposite sides of a huge board-room table and, as we talked, his brow creased in puzzlement. 'So why did the Emperor Qianlong make this lace bark pine a general in his army?' I was asking. 'Was it some kind of joke?'

The pine had been planted in Beihai Park in the Jin dynasty, six hundred years earlier, and one stuffy summer day the emperor stopped to sit under its spreading branches and felt surprisingly cool and comfortable. The emperor promptly knighted it, so it was afterwards known as the White Robe General. Professor Li had been telling me that his institute had spent five years researching the mystery of how the tree achieved its effect. He had spent his life studying Beijing's community of gnarled trees and discovering potions to treat arboreal rheumatism, and now he seemed convinced this was an untapped gold mine of scientific knowledge.

'So tell me about stock options,' Professor Li said impatiently. He was small and wore heavy glasses, and I noticed he had put on a formal suit and a tie featuring a goldfish for my visit. He thought I was playing hard to get. 'It must be easy enough,' he said archly, returning to the subject of the Hong Kong stock market, 'if you know the right sort of people down there.'

But this time he had exhausted my small reservoir of knowledge about stock market listings, patents and product liability, and I tried to steer the conversation back to the greatest of all Qing dynasty emperors. The Emperor Qianlong reigned for exactly sixty years, as a warrior who led his army in battles that had doubled the size of his empire; a romantic who fell in love with a Turkish princess; a poet who composed more verse than any other emperor in history; and it seems a tree-lover extraordinaire. All over Beijing you used to find his calligraphy. Where Qianlong went, he found beauty and could not resist a compulsion to crank out a few more verses. A stonemason would then quickly chisel out an exact copy, leaving future generations to admire both his calligraphy and literary gifts. Professor Li believed that since I worked for a Hong Kong company, I had the entrée into the world of tycoons and could help him navigate the global capital markets. I came to interview him because I had read that many Beijingers were petitioning the municipal authorities to stop planting poplars and to grow ginkgoes instead. The government was planting industrial-scale plantations of fast-growing willow and poplar out of an understandable wish to control the fierce dust storms that plagued the city.

The utopia that Chinese planners wanted to create required avenues with trees regimented like soldiers on parade. Yet people detested these trees. They complained that in April the cotton-like fluff that floated off the poplars caused hay fever. In May another suffocating white snow came from the catkins of the willow trees. Beijingers, great and humble, have always cared to have trees around them. Sprawling Chinese scholar trees or jujube trees are planted in court-yards to create shade. Elms perform the same service in the hutongs. The yellow or purple flowering magnolia is popular for its blossoms and so is the Chinese wisteria, with its purple blossom, and the crab apple tree that produces white sprays. Above all, Beijingers revere irregular trees shaped by their *qi*, that is, by spontaneous natural forces, as well as strangely shaped rocks. They love bizarre species like the Chinese pagoda tree with its twisting, winding limbs or the ugly jujube tree. Even the odd-looking Chinese catalpa inspires great affection, and particularly odd specimens are given individual names, or indeed official honours and salaries. The Emperor Qianlong made a *guazi* pine in the Forbidden City a marquis and penned some verses in its honour. He knighted another pine in Jietan Temple, calling it the Crouching Dragon. It is still there, a beast emerging from a marble balustrade, twisting its scaly mottled trunk and thrusting aside the ponderous marble blocks with hideous strength. Some trees diligently fulfilled their responsibilities, showing that these titles were no mere empty baubles. One cypress in the Temple of Confucius, the 'Cypress-which-offended-the-treacherous-officials', had loyally dropped branches on several scheming black-hearted eunuchs. The movement to resist the 'factory' trees was just part of the great resistance to the modernizing project. An old man, when I met him early one morning in Ditan Park, was furiously slapping a cypress; he explained what drove the combatants in this low intensity conflict: 'Only these kinds of ancient trees have a lot of *qi*, and that is why their life force can nourish your own vitality,' he explained, pausing to catch his breath. Then he rammed himself against its gnarled trunk.

In the early 1980s the city had gone to great lengths to identify its ancient trees. Some 40,000 were given an identity number recorded on a tin plate hammered onto the bark. Metal railings often gave extra protection. Even when so many old buildings were levelled, architects took great pains to ensure the majority of trees were not cut down. The oldest within the old city walls are the cypresses in Zhongshan Park near the moat of the Forbidden City, planted during the Liao dynasty a thousand years ago. My favourites are in the Temple of Confucius, cypresses with twisted limbs held up by metal props, like geriatrics clutching on to their Zimmer frames. Professor Li took a modern and utilitarian view of trees but he explained this was not so new. Emperors liked to plant cypress and juniper trees for practical reasons. Junipers are planted at tombs, not just because their twisted and curling trunks look like dragons but the Chinese once believed that their branches housed strange creatures called *wang liang* that frightened off evil spirits. The seeds and berries of both trees are efficacious in treating heart ailments and were used by Tongren Tang, the former imperial pharmacy. The seeds of the Chinese honey locust tree are good for curing afflictions of the brain. Its leaves are also brewed for an infusion. In times of necessity, the blossoms are stir-fried and the nectar is edible too. During the Great Leap Forward famine, Beijingers relied on the tree to supplement their rations.

Professor Li explained that it was his sound knowledge of Chinese medicine that enabled him to develop remarkable cures for arboreal maladies. If I would only let him explain, I would begin to grasp how his compresses and ointments could make us rich. If, he said, my company would consider investing some capital – here he mentioned a seven-figure sum – then we could market products with a global potential. At this, I had to bring matters to a head. 'There must be some mistake,' I ventured at last. 'I am not in business.' 'Ah,' he replied with a knowing smile. 'But your secretary said something else.' So that was it. The office fixer had been off on holiday and the temporary replacement must have spun him a story just to get him to agree to be interviewed. When I finally convinced him that, although undoubtedly foreign, I was not a foreign investor, he asked about my nationality. 'Ah, so you are English,' he said. After turning this 'Yinguoren' (Englishman) notion around in his mind for a moment, he suddenly and vehemently demanded: 'So what do you have to say about the burning of the Yuanming Yuan [Old Summer Palace]?'

The accusation, and the emotion behind, took me by surprise. Lord Elgin had burnt down the Qing dynasty pleasure gardens nearly 150 years earlier. So much else had happened since and so much more of old Beijing was being destroyed that this attack seemed absurd. As an atrocity it paled into insignificance beside the millions who had died in twentieth-century China. Besides, it had always seemed just another example of how Chinese and Westerners so often have been at cross-purposes. The burning of the Yuanming Yuan, or Garden of Perfect Brightness, in 1860 belonged to the chain of misunderstandings that have bedevilled relations between China and the West.

'Do not forget the national shame, rebuild the Chinese nation', reads a sign outside the eastern entrance to the parklands. In the Communist Party's narrative of Chinese history, the destruction of the Yuanming Yuan marks the start of the modernization project, the beginning of a 'century of shame and humiliation' when the might of modern industrializing nations of Europe first began to force change on the feudal and immobile Chinese empire. No one can fail to be moved by the loss of the Yuanming Yuan, but there is something odd, even puzzling, about the way it has been elevated into such a potent symbol. One day I came to walk among the ruins and saw schoolchildren wearing the red scarves of the Communist Youth League, standing on the ruined stones in military ranks, raising their clenched fists and vowing allegiance to the party and its mission to modernize China and avenge past humiliations.

China's Risorgimento begins with the founding of the People's Republic of China in 1949. The Opium Wars are given the same role in Chinese history as the sacking of Rome by the Vandals, Goths and Huns, mute witnesses to the story of how a proud civilization was ruined by foreign troops, imperialism and aggression. Thus China's decline, and a century of colonial exploitation, begins with the burning of the Yuanming Yuan and the first Opium War, 1839–42. In the minds of many Chinese, the garden has been transformed into an Eden from which they have been expelled by barbarian invasions. One American academic, Norman Kutcher, went so far as to claim: 'The place has a meaning for Chinese akin to that of the Holocaust for Jews: it is an eternal reminder both of what has been lost and of what cannot be allowed to happen again.'[1]

The shattered marble and the lakes and fountains overgrown with reeds speak to one powerfully but it is a long stretch to link it with Auschwitz and its gas chambers. What you find instead is a park given over to a tacky funfair, a dreary zoo, a so-called 'primitive people's totem park' and amusement rides featuring Snow White. The casual ugliness of so much of the Yuanming Yuan makes it hard to imagine its former beauty. Moreover, the only parts worth visiting are the ruins, which actually belong to the rococo palaces and fountains built by resident Jesuits. As it prepared Peking for the 2008 Olympics, the government hesitated whether it was best to restore the ruins or leave them in their original state as a centre for 'education in patriotism'. One conservationist, Liang Congjie, argued that it was best not to try to restore the gardens because the result would be inferior to the original and destroy the evocative atmosphere of the ruins. The government held nearly a hundred meetings on the matter. It then persuaded UNESCO to declare it a World Heritage site, and as such it was obliged under UNESCO rules to preserve it.[2]

The parklands, covering 330 acres some six miles west of the city, once held approximately 4,200 palaces, temples and pavilions. The walled grounds enclosed an area ten times the size of the Forbidden City, and here the emperor travelled between palaces in pleasure boats poled along the network of canals and lakes. Some 240 bridges crossed all these waterways. As far back as the Liao dynasty (907–1125)

Beijing's rulers had built palaces here. When the Manchus conquered China, they so detested the enclosed and claustrophobic life in the Forbidden City that they moved the whole court, and the gardens effectively became the centre of power. The Emperor Kangxi initiated this in 1689 in order, as he put it, to 'avoid the noises and to administrate affairs'. Qianlong defended the cost of expanding the Yuanming Yuan by explaining in an edict that 'Every Emperor and ruler, when he has returned from audience and has finished his public duties, must have a garden where he may stroll about and relax his heart'.[3] The Yuanming Yuan was continually enlarged and came to include three gardens, a vast library, the imperial art collection, audience and banqueting halls, temples, studios, workshops and theatres, as well as palaces and residences. Emperor Kangxi had thirty-five sons and each had his own special part of the garden with offices for his household. All these were controlled by the Nei Wu Fu or Household Department. During his sixty years in office, Qianlong created almost a hundred different scenes in the gardens, replicating whatever building, garden, canal or mountain in the empire took his fancy. The emperor took his ease in such delightfully named palaces as 'Carving the Moon and Opening the Cloud Palace' or the 'Curving Courtyard and Lotus in the Wind', and retired to such edifices as the 'Study History to Understand the Present Complex'.

It was all a fantasy world, a theatrical version of the real world for an emperor who rarely encountered the latter. He could never be seen by his subjects. When travelling, everyone was evicted before he arrived at any place and warned not even to attempt to gaze upon him. Yet his court often tried to recreate life outside the garden. Several times a year the eunuchs created a make-believe town with markets where the emperor pretended to buy things at their shops. Father Attiret, a French Jesuit who lived at the court, reported that it had 'all the markets, all the arts, all the trades, all the bustle, all the comings and goings and even the rogueries of a great city . . . The ships arrive in port, the shops open: the goods are spread out; one quarter is for silks; another for clothes; one street is for porcelain, another for lacquer; everything is there.' The emperor is treated almost like the lowest of his subjects: 'Everyone calls out his wares; they quarrel, they fight; it is the real bustle of the market place. There are even pickpockets. Those quarrelling are taken to a tribunal, examined and judged and one of the men is sentenced to a beating.'4

Other parts of the garden were designed to allow the emperor to pretend he was a hermit enjoying rustic solitude. At times the emperor played the role of a farmer living in Peach Blossom Village, which is the Shangri-La of Chinese folk tales. At the start of spring, the emperor also went to a special field where he pretended to till the earth. The emperor could also pretend to be a sailor when his eunuchs staged mock naval battles with tiny junks that fired on one other with little brass cannons. Just as they played at going shopping, the Manchu emperors pretended to be Chinese emperors. They regarded the Han Chinese as enslaved subjects and forced them to wear pigtails as a sign of their subjugation. Every year, Emperor Qianlong held military parades to celebrate the Manchu military conquest over the Chinese. The Manchu ruling family spoke to each other in Manchu and wrote all official documents in the Manchu script. They kept themselves apart in many ways. Manchu women did not bind their feet like Han Chinese women and continued to wear their own distinctive costume and headdress. Although the Communist historical narrative presents the Manchu emperors as victims of Western imperialism, the Qing empire was a voracious expansionist power, attacking its neighbours and massacring any who dared resist. As Mongol power declined in Central Asia, the tsar in Moscow and the emperor in Peking competed to expand into the vacuum. The Chinese students swearing loyalty to the Communist Party were actually parading on the ruins of the Belvedere Palace, which the Emperor Qianlong built to house a war trophy, the Fragrant Concubine (Xiang Fei), a Muslim princess seized in Turkestan. Qianlong's men had beheaded her husband for resisting their invasion; this is the historical basis for China's current claims to the sovereignty over lands which are now called Xinjiang. The inhabitants, mostly Turkic-speaking Uzbeks, are now called Uighurs, after an ancient nomadic tribe. Even in its final years, the Qing empire did not hesitate to dispatch an army to Korea in order to reassert its control of a vassal state.

The Manchus held together the Qing empire by crushing a succession of large-scale uprisings. In the 1850s the Qing armies emerged victorious from a protracted civil war against the Taipings, a Chinese millenarian sect whose leader claimed to be the brother of Jesus Christ. When the Taiping capital at Nanjing fell, the Qing troops destroyed most of the city and massacred the inhabitants. This may be the worst civil war in recorded history and it cost over 30 million lives. The death toll for all the rebellions in the nineteenth century is thought to total 70 million, causing the population of the empire to actually fall. By comparison, the Opium Wars cost the lives of only a few thousand.

The Emperor Qianlong thought himself without equal on earth and required all others to bow before him. Lord Macartney, who refused to perform this kowtow, was a great exception. During his embassy to China in 1793, he tried to establish the principle that his sovereign, George III, must be treated as an equal. Like other European powers, the British sent embassies hoping to persuade the emperor to agree to open China to British manufactured goods. As the British public had become very fond of Chinese tea and porcelain, London was running a huge trade deficit and was anxious to start exporting and to balance the trade. For a century traders had been confined to a small island in Guangzhou (Canton), and now they pressed for access to the whole market. In his reply to George III, however, the emperor firmly declined to open the door to trade and refused even to allow the establishment of a permanent embassy:

Our dynasty's majestic virtue has penetrated unto every country under Heaven, and Kings of all nations have offered their costly tribute by land and sea. As your Ambassador can see for himself, we possess all things. I set no value on objects strange or ingenious, and have no use for your country's manufactures. This then is my answer to your request to appoint a representative at my Court, a request contrary to our dynastic usage, which would only result in inconvenience to yourself.[5]

Despite this setback, the merchants found they had a ready market for opium. When later the Emperor Daoguang (1782–1850) sent a senior mandarin, Lin Zexu, to Guangzhou to enforce a ban on the opium trade and to seize the merchants' stores, this triggered the first Opium War. Defeat led the Emperor Daoguang to sign the Treaty of Nanjing in 1842 and open five ports to foreign trade. The merchants complained that China was not observing the terms of the Nanjing

Treaty. In 1858 Britain and France sent special envoys to seek an audience with the new reigning emperor, a weak young man known as the Emperor Xianfeng.

A new treaty, the Treaty of Tianjin, was signed in 1858 but the merchants' troubles continued when their properties were attacked and looted. So in 1860 Lord Elgin and Baron Gros appeared at the head of an armed force. The two sides negotiated but the French and British aristocrats accused the Chinese officials of tricking them, violating every agreement, and believed they were too frightened to give the court the messages. When a delegation led by two of Elgin's secretaries, Harry Parkes and Thomas Wade, arrived at the capital under a flag of truce, they were seized and tortured. The infuriated allies then marched to the gates of Beijing and the population panicked and fled. Meanwhile, the young emperor, Xianfeng, was at the Yuanming Yuan. On 6 September 1860 the emperor issued an edict urging people to attack the allies and offered fixed sums for the heads of the barbarians and for the seizure and destruction of their vessels. He had fallen under the influence of Yehonola, a beautiful concubine whom he married. She would later reign as Empress Dowager Cixi. On 29 September the emperor announced he was going on the usual autumn tour of inspection and hurriedly left for Jehol. Yehonola then took charge of the council of war but eventually fled, too, leaving the negotiations in the hands of the emperor's brother, Prince Gong.

When the allies entered Beijing they were incensed to discover Parkes, Wade and the other prisoners half-dead from starvation and wounds at the Yellow Temple in Beijing (which still exists). They also learned that other emissaries had been beheaded as the allies approached. All eighteen mutilated corpses revealed evidence of cruel torture. Lord Elgin decided that the Chinese had to be punished but could not agree with Baron Gros how to do it. The French envoy wanted to destroy Beijing and the Forbidden City: 'As to the destruction of the Summer Palace, a site without defences, it would be, in my opinion, a useless vengeance since unhappily it cannot remedy the cruel events we deplore. The total destruction of the Peking palaces, after removing the archives ... would be a far more expiatory act than the burning of the "maison de plaisance".'[6]

But Elgin felt that retribution should fall on the emperor and his officials, not the innocent citizens of Peking. Eventually his arguments won the day. On 16 October Lord Elgin notified Prince Gong that 'until this foul deed has been expiated, peace between Great Britain and the existing Dynasty of China is impossible'. Lord Elgin explained that the punishment should not fall on the people but exclusively on the emperor, whose direct responsibility for the crime committed had been established, not only by the treatment of the prisoners, but also in the edict in which he entered 'a pecuniary reward for the heads of the foreigners'.

On 18 October British, Punjabi and French troops marched to the Yuanming Yuan and set the palace in flames. The fire burnt steadily for two days, throwing up great columns of black cloud, and pieces of burning and charred wood were carried into the streets of Beijing. One Englishman recorded that 'the world around looked dark with shadow' while in the vicinity 'the very face of nature changed'. Lord Elgin watched with mixed feelings but wrote to Baron Gros: 'This is not an act of vengeance but of justice and I cannot regret the part I took in counselling it.' The Frenchman felt otherwise and he wrote in a private letter to the French Minister for Foreign Affairs that 'This morning we saw the flames which devoured the palace and I have had my heart torn. If I could have foreseen what was to come, I would have refused this mission, even if I had been offered millions . . .'

Some have suggested it would have been better for the allies to have demanded the surrender and execution of those Manchu ministers and generals responsible for the deaths of the foreigners. Yet one of the first English diplomats to live in Beijing, Algernon Freeman-Mitford, later said that the destruction should have taken place in the city. He found most people had somehow believed it was the foreigners who had been humiliated and that they had been made to 'pay an indemnity for leave to withdraw our troops and that we are here in sufferance'. A few days later a peace treaty was signed at the Hall of Ceremonies in the Forbidden City. Soon the British and the French opened embassies in what became known as the Foreign Legation Quarter. So for the first time in history a Chinese emperor was thereby compelled to recognize other monarchs as his equal instead of mere heads of tributary states, but it was a concession made under duress. Forty years later Yehonola took her revenge when she stood by as the

Boxers, a quasi-religious sect who attacked foreigners, besieged the diplomats in the Legation Quarter.

Had they wished, the Western powers could have gone on to take control of China as they did in India, Africa and the Americas. Instead, they preferred to keep the Manchu empire afloat and concentrate on trade. At a critical moment, they even helped the Manchus defeat the Taiping rebels. When news of the burning of the Summer Palace reached Europe, it brought immediate condemnation. Victor Hugo wrote that 'This marvel has disappeared. One day two bandits entered the Summer Palace. The one pillaged, the other burnt. Victory is a thief. That which Elgin did to the Parthenon, he did to the Summer Palace . . . We Europeans, we are the civilized, and for us the Chinese are the barbarians, but look what civilization has done to the bar-barians.' In the eyes of the great French writer, 'Governments are sometimes bandits, the people never.'

Yet some of the people were bandits. As soon as the imperial family abandoned the palaces of the Yuanming Yuan, the Chinese living in the neighbourhood rushed to get ladders and began looting. The French, who had arrived first led by General de Montauban, put guards at the various exits. Lord Elgin and the others came after and the allied troops began grabbing whatever they could put in their pockets. The Chinese joined them: 'Chinese from the surrounding villages crowded in and added their numbers to the voracious looters and hundreds of them going backwards and forwards all day long laden with bundles of spoil . . .' When the foreign troops were sent back to Beijing, carrying whatever they could, Chinese officials re-entered the palace. They executed anyone caught with imperial pos-sessions and many people then hid their stolen works of art. The court officials who repossessed the garden found most palaces untouched or only slightly damaged. 'With a few repairs a large portion of the buildings could be restored to their original beauty,' wrote the English writer Hope Danby in her detailed history of the Yuanming Yuan, *The Garden of Perfect Brightness*. Yet no such orders were given. The emperor Xianfeng died soon after these events and the court was preoccupied with succession intrigues. It was agreed to install a 4-year-old as the Emperor Tongzhi, while the two widowed empresses of Xianfeng would serve as his co-regents. When Yehonola, now named

as the Empress Dowager Cixi, revisited the garden, she was so over-
come with sadness that she refused to speak of it again. The garden
where she had spent her happy youth was left to decay. Like an
enchanted garden under an evil spell, the Yuanming Yuan became a
wilderness. Thieves climbed over the walls at night and took whatever
they could. Peasants smashed up the heavy, polished furniture and
marble, tore out the glazed tiles and wall medallions, took out the
iron rivets and the lead, large trees were cut down for firewood.
The weather took its toll as well, and the garden became wild and
overgrown, the lakes choked with waterweeds.

Yehonola ignored the petitions sent by officials who proposed
restoring it. Then young Emperor Tongzhi thought this was a way of
pleasing his mother and instructed the Lei family, who for generations
had designed and built imperial palaces, to make a detailed proposal.
When in 1874 Yehonola was about to give her consent, the plan ran
into strong opposition from mandarins who raised objections to the
cost and the corruption involved. The project was shelved again and
soon afterwards, the Emperor Tongzhi died of smallpox. Saddened by
her son's death, Yehonola forgot about the Yuanming Yuan, leaving it
guarded by a handful of eunuchs who did little to stop gangs stealing
its bricks, stones and wood.

After Emperor Tongzhi's early death, Yehonola stayed in power by
forcing the court to agree to select the son of her sister, Princess Chun,
as the new emperor. During the reign of the Emperor Guangxu (1871–
1908) she continued to rule. When she turned 60, the court proposed
building her a new Summer Palace, much smaller than the Yuanming
Yuan and the money is said to have been diverted from the budget
for a new Chinese navy. In the meantime, the Yuanming Yuan continued to be denuded and dismantled, in some cases by senior officials
who requisitioned objects for their own houses. Then in 1900 the
Boxer rebels camped in the grounds and destroyed its famous Porcelain Pagoda which had survived in perfect condition until then. In
the 1920s the Christian warlord Feng Yuxiang broke up one pavilion
hunting for buried treasure. When Hope Danby visited the site in 1939
she saw workmen digging through the remaining brick-and-cement
foundations to dig out the thousands of piles on which the buildings
had been supported. She noted that the huge blocks of marble from

the ancestral shrine, the most sacred part of the garden, were being carted off. Over the years objects removed from the garden turned up in antiques markets around the world.

Peasants then occupied the palace grounds, parcelling out fields and breeding fish and eels in the lakes. When the new Qinghua and Beijing universities were founded after 1900 they acquired part of the garden. The destruction continued during the Cultural Revolution, when teams of middle-school Red Guards dug up the stones to help build bomb shelters. Over the years the site was occupied by 600 families, fourteen work units, a state guest house and villa development company, not to mention a rubbish dump. Even in 2000 there were still reports of robbers stealing the stones.

The shabby treatment given to the Yuanming Yuan over these many years suggests both a public irreverence and a healthy scepticism for government manipulation of history. The Garden of Perfect Brightness could just as well be seen as an inspiring symbol of cultural exchange between Europe and China. The Emperor Qianlong had surrounded himself with a group of brilliant European Jesuit priests. By getting close to the emperor, the Jesuits hoped to convert to Catholicism first the court and then China. To do this they offered their services as painters, architects, clockmakers, musicians, cartographers and so on. These exceptional men were in a position to observe everything at the court. Their letters detailed China's wealth and sophistication and circulated so widely in Europe they sparked a craze for chinoiserie.

'Never before had Europe received so powerful and varied an artistic stimulus from a distant civilization,' writes Professor Donald Lach of the University of Chicago in *The Dictionary of the History of Ideas*.[7] The craze for Chinese art objects reached its peak in the early and middle years of the eighteenth century. Some objets d'art arrived as gifts from the Qing emperors but they soon created a thriving export business catering to the desires of everyone from kings downwards who wanted to collect Chinese cabinets, chairs, tables, screens, fans, hangings, porcelains and lacquered bowls. People covered their living rooms with lacquer panels or wallpaper decorated with Chinese designs. In many palaces, royalty demanded a special chamber to house their porcelain collections. The Chinese designed many export items, especially to appeal to the European taste for the exotic. 'As a consequence they often reflected more about the Chinese conception of European taste than about Chinese art itself. Parasols, pagodas, and mandarins were depicted on the wares made in China as the Europeans conceived of them rather than as they actually looked,' notes Professor Lach.

In this imaginary China, the Chinese are graceful, delicate and colourful; they love beautiful gardens, quiet ponds and tinkling bells. Laughter is always gay, the waters are clear and cool, the skies are sunny and the mountains green for this happy people living in their tasteful arcadia. Like many European ideas about pre-modern China, these concepts were exported back to China and embraced, so the Yuanming Yuan became an Eden from which the happy Chinese were expelled by the brutal forces of the modern world. Just as the court of Louis XV became fascinated by China, the Emperor Qianlong conceived a great liking for European art. Qianlong so liked the paintings by the Milanese-born painter and Jesuit Giuseppe Castiglione that he joined him nearly every day that the artist was at work in Beijing and engaged him in long conversations. Qianlong became so fascinated with pictures of European architecture that in 1747 he commanded his Jesuits to make a series of rococo palaces in the style then all the rage in Europe.

In one palace he had a huge room that was filled with Gobelin tapestries, and the machinery for making new ones sent by Louis XV in 1767. 'The European palaces contain only ornaments and furniture. It is unbelievable how rich the sovereign is in curiosities and magnificent objects of all kinds from the Occident,' wrote Father Bourgeois to his friend M. de Latour, printer of the Library of Paris. 'You ask me if the Emperor had any Venetian or French glass? Thirty years ago he already had so many pieces that, not knowing where to put them, he had a quantity of the first quality broken up to make window-panes for his European palaces.'[8]

Another Jesuit missionary, Father Benoît, working at the court, designed and built for Qianlong ornate buildings graced by fountains adorned with classical statuary and complemented by a large maze made of grey stone bricks. The latter is still there. Next to the largest building, the Hall of Peaceful Seas, Benoît built his most complicated fountain: at the top of a pair of staircases stood two dolphins and two lions spouting water that fell into basins and ran down into a large shell. On different sides of the balustrades, fifty-four smaller fountains sent up a barrage of sparkling spray. On each side of the central basin, Father Benoît created a water clock. The whole thing was a masterpiece. It consisted of a group of twelve zodiacal animals representing the different hours of the day and night, in two-hour periods, each animal spouting water at its appointed time. They were the twelve Chinese zodiacal animals, which traditionally exercise an influence on the time that they represent. The horse, for instance, represented the time from eleven in the morning until one in the afternoon. The Hall of Peaceful Seas appeared on the outside like a dignified public building of some eighteenth-century French town, though actually it hid a vast tank lined with lead that fed water into the fountains through an elaborate system of hydraulics. Hope Danby, who interviewed descendants of the Qin family, the contractors in charge of this part of the palace, says that once Benoît died, no one else knew how to maintain the machinery.

Contrary to the impression given by official accounts, Hope Danby says that the fountain was not destroyed by British and French troops; ninety years after it was built, that is, around twenty years before the burning of the Yuanming Yuan, the empress of the reigning emperor, Daoguang, took such a strong dislike to the animals that she insisted on their removal. 'They have completely disappeared,' Hope Danby wrote, adding: 'It is surmised that they were melted down, their metal being remoulded into other ornaments.' Three waterspouts, the heads of an ox, monkey and tiger, one of which had somehow ended up in a Beverly Hills swimming pool, turned up for auction in Hong Kong in 2000. A mainland company bought them in an outburst of self-righteous indignation.[9]

Emperor Qianlong's fondness for trees, especially natural irregular trees, left a deep legacy. Even Lord Elgin noted with some surprise how the trees lent Beijing its charm: 'Peking is so full of trees and the houses are so low, that it hardly had the effect of looking down on a great city. Here and there temples or high gateways rose above the trees but the general impression was rather that of a rich plain densely populated.'[10] The English landscape garden, as it developed, in contrast to the rigid formality of French gardens, with their trimmed and unnatural shapes, owed a great debt to Chinese notions of gardening, especially the Yuanming Yuan. Sir William Temple, a critic of classical, formal gardens, was impressed by how the Chinese sought to reproduce natural effects by following schemes and the concept of what he called 'Sharawadgi', his own rendition of a Chinese or Japanese term meaning 'studied irregularity'. 'On the basis of Temple's remarks the conviction grew that the Chinese example was more important to the evolution of the landscape garden than were Roman proto-types, the semi-formal garden, or a new attitude towards nature in its wild state,' wrote Professor Lach. The English-style parkland, with its studied irregularity and the occasional pavilion, became a success, copied all over Europe, a faint ghostly imprint of the Garden of Perfect Brightness.

7

The Broken Bowl Tea House

Shu Yi, a large, somewhat shambolic man, talked and walked so quickly that I struggled to keep up as he led me around the jumble of dank alleys and two-storey grey brick houses in one of Beijing's oldest districts. When we reached the old vegetable market, the Caishikou, he abruptly raised his arm and pointed out a small pharmacy on the other side of the road with a green cross on its roof. 'At this very spot, the six Confucian gentlemen had their heads lopped off,' he said. 'And that was where the Broken Bowl Tea House stood. After their task was completed the executioners would retire to the tea house for a drink.'

We were now standing at the very spot where in 1898 six men had been executed for daring to put forward a bold blueprint for political and social reform. If the declining Qing empire had not executed them, but rather implemented their proposals, China's history might have been very different. The violent convulsions of the twentieth century and the defeat by the Japanese might never have happened. By extinguishing belief in the Qing dynasty's readiness to carry out necessary reforms, the execution of the reformers was an act of folly that prepared the way for the downfall of imperial China and the 1911 revolution.

'They should have erected a big bronze statue here. One of the most important events in Chinese history took place here. Every schoolboy learns about it,' Shu Yi said. The execution ground where the heads of the reformers had fallen amid piles of old cabbage leaves now supports two six-lane highways choked with traffic.

The six condemned men belonged to a group of young Confucian scholars who, in 1895, presented the Emperor Guangxu with a memorial putting forward an ambitious modernization programme. China was reeling from a humiliating naval defeat at the hands of the Japanese and had relinquished control over Korea and Taiwan to Tokyo. Earlier in the century, the empire had already suffered two defeats at the hands of the British Royal Navy during the two Opium Wars. However, the Japanese victory demonstrated how successful an Asian and Confucian state could be when it committed itself to learning from the West. Japan's root-and-branch modernization programme began soon after Commodore Perry's ships arrived in 1853, but the Qing dynasty had been half-hearted in adapting to the new challenges. It was clear that China had no choice but to follow suit. The scholars won the backing of the Emperor Guangxu, then just 24 years old and trying to escape from the domineering influence of the 60-year-old empress dowager. By then she had effectively been controlling the destiny of the empire for close on forty years, ever since the sacking of the Yuanming Yuan in 1860 by British and French forces. She was counselled by her brother-in-law, Prince Gong, who had negotiated with the Anglo-French expeditionary leaders, and her sinister chief eunuch, Li Lianying. On his own initiative, Emperor Guangxu pushed through the '100 Days Reforms' with a series of edicts outlining reforms covering education, industry, the military and the political system. These ranged from abolishing the Confucian exams to creating a constitutional monarchy. The empress dowager was enjoying life in the New Summer Palace that she had built for her retirement and was alarmed by the reports she received from Yuan Shikai, a powerful general in command of the best troops. (After 1911 this ambitious general seized power for himself and tried to found his own dynasty, an effort that ended with his death in 1916.) The empress dowager acted decisively; she ordered the arrest of the scholars and imprisoned the Emperor Guangxu. With their patron stripped of his power, the six were quickly executed on the afternoon of 28 September 1898. Some fled in time, like Liang Qichao and Kang Youwei, but not Tan Sitong, Kang Guangren (Kang Youwei's younger brother), Yang Shenxiu, Yang Rui, Lin Xu and Liu Guangdi.

The Qing state always carried out death sentences shortly before the winter solstice, so this was known as the 'Autumn Execution' (even today executions are carried out at the same time). The death sentence, signed by the Empress Dowager Cixi, was declared from the top of the Meridian Gate at the entrance to the Forbidden City. Then the condemned were taken through the 'Gate of Proclaimed Military Strength' (Xuanwumen), colloquially known as the Si Men, or 'Death Gate'. They were brought to Caishikou marketplace in the Chinese part of the city which sold vegetables, near Mishijie, the rice market, Guozixiang, the fruit market, and Zhubaoshi, the jewellery market. The carts carrying the condemned stopped outside a tea house; a bowl was taken out to them so they could gulp down a mixture of rice wine and alcohol. Then, the bowl was broken and thrown away – hence the name, 'Broken Bowl Tea House'. A crowd stood and watched as the condemned knelt on the ground and the executioners swiftly wielded their swords. Then the heads were put in a cage and left to rot on the same spot. Soon afterwards, the empress dowager began supporting the Society of Righteous Fists, or Boxers, a quasi-religious anti-foreign sect whose members practised martial arts and began attacking foreign missionaries in northern China and who eventually descended on Beijing and laid siege to the Legation Quarter in the summer of 1900.

The area around Caishikou, the old vegetable market, includes many other sites linked to the fate of the 100 Days reformers. Shu Yi showed me several *huiguan*, or guest houses, run by associations of people from the same town or province. When scholars came up from the provinces to take the imperial exams, they would stay in these *huiguan*. (Even today this tradition continues – government delegations from the provinces always stay at hotels in Beijing operated by the same provincial government.) Near the old coal market, Shu Yi showed me the former guest house where candidates from Guangdong province stayed. It was now a grubby, neglected courtyard house, but this is where Kang Youwei, perhaps the most famous proponent of reform, had stayed while preparing the reform blueprint. Kang Youwei was then in his late thirties and his writings inspired others to join him in founding the Association to Protect the Country. Next door to it, we saw the old Liuyang Guild House where fellow reformer Tan Sitong had survived on handouts from his fellow countrymen from Liuyang in Hunan province. Tan Sitong had called this courtyard his 'Misty Room', and in 1895 he had written a moving anthology called *Verses from the Misty Room*. Although the room, as Shu Yi indignantly pointed out, was designated as a protected historic monument, it was actually the home of a rag-and-bone man called Zhang Futing. As we arrived, he was cooking his dinner on an open-air stove and minding a couple of scrawny chickens. In the great man's bedroom, Zhang stored sacks of old bottles, paper and rags. Zhang's neighbour, grandson of the gatekeeper in Tan Sitong's day, said nobody lived there by choice. 'We wouldn't ask much to leave, there's nothing good about living here,' he said.

The trouble was, the rag-and-bone man helpfully explained, they couldn't touch the buildings because of the preservation order. What had once been a graciously proportioned residence now resembled a slum. Everything about the buildings in this neighbourhood seemed makeshift and provisional. None of these cramped, ramshackle houses had central heating, running water, drains or toilets. Outside, at the communal latrines, residents had to queue up in the morning and the smell pervaded the alleyways. Some forty families were crammed into three courtyards and every household had built its own little wall and thrown up its own crude brick shacks. All around stood heaped piles of rubbish – broken pots and pans, old rusty bicycles, bits of spring mattresses and piles of old wood. The wood was collected to supplement coal briquettes and to burn in the crude stoves everyone used for heating. It seemed not so much a slum, in fact, as a refugee camp, as if the inhabitants, fleeing some war, had stopped here and never moved on.

Shu Yi then brought me to see another neglected building that was hidden behind an alleyway. This is the Yang Memorial Temple where the young reformers had met before presenting their memorial. The temple was originally built to commemorate the fate of a famous scholar-official of the Ming dynasty, Yang Jisheng. He too had been executed after presenting a memorial to the emperor and the temple had a stone tablet that preserved his words:

> The noble spirit returns to the great void,
> The loyal heart remains eternal.
> All my life my debt of gratitude unpaid,
> In heaven my devoted soul will continue to serve.

The later generation of reformers had met in the hope that associating themselves with this venerated martyr would offer some protection. It was not to be. Tan Sitong, only 33 at the time, recited a poem to the thousands who had gathered to watch his death.

> I am yet determined to kill my enemies
> But I cannot escape my fate.
> For the sake of ideals I have been striving for
> I shall die joyfully!

Tan Sitong belonged to the tradition of Chinese intellectuals who believed it was the absolute duty of loyal scholar-officials (like Hai Rui, described in Chapter 3) to give the emperor the correct advice on how to govern the state even at the expense of their lives. Such men never advocated revolutionary change but invariably died professing their loyalty to the existing order. As Confucian gentlemen they were conservatives, constantly looking backward to a mythical golden age and quoting the wisdom of the ancients. This was not surprising. In order to pass the examinations and qualify as officials, they had to spend long years studying the Confucian canon. At first this consisted of the Five Classics: the *Odes*, the *Documents*, the *Rites*, the *Changes*, and the *Spring and Autumn Annals*. By the Tang dynasty (618–907) there were nine works and by the Song dynasty (960–1279), the list had grown to thirteen. These texts had been evolving in oral or written form for centuries before they were designated as 'Confucian', and did not necessarily have anything to do with Confucius himself, but are largely devoted to stories of rulers, good and bad. Many actually cover a range of ideas and sensibilities that have little to do with orthodox Confucianism.

A stone's throw away from the Yang Memorial Temple, Shu Yi took me to see another provincial hostel, the Shaoxing *huiguan*. The famous writer Lu Xun first lived here after arriving in Beijing from Shaoxing, a prosperous town in Zhejiang province. Lu Xun went on to become perhaps the most famous Chinese writer of the early twentieth century and he was promoted as a model intellectual after being adopted by the Communists. Lu Xun's generation were still prepared to sacrifice themselves, though in the cause of radical and revolutionary change. They did not wish to reform Chinese culture but to smash it utterly. The new generation wanted to bury Confucianism and discard the archaic language the classics were written in and which ordinary people could not understand. It would be as if Europeans agreed to cut out not only the study of Latin and Greek classics but the Bible as well. Shu Yi's father, the writer Lao She, was one of those to adopt the new vernacular way of writing and witnessed the May Fourth protests, begun by Beijing students in 1919. These were sparked by the Treaty of Versailles, which gave Qingdao, Germany's colony (called a foreign concession) in Shandong province, to Japan instead of handing it back to China. About 3,000 students started their protest march by assembling at the red-brick building of what was Beijing University, north of the Forbidden City, from where they crossed Tiananmen Square and headed to the Legation Quarter to protest to the representatives of Britain, France, Japan, Italy and the others who had signed the treaty. Turned back at the gates, they then headed to the home of China's Minister of Communications, who was suspected of being a traitor because he was negotiating huge loans from Japan. When they found him absent, the students broke into his house and set it on fire. Others accosted another politician and beat him unconscious. The police arrived and arrested some of them. However, the students went on to organize the first official student union, thereby turning themselves into a potent political force in national politics. And they, too, regarded themselves as the new conscience of the nation.

The May Fourth protests turned into the May Fourth Movement, the name given to the beginning of a literary and cultural renaissance, a Chinese version of Italy's Risorgimento. 'I was given a new soul,' Lao She later said of an event that had changed his life. One of the newspapers founded at that time (which still exists) was simply called *Enlightenment* because it entailed a wholesale embrace of Western political, social, literary and philosophical ideas and institutions that derived from the European Enlightenment. By using vernacular Chinese, the new intellectuals also wanted to cut themselves off from a past which they painted in the blackest colours possible. Lu Xun condemned Chinese civilization as 'nothing but a vaunted banquet of human flesh to be devoured by the rich and powerful'.

As the new Republic struggled to establish itself as a democracy, many of the intellectuals became more and more convinced that the legacy of the past could be destroyed only by violence. Chinese intellectuals believed that in order to 'save China', only the most radical and absolute measures would do. Mao Zedong, who came up from the provinces in 1921, had declared even in 1918, when he was only 24 years old, that 'the country must be destroyed . . . and then reformed'.[1] Lu Xun explained to Beijing students in 1923:

Unfortunately China is too hard to change: just moving a table or repairing a stove tends to involve bloodshed; and even after the blood has flowed there is no certainty that change will be made. Unless a great whip is lashed on her back, China will never be willing to move forward of her own accord. I think such a whipping is bound to come; whether good or bad, it is bound to come, but where or how I do not know exactly.[2]

Some, like Hu Shi, recommended that China should embrace a complete Westernization: 'I unreservedly condemn our Eastern civilization and warmly praise the modern civilization of the West . . . We must admit . . . that we are inferior to others not only in technology and political institutions but also in moral values, knowledge, literature, music, fine arts and body physique.'[3]

Few examples in history compare with China's effort to substitute another culture for its own. The determination to destroy every vestige of the past extended to the most basic symbols of 'Chineseness', like substituting Latin letters for Chinese characters and knives and forks for chopsticks. In the 1980s Chinese leaders, such as Communist party secretary Hu Yaobang, were still talking about the need to do these things. The unsentimental and ruthless determination behind this drive to change China put Shu Yi's quest to persuade the authorities to celebrate the past and preserve historic sites in a most quixotic light. In a society where the past had no value, surely nothing was sacred, not even the memory of the originators of the reform movement. In the end, despite Shu Yi's best efforts, the authorities demolished the building where Kang Youwei had organized the Association to Protect the Country and where the reform programme was first debated.

However, opinion within the Communist Party leadership about conservation and the preservation of historical sites was divided and constantly shifting. When I first met Shu Yi in 1996, he had good grounds for believing that much of old Beijing could still be saved. As the son of Lao She and the director of the Museum of Modern Chinese Literature, Shu Yi had influence and support at the highest levels. Over the years I stayed in touch with him, calling from time to time to ask him for opinions about the fate of this or that building. He sounded as combative as ever but a note of despair began to creep in. His campaign, conducted in the media and in meetings of various advisory boards, changed from a broad effort to protect the old city as a whole to individual battles to defend even a single courtyard house. These battles increasingly ended in defeat. His colleagues in the Museum of Modern Chinese Literature would smile when you asked for news of him, as if his efforts were as pointless as tilting at windmills.

The conservation effort began back in the 1950s when seventy-eight historical sites were listed, including twenty-five areas and streets in Beijing. These sites consisted of the Forbidden City and the princely palaces, or *wangfu*, once owned by relatives of the imperial family, which are concentrated around lakes north of the Forbidden City in an area called Shishahai. After Chairman Mao's death in 1976, the Communist Party formally declared the Cultural Revolution over and admitted that many 'mistakes' had been made. With expressions of contrition, the new leadership began to consider how to conserve what was left of China's cultural legacy.[4] The first thing Beijing did was to order a new survey of its surviving historic relics. It included an inventory of the city's ancient trees and some other gestures, including the rebuilding of one of the great city gates, Deshengmen, which Mao had torn down. Although the new gate is largely made of cement, it signified the municipal government's intention to make amends. The 1982 list was extended to 188 sites which merited national- or municipal-level protection, but Shu Yi complained that this was far from enough. Beijing had seven thousand sites that needed to be protected. Some of these were given local district-level protection, so altogether there were now a thousand listed sites. Invariably this meant nothing more than a plaque being affixed to a wall outside. No money was spent on restoring a building or on other measures to protect it. Shu Yi's ambition to protect seven thousand sites sounded impressive, but old Beijing covered 25 square miles and contained 1.2 million courtyard houses. With history stretching back a thousand years and five dynasties, nowhere was without some interest or significance.

Many army and government work units had occupied historic sites from the 1950s onwards. When Mao Zedong's victorious peasant army marched in, the Communist Party appropriated many of the best *wangfu* for its top leaders and their organizations. Some palaces had been left deserted ever since the occupants abandoned the city in the face of the Japanese advance in 1937. Kang Sheng, Mao's secret police chief, occupied a complex of courtyards that he furnished with enough classic furniture and art to satisfy the most conservative Confucian mandarin. Much of it was acquired by pilfering the collections of his victims. After he ordered the arrest of *People's Daily* editor Deng Tuo in the Cultural Revolution, he took care that his men also carried off Deng Tuo's collection of antiques. Other beautiful *wangfu* were in the possession of Marshal Nie Rongzhen, Marshal Xu Xiangqian, Marshal Yang Shangkun, Yan Jisi, vice-chairman of the National People's Congress, and former vice-premier Yu Qiuli. Marshal Chen Yi, whose troops marched into Shanghai in 1949, took for himself the palace once inhabited by the eunuch Li Lianying, who grew rich by serving as the empress dowager's chief aide for dozens of years. Hua Guofeng, the man who succeeded Mao, lived in the palace that had once been the home of the KMT warlord Zhang Zizhong and later was turned into a small hotel.

The great mansion of Prince Gong, the Manchu who had negotiated with the eight armies in 1900, was the setting of the epic novel *Dream of the Red Mansion*; it had been transformed into dormitories for officials of the Ministry of Public Security. The Temple of Agriculture was being used by a school, a plastics factory, a pharmaceutical research institute and the Xuanwu District Education Bureau. Nearly half the territory of the Forbidden City was in the hands of a dozen work units.

Evicting well-connected organizations was far from simple. Even when the occupant consented to leave, it was hard to find alternative housing because so few new buildings were being built in the 1980s. Work units had to find the money to put up new buildings out of their own funds, and if they could not find new land, they built on the land they already had. The result was that Beijing was being ruined in a haphazard and chaotic fashion by a proliferation of ugly, cheap buildings thrown up without regard to planning regulations or the immediate surroundings.

It was evident that the city's entire infrastructure needed upgrading and large numbers of people and organizations needed rehousing. When urban planning resumed after 1979 there was considerable resistance to radical change. In the mid-1980s, the Beijing government drew up a blueprint with the intention of creating 'a first-rate modern city, a model for the rest of China'. Yet there was within the government resistance to large-scale reconstruction of the old capital. The population was weary of madcap utopian schemes. The first wave of reforms enriched the countryside, not the cities, and Beijing still lacked enough resources to embark on major construction. One of those who came to give advice about Beijing was the famous Chinese-American architect I. M. Pei, who urged China's leaders to preserve the old city centre, with its courtyard houses, as a whole. They had responsibility, he insisted, to preserve a unique architectural heritage.[5]

From 1983 onwards, the party secretary of Beijing was a small dapper man called Chen Xitong, who was quite receptive to this advice. He was neither an elderly revolutionary nor an engineer, but had come up from the provinces just before 1949 to study Chinese literature in Beijing. He was therefore one of the few leaders whose education had given him an appreciation of Chinese culture and he backed those who argued it was not necessary to demolish the courtyard houses in order to develop the city. He told a meeting of the Capital Architectural Commission in 1986: 'Beijing cannot in good conscience honour its ancestors nor face its descendants if the ancient beauty and architectural heritage of the Chinese capital is not preserved ... History would condemn us if we fail to develop Beijing into a modern city with all its ancient beauty intact.'[6] He introduced the Building Height Zoning Act, intended to preserve the surroundings of designated historic sites. The Zoning Act restricted the height of new buildings inside the second ring road. Around the Forbidden City and Shishahai, no buildings could be over 30 feet. Elsewhere they must not exceed 100 feet. Buildings along the second ring road – the former city walls – could not exceed 150 feet. Beijing would be like a bowl, with the Forbidden City at the bottom and surrounded by tall buildings along the rim. Chen Xitong also launched a series of design experiments to show that it was possible to design new residential housing that conformed to the city's traditional architecture code at no great cost. Each district had to build similar model hutong pilot developments. When the time came to rebuild the whole fabric of the inner city, they would provide the model. One of them is the Ju Er Hutong project, a cluster of interlinking courtyards in traditional muted colours which feature comfortable modern apartments with running water, flush toilets and electricity.

Chen later commissioned another plan, called the Beijing City Master Plan, 1990–2010, which also set out to preserve Beijing's unique identity. The plan insisted on 'basically maintaining the original chessboard-like layout of streets and lanes' and 'preserving a part of the traditional vernacular courtyard housing in certain areas', including retaining 'the characteristic city colours'. Under this master plan, Beijing would retain the urban configuration of the Ming and Qing dynasties, namely a square – the inner city – abutting against a rectangle – the outer city. It would also conserve the original network of rivers and lakes. The list of protected sites was increased to 986, including 21 sites at Beijing level and 777 at local government level.[7]

After 1992 China was plunged into a new round of economic reforms intended to spur the growth of the urban economy and win the support of the urban population, who had taken to the streets in the 1989 pro-democracy protests. These reforms created a market for housing for the first time since 1949. The construction industry boomed as investors channelled money into new real-estate projects. Every work unit with its own land ignored the regulations and built what it wanted. Chen was horrified by the new buildings being thrown up. 'The capital is growing increasingly ugly and is steadily losing its Chinese character. Most of the modern high rises with boring concrete façades look like dominoes set down in the landscape without plan and without imagination,' he told top officials in a private meeting. In response, he issued instructions that all these developers must put a 'hat' on their structures. Consequently, the city began to sprout numerous skyscrapers each topped by a sort of Chinese pavilion, and sometimes a sort of dome.[8]

Shu Yi felt considerably heartened by support from Chen Xitong and official recognition that Beijing's courtyards had a value and beauty that deserved preservation. Some wealthy tycoons from Hong Kong had even begun buying up old courtyard houses and renovating them. One of them, David Chu Yu-lin, allowed me to visit a simple house with two courtyards near the Temple of Confucius that cost him nearly US$2 million. From the outside it seemed unchanged, but once beyond the traditional grey-brick walls, the rooms were done up in a kitschy pastiche of chinoiserie that appalled Shu Yi. One living room had a ceiling decorated with brightly painted red-and-gold dragons, which he complained betrayed an ignorance of the basic etiquette of *wangfu* design. 'Only his imperial majesty is allowed dragons,' he sniffed. I confessed that I found the house quite attractive but Shu Yi explained that the building contravened the code that governed *wangfu* construction. The design and decoration of a court-yard house entrance was intended to convey the owner's closely defined social status. For example, the door stones which hold down the swivel of the gate were often carved in the shape of a large drum or square block. They were usually decorated with images of an animal or flower. The top might be carved in the shape of a lion's head or lion-dog's head. Before the entrance to the house of a high-ranking personage, there was also a stone block for mounting or dismounting a horse, called a *mendu'er*, next to a carved stone post on which to tie the reins. High-ranking military officials had a *mendu'er* carved as an entire lion, but only the emperor and his family had a dragon's head. The colours selected to decorate the wooden beams, lintel and door posts and the characters chosen, *ruyi*, meaning 'wishfulness' or *ping'an*, meaning 'peacefulness', all delivered a meaning too.

Of course, the larger the mansion, the higher the status of the resident, but this was not a vulgar demonstration of status. From the outside it is not possible to tell the number or size of the courtyards inside because of a spirit wall that confronts the visitor after the door opens. Due to a belief that ghosts and spirits always walk in a straight line and shuffle their feet when walking, a visitor's way is blocked by a high wall so that after crossing the threshold one has to make a sharp left or right. Such an entrance is called a *tianjing* or sky well. Out of sight, a wealthy man might also build himself pavilions and gardens and a waterway carved in stone for a special game. The players floated cups of liquor down the channels and before they reached the end, the player had to spontaneously make up a poem. Failure meant having to drink the wine inside the paper cup.

In the end, the efforts of Shu Yi and many others made little impact. Appeals to preserve even those buildings directly linked to the modernization project failed as the new city was built at fantastic speed. You can no longer find the home of the great Manchu prince Rong Lu who implemented the empress dowager's orders to execute the reformers; nor the residence of Lu Xun or the home of Cai Yuan-pei, the former education minister during the Republic who, as chancellor of Beijing University, supported the May Fourth Movement. Tan Sitong's old house is one of the few that were preserved. On my last visit to Xuanwu district, I passed near the old execution ground at Caishikou and found it completely changed. It now had a Wal-Mart store, a Sogo department store and a series of office blocks built to house China's coming 'information age'.

fantastic that it is hard to believe anyone took them seriously. He spiced up the stories with descriptions of his own torrid love affair with Yehonola and details of the perverted sex enjoyed by her eunuchs and the debauchery of the Manchu aristocrats in the high-class homo-sexual brothels. Yehonola's faithful eunuch, Li Lianying, emerges as a diabolically clever and malevolent *éminence grise*. In his books, Backhouse plants the notion that there was a secret pro-Western faction in the court, led by Rong Lu, the empress dowager's foremost adviser, and that he was trying to protect the foreigners. Sir Edmund later helped write another volume, *Annals and Memoirs of the Court of Peking*, based on another diary and reports from archives of the Grand Council. This great 'discovery', never actually seen, was the diary Li Lianying kept during his forty years of service as Yehonola's chief factotum. Backhouse claimed it came from the eunuch's great-nephew.

Before foreign powers established their embassies in the Legation Quarter, the West relied on reports sent back by the Jesuits who lived largely with the court in the Yuanming Yuan. Their accounts inspired Leibniz and others to see in China a model of enlightened despotism. Gottfried Leibniz, the seventeenth-century Germany rationalist, thought China enjoyed better social order than European states because its emperors governed firmly with a great respect for law, an efficient bureaucracy and wise counsellors. French philosophers such as Rousseau, Montesquieu and Voltaire praised Confucianism as a rational, self-regulating political system. The great shift, when China came to be regarded as the polar opposite to the modern mundane West, came after the 1900 siege. Europeans were horrified by the brutality of the Boxers, confounded by their mysticism and most of all bewildered by the behaviour of the Qing court. As the British writer Peter Fleming concluded after writing his account, *The Siege at Peking*, 'the most abiding mystery was why it happened at all'.[3]

The Legation Quarter is not on the tourist trail although it is a striking oddity situated just off the east side of Tiananmen Square and close to the Forbidden City. It is fated to disappear completely sooner or later, and China's rulers will be able to bury another part of history they would sooner forget. This island of European architecture still boasts banks built in florid neo-Italian Renaissance style next to step-gable Dutch brick houses; a mock Gothic church beside buildings in the bluff classicism of the Austro-Hungarian empire. Yet much has disappeared as the area is redeveloped with new offices, apartments and hotels – all of them exceeding the heights permitted under zoning regulations introduced to preserve the historic area around the Forbidden City.

The first Europeans to open an embassy in Beijing were the Russians, and their Legation is now the People's Procuracy. By the first Opium War in the 1840s Beijing already had a few Western buildings, including the Russian Orthodox Church at Dongjiao Mingxiang, razed in 1991 to make way for the Supreme People's Court. Another early church was the Nantang, or Southern Church, in Xuanwu district, originally built by Matteo Ricci and the other Jesuits in the sixteenth century. But the arrival of the French and British just after 1860 marked the real beginning of the Legation Quarter and it lasted for a century. The French took over a house that once belonged to a Manchu noble, the duke of Qin. By the mid-1800s the duke's family had become so impoverished they were happy to rent out its dilapidated palaces to the French. The main gate, even then, was guarded by two white stone lions. On the eastern side of the Legation Quarter was a large factory for drying fuel wood called *dajichang*; this area was renamed Customs Street because at its far end lay the inspectorate general of the Chinese Imperial Maritime Customs Service. It was created and run by foreigners to enforce a uniform tariff on China's international trade.

The British took over the palace of Prince Chun, one of Emperor Kangxi's thirty-three sons. Every Chinese New Year they paid the rent by sending out a cart loaded with silver ingots. The State Security Ministry now occupies the site but the gate with the lion and unicorn is still visible and over the wall you can still glimpse the handsome bell tower erected in honour of Queen Victoria's Golden Jubilee. Opposite the British Legation entrance is the former Japanese Legation, which is now occupied by the Beijing branch of the Communist Party and the municipal military garrison.

The Qing dynasty began to treat other nations as equals only after the Second Opium War and for the first time created a proper foreign office called the Zongli Yamen. The former American Legation in fact occupied the site of the 'Hostel of Tributary Nations', built to accommodate foreign embassies who were always treated as delegations bringing tribute to the Son of Heaven. The Hostel of Tributary Nations was established close to the area housing the ministries, or Six Boards, the administrative hub of both the Ming and Qing empires, which is now Tiananmen Square. The Legation Quarter never became a foreign concession, as in Tianjin or Shanghai, with bustling warehouses and factories. When the Boxers laid siege to the Legation Quarter in the fateful summer of 1900, there were twelve delegations and 500–900 foreigners in a city of close to a million. In an empire of between 350 and 400 million people, there were just 10,000 foreigners, half of whom were British or American. The foreigners, together with 3,000 Chinese Christian converts, somehow managed to hold out against some 80,000 Boxers for fifty-five days. The siege finally ended on 14 August 1900 when a detachment of Sikhs entered the Legation. By this time 76 foreigners were dead and 179 wounded. The French writer Pierre Loti vividly described what he saw at that moment:

Here we are at the gates, the double triple gates, deep as tunnels, and formed of the most powerful masonry – gates surmounted by deadly dungeons, each one five storeys high, with strange curved roofs – extravagant dungeons, colossal black things above a black inclosing wall. Our horses' hoofs sink deeper and deeper, disappear, in fact, in the coal-black dust, which is blinding and all-pervading, in the atmosphere as well as on the ground, in spite of the light rain and the snowflakes which make our faces tingle.

Noiselessly, as though we were stepping upon wadding or felt, we pass under the enormous vaults and enter the land of ruin and ashes. A few slatternly beggars shivering in corners in their blue rags, and that is all. Silence and solitude within as well as without these walls. Nothing but rubbish and ruin, ruin. The land of rubbish and ashes, and little grey bricks – little bricks all alike, scattered in countless myriads upon the sites of houses that have been destroyed, or upon the pavement of what once were streets. Little grey bricks – this is the sole material of which Beijing was built; a city of small, low houses decorated with a lacework of gilded wood; a city of which only a mass of curious debris is left, after fire and shell have crumbled away its flimsy materials.

After a few hundred yards we enter the street of the Legations, upon which for so many months the anxious attention of the whole world was fixed. Everything is in ruins, of course; yet European flags float on every piece of wall; and we suddenly find, as we come out of the smaller streets, the same animation as at Tien-tsin [Tianjin], a continual coming and going of officers and soldiers, and an astonishing array of uniforms. A big flag marks the entrance to what was our legation, two monsters in white marble crouch at the threshold; this is the etiquette for all Chinese palaces. Two of our soldiers guard the door which I enter, my thoughts recurring to the heroes who defended it.

We finally dismount, amid piles of rubbish, in an inner square near a chapel, and at the entrance to a garden where the trees are losing their leaves as an effect of the icy winds. The walls about us are so pierced with balls that they look like sieves. The pile of rubbish at our right is the legation proper, destroyed by the explosion of a Chinese mine. At our left is the chancellor's house, where the brave defenders of the place took refuge during the siege, because it was in a less exposed situation.

The horrible part of the siege was that no pity was to be expected from the besiegers; if, starved, and at the end of their strength, it became necessary for the besieged to surrender, it was death, and death with atrocious Chinese refinements to prolong the paroxysms of suffering. Neither was there the hope of escape by some supreme sortie; they were in the midst of a swarming city, they were enclosed in a labyrinth of buildings that sheltered a crowd of enemies, and were still further imprisoned by the feeling that, surrounding them, walling in the whole, was the colossal black rampart of Peking.

They were attacked from all sides and in every possible manner, often at the most unexpected hours of the night. It usually began with cries and the sudden noise of trumpets and tom-toms; around them thousands of howling men would appear – one must have heard the howlings of the Chinese to imagine what their voices are; their very timbre chills your soul. Gongs outside the walls added to the tumult. Occasionally, from a suddenly opened hole in a neighbouring house, a pole twenty or thirty feet long, ablaze at the end with oakum and petroleum, emerged slowly and silently, like a thing out of a dream. This was applied to the roofs in the hope of setting them on fire.[4]

The empress dowager, who seized power after the burning of the Yuanming Yuan, always blamed the foreigners for provoking all the

The doors of a traditional courtyard home are marked for demolition with the *chai* character in one of Beijing's vanishing old hutongs.

Destruction of the hutong districts south of Qianmen Gate began in 2006 to make way for more tourist-friendly shops in preparation for the 2008 Olympics.

The city gate at Xuanwumen before it was torn down. The Xuanwumen area included
Caishikou, the Qing dynasty execution grounds.

The old city wall and gate at Xizhimen, in Beijing's north-west corner.

Emperor Wan Li's tomb at Ding Ling was excavated in the 1950s at the behest of a Beijing deputy mayor who hoped to unearth riches on a par with Egypt's Valley of the Kings.

The site of the tomb at Ding Ling at the time of its excavation in the mid-1950s.

The Bell Tower (*left*) and Drum Tower of Beijing have changed very little in the past fifty years, but the surrounding courtyard homes and neighbourhoods began to vanish in the twenty-first century.

The city wall wrapped around Beijing before it was destroyed to make way for rails and roads, in spite of the preservationist efforts of Liang Sicheng to turn the walls into green spaces.

Cai Jinhua, the Golden Flower concubine.

The Fragrant Concubine, Xiang Fei, as painted by Castiglione.

The home of Cai Jinhua as it appears today.

Emperor Qianlong built a tower for his concubine, Xiang Fei, so she could look west, towards her homeland of Xinjiang.

Wang Shixiang, an antiquities expert, was the first to document and study Ming and Qing dynasty furniture after the Cultural Revolution.

Sun Yaoting, the last living eunuch of China, photographed in 1996 at the age of 96, shortly before his death.

Hopeful preservationist Liang Sicheng and his wife, Lin Huiyin, perch on the rooftop of the Temple of Heaven in Beijing, 1936.

Liang Sicheng with Le Corbusier (*left*) and Oscar Niemeyer (*centre*) at the United Nations Board of Design. In spite of Liang's efforts to preserve Beijing's ancient architecture, the city ended up looking much more like a vision of Le Corbusier's.

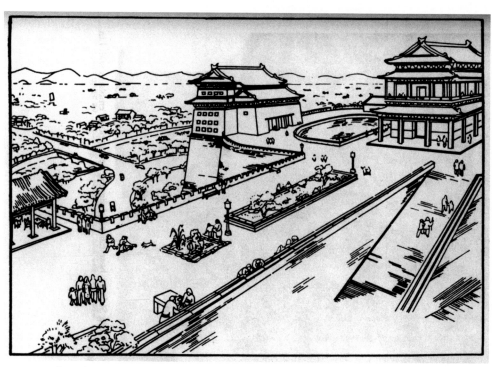

Liang Sicheng hoped that the city walls of Beijing could be preserved as a green city park, but in 1950, even as he proffered plans to improve the city's traffic flow by digging tunnels, the walls began to come down.

A bustling market occupied the heart of Beijing, south of the Qianmen gate, in the late nineteenth century.

Once a devoted Communist, Shi Lu came under heavy attack for this painting, *Shifting to Fight in North Shaanxi*, and was accused of depicting Mao in a hopeless position by showing him too close to a cliff.

The Chinese Central Television building, a prime example of China's bold, postmodern approach to architecture, built at breakneck speed to be completed in time for the 2008 Olympics.

The work of Zhang Dali, also known as AK-47, is visible on many of the buildings slated for destruction, such as this one near the Forbidden City.

troubles that weakened the Qing dynasty. As such, she probably regarded the foreign legations as illegal, something forced on her by what the Chinese government still calls the 'unequal treaties' imposed by the victors of the Opium Wars. By the turn of the century, Yehonola had lost control over tributary states like Korea and Vietnam to foreign powers and had been defeated by Japan. Then she had rejected the '100 Days Reforms', imprisoned the emperor Guangxu and cut off the heads of the reformers. She needed to do something to regain prestige and redirect popular anger against the foreigners, so she supported the Boxers.

They started out by massacring missionaries and their converts in the provinces, acts that the current government of China regards as justified. The official Xinhua news agency reported on the hundredth anniversary of the siege that the missionaries had 'illegally sneaked into the inland to preach their religion, playing accomplices to the imperialist and colonialist invasion of China, committing unpardonable crimes and deserving the punishments they received'. The Boxers attacked shops selling foreign goods, banned foreign kerosene lamps, ripped up the new railways and tore down the telegraph wires. They had a strange mixture of folk beliefs and superstitions. Before descending on Beijing, they had demonstrated to Yehonola that they had magical powers from studying *qigong* and practising martial arts exercises so that they could resist the foreigners' bullets. They also ordered women who were regarded as unclean to stay at home after dark and advised people to cover their chimneys with red paper, which they claimed made them secure against the foreign cannon shells.

The Boxer attacks had the backing of the imperial court but it was, as Fleming points out, hard to understand what the court intended to achieve. All through the fighting Yehonola stayed in the Forbidden City, less than a mile away, and close enough to hear the sounds of the cannon blasts. At one stage she even sent the besieged foreigners a delivery of fruit and vegetables, but she did not use her power to protect them. On the other hand, why did she never order her forces to aid the Boxers and destroy the weakly defended legations? Or at least demand to renegotiate the treaties? Instead, the Qing armies hung back and did nothing – the worst of all possible options. Fleming concludes her intentions are likely to remain a mystery for ever. As the foreign troops arrived, Yehonola fled for the second time in her life, announcing that she was going on an 'autumn inspection tour'. She left at four in the morning disguised as a peasant in coarse blue cotton clothing, taking the captive emperor with her. Before leaving, she ordered his concubines to stay, but one of them, the Pearl Concubine, challenged her authority and in a burst of fury, Yehonola reportedly ordered two eunuchs to throw her down a well. They obeyed instantly and the well is still shown to visitors to the Forbidden City. Most of the Manchu nobility fled, too, leaving their palaces unguarded. Other members of the court were sent into exile, decapitated or allowed to commit suicide by strangling themselves with a silk ribbon.

Three days after Yehonola's departure, the Forbidden City witnessed a victory parade with goose-stepping Germans, Cossacks, Japanese, American marines, Sikhs and British troops. The city was divided into foreign occupation zones as the troops hunted down the Boxers. Foreigners and local residents methodically began to loot the Forbidden City and the Manchu *wangfu*. The Japanese raided the imperial granaries and treasury, carting off some 3 million taels of silver bullion. The Germans grabbed the astronomical instruments built by the Jesuits. These instruments, since returned, are now visible on a tower by the side of the second ring road.

The allies then began to debate what should be done. After protracted negotiations they produced the 1901 Treaty of Peking, which imposed indemnities that continued to be paid for another thirty-nine years. The treaty opened up China to further foreign influence and finally forced the Qing to adopt reforms. Yehonola then returned to the Forbidden City and began to consort freely with the foreigners and even declared herself in favour of railroads, modern schools and other Western innovations. The empress dowager promised the Chinese people a constitution and representative government and outlawed the cruellest Manchu punishments, such as execution by a thousand small cuts. She cancelled many special Manchu privileges and even permitted Chinese people to settle in Manchuria. Before she died, in November 1908, at the age of 73, she ensured an orderly succession. She chose the 3-year-old Pu Yi, son of Prince Chun, who was brought to the Forbidden City in the middle of the night. The Emperor Guangxu was not consulted and, rather conveniently, died the next day at the age of 37, along with his wife.

What actually happened in the 'Great Within' was in some respects weirder than anything 'revealed' by Sir Edmund's imaginary eunuch memoirs. After the end of the Qing dynasty in 1911, genuine court records became available, which should have disapproved Backhouse's twisted account of events. Out of an obsessive bureaucratic urge to record everything, the Manchu court set out to keep a complete record of everything that happened within the empire. The emperors commissioned all manner of encyclopedias and histories, and kept records of every aspect of their own private lives. Almost everything an emperor ever said or wrote was recorded and filed.

No fruit fly was ever put under more scrutiny than a Manchu ruler, and the dynasty left behind intimate records of their sexual activities and medical histories. When the eight allied armies arrived in Beijing to relieve the siege, they destroyed at least half the archives of the Six Boards, the main government ministries. It was only by chance that the rest survived. Then in 1909, the court decided to shift the vast accretion of reports and memorials from the Office of Military Affairs, the Six Boards, the Grand Secretariat and the Ming dynasty archive called the Huang Sicheng to a courtyard within the Forbidden City. A certain scholar called Luo Zhenyu was appointed to supervise the process and began sifting through memorials. He became fascinated by what he found and persuaded the court to house them in a library created inside the Duanmen Gate (located between the Wumen and Tiananmen gates).

Local workmen equipped with pointed sticks to impale the papers were given the job of sorting out the papers and in 1921 officials decided it was no use keeping them and began selling off the archives as scrap. Some 75 tons were crammed into 8,000 sacks and sold for 4,000 yuan to a rag merchant in the Xidan market. One day Luo Zhenyu was out hunting for antiques in Liulichang, a famous street of curio and antique shops, when he came across the original of a congratulatory message from the Emperor Kangxi to the king of Korea. He realized this could only have come from the archives of the Grand Secretariat. After making enquiries, he found out what was happening and decided to buy all the documents from the shop, paying three times the original purchase price. The incident caused a huge scandal at the time and the Palace Museum (as the Forbidden City was now renamed) eventually announced it was creating a new library. It purchased not only Luo's collection but those of others, too. Tons and tons of court documents were turned into pulp, however.

When the Japanese army moved into Peking in 1937, the KMT moved south and took with them hundreds of thousands of documents. Many of them eventually ended up in Taiwan. Some of the archives are now kept in Shenyang, the ancestral home of the Manchu dynasty. The majority, some 10 million documents, are still kept inside the Forbidden City at a building called the First History Archives.

One day I went to have a look. The archives lie just inside the Xihua Gate at the west side of the Forbidden City, in a neglected corner of the palace closed to tourists. Nothing in this area appears to have been touched in eighty years. Nearby, among the brickworks and greenhouses, stood another four-storey Western building of grey brick with shutters, in an advanced state of neglect. This belonged to a now barely remembered claimant to the throne, the general and warlord Yuan Shikai, who built it as his residence before he died in 1916, after having himself proclaimed emperor during a ceremony inside the Temple of Heaven. I followed one of the marble-lined canals, filled with rubbish and flowing with a copper-green water across a white bridge of unblemished stones protected by dragon-headed gargoyles, to find forgotten courtyards overgrown with grass. Through grimy windows, I was peering into imposing halls padlocked with rusty chains when a surly watchman suddenly startled me. Brusquely, he volunteered an explanation. Li Zicheng, the peasant rebel who had brought down the Ming dynasty, had lived here, making this his headquarters, before he was defeated by the Manchus. The archives, built in the 1970s, had the familiar smell of a Chinese government office, a mixture of Lysol and rat poison. The polite librarian took me down a corridor to a steel door through which she led me into a windowless vault filled with rows of steel filing cupboards stacked with documents wrapped in yellow silk coverings. One of them, almost three feet thick and made from thick palace paper, was the genealogical family tree of the Manchu imperial family, the Aisin

Gioro clan. It stretched back over 450 years and had been updated once every ten years.

A Manchu ruler like the Emperor Kangxi read at least fifty memorials a day, sometimes as many as five hundred, correcting and annotating each with vermilion ink. Slow communications meant that the emperor read reports on events weeks or sometimes months after they took place. The archives hold secrets, maps and treaties that are still being mined by scholars. There are detailed reports on the movements of Ambassador Macartney as he led his English trade delegation through China to meet the Emperor Qianlong, completed with comments inscribed by the emperor himself. Also here are the secret police files that the Grand Secretariat of the Qing court kept on all foreigners, such as the German Jesuit priest Adam von Schall who worked at the court for forty years and is buried in the city. From these records we now know details about the mysterious great *dedans* – the secret interior – which might have surprised Backhouse or René Leys. We know exactly how the empress dowager was treated for flatulence, nervous facial tics, diarrhoea and irregular menstruation. She employed more than two hundred doctors, some specializing in preserving her white complexion and lustrous hair from the ravages of age by concocting herbal baths and shampoos, and tonics with optimistic names like Eternal Spring Longevity Pill.[5] The detailed prescriptions are now the basis of a small cosmetics industry that produces face masks made from crushed pearls and potions using rare pollens and royal jelly.

Even the daily menus are preserved in the archives. We know, for instance, that on the seventh day of the tenth lunar month of the tenth year of the reign of the Emperor Guangxu (1876), the empress dowager was served the following for breakfast:

2 Hot-pots of Eight Treasures Suckling Pig, Gold and Silver Duck.

4 Big Bowls of Duck Roasted with Bird's Nest, Fatty Chicken with Bird's Nest, Red and White Chicken Julienne with Bird's Nest, Mixed Chicken Julienne with Bird's Nest.

4 Side Bowls of White Chicken Julienne with Bird's Nest, Honey-baked Sea Cucumber, Pigeon Eggs with Ham, Elm Fungus Braised with Stir-fried Meat.

6 Dishes – Chicken Julienne Roasted with Bird's Nest, Fish Slices with Mushrooms, Tender Meat with Young Bamboo Shoots, Sliced Meat Braised with Dried Young Bamboo Shoots, Chopped Duck, Fresh Prawn Cakes.

2 Side Dishes – Roast Duck, and Roast Pork.

4 Maize Cakes.

The sexual practices of the imperial court make for the oddest reading. Court astrologers were employed in determining the optimum hours for sex, based on cycles for *yin* and *yang*, in the belief that with the right timing the result would be a boy. Then, after the second meal of the day, a eunuch would present the emperor with a silver tray with bamboo slips, each with the name of one of the concubines. The emperor would turn over the name of his choice and she would then be brought at the correct time, wrapped in a blanket. It was the duty of the eunuch standing in the alcove to shout after a decent interval, 'Time is up', followed by the advice: 'Preserve your imperial body, Sire!' If there was silence after the third call, then the eunuch would step in to carry the woman out, only pausing to ask if the emperor wished her to bear a child. If the answer was yes, then he would record all relevant details in a notebook.

It is not surprising that so many emperors went mad growing up in a court where every courtier became intimately familiar with the Son of Heaven's bodily failings. The American writer George Kates related what he saw when he went to inspect the Emperor Guangxu's private bedroom in the Ying Tai, the island in Zhongnanhai where he was held prisoner by Yehonola after the failure of his reform movement.

One could . . . see where the cupboard-like partitions had been built into the walls, one at either end of the imperial *k'ang* [a bed heated from below]. Each, it was said, was contrived to permit a eunuch to stand concealed, during the night watches. His duty in this uncomfortable position was to inscribe in a register whatever transpired in the imperial alcove. Each of these was brought to the Empress Dowager every morning.[6]

The eunuch's job was to prevent the emperor wasting his semen, for fear that it might weaken his *qi* or vital forces. The records show that many emperors required special treatments to maintain their sexual vigour and regulate their seminal emission. This appears to have been a matter of particular concern for the Emperor Guangxu. Dr Detheve, Ségalen's predecessor at the French Legation, was brought in to examine him. The Son of Heaven had complained about problems with his kidneys and urinary tract and the French doctor diagnosed nephritis, a chronic inflammation of the kidneys: 'His Majesty stresses his ejaculations, which come at night and are always followed by voluptuous sensations ... These nocturnal emissions have been followed by the lessening of the faculty to achieve voluntary erections during the day.'

The files in the imperial archives revealed the medicinal concoctions used to treat his chronic nocturnal emissions, premature ejaculation, scrotum eczema and other embarrassing ailments. One of the accusations that Kang Youwei levelled against Yehonola was that, when she had the Emperor Guangxu arrested and imprisoned after crushing the 100 Days Reforms, she set out to poison him. Certainly, doctors found him feeble, thin and depressed in his island prison, but the archives offer no evidence of actual poisoning. On the other hand, the French doctor's medical reports were made public and no ruler, especially one who claimed to be so divine that no ordinary mortal could look upon his features, could preserve his aura of majesty and mystery once his impotence was made known to the world.

Immediately after the siege some foreigners had proposed razing the Forbidden City and pulling down the city walls. Instead, the Foreign Legation Quarter was expanded, the Chinese residents evicted and the area fortified by a new wall and glacis, a protective embankment. Each legation built barracks to house a permanent military detachment and there was a large parade ground for the troops to exercise. The British Legation tripled in size to 36 acres, which covered the land occupied by many of the ministerial offices that the Boxers had burnt. These included the Imperial Carriage House, the Board of War, the Board of Ceremonies and the Hanlin Academy, which had housed an enormous library dating back to the Ming dynasty.

The French Legation still stands, as do the stone lions that Pierre Loti noted when he arrived with the victorious troops. You head east past the old Banque de l'Indochine et de Suez, which is easy to spot even though it has been taken over by the municipal fire department.

From there you walk past the old French post office with its official grey bricks and square windows. It is now a restaurant and the day I came by a girl in a bright red silk *qipao* and high heels was standing outside inviting customers in. Past the site of the former German Legation, you find a pair of grand doors painted bright red beneath an imposing archway and high defensive walls guarded by a pair of sentinels who stand on twenty-four-hour guard. Through the doorway, rock gardens and some handsome new buildings are visible. The French barracks, on the other side of the Rue Marco Polo, are now the Beijing Workers Union Centre. Past the guards, one can spy some square three- or four-storey brick buildings built in the colonial style with red tile roofs and arched windows. Ségalen's children attended the French school, adjacent to the handsome grey Gothic spires of St Michael's, which is also still there. The classrooms are now divided between a restaurant, an advertising company and the Cambridge Young Learners English Test Centre. Across the street are the high, green steeple-pitched roofs of the old Belgian Legation, which lend a touch of medieval Flanders. And at the end of Rue de la Brouse, where the German Hospital once stood, is now a massive modern hospital block rising to more than twenty storeys.

The new legations were so large that when Vare saw Italy's building for the first time, his impression 'was one of astonishment at their size. I could not help asking "why so enormous?"'. It was all due to the ingenuity of Marchese Salvago Raggi, the Italian minister, he said, who in the middle of the night had enclosed a large plot with stakes bearing the legend 'Legazione d'Italia'. This infuriated the ministers of France, Belgium, Germany and Austria who went to him indignantly, accusing him of taking over all of Beijing. 'The Italian Minister smiled blandly and answered that doubtless the matter could be amicably settled and ceded some.' Vare's wicked anecdotes capture the tragicomic aspects of life in the new Legation Quarter. When a fire that broke out in the German Legation threatened to spread, the Italians were asked to save the Belgian Legation, but the hose of their new Fiat fire engine was lowered into the cesspit instead of the well. 'The results can be better imagined than described,' Vare wryly noted.

The foreigners, he noted, spent too much time entertaining each other and too little trying to understand the events unfolding outside.

Of a meeting of the Legation Quarter's governing council held in the British Legation, he wrote:

The windows opened to a small courtyard where the lilac blossomed in the spring and the legation parrot used to sit out there and join in our discussions (sometimes very aptly) with a hoarse guffaw, or a subdued chuckle, or a sudden screech. He was a talking parrot but he only spoke Chinese so that his remarks were unintelligible to most of the assembled diplomats.

When he returned for a second stint in 1927, Vare proposed founding an 'Anti-Dinner League': 'Dinners in Beijing were peculiar in this way, that as the foreign community was small and our relative importance fixed by protocol, it happened that the same people would sit next to each other night after night, and some of us made no mystery of the fact that we would rather have stayed at home.' When Ségalen returned for his second posting in 1917, he had a different reaction and found the new China much less to his taste. A new parliament had been built and schools, hospitals and universities, like Beijing and Qinghua, were flourishing. The city boasted electric lights, motor cars, tramlines, cinemas, newspapers, department stores and telephone lines. In his *Essay on Exoticism*, Ségalen complained about 'everything we call Progress' and the prospect of creating a classless society where there is no difference between 'the son of heaven and the people'. He warned that we would all be the poorer if the 'rule of the people brings with it the same customs, the same functions everywhere'.

In some respects Ségalen was right when he predicted that progress would decrease 'the exotic tension of the World' and that travellers would soon be hurrying to visit 'one strange place after another before the world runs out of places whose remoteness still offers the promise of mystery'. We need to preserve a sense of the mysterious from the growing banality and boredom of modern life and he was right to say that we cannot do without exoticism in our lives, per-haps, as he theorized, because it is 'a source of Energy – mental, aesthetic, or physical'. Yet as I walked around the Legation Quarter, I wondered if he had been correct in predicting that Beijing or China would lose its exotic character. What could be more mysterious or exotic than Mao's China? Hordes of fanatical Maoist Red Guards besieged the foreign embassies in their new Legation Quarter built in the Jianguomenwai district, just as the Boxers had done. Inside their new embassies, the baffled foreign diplomats tried to understand the actions of the Red Guards. They tried to interpret the meaning of the enigmatic signals emanating from Mao's court with the same puzzlement that their predecessors tried to decipher the empress dowager's intentions. And French writers like Simone de Beauvoir who visited Mao's China returned reporting a fantasy of happy Chinese living under an enlightened Marxist despotism.

Ségalen returned to France where, at the age of 41, he was found bleeding to death under an oak tree with a copy of *Hamlet* by his side. The posthumous publication of *René Leys* lifted his reputation as an important writer and poet. Backhouse took refuge in the vacated Austro-Hungarian Legation during the Japanese occupation and died in 1943, still spinning his fabulous tales of Manchu decadence to eager listeners. Meanwhile, in the 1970s the French Legation became the residence of Cambodia's exiled Prince Sihanouk. Mao had backed Pol Pot's Khmer Rouge revolution but inexplicably also gave refuge to the prince after Pol Pot's followers murdered most of Sihanouk's family. Cambodia's nightmare and the terror of China's Cultural Revolution, events more mysterious and monstrous than anything imagined by these earlier writers, cast a different light on the past. The tales of Manchu decadence and even the siege of the Legations now seem to belong to a more innocent age.

9

The Last Manchus

Pu Ren, a bespectacled figure with a head of white stubble, shuffled around his home with the dazed and apologetic air of a refugee. For more than four hundred years his family, the Aisin Gioro dynasty, had been the richest and most powerful in China, and, as he led me past a courtyard where wild flowers grew among piles of broken bricks, I wondered what had happened to him. Inside the sitting room, the whitewashed walls were dark with grime and so, I noticed, were his fingers. While we sat on folding plastic stools, drinking from tiny teacups poured from a green plastic vacuum flask, I could hear his wife coughing in her bed in the adjoining room. The rooms looked as if he and his wife had recently arrived and might decamp at any time. Stuff lay in heaps on the floor, covered by cloths. The rest was dumped in cardboard boxes and piled on top of a wooden wardrobe and a large white refrigerator, their most impressive possession. Much of what they had seemed new – an aluminium cooking pot, a red plastic bucket, a lamp holder shaped like a panda and a plastic snow globe with a tiny Father Christmas trapped inside. I wondered if the house would survive their death. It was located down a narrow hutong in an area that was being rapidly demolished and redeveloped. Soon Pu Ren would be living in the shadow of some giant steel and glass towers.

As the brother and nearest surviving relative of Pu Yi, China's last emperor, and at 85 the oldest member of the Aisin Gioro clan, Pu Ren was probably the nearest there was to a legitimate claimant to the Manchu empire. In fact, he had spent most of his life as a primary school teacher in the countryside around Beijing and still spoke in a commanding schoolmasterly voice. When I visited him in 1999, he kept referring to himself as 'Teacher Jin'. Jin, the Chinese word for gold, forms part of the Chinese transliteration of Aisin Gioro, his Manchu name. When Henry Pu Yi vacated the throne, some 2.1 million ethnic Manchus ruled an empire of 350 million, scattered in enclaves and garrisons in all the major cities. Once Beijing had between 400,000 and 600,000 Manchus, by the far the majority of its inhabitants. In 1911 many still spoke and dressed as Manchus. Now they seem to have all but vanished; seeing a Manchu is as unlikely as spotting a Hittite or an Inca on the street.

For centuries Westerners referred to Beijing not as a Chinese city but as the 'Tartar City', after the word used to encompass all central Asian nomadic tribes. By law the Chinese, or Han Chinese in today's parlance, were restricted to an area south of Tiananmen Square called the Chinese City. The Manchus lived in the Inner City around the Forbidden City, protected by a wall. This area was called the Huang Cheng, or Imperial City, and its wall was demolished only in the 1960s. A small section has now been restored and exists as a garden promenade. It is not just that the Manchus have disappeared but their homeland, Manchuria, has, after four hundred years, been deleted from the history books. It is not to be found on any map either, and has been removed from the Chinese vocabulary. It has simply become *Dongbei*, or China's north-east, and is divided between three provinces. When one of Pu Ren's brothers, Pu Jie, was finally allowed back to Beijing in the 1980s, he always made a point of telling interviewers that he was pleased that the Manchus had disappeared. 'I was like a drop of dirty water,' he would say. 'Now this drop of dirty water has been returned to the ocean of one billion people.' Manchu, too, the official state language for more than three hundred and fifty years – used to write millions of documents – has been forgotten as if it never existed. Only a few elderly villagers living on the Amur River bordering Russia can still speak it.

Apart from the direct descendants of the Aisin Gioro family, there were other Manchus still living in Beijing, some working and living in the same street where their ancestors had settled when bannermen – military regiments – and imperial guards lived around the Forbidden City after riding victoriously into Beijing in 1644. The more Manchus I met the more I realized the depth of their impact on Beijing and indeed on Chinese culture. Much of what has come to be thought of as typically Chinese, like the sexy figure-hugging *qipao* dress, is in fact Manchu. Now a short-sleeved dress with a long skirt slit to the thigh, it was originally a baggy silk robe which a bannerman wore over trousers. The Chinese called the Manchus 'bannermen' or *qi ren* when the conquerors first arrived in Beijing because they were organized in military banners or regiments (also known as *qi*).

It was the Manchu bannermen rather than members of the court itself who gave Beijing a flavour like no other part of China. As a hereditary leisured class, they developed interests and tastes somewhere between the working class and the aristocracy, which spread and created a general Beijing culture. They introduced popular dishes like *dajiang mian*, a noodle dish with various sauces, and *sacima*, a fried sweet rice-bun, as well as sliced mutton hotpots, roast Peking duck and flat wheat-cakes. The soldiers brought with them a taste for hunting, riding, hawking, fishing and caring for steppe birds, pigeons and swallows, and breeding exotic creatures, tiny lapdogs and goldfish with exaggerated fins and bulging eyes. The bannermen liked all kinds of harmless boyish pastimes, which they called 'small games', like cricket fighting or collecting carved whistles to attach to tails of swallows and pigeons. They also enjoyed a low-life comedy patter routine called 'cross-talk' in which two characters talk at cross purposes raising laughs with verbal puns. It is particularly funny in the Beijing dialect in which the end of words are all mumbled in a rustic burr of 'rrrs', a verbal tic from the consonant-rich Manchu language. Over time I came to realize it was the bannermen who had created much of what I had come to love about Beijing's vanishing culture.

The Manchu soldiers who conquered Beijing belonged to eight banners, or regiments, and each regiment was allocated a particular quarter of the Tartar City. You could still find some of them living in their original quarters until the late 1990s. Tang Qiliang's family had always been Blue Bannermen and Tang still lived in a small shabby courtyard house in the Guozi Jian Hutong, near the Temple of Confucius, where the Blue Bannermen families had always lived. When I first knocked on Tang's door and stepped over the threshold, his granddaughter invited me into one of his two small rooms. Tang was large, like many Manchus, and dressed in loose white vest and baggy blue trousers that revealed his large frame. He immediately fished out his business card. It identified him simply as a 'toymaker' and I looked back up at his large domed cranium and caught a brief humorous twinkle in his eyes.

Tang, who was by then 83, explained that his family had lived in the same hutong for three hundred and fifty years, but only recently had they turned to making toys. As palace guards, the bannermen had always been able to trust the emperor to provide them with wages and grain straight from the imperial granaries, grain that had been pulled by barges all the way up the Grand Canal and stored in large, grey, brick warehouses nearby.

'When the emperor [Pu Yi] ran away [after 1911], nobody supplied us with grain or clothes, so we had to find another way of making a living,' he explained. Then he picked a big grey rat from the shelf, wound it up with a small key, put it on the floor and laughed as he watched it run across the room. Beijing was still home to a large and pugnacious breed of rodents that no number of 'rat extermination days' had ever managed to eradicate. 'Children still like them,' he said simply, although he admitted that too many young boys and girls were beginning to prefer new toys. Most of the world's toys are made in China and the industry is now worth US$ 40 billion a year.

The industry had started up after the Boxer Rebellion. When allied troops entered Beijing to end the siege and the empress dowager fled, the income from annual grain-taxes levied on the Chinese peasantry stopped for the first time since 1644. The bannermen had to find new ways to earn their keep, and some naturally turned to the skills they had learned with their pursuit of 'small games', so the Blue Bannermen started making simple toys out of papier mâché, string, bits of wood and rubber bands.

At the time the concept of 'childhood' was still new to the Chinese and toys made specially for children were a novelty. Chinese culture had changed so much and so much from the past had been jettisoned that the significance of some of the toys Tang made was lost. They might as well have been African totems. One he pulled down from the shelf to show me was an odd-looking cart with little bells on it. On the side, he had painted the warning 'Check your goods after leaving, no refunds'. This, he explained, was supposed to be the sort of cart that street peddlers pulled around Beijing and this particular one had been used by peddlers who offered to repair broken fans. It was very pretty, but no child would recognize it. Once Beijing streets had been enlivened by an orchestral medley of cries, clangs and bells, each the distinctive call sign of peddlers offering a vast selection of goods and services. Yet the peddlers were banned soon after 1949 and when they made a comeback after 1979 Beijing's authorities made every effort to shunt them off the streets. Even the farmers' markets had been closed down in the 1990s because they might give the impression to Western visitors that China was still not modern enough to have supermarkets.

Another toy that Tang still made was a model of an emperor's carriage. A third type was a cart designed for Zhu Bajie, the legendary pig-like character in the Chinese classic *Journey to the West*. This book is still in circulation, and supposedly a children's story, but the symbolic account of a monk's journey to India to gather Buddhist scriptures, and his battles with malevolent Daoist spirits, is rather gruesome. Western fairy tales translated and introduced in the 1920s, such as the story of Snow White, are now far more familiar to Chinese children.

Toys like Tang's were sold at temple fairs, formerly held regularly in every quarter of the city to mark local festivals. Reviving the festivals is impossible because the folk culture around them has been deliberately suppressed. Tang pulled from a shelf a small statue of a foal he had made, which had a gold coin on its back. He explained that outside Zhangyi Men, the city gate now called Guangmen, there used to be a temple called Wu Xian. On the second day of the spring festival (New Year) worshippers would go there to pray for good fortune. They would buy a golden foal to put in the niche reserved for the Kitchen God. Every year it was the duty of the Kitchen God to report the family's doings to the heavenly authorities, and the foal's gold coin was a bribe meant to 'encourage' positive reports.

Another forgotten story lay behind the images of hares that Tang had made from clay. The Chinese believe that the moon is inhabited by a toad and a hare. Beijingers once considered the Lord Hare to be the city's patron god. In the old days, a clay image of the Hare dressed up as a magistrate, right down to his pointed mandarin shoes, was often bought as a charm. Once, when the city had been plagued by pestilence, the populace burnt joss sticks to implore Chang'e, the Moon Goddess, for help. She sent the Jade Hare to help cure them and in return the Hare was given gifts of small round red or white flat cakes. Just before the mid-autumn festival, Beijingers presented each other with all kinds of round 'moon cakes' filled with fruits or vegetables like lotus root or watermelon, which hares (supposedly) enjoy. These moon cakes are still given as gifts, but they have become a sort of burden, passed around like old Christmas fruitcakes that no one likes to eat or throw away.

After 1949 the new Communist government stopped the toymaking, along with hundreds of other handicrafts and trades, and gave the toy craftsmen new jobs. Tang became a labourer, and only after 1979 could he start making toys again, but by then it was no use. 'No one buys these handmade products any more, just a few foreign friends,' he said. The rest of the toymakers from his generation went to work at the Beijing Toy Factory, which made 300 different kinds of products. 'This might be the last time for you to see all these toys,' Tang said. 'No one will make these kinds of handmade toys any more once I am gone.'

After 1911 the Manchu aristocracy were too proud to make toys or go into business; instead they became artists like Pu Ziwei. A petite, fine-boned woman with pale skin, she lived in a red-brick block of buildings with her 85-year-old father, Pu Zong, a direct descendant of the Emperor Daoguang, who ceded Hong Kong to Britain in 1842. 'We are all very artistic. From generation to generation we had a tradition of learning to play instruments and chess, to use a brush for elegant calligraphy,' she said, as we chatted in her small bedroom, dominated by a large easel. Her father had worked as an art college teacher in Tianjin after 1949. When the Communists came to power they introduced a new nationalities policy designed to win over China's fifty-five recognized minority ethnic groups. This had at first benefited the Manchus, who had been discriminated against after the downfall of the dynasty. At that time, some opted to hide their identity by changing their names or abandoning the Manchu language, and in a Republican era census as few as 100,000 dared register as ethnic Manchus.

'The Nationalists had treated us rather badly but the new government treated us well after 1949,' Pu Ren said. 'The new government offered privileges to the Manchu nationality.' These privileges included reserved jobs and university places for members of minorities. Pu Ren also said that Mao Zedong was a strong admirer of the great Manchu emperors, such as Kangxi. 'Mao said the Qing dynasty had made some contributions to the country by expanding its territory. This encouraged us greatly,' he said. Premier Zhou Enlai recruited twenty students to study the language so they could read the imperial Manchu archives, because military-related documents, such as border treaties negotiated with the Russian tsars, were always exclusively written in Manchu. It was now vital to be able to read them in order to deal with Stalin, who was trying to hold on to much of Manchuria. From the 1960s onwards, as relations with the Soviet Union turned to hostility and China began to prepare for war, Mao changed his attitude towards minorities; now he wanted to force them to abandon their separate identity and to assimilate. As life for the Manchus became intolerable, the number of those registered fell sharply.

In Tianjin, Pu Ziwei's family were sent into exile in the countryside, where her aristocratic father was made to clean toilets. Yet her father did not change. The older generation of Manchus often shared a fatalistic attitude that bordered on recklessness. 'He always tried to enjoy himself by going off fishing,' she recalled. 'He also taught us three things: never save money, study hard and contribute to the country.' André Malraux, the French writer and former culture minister, once remarked that a particular gift made by the English was to provide a new definition of what a gentleman should be. The same could be said about the Manchus, and it was especially noticeable with men like Pu Ren or Pu Ziwei's father. Prince or pauper, they exhibited an amused tolerance of life's ups and downs, a pronounced courtesy and the dignified good manners that went with a slow and unhurried approach to life. This special sense of how a gentleman should behave was not a matter of class but had everything to do with old Beijing's culture. Moderation and enjoyment of life's pleasures, a humorous, cynical reserve, were inimical to strong political obsessions or the frantic race to get rich.

After Deng Xiaoping came to power in 1978 the state restored some of the privileges of the minorities. They could, for instance, claim exemption from the one-child policy and this is one reason why there are now officially 10 million Manchus in China, which means they outnumber both Tibetans and Mongols. However, the Manchu sense of self-identity is far weaker and life is still difficult.

Pu Ziwei's family left the countryside and returned to Tianjin, but she found it hard to find a place in society. As the family were judged to be class enemies in the Cultural Revolution, she had missed out on her education and had not been allowed to attend school. Without qualifications, she could not find a job. Often she ran into people who hinted they might help but would first ask her to draw a picture as a gift. Once they had it, the job disappeared. 'I was cheated many times,' she said. Like other Manchu ex-aristocrats, she found herself eking out a precarious existence on the line separating celebrities and circus freaks. Later Pu Ziwei found she could live off sales of her paintings and calligraphy and opened a small shop in Curio City, a centre for antiques. As the Aisin Gioro family members slowly made their way back to Beijing, they attempted to salvage something from their heritage. Some families had adopted Chinese family names to escape persecution. A few resorted to consulting the First Historical Archives in the Forbidden City to trace their real identity in one of the huge volumes that delineate the vast Aisin Gioro family genealogical tree. The state, however, still regarded the imperial family with suspicion, so members of its many branches dared not assemble, not even to sweep ancestral graves at the Qing Ming festival.

One member of the family who suddenly emerged from obscurity in the 1990s was Li Shuxian, the widow of the last emperor, Henry Pu Yi. A frail woman in her early seventies, she was dressed plainly in a blue Mao jacket beneath a black coat. She wore the same short hair as in her wedding photographs and looked wan despite applying thick make-up. We met at the Hua Long Imperial Cemetery, where she had come alone to sweep her husband's grave on Qing Ming. Inside the meeting hall, a Hong Kong businessmen of the kind who popped up everywhere in the early 1990s, when China's boom was getting under way, greeted her effusively. A portly man with a blue fishtail tie who spoke garbled Mandarin and English through a thick

Cantonese accent, he had persuaded her to have Pu Yi's ashes reburied in the commercial cemetery that he had invested in. Funerals had again become big business in China and many people, especially in the south, chose to rebury their parents in style. In provinces like Fujian one can see hillsides covered by large white horseshoe-shaped family tombs.

The cemetery lay among pleasant wooded hills, several hours' drive from Beijing, at the Western Qing tombs in Yixian County. Five Manchu emperors are buried in the Western Qing tombs, along with many wives and concubines; the other emperors, including the Empress Dowager Cixi, lie in the Eastern Qing tombs. The last ancestral sacrifices were held there in 1924 and only four years later soldiers of a warlord, Sun Tianying, desecrated the tombs of Emperor Qianlong and Cixi. Sun Tianying's men dynamited them open and hacked the corpses to pieces. Cixi's cadaver was later found almost stripped of its clothes with her silk pantaloons half pulled down. Descendants of the Manchu bannermen who had been settled there with their families to guard the tombs are still living at the Western Qing tombs. The tombs had a neglected air: rows of stone spirit guardians stood forlornly in dense thickets of wild grass and bushes; and the inhabitants struggled to make a living in a designated poverty area. They resorted to growing corn in the marble-lined empty canals and moats.

The Hong Kong businessman had brought investment to the area. On nearby hillsides, I could see rows of empty plots that he was hoping to sell to newly rich Chinese, attracted by the aura of royalty. Commercial cemeteries were then a new thing in China, though highly sought after. Hitherto everyone had been obliged to take their relatives to be cremated at just one crematorium at Babaoshan on the western side of the city. After 1949 the Communist Party had outlawed the custom of holding costly funerals and building lavish tombs. Babaoshan, however, was a soulless, dreary place, even for an atheist state. The dead were dispatched in a matter of minutes, the still-warm bones and ashes emptied into an urn for the dispirited relatives to take home. Often Babaoshan was overbooked and there was a long waiting list. It was especially hard to dispose of the dead at weekends and during public holidays when hospital workers or undertakers were absent.

'Sometimes people queue up for a long time with the corpse,' said one friend, who was shamed by his failure to send off his deceased father with a modicum of respect and propriety.

The businessman had volunteered to spend his own money on reburying Pu Yi's remains in a new tomb, no doubt hoping this would help lure customers. So now a small group of Chinese photographers and myself stood beside Henry Pu Yi's tomb, watching his widow. She clutched a fist to her chest, bowed low and laid a small bunch of flowers on the grave. The tomb, made of white stone and framed by four diminutive carved dragon posts, seemed pathetically modest beside the nearby tombs of his forefathers. It had a brass plaque with 'Aisin Gioro Pu Yi' written in plain characters. Her prostration completed, Li Shuxian turned and started to express her frustration at the lack of official recognition. 'He was never an ordinary citizen, even a movie based on his life won nine Oscars,' she started up. 'They should have put a title before his name. They should have said he was the Last Emperor, like in the film.' At the very least, his Communist-era titles ought not to have been forgotten. After all, he was, as she said, both a member of the Chinese People's Political Consultative Conference and a research fellow of the History and Literature Bureau.

In fact, it seemed unlikely that his new resting place contained any of his remains. Pu Yi had died in 1967 at the height of the Cultural Revolution. An official report said he had kidney cancer but it seems the truth was probably very different. He had taken refuge from the tumult on the streets by checking into a hospital, a common ruse for officials to lie low. Red Guards heard where he was and tried to force their way into his ward. They wanted to question him because they were convinced he had hidden some palace treasures somewhere and had already searched his house three times. The doctors and nurses allegedly linked arms to keep the Red Guards out, but whether they really protected him we do not know. The timing of his death was suspicious and he was immediately cremated at Babaoshan. It was not permitted to keep anyone's ashes in the columbarium for longer than three years because of the pressure on space and Li Shuxian provisionally reburied his remains in a public cemetery.

In the 1990s she revealed other facts that contradict the official version of his life detailed in the ghost-written autobiography, *From Emperor to Citizen*, the book that inspired Bertolucci's film *The Last Emperor*. Li Shuxian was one of a dozen brides introduced to the emperor as prospective mates and in the book she is described as a respectable nurse. The truth was different. She was a former taxi-dancer from a Shanghai nightclub who had already been married twice when she was introduced to Pu Yi by a reformed prostitute. Li Shuxian told me that for both of them it was love at first sight. 'Of course, at first I was worried because I thought all emperors had violent tempers, but then I realized he was not like one of those figures in operas,' she said. 'He had a kind heart and loved children.' If it had not been for the Cultural Revolution, Li Shuxian said, she thought her husband might have lived a few years longer and they might have started a family. 'In the courtyard house where we lived, all the children would run after him and call him "little emperor",' she recalled.

Li Shuxian was twenty years his junior, and the marriage was inevitably a misalliance. Within a week of marrying they had their first quarrel after she squandered their entire monthly income on a bottle of perfume. She had probably believed the stories that Pu Yi was still rich and had somehow stashed away a small part of the imperial treasures. Furthermore, Pu Yi is now alleged to have been a homosexual, never likely to father children. One day Li Shuxian followed him to a hospital where she discovered he was getting hormone injections to cure his impotency. She even petitioned for a divorce, an appeal that was rejected.

Still, it struck me as curious that no other members of the vast Aisin Gioro clan had turned up on Qing Ming to pay their respects to Pu Yi. Certainly, Pu Ren thought Li Shuxian was common and spoke of her with undisguised contempt, but there was more to it than that. The family had long ago split into two factions, with one side backing Pu Yi's effort to preserve their Manchurian homeland and identity, and the other side, which included Pu Ren and Pu Jie, resigning themselves to being absorbed into the great ocean of China: Pu Jie's 'drop of dirty water'. The Communists regarded Pu Yi as a traitor to the Chinese who had sided with the invading Japanese, but some Manchus even now saw him as a patriot. Pu Ren and Pu Jie refused to join their brother when, in the early 1930s, he accepted the throne of the Japanese puppet state of Manchuguo. After 1949 Pu Ren and Pu Jie were initially well treated by the Communists, while Pu Yi's followers were not allowed back from exile until well into the 1990s.

Pu Yi was raised in difficult circumstances, always at the mercy of historical events taking place outside the court, which makes it hard to think of him as a resourceful leader. He grew up in the Forbidden City as an isolated child with no playmates until he was 7. Instead, he was largely raised by eunuchs. By the end of her reign, the Empress Dowager Cixi employed 2,000 eunuchs in her court and her most important servant and counsellor was Li Lianying. It is said that he was born into a poor peasant family in Hebei, near Beijing, and first won her favour by skilfully styling her hair. In his autobiography *From Emperor to Citizen*, Pu Yi wrote that he never liked the eunuchs. 'By the age of eleven flogging a eunuch was a part of my daily routine . . . Whenever I was in a bad temper or feeling depressed the eunuchs would be in for trouble.' On one occasion he ordered a eunuch to eat some dirt on the floor. Another time, he wanted to hide some iron filings in a cake so that a eunuch would break his teeth eating it, and was only stopped from doing so by his kindhearted nurse. Yet the eunuchs played a role in moulding his character, and some think his homosexuality may have been linked to the strange palace atmosphere. The eunuchs played on the poisonous female rivalries, cattish jealousies and ambitions that festered in the hothouse atmosphere of the harem. With several thousand women all competing for the emperor's attention, a clever eunuch could help or defeat them in their ambitions. Some joined forces with a scheming empress or concubine in dark plots. It is not surprising that neurotic behaviour flourished in such an atmosphere of repressed sexuality.

When Pu Yi abdicated at the age of 6, he continued to live inside the palace until 1924. Outside its walls, some still plotted to restore the Qing dynasty, but other Manchus wanted to preserve the independence of their homeland. Until 1900 Han Chinese were forbidden to settle there and much of it remained a wilderness, empty of people other than Manchu or Mongol herdsmen. The construction of railways, especially the Trans-Siberian and its extension through Manchuria to Beijing, encouraged large-scale migration of Chinese,

Russians and Koreans. New multi-ethnic cities like Harbin sprang up. Russia and Japan both vied to lay claim to this rich, empty land. After 1931 the League of Nations devoted fruitless efforts to determining who had a rightful claim to the region. As diplomats dithered, the Japanese military created a modern city in Changchun (now capital of Jilin province), which was to be the capital of a great colony where millions of Japanese would be settled. The Japanese diligently set about cutting down the virgin forests, damming the rivers and mining coal and iron to create a modern industrial economy.

The Japanese solution to the disputed sovereignty question was to install the by now friendless Pu Yi as the ruling sovereign of Manchuguo. His brother, Pu Jie, was encouraged to marry a member of Japan's ruling imperial clan, Saga Hiroshi, thereby binding the two dynasties together. From Pu Yi's perspective, the alliance with the Japanese offered the sole prospect of preserving something of the Manchu heritage. These hopes did not entirely end with Japan's surrender in 1945. Soviet troops marched in and continued to occupy much of Manchuria even after 1949. Stalin toyed with the idea of creating a Manchurian buffer state and kept Pu Yi and his followers in a Soviet prisoner-of-war camp for five years. Stalin had already made one buffer state out of Mongolia (which Mao wanted), which was recognized as a separate country by the United Nations after a plebiscite on independence was held in 1946.

After Stalin's death in 1953 the idea was abandoned and Pu Yi and his followers were transferred to a Chinese camp after the Soviets withdrew. Mao then settled tens of millions of Chinese in Manchuria, many of them political prisoners who lived in camps felling trees and draining marshes. Fifty years later the three provinces that make up former Manchuria are home to 110 million Chinese. There are still those living in Beijing in the 1990s who continued to believe Pu Yi had acted rightly all along and remained faithful to his ancestors: one was the last eunuch to serve him, and the other was a claimant to the throne.

I found Jin Hengkai living in a one-room hovel near the Drum Tower, not long after his return from exile in the late 1990s. A stunted figure, almost a dwarf, with big hands and a large head, Jin exuded an unexpected air of dignity and showed a defiant pride in his ancestry.

After a life of almost unbelievable misery, he was making a living as porter for a property company run by local party officials, the Beijing Shichahai Economic Construction Development Company, building modern courtyard houses to sell to the new moneyed classes. It was the price he and his father Yu Yan had paid for remaining loyal to Pu Yi. While in a Soviet labour camp, where the last emperor spent five years, Pu Yi had rewarded Yu Yan, his most faithful follower, by naming him as his heir. Pu Yi's failure to produce an heir after numerous marriages had left him no other choice. As Jin Hengkai was the younger of Yu Yan's two sons, he was therefore second in line to the Dragon Throne. 'Pu Yi was a good man, he was no traitor,' Jin Hengkai insisted. 'He was an example to his family.'

His father, Yu Yan, is better known as 'Little Jui' in Pu Yi's autobiography and was the son of Prince Tun, one of Empress Dowager Cixi's chief counsellors, who had supported the Boxer Rebellion. When master and servant were transferred to a Chinese labour camp, Yu Yan went on to betray his master. He revealed to his new jailers that the emperor had sewn jewels into their clothes and stashed valuables beneath a false bottom in a suitcase. The betrayal did not save Yu Yan from spending a total of thirty-two years in various prisons. He was permitted to return to Beijing only a few years before his death in 1999.

As we sat on his bunk bed leafing through a photograph album, Jin talked about his life. He paused at a black-and-white image of his mother, smiling as she posed in a silk *qipao*. She died aged 27 from tuberculosis while her husband was in a penal camp. She had moved into Pu Yi's former residence in Tianjin, and when she died her two young sons were brought to Beijing to live in the care of an elderly uncle who was living in a princely courtyard house near Houhai Lake, just north of the Forbidden City. Soon afterwards their guardian died. When the authorities were about to send the boys to a state orphanage, an official objected. 'They rejected us because we could not be orphans when our father was still alive,' Jin said, with mordant humour lifting up the corners of his mouth. China was then in the grip of the Great Leap Forward famine, when 30 million perished of hunger. Mao had forced the peasants into communes and created nationwide food shortages. The boys starved. 'We didn't even know how to use the ration tickets,' he explained. They could get nothing to eat and the legacy was his stunted physique. Neither he nor his elder brother, Jin Hengzhen, could attend school, nor could they find work, even as farm labourers, because everyone rejected them on seeing their emaciated bodies. Soon after their father was released from prison the Ministry of Public Security arrested all three of them. By 1961 his elder brother found himself in the Xinjiang Border Guard and Construction Corps, several thousand miles from Beijing. He was not permitted to return to Beijing until 1998 when he found work as a nightwatchman.

Pu Yi was also released in 1959 from the 're-education camp' outside Lushun in former Manchuria and sent to work in Beijing's botanical gardens. He was given part of an old courtyard house inside the Guanyin Temple in Xizhimen to live in, furnished with a sofa, a carpet and a special telephone. The carpet was only made available when he received visits from foreign journalists and diplomats. In propaganda he was often presented as having been 'reformed' so that he could live the life of an ordinary citizen.

In the meantime Jin Hengkai was sent with the father he barely knew to a labour camp in Daxing county outside Beijing, where they worked together in the same labour brigade. There his father spent twenty-two years as a labourer. His son was given better treatment. 'I was considered capable of remoulding,' he laughed softly. He became a trusty in the camp and when the Cultural Revolution turned the world upside down and the prisoners put their jailers in prison, he unexpectedly rose to a position of authority. 'I was in charge of the Committee for the Ideological Remoulding of Cadres,' he said with dash of pride. Although he was with his father for these long years, the two never dared speak openly to each other about their family or their patrimony. 'We could not speak of such things. He was always under suspicion as a class enemy and went through a complete brainwashing.'

On his release in 1975, Jin worked as a handyman in a hospital and there he met his wife. Even when they married, he avoided using his real name, fearing this would frighten away his bride. 'During the years of class struggle no one would think of marrying a man like me with my background,' he explained. Now they had a son of their own who they hoped would have an easier life.

For a long time I had heard rumours that one of the old palace eunuchs was still alive somewhere in Beijing. He would have to have joined in the last days of the Qing dynasty and worked for Pu Yi, making him at least 90. Sometimes when walking through the hutongs around the lakes north of the Forbidden City, I would peer inside a courtyard house, hoping to see – past the piles of coal briquettes and lumber – the ruined halls of the residence of a Manchu prince. Or I would glance up at the windows of one of the drab four-storey dormitory blocks thrown up in the 1960s and wonder if he might be hanging on, a forgotten remnant of imperial grandeur. More likely, he would have chosen to live in one of the hundreds of half-ruined temples that one stumbled across in Beijing's back streets, which had been turned into a factory, a warehouse or a printing press. A Chinese writer, Jia Yinghua, who had researched and written many books about the end of the Qing dynasty, finally introduced me to Sun Yaoting, the last eunuch. He lived at the back of the Guanghua Temple in the headquarters of the state-run Chinese Buddhist Association, near the imperial lakes. It had been closed to foreigners for twenty years, but in 1996 Jia agreed to smuggle me in. Early one Saturday morning we arrived at a busy street in front of a high wall painted a deep red. After glancing conspiratorially from side to side, Jia knocked three times. A small door inside the gate opened and, negotiating the usual piles of coal briquettes and cabbages stacked in the hallway, we found ourselves in an airy courtyard.

'I've been worried these last days, he's not been eating properly,' whispered a man in a dirty white vest. Jia looked concerned and explained that this man – from a village near the eunuch's birthplace in Hebei province – had been hired by the monks in the temple to help look after him. When we entered his bedroom Sun was still in bed and he scrabbled around his bedside table to find his spare teeth, bending fingers with joints swollen and stiff from arthritis. As he struggled into his clothes (a coarse blue Mao suit), a telltale whiff of stale urine filled the air. Beneath the white stubble still covering his head, his watery eyes looked out alertly at the foreigner but he did not seem alarmed. His cheeks were sunken but not especially beardless or womanly. All in all, his lean frame bore little resemblance to the grossly fat, vain peacocks with rouged and powdered faces who cackle their way so prominently through Chinese literature. Sun looked rather sharp, especially for a man his age, and it was not hard to imagine that in middle age he had been plump but a little wrinkled. It was hard, however, to know what to ask this traveller from a country of the nether sex.

'These days my health and my circumstances are not so good,' he confessed in a high piping voice. Then he looked around the small grubby room that had been his home for the past fifteen years, as if a little surprised at these plebeian surroundings. He shared with Pu Ren that sharp but kindly humour of old Beijing. He wore striped pyjamas over which he now buttoned his Mao suit. He sat on the bed while we occupied the two armchairs and sipped tea that his carer poured from a thermos flask.

'Let me see, I suppose I am now 96 years old,' the eunuch quavered as I politely enquired after his health. 'But my memory is not so good,' he added. It was difficult to make conversation without being inter-rupted by the know-it-all Jia. If only I had just come a year or two earlier, Jia said, 'when Sun still had all his faculties intact, oh what secrets he would reveal, what dark palace intrigues!' Instead, the interview con-sisted of me asking a question with Jia repeating it in a loud voice, then both of us straining to interpret the response. It went like this:

'Have you been back to the Forbidden City?'

'The foreigner wants to know if you want to go back to the Palace Museum.'

'The what?'

'This foreign devil wants to know if you want to go back to the Purple City.'

'What kind of a foreigner is this?'

'An Englishman.'

'Oh, yes, there was another Englishman in the old palace – I forget his name.'

And so it went for nearly an hour without inducting me further into the mysteries of eunuchhood. Somehow, it seemed too ill-bred to pose probing questions to such an old gentleman, as if he were a circus freak. Jia said that Sun had once told him that despite being emasculated, eunuchs still had felt strong sexual urges and that even at the age of 90 these had not completely disappeared. 'It was only a longing,' Sun told him. Those who had been castrated before puberty were notorious for suffering from bouts of ill-temper and spiteful anger. 'Some eunuchs became sadists, satisfying their frustrated desires by inflicting physical pain on women,' Jia said. Other believed their genitalia could regrow, like a lizard's tail, if they ate the still-warm brains of executed criminals.

Sun was just 8 when his father, Sun Huaibao, a mendicant pancake-seller, got into a fight with a local landlord in Jinghai, near Tianjin, and was put in jail. Sun's family lost their plot of land and fell into such misery that a career in the palace offered a way out. Besides, it was a tradition in the villages of the north China plains. By contrast, the mandarins usually came from the wealthy families in the Yangtze valley who could afford the expense of putting their sons through the gruelling examination system.

His father and uncle performed the operation at home. With one sweep of a razor, they cut off his entire genitals and he fell into a coma. Then they covered his wounds with a dressing of paper soaked in an oil in which peppercorns had been fried. His father then inserted a catheter, probably a goose quill, into the urethra to allow the passage of urine. The 'three precious' were briefly fried in a wok, then wrapped in a piece of oil paper and bound up in a package usually called a *sheng* – meaning promotion, a reference to the hoped-for rise through the ranks of the imperial household.

Just a month later the Qing dynasty dissolved and China proclaimed herself to be a Republic. Sun nevertheless managed to be accepted and spent six years in the Forbidden City. His first post was in the household of Prince Zai Tao, the seventh uncle of Pu Yi. A year later, when Sun was 16, he joined the 1,221 eunuchs serving Duan Kang, the high consort of Pu Yi. Court ladies particularly favoured young boys, whom they treated more like pets and companions than domestics. He worked in her opera troupe before being apprenticed to the chief bookkeeper.

His career flourished. In the spring of 1922 he was promoted to wait on Empress Wang Rong, Pu Yi's wife. Just months later, however, Pu Yi decided to expel all the eunuchs. Sir Reginald Johnson, the upright and fiercely monarchist Scottish tutor of the last emperor, blamed the eunuchs for starting a fire in the palace to hide the evidence that they had been secretly selling works of art from the imperial collection. A couple of months later the vacillating ex-emperor relented and allowed the eunuchs back until, in November 1924, the warlord Feng Yuxiang resolved the matter once and for all. He evicted not just the eunuchs but Pu Yi and the entire imperial household from the Forbidden City.

Sun followed Pu Yi to Manchuria but ill-health forced him to return to Beijing, where he worked for a salt merchant until 1949. Then he settled in the Xinglong Temple near Zhongnanhai, which had been built by a powerful Ming eunuch and later served as a retirement home for many eunuchs. Sun possessed a good memory and an aptitude for figures and there he was put in charge of collecting the revenues from the land owned by all Beijing temples. He moved to Li Ma Guandi Temple. It was a slum, barely recognizable as a temple when I saw it in the 1980s, lost in a wasteland by a new motorway. The once grand courtyards were now indiscernible among a higgledy-piggledy collection of crude shacks built by families who had been squatting there since the 1960s.

After 1949 the eunuch-monks had to donate all their property to the state and were brought together to live in one temple. There, the dwindling community became caught up in Mao's increasingly violent political campaigns. Sun became a target of the 1962 national anti-corruption campaign and was found guilty of forging the ledgers recording grain stocks. In the Cultural Revolution, Red Guards shaved off half his hair and hung a board around his neck that said 'landlord'. A search of his belongings turned up the last 7 ounces of gold he had hidden. The Red Guards sent Sun back to his Hebei village. Later he was returned to Beijing and brought together with the other surviving eunuchs at the Guanghua Temple. There, they took part in ideological study sessions, competing to berate each other for serving the feudal oppressors of the labouring classes and to praise Mao. Yet Sun never stopped lamenting the fall of the Manchu dynasty. 'That regret stayed with him all his life,' Jia said. 'All his life Sun said he wished to see it restored.'

Even so, he returned only once to the Forbidden City, when Jia insisted on driving him and filming his reactions. On the shaky film, in which Jia himself constantly intrudes in every possible shot, fussing over his prize, Sun can be seen in a wheelchair being pushed from courtyard to courtyard by a shy young peasant girl, his youngest niece, animatedly recalling where Pu Yi played tennis or swung on a swing, or where the doorstep was removed to allow him free access on his bike. 'I don't remember the walls being so red,' he told me, as if somehow the seventy years that had passed had also faded the vivid colours in the images he carried around in his head.

A few months after our interview in spring 1996, Sun died peacefully in the temple. After his death his family came to lay a gold cloth across his face, put rings on his fingers, and shroud him in white silk embroidered with the imperial emblems of the dragon and phoenix. Then he was taken for burial near his ancestral village, and his remains, minus his three treasures, were placed under a tall marble tombstone. Hundreds of relatives and onlookers gathered to pay their respects and even the police arrived to stand guard. Although I was far away in England when the news broke, seeing the photograph taken at our meeting I felt a twinge of sadness. A last ember from the glow of old Beijing had finally died out.

In the meantime, Jin Hengkai was in the midst of a terrible struggle to save his son's life. His kidneys had failed and they urgently had to find enough money to pay for expensive dialysis treatment. It was costing them hundreds of thousands of yuan every year to keep him alive and his father's monthly salary was only 800 yuan (US$ 90). As a last resort, Jin Hengkai went public, revealed his true identity and begged for public charity.

'Many people came forward,' Jin said. The Beijing University hospital eventually found a donor for the boy, by then 22, and carried out a kidney transplant gratis. When I met the son, a plump bashful boy, his face was covered by a rash of pimples, a side effect of his illness. He said he didn't know where the kidney came from but it was easy enough to guess the source. It must have been from the warm body of a prisoner, one of the ten thousand or more executed in China every year. China's sprawling penal system, which had consumed the lives of so many members of the family, had kept him alive. The family was still too poor to afford the drugs that keep the body from rejecting the transplant. 'We have nothing, but we are together,' Jin said, 'back where we belong.'

In 2006 Pu Ren, then 88 and still living in a house surrounded by new gleaming office blocks, had been reduced to engaging in a succession of legal battles to defend the name and reputation of Pu Yi. He had launched one lawsuit against the writer Jia Yinghua, accusing him of defaming Pu Yi in his books; and another against the administrators of the Palace Museum. He claimed that the family possessed copyright over Pu Yi's images and the museum had no right to exhibit his pictures without permission. The courts had rejected the charges in both cases. Pu Yi and his history now belonged to the state alone.

10

In Search of the Golden Flower

Soon after Lili and I had settled down on the sofa of the KTV saloon in the 'Rich Man's Club', we established a mutual sympathy. The girl wore a purple cocktail dress over her whippet-thin body, which was buttressed by a thickly padded bra, and sat modestly with her knees pressed together. In front of us was a giant television screen with a karaoke machine, which gave the establishment its name and was now showing a happy girl standing on a tropical beach mouthing a song. In front of us was a table with our drinks and a large box of tissues in a gold-coloured box. Lili had begun by enquiring after my nationality and then generously volunteered the opinion that Englishmen were 'noble' and 'honest'. Chinese people, she was certain, were much more dishonest than foreigners. 'How long have you been in China? You must be tired, working so hard, and lonely without your family,' she said oozing concern. Then she shyly put a smoothing hand on my brow and told me I was lucky to have such soft skin.

Lili was also all alone in a big, strange city. She had recently arrived, a poor factory girl from a family of workers in Shenyang, the old Manchurian capital, where everyone had lost their jobs in a bankrupt state munitions factory. She was hoping to support her entire family, including a sick brother, by working as a *san pei xiaojie*. The term seems to be a new one and literally translated means 'three accompany miss'; it refers to a hostess who accompanies clients in drinking, singing and dancing. From time to time Lili topped up my glass from a bottle of beer or hastened to light a cigarette. Now and again there would be a discreet knock on the door and a waiter in a bow tie would enter, politely offering to bring more drinks, a platter of fresh fruit and hot towels. If I declined to buy Lili a fresh drink, she played a spoilt little girl, pouting, and told me, with a charming lisp, that regular customers, meaning proper gentlemen, drank French cognac and kept their own bottle in a fine mahogany dark cabinet. Whenever the door swung open, I could hear uproarious bursts of laughter from one of the other rooms along the corridor. One party was having fun playing the old finger number guessing game in which the loser has to down a glass; in another room a male voice wavered unsteadily, trying to reach a difficult high note, to the great amusement of the company.

You were not really supposed to hire these karaoke or KTV rooms on your own. When I arrived at reception, passing between gilded statues of helmeted Roman conquerors and bare-breasted Greek nymphs, the manager seemed uncertain what to do with me. He had shown me to the room and brought a string of girls for me to select, hinting strongly that it would be more jolly if I hired two or three at once. After 1949 the Communists had closed Beijing's brothels in a great show of puritanical indignation. They declared them 'unworthy of a civilized nation', 'feudal relics of capitalism' and 'a blot on the newly awakened Chinese people'. The noted Chinese journalist Xiao Qian, who had reported during the Blitz from London, where he became friends with E. M. Forster, was back working in Beijing at the time and witnessed the clean-up of Beijing's famous red light district in the Bada Hutongs:

One afternoon, several dozen trucks arrived and surrounded [Bada Lane]. The prostitutes of each and every grade, the madames, the waiters, the servant boys – the whole lot of them were chased into trucks in one smooth operation. It was done as dextrously as a post office sorts letters, so that in only a few days each person on the truck was in his or her proper place. The prostitutes were in their study classes and the pimps and procuresses were in jail.[1]

Afterwards a great fuss was made of re-educating the prostitutes and then demonstrating how they were now capable of taking part in productive labour. David Kidd, an American writer who stayed on after 1949, saw astonishing scenes of mass hysteria when the former prostitutes were put on stage to re-enact their liberation. Now dressed in sensible blue tunics and employed in button factories, the girls performed in agitprop shows, cast as innocent victims of a corrupt bourgeois society, in front of an audience of students. Kidd reported how the students went into fits and convulsions and had 'tears streaming from their eyes' and had 'faces contorted in agonies of fury and uncontrollable despair'. Yet, as he wickedly observed, the trade continued, albeit in a more discreet manner. Taking a rickshaw one day he was taken aback by the driver who asked him if he wanted to visit a 'black gate', the newly coined euphemism for the independent prostitutes who were still plying their trade.[2]

The end of prostitution and the rehabilitation of the girls served Communist propaganda in various ways. It was central to the goal of establishing a new morality for the New China that contrasted with the decadent laxity of the Republican era. As in Germany's Weimar Republic, everything about the Republican era has been rejected. The 1920s and 1930s are now considered a disastrous and failed experiment in liberal democracy that led to warlordism and political chaos. In popular fiction, Beijing's brothels were like Berlin's cabarets, symbols of a decadent and corrupt era that led to revolution. In the place of the warlords with their courtesans came austere and dedicated revolutionaries who upheld high moral standards in their private and public life.

As old Beijing was rebuilt into a modern city, the buildings from the Republican era, apart from a selected few, were ruthlessly demolished. It was part of the selective manipulation of China's memory but, until the late 1990s, I found it astonishing how many sites which had been famous in their time could still be found. The building that housed the country's first (and only) elected parliament building still exists but is now hidden inside the headquarters of Xinhua, the state news agency, not far from Tiananmen Square. In recent years it has mostly been used as a library and is closed to the public. The home of Li Yuanhong, China's second president, still stood until bulldozed away in 2001, despite being earmarked for preservation. One day I even found that Beijing had once possessed its own stock exchange. While looking for one of the old pleasure houses, I stumbled through a door in a hutong which led into a cavernous hall. Inside the dim hallway was a scene straight out of Dickens; everything was dusty and broken but one of the occupants, an ancient crone who lived in an old office, told me what it had once been. An equally neglected survivor is the red-brick Republican-era building which was the original library of Beijing University, where in 1919 students started their protest march and where Mao Zedong had worked as a librarian and first attended lectures on Marxism.

Beijing was once full of grey-brick Western houses, built in the early years of the Republic (1911–49) when Beijing was still China's capital. In the first part of the century its appearance had rapidly begun to change. It was lit up with electric and neon lights. The dusty roads were beginning to be paved and there were trams, buses and trains. Telephones, gramophones and the telegraph became commonplace. Far from being a failure, the modernization of Chinese life was in full swing. Out went ancient practices like foot-binding and concubinage and in came Western customs of marriage, divorce and funerals. Chinese brides began to wear white when they married, although white clothing had traditionally been reserved for mourning. Many Chinese threw themselves into learning Western music, classical and modern, ballet and ballroom dancing. Even as the Communist army marched in, Beijingers were still dancing the hokey-cokey and the cha-cha. Popular and mass culture flourished in China's cities. Beijingers went out to nightclubs, theatres, literary salons, concerts, tea houses, restaurants and dance halls as never before. People could live where they wanted and go where they wanted, either for study or pleasure. Memoirs written at that time are full of stories of days spent at the races, picnics in the Western Hills, paperchases, dinner parties and polo games.

Unlike the ports of Shanghai and Tianjin, Beijing never became an important business or industrial centre. Old Peiping 'was a delightfully idle, merry place', as Jacques Marcuse, a French journalist, wrote in his sardonic memoirs, *The Beijing Papers*. 'Everyone agreed that Puritanism and Peiping didn't mix well,' he wrote, as he struggled in 1962 to reconcile its ghost-like drabness with the place where once 'life was an endless string of parties'.[3] Many in Beijing enjoyed more political freedoms than at any time in China's history. A civic society sprang up which was happily and proudly bourgeois. With the removal of the deadening hand of the centralized imperial authority, citizens could associate freely in trade unions, student unions, political parties and charitable organizations. Instead of the old trade guilds and their temples and rituals, businessmen began to meet for business lunches at the Rotary Club. Universities became autonomous and professors could say what they wanted. A lively commercial press sprang up, publishing books, magazines and newspapers. Modern schools and universities opened for the first time, affording opportunities for women's education. Despite its many failings, for twenty years the Republic held regular elections, and parliamentary assemblies convened to pass laws and draw up budgets. In the rebuilding of Beijing the whole history of China's abortive experiments with liberal democracy has been deliberately buried and the very existence of the parliament building deliberately forgotten.

The Beijing government also forbade tour guides to take curious visitors to see the old brothels, which in their time (the 1920s) had become as popular a tourist attraction as the Forbidden City. When I called the Beijing Tourist Office to ask if the Xuanwumen district authorities planned to preserve the old red light district, a certain Mrs Zhao, who answered the telephone, was stern and definite; 'The history of the Bada Hutongs represents the dark side of China, its former backwardness. This will not be protected.'

The Bada Hutongs – 'the eight great hutongs' – are in Tianqiao, just south of Tiananmen Square, in a warren of bustling alleys formerly packed with tea houses, opium dens and opera houses. The 'lanes of flowers and willows' (a reference to the beauties who worked there) date back as far as the Ming dynasty (1368–1644), when imperial princes sneaked out of the palace in disguise in order to enjoy their attractions. The tradition continued in the following Qing dynasty, and the Emperor Tongzhi, son of Empress Dowager Cixi, reportedly caught syphilis during a visit there. After 1900 the brothels became highly regulated, inspected and graded into first, second and third class institutions. Working girls had to register with the police, and income was taxed. A 1906 survey of Tianqiao listed 699 opium dens, 308 brothels, 301 inns, 247 restaurants and 246 tea houses. The Chinese writer Lin Yutang, whose works helped introduce China to Western readers, said that girls in the Bada Hutongs formed a distinct class and were not to be compared with common prostitutes. 'Their function and training are exactly similar to those of Japanese geishas. They are entertainers. Singing is their main accomplishment. The girls were sent for to grace a public dinner, like the Greek courtesans.' And he quoted Professor Ku Hungming's verdict: 'If you want to see the true spirit of Chinese civilization you must visit the Bada Hutongs and see the essential grace, courtesy and feminine dignity of these singsong girls and in particular their ability to blush at obscenity.'[4]

John Blofeld, an English writer who lived in Beijing during those years and later became a great scholar of Buddhist philosophy, described being taken to the 'House of Springtime Congratulations', to be greeted by a male functionary known as the Big Teapot. Then he and his companions, two elderly academics, were brought to a sitting room where they drank tea and cracked melon seeds. After a long wait three breathtakingly pretty girls ran into the rooms. 'They were so far from my concept of alluring courtesans that, had they been more shy, I could have taken them for a professor's daughter.'[5] A man might visit quite a number of houses in the course of an evening, and a girl would die of shame if the guests started asking the price for a night. Instead, the Madame would come to 'borrow' money on some well-tried pretext, like putting up new mat-sheds or buying new stoves. A man who became an intimate of the house was supposed, to the best of his ability, to pay in vague undefined ways for jewellery, dress-making or restaurant bills, especially around the three big festivals. Sometimes, as Professor Gu explained, boorish asses from the countryside might spend thousands of dollars and still find themselves excluded from a girl's favours. Beijing was not, he explained, a prudish place and never was. As Professor Gu put it, it was as natural for wealthy men to take multiple wives and concubines as for a teapot to serve many cups.

I discovered that the bicycle rickshaw drivers who hung around the nearest tourist attraction, the Lao She Tea House south of Qianmen, which offered a very tame version of old Beijing's pleasures, seemed happy to ignore the interdiction.

'Can you take me around the brothels?' I asked one man reclining on the passenger seat of his vehicle. He looked like Lao She's most famous fictional hero, Camel Xiangzi, a rickshaw driver. He had a round, shaven skull and thick torso wrapped in a dirty sheepskin overcoat. Getting up lazily, he asked hopefully, 'Do you want to see them *all*?' 'I am looking for the House of the Golden Flower,' I replied.

CITY OF HEAVENLY TRANQUILLITY

'Ah, I know that one and all the famous houses; let's go.' We set off through narrow streets which preserved the distinctive feel of Republican-era China with their red-brick villas, although the layout of these streets actually dates back some eight hundred years, to the Jin dynasty.

We set off to find the house of pleasure once owned by Cai Jinhua, the Golden Flower, who achieved fame as a national hero. She was born as Cao Menglan in Suzhou, the southern city famous for its beauties, and while still a young girl was sold to a local brothel. There she had come to meet and bewitch a great scholar and official, Hong Jun. When Hong Jun was chosen to be the Qing dynasty's first ambassador to Berlin, she accompanied him as his concubine. Once in Berlin she learned to speak German and was such a great social success that she was presented at the court and made friends with the Kaiser's mother. Cai Jinhua's talents came to the fore after 1900 when the 'eight-nation' armies arrived in Beijing to lift the siege of the Legations under the command of Field Marshal Count von Waldersee. By this time Waldersee was 68 and in retirement, but he was a tough man whom the Kaiser trusted to do his duty and inspire fear and respect. In a speech made before the German expeditionary troops set off, the Kaiser told them: 'Give no pardon, take no prisoners! Just as a thousand years ago, the Huns under King Etzel made a name for themselves, now you will ensure that for a thousand years the name "Germans" will cause the same fear so that never again will a Chinese even dare to look askance at a German.' The Germans obeyed the Kaiser's wishes. After the empress dowager and her court fled the city, the allied forces divided it up into eight different occupation zones. Soldiers moved through the city executing anyone suspected of being a Boxer and looting the abandoned palaces, taking jewellery, antiques, furs and other valuables. The Germans even seized the astronomical instruments of the Chinese Imperial Observatory, which had been made by the Jesuits two hundred years earlier, and sent them to Berlin. Count von Waldersee also mounted forty expeditions into the countryside around Beijing, ostensibly to search for more Boxers but often in search of more loot.

While the foreigners were pondering what other retribution to inflict (one idea was to demolish the Forbidden City), Cai Jinhua arrived in

Beijing. She soon put her German-language skills and her charms to good use. Even the crusty old Prussian *Junker* could not help but fall madly in love with her. One night when a fire broke out in the Forbidden City they were discovered there in bed together. Although Count von Waldersee stayed in China only for nine months, Beijing legend credits Cai Jinhua with having 'civilized' the German to the extent that he agreed to restore law and order to the terrified city.

Armed with her new fame, Cai Jinhua went back to Shanghai and Suzhou to recruit a number of beautiful women and then opened her house, the Yi Xiang Yuan, at Number 32 Shaanxi Hutong. My pedi-cab driver knew exactly where it was and we quickly arrived in front of a large grey-brick building. It was now the Shaanxi Guest House and had been beautifully restored. The doorkeeper reluctantly allowed me to take a peek inside. Overlooking an interior courtyard were balconies rising four or five floors with rooms leading off them. The wood was all painted a raffish red. Of course, there was no reminder of Cai Jinhua nor any indication of its original purpose. Later in life Cai's fortunes took a turn for the worse. She got into trouble with the police and was accused of beating one of her girls to death. Thanks to her political connections, she got off lightly and retreated to Shanghai, where she married a wealthy man. When he died a few years later, she returned to Beijing. By then in her late forties, she became a devout Buddhist and died peacefully in her house in Tianqiao at the age of 65.

Next the rickshaw man brought me to another famous house of pleasure, hidden in a back alley leading off the Shaanxi Hutong. 'Yes, this is Little Fengxian's house,' admitted an elderly woman when I knocked at her door. Beaming with pride, she opened it up to offer a glimpse of high ceilings and marble floors. The original building had been a gracious structure but it was hard to see what it once looked like. It was now a slum tenement which numerous families divided among themselves and each of them had encased the exterior, like barnacles on a ship's bottom, with piles of haphazardly hoarded clutter and rubbish.

Fengxian had once succeeded Cai Jinhua as Beijing's most famous madame and her deeds were even immortalized in a propaganda film called *Zhi Yin*. She possessed a fine singing voice and accompanied herself on many instruments. Numerous courtesans became so famous that picture postcards of them were sold. There is one of Little Fengxian, but it is hard to see her allure as a pin-up. She is posed sitting wrapped in a lumpy embroidered coat folded up to her throat, next to a flowerpot with her hands on her lap. Her plain oval face, topped by a half-moon fringe around the forehead, has a solemn expression. Yet many powerful men fell for her and she used her influence to play a key role in helping to stop Yuan Shikai's attempt to found a new dynasty in the first years of the Republic. Fengxian's father was a high official in the Qing dynasty who was executed by General Yuan Shikai, the trusted adviser to the empress dowager, when he obeyed her orders to crush the 1898 reform movement. After the empress dowager's death and the 1911 revolution, General Yuan commanded the most powerful army in northern China. He summoned the Yunnan warlord, General Cai Er, a handsome man in his thirties with a Prussian moustache, to Beijing and demanded his support. In the capital, General Cai fell for Little Fengxian's charms and stayed in her house. When he decided to oppose General Yuan's ambitions and support the Republic, she helped him escape from Beijing and get back to Yunnan where he led his troops against Yuan's short-lived government. Yuan's dynasty lasted just eighty-three days and the square Edwardian-style villa that he built for himself in the Forbidden City still exists, but has been left a ruin.[6]

From 1916 onwards Beijing fell under the control of a succession of warlords whose armies marched in and out. The administrative headquarters of the Beijing government during this warlord era still exists but is divided up into housing for retired university professors, offices and dormitories. Its architecture is a curious mixture of Gothic Revival and Art Nouveau. Set around lawns and quadrangles with high arched windows, it has the look of a red-brick university aspiring to rival an Oxbridge college.

After Yuan Shikai, Beijing was controlled by his former Minister of War, Duan Qirui. He became China's prime minister from 1916 to 1920 and moved into a vast sprawling residential palace that had been built by Emperor Qianlong's powerful prime minister, He Shen. It was originally not much smaller than the Forbidden City, but it took time to find it. No effort has been made to preserve the palace, perhaps because Duan Qirui is regarded as a traitor. He is held responsible for the decision taken at the Versailles Peace Conference to give Germany's colonial possessions in Shandong province, including the city of Qingdao, to Japan. This was felt to be an injustice and a humiliation because China had sided with the Allies and declared war on Germany. Duan's residence had been broken up into pieces. A garrison of the People's Liberation Army occupied one part and another had been demolished to make way for a coal briquette factory. Various brick buildings which had once served as barracks and stables for Duan Qirui's guards remained. The large walled garden that belonged to the residential palace had survived too but it had been divided up to provide slum-like housing for sixty families. On 4 May 1919 Beijing students took to the streets to protest against the Versailles Agreement and marched on the home of Duan's Minister of Communications, Cao Wulin. His residence, which lies hard by Duan Qirui's palace, can still be seen although it has been turned into a government hostel.

The next warlord to leave his mark on Beijing was Zhang Zuolin, the diminutive general whose forces controlled Manchuria. Oddly enough, his mansion has been carefully preserved, although he was aggressively anti-Communist. In 1927 he ordered his men to raid the Russian Embassy, which still exists in the Legation Quarter, and broadcast slogans such as 'Absolutely Destroy Communism'. In the Russian Legation his men arrested Li Dazhao, co-founder of the Chinese Communist Party. Then Zhang Zuolin hanged Li Dazhao and nineteen of his followers. Yet the authorities took the trouble to remove the house where Zhang had lived for four years from its original site and rebuild it as a historic monument in Chaoyang Park, newly established on the eastern side of the city. The reason is that his son helped the Communists at a critical moment. The Young Marshal, as he was called, took over after June 1928 when the Japanese assassinated Zhang Zuolin by blowing up his train as part of their progressive annexation of Manchuria. In 1936, the Young Marshal Zhang Xueliang was in Xi'an with his forces when Chiang Kai-shek paid a visit there. Zhang's men kidnapped Chiang and released him only after he agreed to enter a united front with the Communists against the Japanese. Somewhat strangely, the

Western-style villa where Chiang Kai-shek lived on his visits to Beijing has recently been turned into a Japanese restaurant.

Life in Beijing was no longer so much fun in the 1930s, as the Japanese forces moved further south and threatened to take the city. After 1929 Chiang Kai-shek formally moved the central government to Nanjing, and Beijing was renamed Beiping, Northern Peace. Chiang shipped Sun Yat-sen's bronze coffin to his new capital from Beijing, where it had rested after his death in 1925. As he consolidated power, Chiang and his followers launched a puritanical movement, the New Life movement, that targeted such pleasures as horse racing, gambling, opium, spitting and prostitution, and began to end freedom of the press and freedom of association. Chiang encouraged students to join his Blue Shirt youth organization.

In the dead of night in February 1933, the palace art collection was secretly shipped out of Beijing; lines of wheelbarrows, one after another, made their way from the Forbidden City to the railway station. Early next morning the piles of wooden crates were sealed with strips of paper and loaded onto two trains for Nanjing. Some 700,000 works of art then made their way south, keeping one step ahead of the Japanese. By 1936 the Kuomintang (KMT) had finished building a new museum in Nanjing to house the collection but it had barely opened when fighting broke out in Shanghai. Beijing's fate was sealed by the Marco Polo Bridge incident, when Japanese troops from Tianjin moved to take over the small walled town of Wanping, outside Beijing. Fighting began when the Chinese garrison resisted at a railway bridge over the Yongding River. It is still there and at the site is a small museum dedicated to the start of what is known in China as the Anti-Japanese War of Resistance. On 8 August 1937 the American journalist Graham Peck watched the Japanese Kwantung Army stage a triumphal march through Beijing, beginning seven years of occupation:

Through all the morning a long column of troops, trucks and tanks filed into the city through Yongdingmen [gate] parading up the central avenues before they divided to occupy the barracks vacated by the Chinese . . . Up Hatamen [gate] rolled a thundering column of trucks loaded with food and ammunition. All of them were draped with coarse netting in which cornstalks and foliage had been woven for camouflage: even the grim dust covered drivers wore on their helmets small nets like lettuce bags, into which leaves and grasses, and sometimes flowers, were twisted with an unexpectedly coquettish effect.[7]

Beijing was soon forgotten as Chinese and Japanese forces battled for Shanghai. Chiang Kai-shek's troops put up a stiff resistance but were defeated, and retreated to Nanjing. In December 1937 the Japanese entered the city and massacred more than 300,000 Chinese. The Nationalist forces staged a retreat, passing through Wuhan, and finally moved up the Yangtze to settle in Chongqing (Chungking), Sichuan province. Those who could fled Beijing, some heading to Chongqing, where Chiang established his new capital, others joining the Communists in their headquarters at Yan'an in Shaanxi province. Few were left to witness the Japanese occupation; even the foreign residents were interned. By late 1945 the Japanese were gone, and American marines and the Nationalist forces arrived. Four years later it was the turn of the Communists to stage a victory march. As one army marched in and another left, Lin Yutang was confident that nothing would change: 'What are centuries elsewhere are but short moments in Beijing . . . Conquered many times, it has ever conquered its conquerors, and adapted and modified them to its own way of living.' He seems to have been proved right. Half a century later, the Communist austerity has gone and sexual prudery has given way to a licence far in excess of the 1920s. The first private bar opened only in 1988 but by 2005 Beijing had an estimated 300,000 girls working as masseuses, *san pei xiaojie* and prostitutes in an archipelago of KTV saloons, nightclubs, saunas and foot-massage salons. In some of these places you can do almost anything: order a meal, have a massage of various kinds, play mah-jong or cards, or just relax and sleep. Even so, the extent of the prostitution is evident. Most hotels have a brothel attached to them, masquerading as a beauty salon, and in 2001 some Chinese academics, such as economist Yang Fang, reckoned there were 20 million working girls in China.

In Republican China, sex and politics mixed so often that famous courtesans reputedly knew better than anyone what went on behind the scenes. In her house, a courtesan would entertain a powerful

client's friends and associates at dinner parties, facilitating the trans-
action of many delicate negotiations. Equally, there was often gossip
that rivalry for the favours of some sought-after beauty had led one
warlord to fall out with another.

As Lili and I talked, it seemed that this, too, had not changed.
Many nightclubs thrived on the patronage of state cadres. Entertaining
patrons had even become a legitimate business expense and KTV
salons issued official expense receipts; indeed, many establishments
are popularly believed to be owned by the Ministry of Public Security.
As it became common for leading officials to maintain mistresses,
some found themselves caught in a trap between the official standards
of Communist morality and the new era of sexual freedom. Lili knew
all about the politics of Beijing and told stories that cast a revealing
light on some major political events in the city. In 1995 the powerful
and well-entrenched party secretary of Beijing, Chen Xitong, fell from
power. President Jiang Zemin ordered the secret police to investigate
Chen's affairs in the hopes of unearthing evidence that could destroy
him. 'No one dared help with the investigations, they were too afraid,'
Lili explained, nodding sagely. His deputy, Wang Baosen, who was in
charge of the city's finances, was found dead in a hunting park in the
hills. He was said to have shot himself but no suicide note was ever
found. 'In the end it was Chen Xitong's wife who betrayed him.' His
wife had produced hard evidence of his misdemeanours by digging
out statements from secret bank accounts held in Hong Kong. 'But
why did she do such a thing?' I asked. 'Well, she was furious with him
when she discovered that he had given his mistress far more money
than he had given her. She wanted revenge.'

The state media went on to report that Chen Xitong had embezzled
US$2.2 billion, some of which he spent on building himself villas,
and one of his mistresses was supposedly a lion-tamer in the Beijing
circus. Three years later television news broadcast scenes of Chen
Xitong standing impassively in court as a sixteen-year jail sentence was
handed down, interspersed with pictures showing a large collection of
watches and expensive knick-knacks that he had allegedly accepted
as bribes. A few years later I thought again of Lili and wondered if
she had revealed the truth behind Chen's downfall. The media
reported the dismissal of another top Beijing official, a deputy party

secretary in charge of construction. By this time Jiang Zemin had retired and his successor wanted to replace the leadership of the Beijing municipality. It was said that top officials were ordered to attend a meeting in a room, when suddenly the lights were dimmed and on a large screen a video film was shown. The official in question had been secretly filmed cavorting in bed with two of his mistresses.

11

Mao and Beijing

Thirty years after Mao left Beijing as an aimless, impoverished library clerk, he returned triumphantly in 1949 at the head of a huge and powerful army. In 1919 he had slept crowded on a heated brick *kang*, squashed between seven others from Hunan; now he chose a secluded courtyard house on an island in the imperial palace gardens. In 1918–19 he spent six months in Beijing working under Professor Li Dazhao at Beijing University. Mao was by then 24 or 25, and the 'Three-Eyes Well Hutong' where he stayed still exists, as does the handsome red-brick university building where Professor Li set up the first Society for the Study of Marxism. By this time Mao was already convinced that the Chinese had to be transformed and their culture discarded, but in 1949 it was not obvious that he intended to rebuild Beijing. We know that in the 1930s Mao had rhapsodized about the city when he briefed his American biographer Edgar Snow about his early life:

My own living conditions were quite miserable, and in contrast the beauty of the old capital was a vivid and living compensation . . . in the parks and old palace grounds I saw the early northern spring; I saw the white plum blossoms flower while the ice still held solid over the North Sea [Bei Hai Lake]; I saw the willows over Bei Hai with ice crystals hanging from them and remembered the description of the scene by the Tang poet Chen Can, who wrote about Bei Hai's winter-jewelled trees, 'looking like 10,000 peach-trees blossoming'. The innumerable trees of Beijing aroused my wonder and admiration.

This refined poetic sensibility of Mao, contrasted with an utter ruth-lessness, often confused people and still makes his character difficult to comprehend. Shortly before the Red Army encircled Beijing, he had allowed some 300,000 residents of Changchun to perish in a three-month siege. Yet when the 8th Route Army moved south and closed in on Beijing in late 1948, they seemed determined to preserve the city's architecture from destruction.

Behind Beijing's high walls, the Nationalist Party General Fu Zuoyi, commander-in-chief of the Kuomintang's Northern China Bandit Suppression Headquarters, waited with 200,000 men and prepared for a prolonged siege. He razed private houses around walls, built gun emplacements along the great Ming walls and dug trenches alongside the old moat. For the terrified residents, the walls turned the city into a death trap from which there was no escape and little to eat. Refugees fleeing from the north had swollen the population. Some were living in the Temple of Confucius, sheltering behind latticed doors and windows covered by old newspapers and mats amid heaps of smashed furniture. The only way in or out was on the aeroplanes that sometimes landed on an airstrip at Dongdan, on the former glacis of the Legation Quarter, or another that the KMT built at the Temple of Heaven by cutting down 20,000 trees, including 400 ancient cypresses.[1]

In the summer of 1948 Beijing had still seemed a lotus land to some of the foreign residents. As the Communists approached from Manchuria, one American wrote that it was a 'ripe Camembert' baking in the summer heat of the north China plain, 'fragrant at night with ancient Jasmine scents and the pungent smells of Peking cooking, odours underscored by the night soil transported daily out of the city in honey pots'.[2] By the onset of winter, the Dutch writer and diplomat, Derk Bodde, noticed that the night soil carts dared not leave for fear of being pressed into forced labour by one of the armies. At the Dong An market, a huge crowded shopping arcade, he saw crowds struggling to get rice and buy flour with ration cards.

One morning, Bodde, woken up by an unfamiliar sound, looked out and saw eight planes looming through the morning mist and landing in the middle of the city. Often the Communist guns made it difficult to land and the KMT could relieve the food shortages only by dropping bags of rice and flour onto the ice of Bei Hai Park, occasionally hitting or injuring those below. Five bombs fell on the campus of Qinghua University, where Professor Liang Sicheng was advising the 8th Route Army officers waiting outside the city walls what buildings must be protected.[3] Peace talks began in January 1949 and General Fu was given an ultimatum: if he did not surrender by 2 p.m. on 22 January, the 8th Route Army would storm Beijing regardless of the cost. A few hours later General Fu surrendered rather than continuing with a futile defence that might destroy the ancient capital. Bodde felt the Communists enjoyed considerable support and noted that the walls and telegraph poles were plastered with posters exhorted the population to conduct itself peacefully and work for the building of new China. Students daubed his gate with the slogan 'Down With American Imperialism'.

On 31 January the KMT troops marched out and the PLA marched in. A truck drove up Morrison Street (Wangfujing), continuously blasting the refrain, 'Welcome to the Liberation Army on its arrival in Peiping! Congratulations to the people of Peiping on their liberation.' Behind it marched 300 soldiers in full battledress.

'All had a red-cheeked, healthy look and seemed in high spirits. As they marched up the street, the crowds lining the sidewalks . . . burst into applause.'[4] They carried two large portraits of Zhu De and Mao Zedong. Then finally a long line of trucks came carrying more soldiers, students and civilian administrators. In about ten minutes the parade was over. A second and bigger grand victory parade took place on 3 February, but a dust storm tore down all the banners and portraits. The spectators saw bands of stilt-walkers and cheerleaders orchestrating groups that chanted the PLA's famous 'eight points of discipline'. Beijingers were introduced to the rhythmic Yangge planting song, one of the folk dances invented by the Communists which is still performed on the streets today. The PLA also paraded 250 heavy motor vehicles, tanks, armoured cars, trucks mounted with machine guns, heavy artillery, jeeps, and ambulances, virtually all of them American-made and captured from the KMT over the previous two years. Later 200,000 people attended a mass meeting in Tiananmen Square, where Chiang Kai-shek was shown as a huge turtle being ridden by Uncle Sam. The United Press International correspondent reported that the locals had an attitude of wait and see, and thought the welcome given to the Communists was scarcely different from that accorded to each of the six other armies that had marched into the city over the previous forty years. The Associated Press reporter wrote that 'in the same way in which when Japan occupied Peiping, it welcomed the Japanese; when the Americans returned it welcomed the Americans; when the KMT returned, it welcomed the KMT; and even as several hundred years ago it welcomed the Mongols'.

Mao himself waited outside the city throughout most of 1949, staying in a heavily guarded military camp near the temples of Ba Da Chu in the Western Hills. Already treated as a demi-god, he did not show himself in public until the brief ceremony for the founding of the People's Republic on 1 October. Even so, he limited himself to a few brief sentences, did not mingle with the crowds and quickly disappeared from public view. The gardens of Zhongnanhai, like the rest of the former imperial domains in Beijing, had been open to the public to stroll around, but in September 1949 Mao and his entourage moved into Zhongnanhai and established themselves in the Ming era pavilions, courtyards and former temples. Just why Mao decided to make Beijing the capital of the new state has never been made clear in any official explanation. One can only guess at the reasons. Nanjing would have been tarnished by its association with the Nationalists and the shame of the 1937 massacre. Shanghai was largely a city created by the Western imperialists. Changchun had large and beautiful administrative buildings but these were designed by the Japanese for the new Manchuguo. Perhaps Mao wanted to associate the new state with the glory of the Ming dynasty, the last great ethnic Chinese dynasty. Some say Mao identified himself with the founder of the Ming dynasty, Zhu Yuanzhang, and the comparison between the two began to fascinate Wu Han, the deputy mayor of Beijing. Perhaps it is true to say that Mao signalled that he wished to be regarded as an emperor by moving into Zhongnanhai and establishing the head-quarters of the regime at the symbolic centre of imperial China. 'The emperors lived in Zhongnanhai, why can I not live there?' Mao reportedly said. Soon all the top officials were moving themselves into the minor palaces, or *wangfu*, of the Qing aristocracy.

The Communists claimed that Beijing had been 'liberated' in a 'revolution' but it was in reality a straightforward military conquest by a superior and heavily armoured mechanized force. As in most invasions in Beijing's history, the invader descended from the north, and in some respects it was a foreign invasion since without Stalin's backing the Red Army could never have succeeded. Although, as Bodde noticed, the Communists had some supporters, especially among the students, the party did not have broad popular support; indeed it acted as if a large part of the population was hostile to it. The entry was immediately followed by a reign of terror with large-scale arrests and summary executions. Peng Zhen, the first party secretary after 1949, approved more than 10,000 executions in the early 1950s. In *Mao: The Unknown Story*, the authors say that in Beijing there were 30,000 sentencing and execution rallies attended by nearly 3.4 million people. 'A young half-Chinese woman from Britain witnessed one rally in the centre of Peking, when some 200 people were paraded and then shot in the head so that their brains splattered out on to bystanders. Even those who managed to avoid such things could not always avoid seeing horrifying things, like trucks carrying corpses through the streets dripping blood.' Most were condemned without trial, as the existing courts were closed, and large numbers of other 'class enemies' were dispatched to labour camps, often in Manchuria. Even some foreigners were arrested and executed after being accused of plotting to assassinate Mao.

The Communists proved themselves to be as ruthless as the Mongols and in some respects more so. While the Mongols and Manchus had been tolerant of the customs and beliefs of their subject peoples, the Communists set out to interfere with and change every aspect of their private lives. They began drilling the indolent residents until they became a semi-militarized workforce. Political meetings absorbed all leisure time as the state, backed by a huge army of informers and secret police, clamped down on 'bourgeois' pursuits. The Communists banned the traditional 'small amusements', targeting their pets: crickets, pigeons, goldfish and most of all dogs. The party claimed that the Americans had infected the dogs with germ warfare, so it organized teams of dog executioners to patrol the city.

David Kidd, an American who had studied poetry at Yenching University and married the daughter of the former chief justice of the Supreme Court, was living in the sprawling Yu family mansion west of the Forbidden City. One night when he was in the garden, at around 11 p.m. he spotted a shadow: 'Surreptitiously the shadow of a man had joined that of the [decorative roof tile in the shape of a] fish on the rooftop nearest us. Then we saw the man's shadow glide up and across the ridge and disappear down the far side.' Soon the family discovered, as he wrote in *Peking Story*, that Baldy, their trusty watch-dog, had disappeared. 'The Communists really hated dogs because in a very tangible way the dog, loyal to individuals and not to beliefs, represented the last defence of the private citizen against the increasing nosiness of the police, the community, and the state,' wrote Kidd.[5]

Another night David Kidd woke up, turned on the light and saw a weird tableau: ten men illuminated on the garden terrace frozen for a moment in a parody of stealth, half of them carrying weapons. These were the 'night people' – a group of black-clad ex-burglars and acro-bats the police employed to scale the walls of private houses and go onto the roof to listen for the clatter of mah-jong tiles or pick up the smell of opium, both of which had been outlawed. Each night the 'night people' staged raids in a different section of the city. On one occasion members of the Yu household awoke to the cold touch of a carbine muzzle at the back of the neck when the police sneaked into their bedrooms. The police agents then demanded to see everyone's registration papers. David Kidd found himself being marched to the local police station, which he found crowded with other people in dishabille. He also described how the Yu family valiantly tried to adapt to their new circumstances and undertake such proletarian activities as breeding pigs in the garden and turning the ancestral mansion into a factory. (I later found the old Yu family mansion and discovered that Marshal Lin Biao, Mao's second in command, had used it as his private residence and built a four-lane-wide tunnel leading to a nuclear bunker. It now serves the Zhongnanhai guards as their barracks.)

The atmosphere of suspicion, spying and paranoia spread through-out the city. No one escaped this, no matter how high they rose or how low they fell. One political campaign and purge followed another year after year and no one was safe, not even those in the upper leadership round Mao. The educated classes were targeted in the Anti-Rightist Movement of 1957, when from 500,000 to a million intellectuals were sent to the labour camps, accused of disloyalty on the basis of false accusations and fabricated allegations. A great many of them did not return to their homes and jobs for another twenty years.

The terror and fear can be explained partly by the nature of Chinese Communism and its deliberate attempt to copy everything from the Soviet Union, but another part of the explanation may lie in Mao's character. When Wu Han (1909–69) writes of the early years of the Ming dynasty in his biography of Zhu Yuanzhang, he might well have been describing Mao. After Zhu became emperor, 'he felt everyone was trying to destroy him, everyone was ridiculing him' and 'he suffered from intense stress, paranoia, and pathological fears'. Wu Han explains his purges in psychological terms, saying that 'the disease that afflicted him was a form of compulsive sadism that drove him to use the sufferings of others to lessen his own sense of terror'. When in 1965 Wu Han was forced to rewrite his biography, this was changed; instead, the book explains Zhu's actions in terms of class conflict and maintains that the victims deserved to be punished.[6]

Policy disputes between Mao and his chief lieutenants turned into plots and Mao's paranoia grew. There were many issues over which the Maoists and moderates fell out: from the Korean War, to the rift with Moscow, to the drive to reach Communism overnight, called the Great Leap Forward. Mao embarked on the latter against the advice of his colleagues and nearly destroyed the regime. At least 30 million died in a nationwide famine and the economy collapsed. When his leading general, Marshal Peng Dehuai, dared question his policies, Mao responded with another savage purge but was temporarily forced to relinquish some power as the party struggled to restore food production.

The fate of Beijing was another source of friction, albeit a relatively minor issue. Although Mao lived in the Ming palace, it did not mean he wanted to preserve these symbols of the old order or the city itself. Possibly, from the beginning, he had intended to rebuild the city from scratch. A start was made immediately after 1950 and the whole area around Tiananmen Square was demolished and rebuilt according to Soviet designs. At that time, the Soviet Union was China's big brother and some sixteen Soviet advisers on city planning arrived in the early 1950s. They recommended creating a copy of Moscow's Red Square, which would provide a huge parade ground for mass gatherings. To create this vast space, the authorities demolished major gates (Chang Yongmen and Chang Youmen) at the T-intersection in front of the Gate of Heavenly Peace. In imperial times these had allowed officials access from the east, west and south to all the former ministry buildings. Along with the gates, two ornate *pailou* (memorial archways) disappeared and a reviewing stand was built at the Gate of Heavenly Peace. On each side of Tiananmen two monumental buildings with flat roofs, the National History Museum and the Great Hall of the People, were finished by 1959 for the tenth anniversary of the People's Republic. The municipal party administration was installed nearby in the former Legation Quarter.

Giant parades were a vital part of the new state's rituals. The first grand military parade took place in 1953. Three million people were marshalled to perform in the 1 October parades and the populace was also regularly turned out to welcome foreign leaders. Millions lined the streets all the way from the airport, so that wherever he went a visiting leader would be greeted by cheering crowds. On reaching the square itself, a foreign leader would be astonished to see a vast kaleidoscope made up by troupes of dancers. To accommodate these vast spectacles, it was necessary to build a grand avenue that ran from east to west. Beijing's existing north–south axis ran through the Forbidden City and along a line of great halls, gates and towers that included the Drum and Bell towers. This was interrupted to make way for the square, and the Zhonghua Gate was pulled down. Now a new axis went through the centre of the city by widening Chang'an Jie, the Avenue of Eternal Peace, and replacing the runway of the small Dongdan airport, used by some to escape the siege. Beijing's party secretary Peng Zhen created a ten-lane boulevard, wide enough to accommodate a million cars, but it also cut the city in half. The French journalist Jacques Marcuse described it as an 'idle stretch of an important highway linking two major hypothetical towns which leads nowhere and at both ends turns into a primitive country road with a bad surface'. Driving down it, Marcuse noticed with amusement how the boulevard had an elaborate system of traffic lights operated by hand. As he went past, policemen in wooden huts picked up the phone to report his passing. The creation of Chang'an Jie allowed the state to hold Soviet-style parades of troops, tanks and

Katouschka rockets mounted on trucks, which went on for twenty-four years with the exception of 1960, the nadir of the famine.[7]

After 1949 Mao made it clear that Beijing should be transformed from 'a city of consumption to a city of production'. Everything else followed from this view. 'Chairman Mao wants a big modern city: he expects the sky there to be filled with smokestacks,' Peng Zhen once told the eminent architect and historian Liang Sicheng as they stood on Tiananmen Gate looking south. With Peng Zhen's support, Liang and his colleagues had drawn up plans to preserve the old Ming city and establish the central government in new buildings outside the old city walls. The narrow streets of old Beijing and the medieval courtyards were clearly unsuitable for modern transport and communications. Mao rejected the entire proposal to move out of the centre. 'I spent twenty years fighting to get in, now he wants me to leave,' he said of Liang. He wanted neither to retain the old architecture, nor for the new buildings to be designed with any traditional features. The municipal government enlisted a team of experts from the Cultural Relics Bureau and drew up a list of 8,000 buildings that had historic, religious and artistic value; they decided to preserve seventy-eight of them for posterity.

Mao also insisted that Beijing should become an industrialized city because only 3 per cent of the population counted as the industrial proletariat, while in Moscow the figure was 30 per cent. Six thousand factories, big and small, were established in a city that was fundamentally unsuited for such a role by its location and by its lack of water, power and other key resources. Many factories were constructed in the heart of the old city. Outside the walls, the population was mobilized to create a new water source by damming rivers and excavating the Miyun Reservoir. Over time, Beijing municipality, an area the size of a small province, developed into a centre for steel, chemicals, machine tools, engines, electricity, vinegar, beer, concrete, textiles and weapons, everything needed to make it an economically self-sufficient 'production base'.

The Great Leap Forward was an attempt to accelerate the industrialization of China and millions of peasants were brought into Beijing to work in factories and on construction projects. By 1958 Mao decided the urban population, like the rural, should be organized into communes where all private property was abolished. Members of the urban communes were intended to live in a new type of building called 'Communist Mansions', specifically designed for communal living. Some prototypes were built around a twelfth-century pagoda near a hutong called Gongmen Kou Heng. These red-brick blocks of flats are still occupied, although the small apartments lack kitchens. The residents had to eat in communal canteens, wash in communal baths, clean their clothes in communal laundries and so on. Current residents told me that the communal kitchens lasted only two years because there was nothing to eat during the three-year famine that the Great Leap created. The party's grip on power had been dangerously undermined by a man-made disaster on a monumental scale.

Mao could not avoid shouldering some of the responsibility and his monstrous failures gave Beijing's architecture a temporary reprieve. In the end there was no money left to rebuild the city. The plans to rebuild it were never carried out and only a few of these newfangled 'mansions' came into existence. However, in the country-side party officials destroyed as much as they could, confiscating all private possessions of the peasants, everything from their work tools to their pots and pans. The walls surrounding old towns and villages disappeared, as did many temples, shrines and individual houses, not to mention furniture, paintings and jewellery. Only a few buildings that were listed as being of national historical value came under protection.

After 1961 the moderate leader Liu Shaoqi became China's president and together with others, including Deng Xiaoping, ended the famine through a number of temporary measures that allowed peasants to grow extra food on small plots of wasteland and sell it in markets. There was a similar liberalization in other areas, including the arts, and a number of writers, under the protection of Peng Zhen, were able to publish thinly veiled attacks against Mao. One such work was a play, or rather an opera, penned by Wu Han, deputy mayor of Beijing and Ming historian, who had authorized the opening of Emperor Wan Li's tomb. In *Hai Rui Dismissed from Office*, the upright Ming official (who in real life had reprimanded Emperor Wan Li and Emperor Jiajing) is dismissed after attacking the emperor for vain projects which had caused mass starvation. This was clearly an attack on Mao's dismissal of Marshal Peng Dehuai after he had warned him in 1959 of the mass hunger in the countryside.

Mao, however, felt that he was being forced out of power and believed he had been let down by a conspiracy of 'capitalist roaders', namely Liu Shaoqi and Deng Xiaoping, and he also blamed his failures on the shortcomings of the Chinese people, who clearly could not embrace utopia because they were still too rooted in the past. Mao plotted his return to power, and his first objective was to seize control of the capital and remove Peng Zhen. In 1964, with the help of his wife, Jiang Qing, he drew up a list of thirty-nine artists, writers and scholars that he considered 'reactionary bourgeois authorities' and whom he suspected of having cast doubts on his utopian fantasies. At the top of the list was Wu Han and the Peking Opera star Xun Huisheng; they and the others were soon arrested and held in a house in the outskirts.

In February 1966 Jiang Qing began orchestrating the publication of a series of vitriolic articles targeting Wu Han. Party leaders, however, still had no inkling of the scale of the movement that Mao was about to unleash. Official records term the Cultural Revolution as the 'years of chaos', but this is misleading. Mao deliberately bypassed the party to rally support among the students. Nearly everything that happened was orchestrated from above and staged with careful planning. In May of that year, Nie Yuanzi, party secretary of the philosophy department at Beijing University, wrote a revolutionary big-character poster warning that the university was controlled by the bourgeoisie. The poster called for an all-out attack against elitist forces. On Mao's order, the poster was read over national radio on 1 June 1966. He also authorized editorials denouncing bourgeois elements in society. Soon Peng Zhen came under direct attack and was seized.

On the night of 29 May 1966, a group of teenagers from the middle school attached to Qinghua University held a secret meeting in the nearby Old Summer Palace and took an oath to protect Chairman Mao. They named themselves 'Red Guards', dressed up like guerrilla fighters with red armbands and brass-studded belts, and began putting up posters attacking certain senior party leaders and their own teachers. The threatened leadership responded to the growing unrest in the universities by sending in 'working teams' often composed of senior officials, but Mao reacted by ordering students to make physical attacks on his enemies at all levels.

On 8 June three girls at the middle school attached to Beijing Normal University beat their deputy head, Liu Meide, with a plank two inches thick. It broke after three hours of fierce beating. The headteacher, Bian Zhongyun, was tortured for more than four hours during a 'struggle meeting'. 'I was forced to wear a high hat, lower my head (eventually, bending over at a ninety-degree angle), and kneel on the ground. I was beaten and kicked. My hands were tied behind my back. They hit me with a wooden rifle that was used for militia training. My mouth was filled with dirt. They spat in my face,' she later wrote in an appeal for protection. It was ignored and in August her students beat her to death.[8]

At Qinghua University students on 11 June organized a 'dog-beating team' to beat those who had been accused of being 'members of the black gang or other enemies'. They insisted that such people were 'dogs' and not humans. On 28 July the city's Municipal Party Committee admitted defeat and issued a 'Resolution on Withdrawal of the Working Groups from Colleges and Middle Schools'. At the start of August 1966 Mao showered praise on Qinghua students by writing a public letter, which said:

Red Guard comrades of Qinghua University Middle School: I have received both the big-character posters which you sent on 28 July as well as the letter which you sent to me, asking for an answer. The two big-character posters which you wrote on 24 June and 4 July express your anger at, and denunciation of, all landlords, bourgeois, imperialists, revisionists, and their running dogs who exploit and oppress the workers, peasants, revolutionary intellectuals and revolutionary parties and groupings. You say it is right to rebel against reactionaries; I enthusiastically support you.[9]

After this the Red Guards took over and teachers began to be beaten and murdered on a large scale. On 24 August 1966 the children from the Qinghua University Middle School brought in truckloads of Red Guards from twelve other middle schools in order to beat up the university administrators and professors, including Liang Sicheng. Millions of Red Guards descended on Beijing for the first mass rally on Tiananmen Square, on 18 August 1966. There, Mao allowed Song Binbin from the girls school attached to Beijing Normal University, a teacher training college, to put a Red Guard armband on his sleeve. He called on the students to 'bombard the headquarters', that is, to attack his opponents within the party headquarters. The students responded and besieged Zhongnanhai, trying to kill the head of state, Liu Shaoqi, and many other top officials. They later threw the eldest son of Deng Xiaoping – 'the number two capitalist roader' – who was studying physics at Beijing University, out of a fourth-floor window, which left him a paraplegic. Red Guard groups sprang up everywhere and thousands were killed in Beijing's 'Bloody August'. Schoolchildren daubed the slogan 'Long Live the Red Terror' on a wall near the Forbidden City. Later the slogan was repainted using brushes dipped in the blood of their teachers.

Mrs Wang Youqin, now a senior lecturer at the University of Chicago, was at the Middle School of Beijing Normal University on 18 August when Chairman Mao Zedong issued his famous proclamation to 'bombard the headquarters'. Mrs Wang was at her books when she heard a cry go up that the headteacher, Bian Zhongyun, was being attacked. Mrs Wang ran to the sports field, where she found a scrum of girls wielding bats, table legs and belts – the wide straps used by soldiers – around the headmistress and a few other teachers. The girls, all daughters of politburo-level party officials, were forcing the teachers to clean the track with their bare hands and later to scratch the excrement from toilets with their nails. Mrs Wang witnessed well-brought-up girls spitting on their victims, whipping and kicking them with their boots. They acted liked crazed animals, she said, and the beating went on for four hours. Bian finally died, lying at the bottom of a dormitory stairway, her blood splattered on a wall, after one girl smashed a bench leg on her head.

Now a historian of these events, Mrs Wang has pieced together accounts of what happened. In August and September 1966 a total of 1,772 people were killed in the capital, according to a report published by the *Beijing Daily* after 1979. The numbers exclude those beaten to death as they tried to escape Beijing on trains after their registration cards as residents of the city were suddenly cancelled. On certain days during Beijing's 'Bloody August', Red Guards murdered over a hundred people. On 26 August, 126 people; on 27 August, 228 people; on 28 August, 184 people; on 29 August, 200 people; on 30 August, 224 people; on 31 August, 145 people; on 1 September there were 228 victims.

In one incident, on 19 August, students from Beijing's Fourth, Sixth, and Eighth middle schools held a 'struggle meeting' in the Zhongshan Concert Pavilion in the Forbidden City. On a stage in front of an audience of thousands they whipped and kicked more than twenty 'members of the black gang' from the three schools and the city's Education Bureau. Sun Guoliang, head of the municipal education bureau, suffered three fractured ribs. Wen Hanjiang, vice-principal of the Eighth Middle School, lost consciousness as he bled on stage. According to an interviewee, all were so severely beaten that they 'no longer looked human'.

Eric Gordon, a British journalist from the *Daily Worker*, who was being kept under arrest in the Xin Qiao Hotel in a corner of the old city, felt that a wild beast had been unleashed:

For if one could not see the revolution, one could hear [it] in the evenings carried out across the Peking sky. The sound was the angry, shrill shouting of slogans often accompanied by the beating of drums and the clashing of cymbals. It poured out of the hundreds of meetings that were being held throughout the city, meetings that began late at night and carried on until the early hours. You could not escape from the roar of the meetings: it was like the moaning of a gigantic animal crouching over the city.[10]

Xiao Qian, in *Traveller without a Map*, recalled what he saw. His family had already been forced to live in one room with a ceiling made from newspapers which leaked in the rain, when his house was wrecked by workers from a nearby plastics factory. They even smashed his collection of gramophone records. One day in August he found six corpses in a pile at the end of the alley. His eldest son came home and described how a dedicated teacher at his school was accused of class crimes and beaten to death. 'Afterwards the school principal was forced by the rebel faction to mount a balcony where he could be seen, to put his arms around the corpse and dance with it. He jumped to his death. For many people in those days death was pleasanter than life,' Xiao Qian wrote. The Red Guard schoolchildren had set up a 'water dungeon' where they kept their prisoners half-immersed in a basement. Many of them died.

Xiao Qian tried to end his own life with a bottle of sleeping pills. His wife was accused of being a spy because her elder sister had married an American professor. His wife's 70-year-old mother hanged herself and his wife was made to stand before the corpse, chanting 'The death of Wan Peilan has relieved the world of another stinking scourge'.[11]

The movement was officially called the 'Great Proletarian Cultural Revolution', though it was more about education than workers or factories. Mao not only asked students to destroy the education system, but to 'smash the Four Olds: old ideas, old culture, old customs and old habits, and erect the Four News' (*po sijiu, li sixin*). The students rampaged through the city, searching houses and destroying anything that looked old. In one month alone, the 'Bloody August' of 1966, they ransacked 33,000 homes and destroyed 3 million tons of books.

Mao's heir apparent, Marshal Lin Biao, gave a speech, 'Why we need a Cultural Revolution', in which he explained what was meant by 'old culture and ideology':

We can use a great many words to express it and call it old culture, old ideology, poisonous weeds, ox-monsters and snake-demons, reactionary authorities, old academia, old morals, old art, old laws, old education systems, old world outlook, etc. The most essential oldness of these things lies in them being old in one particular respect, namely as part of the system of private ownership.[12]

A moneyless, propertyless and classless utopia had not instantly emerged from the People's Communes because the Chinese people, including his own colleagues, were still coloured through and through by their great cultural heritage. This could not be Mao's fault but could only be blamed on the shortcomings of the Chinese people. They had let him down. All traces of that heritage had to be destroyed for a new China to be born. This idea was not very different from the all-out Westernization ideas current in the 1920s, when Mao was a university library assistant in Beijing. The left-wing writer Lu Xun himself had warned that China would only change if there was mass violence – a great whipping, he called it.

The fount of these ideas was Marx. 'The alteration of men on a mass scale is necessary,' Marx had insisted, otherwise his revolution could not succeed. In his view, history consisted of a preordained succession of conflicts between different classes. The improvement of the human condition could only come from the victory of one group over another. Given such a perspective, individuals counted for nothing. 'There is no such thing as an abstract independent individual,' declared Marshal Lin Biao. Individuals were moulded by forces like culture and history. 'Man has no nature; what he has is history,' as the Spanish thinker José Ortega y Gasset remarked in 1935. If that history could be erased from the collective memory of the Chinese people, then you could replace it with whatever you wanted. Human nature was just so much infinitely malleable putty, so any individual could be brainwashed and any society taken apart and rebuilt. 'It is on a blank page that the most beautiful poems are written,' Mao once wrote. 'A blank sheet of paper has no blotches, and so the newest and most beautiful words can be written on it, the newest and most beautiful pictures can be painted on it.' Mao made it clear that the more ignorant the Red Guard students were, the better. Students who handed in an empty sheet of paper for their examinations were the best students. 'What is there to learn in school?' Mao demanded of the Qinghua University Red Guard leader Kuai Dafu when they met in July 1968. 'What is the use of studying philosophy? Can one learn philosophy in college?'

As Mao pointed out, Stalin never went to university and Jiang Qing only had six years of schooling. 'The more one studies, the narrower one's mind gets,' added Mao's deputy, Lin Biao. It became a catch-phrase; the more one knew, the more stupid one became. The effort to create a blank sheet of paper required the destruction of traditional Chinese culture, but also turned against all Western and foreign culture. With each new phase of the movement, the violence spread until it consumed everyone, even the Red Guards.

As Chairman Mao dangled the prospect of real political power in front of the Red Guards by inviting the students to join revolutionary committees, the rivalry between different factions broke out into the '100 days war'. In 1967 Qinghua students split into two rival factions. The ultra-leftists, called the Jinggangshan Regiment, were led by Kuai

Dafu. He believed all senior party officials should be persecuted as 'capitalist roaders'. On the other side was the April Fourteenth Faction, the moderates who believed that only a minority of Mao's enemies needed purging. Militants from both sides, known as 'rods' – perhaps because they were considered 'straight and strong' – progressed from using spears and knives to revolvers and rifles, and finally ended up using machine guns, mines and even tanks. The students not only used these weapons against themselves but also killed workers and soldiers who had been sent to stop the fighting and expel the students. Altogether about 800 people were killed in the fighting at Qinghua University, including some members of the architecture faculty.

The worst outburst of violence against the staff took place in 1968 during the 'Cleansing of the Class Ranks' campaign, which caused the deaths of many senior leaders. Teachers were detained on campus for months or years and some of them were beaten by students again and again. Many committed suicide. To celebrate the start of the violence on 18 June 1968, the Qinghua faculty had to walk in single file along a path across the campus; students and others who stood on either side of the path beat them with clubs and whips. These older Red Guards also went out to attack foreign embassies. On 1 April 1968 the *People's Daily* ran an article justifying the Boxer Rebellion by describing the Boxers as predecessors of the Red Guards. The Jinggangshan Regiment stormed China's Foreign Ministry. The April Fourteenth Faction had tried to trump them by sacking the British Embassy in August 1967.

The chargé d'affaires, Donald Hopson, recounted in official papers how the staff refused to be rattled, embarking on a surreal evening of entertainment while 20,000 massed outside. 'After dinner of tinned sausage and claret, I went to the first floor to play bridge while those of the staff who were not at work watched Peter Sellers in a film entitled, not inappropriately, *The Wrong Arm of the Law* ... At 10:30 pm I had just bid three no-trumps when I heard a roar from the crowd outside. The masses had risen to their feet and were surging like an angry sea against the small cordon of soldiers who linked arms three deep before the gates,' he said.[13] 'I only had time to throw on my jacket before the mob poured through and over the gate like monkeys,' he wrote in his official dispatch home. The eighteen men and five women in the embassy 'were hauled by our hair, half-strangled with our ties, kicked and beaten on the head with bamboo poles,' he said. 'The girls were not spared the lewd attentions of the mob ... So much for the morals of the Red Guards.' Outside, the mob hung posters that said 'Hang Wilson' and 'Burn the Wily Anglo-Saxon' and 'Crush British Imperialism'. The Reuters correspondent Antony Grey was imprisoned in a room and would not be freed for another two and a half years.

Order was only restored on Qinghua's campus by the army. They marched in and took control of almost every institution in the city and disarmed the students. From late 1968 Mao expelled 12 million youths from all the cities. These were the students who belonged to the *lao san jie*, the name for the high school classes of 1966, 1967 and 1968, who were packed off to the countryside to learn from the peasants. Their three years of freedom to do whatever they wanted, including the rare freedom to say and publish, to travel and associate as they pleased, was over. The children of high-ranking cadres, many of whom had committed the worst atrocities, were held in a special labour camp. Beijing became strangely quiet. During the three previous years some 9 million Red Guards from all over China had invaded the city, camping out in people's homes or in makeshift dormitories in schools and other public buildings. The schools, universities and many other institutions, including museums, remained closed. The Forbidden City was closed, too, and over the next seven years became a wilderness. Only a small unit of soldiers guarded it. The grass grew long in the courtyards and it became a home to rabbits, wild foxes and flocks of sparrows. The outward appearance of Beijing changed for ever; even the old familiar places were altered to give them a new revolutionary flavour.

The army was present everywhere, but, emptied of half of its population – many officials were sent off to re-education camps – Beijing began to take on the atmosphere of a village. The trams no longer ran, work in the factories came to a standstill. There were no markets, no peddlers and no restaurants. Most people still lived in pre-Revolutionary Qing dynasty buildings although the housing had been reallocated, again in the spirit of absolute egalitarianism. China's civilization developed in its cities and Mao's revolution was an assault on urban China, an effort to erase the differences between town and countryside in the name of egalitarianism.

'It is an excellent place for an experience of complete loneliness. Here one will find not even ersatz understanding, or a soothing quasi security of the coffee house or cinema. Peking is an ideal post for the philosopher,' wrote Dutch diplomat Douwe Fokkema. 'Without contact with the outside world, a person will be alone with the reminiscences of the traditions of his own country.'[14] This phase of quietude changed when Mao decided to distract the country by starting a war with the Soviet Union. In 1969, his troops launched unprovoked attacks on Soviet troops on an island in the Amur River in the far north. China was put on a war footing and Beijing's inhabitants were mobilized to dig nuclear bunkers. The country's top leadership was dispersed to remote areas. The authorities drew up plans to evacuate 60 per cent of the population, mostly the young and elderly, and to dig shelters to house the remainder. Each person was to be allocated a space of approximately 63 square inches. Archive propaganda film is still occasionally aired showing how the citizens could comfortably survive a nuclear attack and continue to live beneath a radioactive wasteland. As in an early science fiction fantasy, one sees trucks driving up and down two-lane underground roads, workers sitting at lathes churning out goods in subterranean factories, peasants growing mushrooms, raising chickens and breeding edible algae in cellars. Behind enormous steel doors, rows of neat children are shown calmly studying in classrooms and athletes performing gymnastics or playing table tennis in subterranean gymnasiums.

The shelter building went on for nearly ten years and much about it remains shrouded in secrecy, but there is said to be a maze of 34 miles of tunnels under Beijing. In the surrounding countryside, one can still come across caves hollowed out to house tanks, as well as hidden factories, underground bunkers and warehouses. The military built its own shelters, strong and deep enough to withstand a direct nuclear hit. These were linked by two underground railway lines; a circular line that runs roughly along the route of the city walls, and another, which leads from Tiananmen Square in a straight line westward, for the leadership to be evacuated to the military garrisons in the Fragrant Hills, where there is an underground airstrip. The 31-mile circular line, now Beijing's Number 2 Metro Line, runs directly beneath the former Soviet Embassy, and diplomats sitting on the toilet can clearly feel the rumble of passing trains.

The civilian nuclear defence network was built to far inferior standards and would probably only protect residents from some missile attacks or perhaps from biological or chemical weapons. As early as 1972 the authorities took visiting American journalist Joseph Alsop to inspect the shelter dug beneath the streets of the Bada Hutongs in Tianqiao. Behind the counter of a clothing shop, the saleswoman pressed a button and a trapdoor opened to reveal a concrete staircase descending deep into the earth. Hundreds of feet beneath the surface one can still find a cinema, a restaurant, and dormitories that have been turned into hotels.

Underneath Ditan Park – the former Ming dynasty Temple of the Earth, just to the north of the Temple of Confucius – local residents excavated a huge underground grain store which is now the biggest ice rink in the city. You buy a ticket and then descend through a tunnel wide enough for two trucks to pass each other to find hundreds of youngsters racing round the oval rink to the sound of Elvis Presley blaring from the loudspeakers. The network of tunnels beneath Yuetan – the Temple of the Moon – in the west of the city is now a huge emporium filled with stalls selling underwear, haberdashery and fake Rolex watches. Previously the tunnels had served as shooting ranges and dormitories. After 1978 the shelters provided 40,000 beds and two-thirds of Beijing's visitors had to sleep in them because of a shortage of hotels.

In addition to these giant projects, every household was also ordered to build its own crude shelter. These were excavated by hand, using shovels and buckets, in nearly every courtyard house, including Lao She's home as well as ancient mosques and temples. Nowadays, officials admit that most of these shelters would have been useless in any real nuclear war. Even the larger ones lacked any mechanisms for filtering air. Everyone except those in the military bunkers would have died immediately or shortly afterwards from the blast, heat and radioactive fallout.[15]

Once Mao had put the country under a wartime state of emergency after 1969, the last of the city walls were pulled down. Schoolchildren were sent to demolish the remaining stretches; they used the bricks to build air raid shelters and even used the stones from the ruins of Emperor Qianlong's fabled Yuanming Yuan. Where the wall had once run is now the second ring road, a six-lane concrete motorway. Only the names of the bus stops recall, in ghostly fashion, those of the famous gates that had stood for six centuries.

When Mao died in September 1976 many people were sleeping out of doors, afraid to stay in their homes after a massive earthquake hit Tangshan, a coal-mining town near the coast. The July earthquake shook houses in Beijing, cracking walls and dislodging tiles. This all added to the air of destruction and neglect that by then pervaded a dingy industrial city choked by smoke and dust. Even with his death, Mao was not finished with Beijing. His corpse was secretly moved around the city's underground roads and quickly pumped full of formaldehyde, but the body began to disintegrate. His followers hastily erected a huge mausoleum in the centre of Tiananmen, directly on the north–south axis of gates and palaces. At first a wax dummy was made after experts went to Madame Tussauds in London, until a panel of scientists found a way to restore the skin to a more natural appearance. Mao is now on show for part of the day, but his sarcophagus, filled with inert gas, is mechanically lowered into a vault beyond the reach of harmful solar radiation. Every two days the sarcophagus is opened and sprayed afresh with a special mixture of chemicals designed to preserve him intact for at least another century.

12

History in Stone

It was like this for many people in Beijing. They spent much of their lives forced to live next door to neighbours who had taken part in their persecution and the death of their family members. For Zhu Lin in particular, the memories must have been even more painful. Many of Qinghua's leading Red Guards were now running the country and still intent on completing the destruction that Mao had demanded during the Cultural Revolution. Even then it was still hard to talk openly about the past, to lay to rest the demons that had been unleashed in the explosion of violence and terror.

When we met in 2002, Zhu Lin was in her seventies. She wore thick glasses and her hair had turned grey, but she walked with a firm step around the neat lawns of Qinghua University, pointing out the places where her husband, the architectural historian Liang Sicheng, had faced the fury of the Red Guards. 'That's where we lived when the Red Guards took my husband away,' she said as we stopped outside a row of two-storey town houses. It was now occupied by some of those, now senior university administrators, who had persecuted them. She scrabbled to open a small pack of paper handkerchiefs and dab a tear that sprang from her eye. The house was just a few hundred yards down from where she now lived alone in a ground-floor flat with a piano and a collection of classical music. 'By then he was half dead from the tuberculosis that had killed his first wife,' she said, referring to Lin Huiyin, the charming and talented hostess of the Crescent Moon Society's literary salon. 'At these meetings, they forced him to stand up and someone had to hold him up on either side.'

'This is the place where Jiang Qing came and spoke to the crowds,' she said, in front of a big square at which a parade of new buildings ended. 'And this hall', she said, pointing to a neo-classical building with white pillars, 'is where the struggle sessions took place. It was copied from the campus of the University of Virginia. And this is the science building, one of the oldest parts of the campus,' she continued as we paused before a four-storey block of red brick overlooking a well-kept lawn.

At the height of the '100 days war' in Qinghua University, rival gangs of Red Guards fought each other with machine guns, home-made bazookas, Molotov cocktails and even tanks. One desperate band of Red Guards, besieged in the science faculty, had tried to escape by digging a tunnel. When an American writer, William Hinton, arrived three years later and inspected the scene, he could still see buildings pockmarked by bullets and shells, and nuts and bolts fired by huge slingshots made from bicycle inner tubes, as well as trenches and the underground tunnel built by the April Fourteenth Faction of Red Guards as they tried to escape from the science faculty.[1]

'I never saw this fighting, but before the troops arrived in July 1968, it was very dangerous, very chaotic. Anyone could march into your house and take anything they wanted at any time. They destroyed everything,' Zhu Lin said. 'Liang Sicheng had a collection of Buddhas with samples from every period and they took this as evidence of superstition. We were reactionaries so they could do whatever they wanted, even force us out of our home.' They were forced to live in a tiny apartment with Liang's two grown-up children. All the windows were smashed and they shivered through the winter when temperatures fell far below freezing. Shut up in a tiny room of just 258 square feet, he designed and made bookcases and wardrobes to fit. Liang could only leave his apartment wearing a huge black placard across his chest that said 'Reactionary Academic Authority Liang Sicheng'. Finally, Zhou Enlai ordered him into a hospital, where he had to join a group of patients who studied Mao's thoughts, and where he kept writing self-criticism to the last. Just before he died in 1972 he was readmitted into the party.

When Liang Sicheng left the University of Pennsylvania in the late 1920s, a slim, dapper figure with glasses and a double-breasted white suit, he had every reason to expect a career filled with glowing achievements and international recognition. He was the son of the famous

Liang Qichao, one of the 100 Days Reformers and one of the most influential of the intellectuals who called on the Chinese to modernize and become a 'new people', and he had married Lin Huiyin, one of the most sought-after beauties of the day. While his father called for radical change, the son plunged himself into the study of the past. He returned to China and embarked on his life's work, A History of Chinese Architecture.

Until he finished his great work, in the closing months of the Second World War, the leading experts on Chinese culture scorned the very notion that such a thing was worth examining. The modern study of China's ancient culture began in earnest at the beginning of the twentieth century, just as Chinese intellectuals became obsessed with copying from the West as much as possible. Few thought there was much worth preserving from the past and many shared with Western scholars the belief that China's greatness lay in its literature and fine arts. 'Chinese civilization did not lodge its history in buildings,' noted the Princeton historian Professor Frederick W. Mote. Architectural historian Ann Paludan thought that in China, 'there is no need for an architect' . . . and not much room for genius.[2]

Even great enthusiasts for ancient Chinese culture, like Victor Ségalen, thought that China, when compared with Rome, Greece or Egypt, had little to offer. He concluded that its buildings, made of perishable materials, had a sort of built-in obsolescence necessitating constant repair. From this, Ségalen concluded that 'eternity does not inhabit the architecture but must inhabit the architect himself'.[3] Until Liang completed his research, only a German, Ernst Boerschmann, and a Swedish art historian, Osvald Sirén, had produced studies – in 1923 and 1925 – which examined urban architecture, but only in a fairly amateurish way. Liang Sicheng's father gave a big impetus to his research when he gave him an 800-year-old manuscript that had recently come to light. It was a treatise on Song dynasty building techniques by a man called Li Jie. At once it offered him a huge insight into the evolution of architecture in China.

During the Republican period architects of all nationalities made some efforts to incorporate Chinese elements into modern buildings, but after 1949 interest in Chinese architecture dwindled away entirely. There are, it must be admitted, some genuine reasons for denigrating

Chinese architecture. Whether it is a temple, a palace, an official's *yamen* or a peasant house, no matter what the dynasty, it all seems to consist of variations of the same unit. The basic design and structure of a peasant house is strikingly similar to that of the greatest palace in Beijing. Once I stayed in a little hamlet under the shadow of the Great Wall and watched how the locals fixed up a house that had burnt down. A cheerful team of men rebuilt the roof and the walls without an architect or a blueprint. Between the timber uprights, the men, stripped to the waist, packed a mixture of earth, stones and straw to form the walls on a square raised platform of mud. The roof was simple, too. Few timbers were used, just some white branches, laid end to end across the roof beams, which were just strong enough to support grey roof tiles. In this village, the older buildings had thatched roofs, but, whatever the material used, the roof extended over the walls to cover a small porch supported by plain wooden pillars, usually painted bright red. The overhanging eaves kept the walls dry, otherwise the rain might wash them away. In better houses, purlins help tip the roofs upwards at the end, giving graceful floating eaves that draw the eye.

It is the dimensions of the roof that lend Chinese buildings elegance and distinction. The windows always face south, and for this house the builders did not bother putting in windows in the other three walls because it backed onto a hillside. Richer village houses had grey stone walls enclosing a forecourt, with relatively minor buildings flanking the eastern and western sides. The entrance was through a small gate adorned with tiles and other decoration. Inside one felt snug and private, but walking between the houses and their walls, especially in villages enclosed by a protective wall, could feel claustrophobic. The size of any traditional Chinese building is determined by the number of *jian*, the unit of measurement for each partition, and the size of a house is determined by the number of courtyards. A large prince's palace (*wangfu*) and even the Forbidden City itself become merely an agglomeration of courtyards. Ming dynasty regulations specified for each grade in the bureaucracy how many columns, *jian* and courtyards a man could have for his residence. Ordinary dwellings contained three to five *jian* but the higher the status of a man, the more court-yards and the bigger the space they occupied. Superstition also played a role: odd numbers are considered lucky and houses using the numbers four or six inauspicious, with four (*si* in Chinese) being particularly bad because it is a homonym for death. Qing dynasty regulations specified that commoners could not occupy houses with more than three *jian*, but officials could have seven, temples not more than nine and palaces as many as eleven. Chinese buildings are therefore intended to reveal not much about the individuality of the owner but more about his status.

However, the charm of China's ancient cities, like Ming dynasty Beijing, derived from conformity enforced by state regulations. Both the universality of the architectural design and the uniformity of the materials combined to lend a sense of great harmony. Few buildings rose more than two storeys – the only exceptions being the Drum and Bell towers and a few key religious buildings, like the Temple of Heaven or the white pagodas, a design imported from India. Even palaces were not intended to be works of architectural creativity. The Forbidden City was designed by an Annamese eunuch called Ruan An, who followed the same palace designs used in previous dynasties. Even in the centre of the Forbidden City the great halls are still only one storey high. The city was also colour-coordinated to designate rank. Imperial residences had yellow tiles and vermilion walls. Ordinary folk had their walls painted grey.

Despite the strict building code, individuals went to great lengths to decorate their homes. The craftsmanship of old China was remarkable and the sense of detail that went into the carving of wooden window trellises, doorways and all kinds of everyday household objects is a world away from the plain uniformity of the mass-produced factory products that filled people's homes after 1949. It was easy to see, just by walking past the entrance, how an owner expressed his individuality. At the doorstep, Beijingers would place a pair of lions, or drums or some other stone object, each beautifully carved and often decorated with a magnificent diversity of themes. The doorposts, lintels, and the cantilevered beams holding up the eaves were also gaily painted in five sacred colours in a variety of designs. The roof tiles were also decorated with a succession of mythical beasts or guardian figures, each of which commemorated a story from Beijing's past. All the patterns, shapes and meanings of old

Beijing, from the roof tiles to the hand-painted blue-and-white porcelain cups, were invested with religious and cultural significance that the residents understood.

It is also true to say that Chinese buildings are both cheap and simple to repair. Travelling around China in the 1980s and visiting temples that were being repaired after decades of neglect, I often saw workmen using stencils to paint patterns and even scenes on roof beams and pillars. Some of the work was repetitious and mechanical – one might hesitate to call it art or craftsmanship. These traditions, however, meant that Beijingers inhabited an integrated world in which all the details conveyed a meaning that they readily understood. The very design of the city had meaning because it was supposed to represent a map of the universe. Further, the designs were also practical. People lived in buildings adapted to the local climate so that Beijing's walls gave shelter from the winds, the many trees gave shade and the courtyards gave sunshine. The low-level buildings, the human scale of the architecture, the intimate seclusion of the inner courtyards and the greenery of the city were pleasing and comfortable even in the hot summers.

Once a building is finished in China, little money or effort is spent on maintaining it, and there seems little respect or veneration for the structure per se. After a while, new buildings begin to look as old as any other. Within two years, the new houses in the Great Wall village seemed indistinguishable from the others. Even in Beijing, many apparently old buildings are actually quite new, like the Qianmen Gate, the Temple of Heaven, the Deshengmen Gate – all rebuilt in the last hundred years. Although the design of the Forbidden City dates back to Emperor Yong Le (d. 1424), physically the buildings are rarely older than the eighteenth century. The originals were destroyed by frequent fires, and identical buildings then reconstructed.

When Liang Sicheng finally produced his *History of Chinese Architecture*, he challenged the low esteem accorded to Chinese architecture, but it was almost too late. As Liang and his students began to search old China for traditional buildings, they realized they had to hurry before everything vanished. He felt he was racing against time, 'like a blind man riding a blind horse', wrote Wilma Fairbank in her book *Liang and Lin: Partners in Exploring China's Architectural Past*.

While Lin Huiyin was hosting her literary salon in the 1930s, he was busy making field trips across the country, eventually recording some 2,000 sites. Sometimes his wife came along. 'They bounced for days crossing rutted mud roads with a vision created by some literary sources of some wonderful old monuments only to find after hundreds of miles, a few roof tiles and stone column bases,' wrote Wilma Fairbank.[4] The couple's greatest ambition was to discover an intact Tang dynasty wooden temple. Among the many forgotten marvels they found was an ancient stone span bridge dating from AD 600 and, in Beijing itself, they made the remarkable discovery of a Liao dynasty pagoda, the Tianning Temple, or Temple of Heavenly Tranquillity. Then, in 1937, just before they fled Beijing and embarked on a ten-year odyssey to south-west China, the Liangs made their most extraordinary discovery: a temple on Wutai Shan, the Buddhist holy mountain in Shanxi, which they dated to AD 857. It had survived intact for 1,100 years. Liang's research enabled him to identify six stages in the development of Chinese architecture stretching over 3,500 years and find examples of sophisticated engineering achievements that rivalled those of the Romans.

Meanwhile the entire campus of Qinghua University prepared to decamp ahead of the Japanese invaders. Liang Sicheng and his Institute for Architectural Research had to go as well. Liang and his wife tried to remain as long as possible, but eventually they joined the trek westwards. They ended up in Chongqing, the wartime capital of the Nationalists, but most of the time they lived in a small village downstream. There, Lin Huiyin became weaker and weaker from the tuberculosis that would eventually claim her. After Japan's surrender the Liangs moved back to Beijing and settled again on the Qinghua campus. They also went to America and spent a year at Yale University; they could have stayed in America or followed the defeated KMT to Taiwan. Instead they returned to Qinghua University, where he opened the architecture department, and the Communist siege of Beijing found them there hard at work.

By then even the unworldly Liangs must have known enough about the Communists' attitude towards Chinese traditional culture to be able to judge whether they should stay or flee. Neither seemed to have entertained much regard for either the Communists or the

Nationalists, seeing them as similar as two peas in a pod. In one unguarded moment, Lin Huiyin confided to her American friend Wilma Fairbank: 'The stupid thought-control of the right, the purposeful thought-manipulation of the left are enough to leave one very thoughtful and speechless for a long time.'[5]

Yet Liang must have felt he would be able to contribute to his country under any government. During the Second World War, he sent Zhou Enlai lists of historical sites that needed to be preserved and even marked out sites in Japan, like Nara and Kyoto, which the Americans should avoid bombing. Perhaps he thought it his duty to stay and save Beijing. During the siege, a PLA officer even came to him with a map of the city and asked him to designate areas where precious buildings and cultural relics ought to be preserved if things came to the worst. By this time Liang Sicheng was an international figure in the world of architecture. He was invited to join the United Nations Board of Design as a consultant in the design of the United Nations building in New York. The Communists felt that such figures lent them prestige and international credibility. At first things went well. After 1949 the Communists continued to treat him with great respect, giving him titles and consulting him on a wide range of issues. They even appointed Liang and his wife to committees that designed the new national symbols, including the national flag and state emblem.

All these honours helped give Liang Sicheng some authority to speak out when he found himself in a treacherous battle to preserve Beijing and its architecture. Liang considered it was vital to preserve Beijing as an integral whole. Piecemeal preservation would be meaningless. And it was essential to win the battle for Beijing because officials across China would take their cue from what happened to the capital. The protection of China's entire architectural heritage, therefore, hung on the fate of Beijing. When Liang became vice-director of the Beijing City Planning Commission, he made a series of recommendations. First, that the city should be a political and cultural centre; he insisted that all industry must be absolutely barred from the walled city, for industry, he argued, would cause traffic congestion, environmental pollution, a rapid and excessive growth of population and a shortage of housing. Further, he emphasized that the Forbidden

City should be strictly preserved and all new buildings inside the city walls should be limited in height to two or three storeys. Lastly, he put forward a plan to create a new administrative centre with government buildings along a north–south axis, established west of the Forbidden City.[6]

He prepared, printed and distributed at his own expense a plan for the new administrative centre which would allow the new construction to take place without disturbing the traditional central axis of the city. He wrote articles like 'Peking – a Masterpiece of Urban Planning', which he hoped would win his cause public support. Liang suggested that Beijing should become like Washington DC, largely a tourist city, and reminded the new leadership that architecture is 'history made of stone'. We may deny history, he warned, but we cannot cut ourselves off from it. In the illustrations that he drew, Beijing is shown as a gigantic museum. The flat wide tops of the battlements became a continuous public park with flowerbeds and garden seats. The gate towers and corner towers with their up-swept double roofs were turned into museums, exhibition halls, refreshment kiosks and tea shops. The moat around the city was transformed into a beautiful green belt where 'the great masses of the working people' could go fishing, boating or ice-skating. The walls of Beijing, he said, are not only China's national treasure but also the cultural relic of the people of all nations. 'We have inherited this priceless and unique historical property; how can we now destroy it?' he pleaded.

Liang Sicheng sometimes appeared to make headway in convincing China's new rulers that architecture mattered. When the party considered what the new national emblem and flag should be, the Liangs argued the case for some Chinese characteristics, so instead of the hammer and sickle, the national emblem is still an image of an architectural design, a representation of Tiananmen Square in red and gold. Liang was also consulted on the design of the Monument to the People's Heroes, which was finally erected in 1958. He persuaded the government that it should be like a traditional memorial stela and of a height and dimension in keeping with the Ming gates. Liang was determined to persuade the new government to relocate its headquarters from the historical centre to a new site to the west of the city. In the 1940s the Japanese had already drawn up plans, and constructed a few roads and buildings in Gongzhufen near the Temple of the Moon. Together with another foreign-trained architect, Chen Zhanxiang, Liang drew up a detailed plan to relocate the ministries and the residential quarters for the officials who worked in them. They produced a number of designs to satisfy the desire for large new buildings, using steel and concrete, but which also exhibited a Chinese style. Architects in the 1920s had put up such buildings, which were four or five storeys high, with concave roofs and overhanging eaves. Liang now designed skyscrapers embellished with similar Chinese roofs.

As one political purge followed another, Liang Sicheng worked tirelessly to protect Beijing in what must have been an intimidating and morbid atmosphere. As he worked, Lin Huiyin lay in the bedroom next door dying. She died in 1955 at the age of 51, but not before vowing to kill herself in front of the city gates if the party decided to pull down the walls. The destruction began in 1950. First to go were the city's fifty-five beautiful *pailou*, the elaborate tiled and wooden ceremonial arches built over the centuries in memory of chaste women and upright generals. The excuse was always that they impeded the traffic or posed a fire hazard. Often the authorities, knowing that the citizens were against it, ordered the demolition to be done at night by gangs of peasants brought in from outside. Next to go were the city gates and the walls. One of the most beautiful gates, Xizhimen, was first secretly set on fire because only then could it be demolished as a hazardous building. Liang Sicheng had likened the wall to 'a necklace around the neck of Beijing', but the authorities called it 'a chain around Beijing's feet'. Although he drew blueprints to show how one could dig road tunnels under the walls so as not to disturb the gate towers, and to preserve the integrity of the walls while still improving traffic, it did no good. The walls, the towers and the moat all disappeared. 'When a city gate was demolished, it was like cutting a piece of flesh from me, and when the bricks of the outer city wall were torn down, I felt as if my own skin was being stripped off,' Liang said.

The Party regarded the defence fortifications as relics of a feudal empire which obstructed traffic and restricted development of the city. It was better for the bricks to be used to pave new roads. The idle Beijingers whom Liang Sicheng had fondly imagined in his preservation scheme going fishing in the moat or visiting art galleries had by this time been transformed into a highly drilled and semi-militarized workforce. In the end, Liang failed in almost every way to achieve his aims and barely survived the increasingly savage purges of the 1950s. He became the target of a campaign of criticism in 1955 and spent months writing confessions, even having to criticize his father, Liang Qichao. He caught tuberculosis himself and fell into a depression. In 1957 he was again targeted while his colleague Chen Zhanxiang was exiled to the countryside. Liang's enthusiasm for an indigenous style, a fusion of modern and ancient architecture, came under harsh attack too. Large roofs covered with glazed tiles were condemned for being a waste of money and for smacking of 'formalism and reactionism'. His ultimate defeat came when the Great Leap Forward was launched in 1958, and the party dropped its last qualms about preserving old Beijing. Millions of peasants were drafted in from the countryside to make steel and start the reconstruction of the city. A new plan was drawn up to approve the destruction of 80 per cent of old Beijing over the following ten years. The walls would be pulled down and a series of ring roads would encircle the city. The plan to build a new administrative capital in Gongzhufen was dropped. Architects instead prepared plans to demolish the Forbidden City and to create a new set of modern residences and offices for the central leadership.

It was inevitable that Qinghua and especially its architectural faculty would become a key battleground in the Cultural Revolution. Like Beijing University, Qinghua was one of the main crucibles of the modernist movement. It was tainted by the past as it was founded with the indemnities China paid to the United States after the Boxer siege of the Legations. In 1968 professors were forced to pull down the triple-arched memorial commemorating the university's founding in 1905. And Qinghua's architectural faculty, where Liang and his students researched the history of Chinese architecture, was a centre for opposition to Mao's plans to destroy old Beijing.

Rather like in Lao She's play, *Tea House*, where in each successive act and each generation the same characters appear condemned to play the same roles, Qinghua alumni and staff continued to fight the same battles long after Mao's death. On one side were Lao She's son, Shu Yi; Liang Sicheng's son, Liang Congjie, a history professor and leading environmentalist; Liang's widow, Zhu Lin; and one of his disciples, the leading architectural professor, Wu Liangyong.

On the opposing side were the Red Guard generation. By the late 1990s the top positions in the Communist Party were filled with former Red Guards, including a group of forty Qinghua alumni, many of whom took part in the '100 days war'. Many were leaders of the moderate April Fourteenth Faction, including Jia Chunwang, who in 1966 was a member of the Cultural Revolution Preparation Committee at Qinghua. Jia Chunwang, who had been captured and tortured by the Jinggangshan Regiment, rose to become Minister of Public Security in charge of the police and prisons. Another former Qinghua militant was Zhang Fusen, who became Minister of Justice. For a while the chancellor of Beijing University was Ren Yansheng, one of the notoriously violent 'rods' during the '100 days war'.[7]

The man who in 2002 succeeded Jiang Zemin as the head of the Communist Party was another Qinghua engineering student. Hu Jintao graduated from Qinghua in 1964 with a degree in hydropower engineering, and when the Cultural Revolution broke out he was working on the campus as an assistant political instructor in the Communist Youth League. He almost certainly participated in some initial Red Guard activities and put up posters attacking faculty members for belonging to the wrong class or for advocating 'feudal ideas'. After 1968, when the army arrived to end the fighting, he was rounded up and imprisoned for several months before being expelled, like many other troublemakers, to the countryside. Many of the middle school students who had attacked and in some cases murdered their teachers were also in positions of power. Among those who had been in Beijing's middle schools during these years are Bo Xilai, son of veteran revolutionary and sometime kingmaker Bo Yibo, who became the Minister of Commerce after 2000; and Deng Rong, daughter of Deng Xiaoping, who was a student at Beijing Normal University Girls School when the headteacher was murdered.

After 1998, as the destruction of old Beijing gathered pace, Zhu Lin and the others continued a last-ditch campaign to preserve the old capital's architecture by writing letters and petitions. They lobbied in vain to persuade the authorities to honour Liang Sicheng's memory by proposing to put up a statue on the campus in his memory or to name a garden after him at Dongbianmen, where the last remaining stretch of the Ming era wall was restored. With a government dominated by engineers and former Maoists, all these proposals fell on deaf ears and the curtain fell on the last act as historic Beijing was bulldozed into rubble.[8]

13

The Strange Death of Lao She

The violent events that led in 1966 to the suicide or murder of Lao She, Beijing's most famous modern writer, began in the Temple of Confucius. It is now a calm and soothing sanctuary from where the snarled traffic and impatient crowds seem far away. One crosses marble paving stones, worn smooth by generations of earnest students, to rest in the shade of ancient cypress trees or loiter to examine the lists of names chiselled on stone tablets. The 198 stelae record the names and home towns of the 51,624 candidates who, over the centuries, passed the imperial examinations and entered the highest ranks of mandarins staffing the state bureaucracy.

This temple was first built by the great Mongol conqueror Khublai Khan in 1306, along with the Imperial Academy next door. It lies on the Guozijie near the Lama Temple at the north-east corner of Beijing, on a street graced by one of the city's last remaining *pailou*, which were among the city's best-loved ornaments. This green-and-yellow tiled *pailou* commemorates 'Perfecting Virtue Street', because this is what scholars were supposed to be doing by studying Confucius. The temple is entered through the Gate of the First Teacher – a reference to Confucius, the patron of all mandarins and the creator of the state ideology that served China for more than two thousand years. To pass just the lower-level provincial exams, an official had to spend long, weary years in study. The most successful then came to Beijing to sit for the highest examinations, held every three years under the direct patronage of the emperor himself. Each aspirant took the written examination locked in a cell for three days. To triumph in this 'examination hell' brought everlasting renown to the scholar himself, his family and his home town.

Next door to the Temple of Confucius is the Imperial Academy, the highest seat of learning in China; it is hard to find a more refined or private spot in the city. At the heart of the Academy is the Bi Yong, a pavilion set on an island linked by four delicate marble bridges. Here, the emperor would come each spring to lecture the students in person on the Confucian canon. The texts of the thirteen Confucian classics, which the candidates had to memorize, were chiselled in stone under the orders of the great Qing dynasty emperor Qianlong. At times the Imperial Academy housed as many as 13,000 students. So deeply admired was the Chinese system of government and its brilliant civilization that students came to study here from all over Asia, especially from Thailand, Vietnam, Korea and Japan. The whole Confucian tradition was jettisoned after 1911 when China embraced Western modernity but in South Korea and Japan temples still exist where robed Confucian priests carry out rituals honouring the great sage. Almost no one visits the Academy any more. The examination sheds were demolished in the 1920s, and throughout China almost all the temples once honouring Confucius have disappeared.

Beijing's most famous modern writer, Lao She, was just 6 years old when in 1905 the last Confucian examination was held, and was 66 when, in August 1966, he was shoved off a truck and frogmarched through a scrimmage of screaming schoolgirls in the grounds of the Imperial Academy. The 15- and 16-year-old middle school girls, who wore red armbands over their sleeves, began using their fists, sticks and belts with heavy brass buckles to hit the venerated writer. 'Down with the counter-revolutionary black gang!' the girls screamed. 'Down with the anti-party elements! Those who oppose Chairman Mao will have their dogs' heads crushed!'

Lao She, a slight, bespectacled figure with a taste for tweed suits acquired during his days in London as an associate of the Bloomsbury literary set, stumbled out of the tunnel. Then he was thrust in front of a bonfire and made to kneel. A thick column of smoke rose from a burning pile of embroidered silk gowns, mortarboard hats and belts worn by mandarins and the fans and parasols used by emperors in the Ming dynasty. These were taken from a nearby store of props that had been used by Peking Opera, after performances were forbidden at the start of the Cultural Revolution and replaced by modern revolutionary operas. In front of the Pavilion of Exalted Literature, Lao She joined a kneeling row of twenty-eight other prominent writers, historians, poets and scholars. Over their bowed necks, the Red Guards hung placards labelling them as 'active counter-revolutionaries' and 'feudal reactionaries'. An official photographer was at hand to record the artfully staged scene. Over the next three hours the teenage revolutionaries, who 'struggled'* the writers, worked themselves into a self-righteous frenzy. As they hit them with Ming era swords and halberds, they cursed the 'villains' and 'black-guards' who were resisting change. Then two days later an early morning riser out exercising in a park outside the old city walls found a dead body. It was floating in a lake (Taiping Hu) inside the park and was soon identified as Lao She. What exactly happened in those three days remains a mystery: did Lao She drown himself? Confucian scholars had a tradition of resorting to suicide as means of protesting against some wrong committed by an unjust emperor. Or was he murdered on the orders of Mao? Or perhaps Mao's wife, Jiang Qing? The ex-Shanghai actress hounded many of her former colleagues to death.

Beijing's streets are haunted by many unrequited ghosts from the past. Thousands of other intellectuals killed themselves during the Cultural Revolution, some by drowning, others by throwing themselves from high buildings. Throughout the centuries many princes and mandarins took their own lives using a silk scarf, or were tortured or executed as victims of some court intrigue. On Coal Hill, which overlooks the Forbidden City in the north, tourists are taken to the spot where the last Ming emperor, Chongzhen, despairingly hanged himself from a pine tree as peasant rebels burst triumphantly through the city gates. In Zhongnanhai, where the current leadership lives, there is a tower where the Fragrant Concubine, whom the Qing emperor Qianlong loved to distraction, killed herself with a silk scarf. Tourists guided through the Forbidden City are shown the well in which the Pearl Concubine was thrown when in 1900 Yehonola, hastily fleeing Beijing ahead of the allied armies, fell into a fury when the concubine pleaded to accompany the Emperor Guangxu.

---

* A term used in the Cultural Revolution. The victim is beaten up and forced to confess his political crimes and accept the party's teachings.

Yet with the levelling of old Beijing, the streets, houses and buildings invested by so many other spirits have been exorcised, powerless now to tug at the thoughts of new generations. Lao She is an exception. Forty years on, Beijing honours in many ways the memory of the most accessible of China's modern writers, once tipped to become China's first Nobel laureate in literature. The municipal government has turned Lao She into what James Joyce is to Dublin, Victor Hugo is to Paris and Charles Dickens is to London. Foreign heads of state are brought to the Lao She Tea House to be entertained by skits from Peking Opera performances as they drink tea and eat jujube dates like one of the characters from his most successful drama, *The Tea House*. Shoppers in Wangfujing, the equivalent of London's Oxford Street, pose on the bronze rickshaw pulled by a statue of the leading character from his most widely read novel, *Rickshaw*. His fans can now visit the Lao She Museum located nearby in his former courtyard residence. While he has no statue, there is a Lao She film gala and also the biennial Lao She Memorial Literary Prize. Yet the cause of his death remains an unresolved mystery and the reasons for his persecution are hard to unravel. Lao She was neither a martyr nor a hero, but the story of his life sheds light on why the old Beijing he loved so much has been destroyed.

Although the Red Guards cast him in the role of being a hangover from the imperial past, he was anything but that. He was born into Beijing's underclass, a world he vividly brings to life in *Rickshaw*. His father was a palace guard who died in the fighting as the foreign armies lifted the siege of the Legations in 1900. Afterwards, his mother raised the family by taking on the most menial jobs. As soon as he was old enough, Lao She was sent out to work, but he managed to get an education and graduate from Beijing Teachers College. Far from being a symbol of the old order, Lao She was a product of the May Fourth Movement. He wrote in vernacular Chinese, in his case the guttural Beijing dialect, and discarded the archaic Chinese used in the Confucian examinations. Many of the brightest students went abroad to seek knowledge that they could use to help change China. Lao She spent the years from 1924 to 1929 in London, teaching at the School of Oriental and African Studies (SOAS). He lived in Russell Square, close to Bloomsbury, where he started his first novel, loosely based on his life in London. When he returned to China, he joined a coterie of like-minded writers, including Xiao Qian, who had ties with the Bloomsbury Group and its leading lights: Virginia Woolf, Leonard Woolf, Lytton Strachey, Roger Fry and E. M. Forster. Xiao Qian returned with a collection of eighty letters that he had exchanged with Forster, although he burnt them all in the Cultural Revolution.

Beijing became one of the centres of a literary renaissance that swept China and was home to a clique of writers as important as the Bloomsbury crowd or the Paris Left Bank. Many writers began to translate the Western canon of literature for Chinese readers and others embraced the modern literary trends being pioneered in Europe. As the centre of politics moved to Shanghai, Nanjing and Guangzhou (Canton), where the new China was being forged, Beijing declined into a delightful backwater. Its abandoned palaces and temples produced a decaying and dreamlike atmosphere that attracted a Bohemian crowd and its thriving universities offered many intellectuals a comfortable home. Foreign aesthetes like Harold Acton and William Empson came to settle there. Eminent figures such as George Bernard Shaw, Bertrand Russell, Osbert Sitwell and the architectural historian Robert Byron all made their appearances for longer or shorter periods. Harold Acton, the acknowledged leader of the *Brideshead* generation, felt completely at home in Beijing. He taught literature at Beijing University from 1931 to 1937 and lived off Wangfujing in a courtyard house with a swimming pool. Acton loved everything Chinese, and this shines through in works such as *Peonies and Ponies*. He translated Peking Opera plays, but they never became the success on the London stage that he hoped. The American journalists Edgar and Helen Snow lived in a courtyard house outside Yenching University (now Beijing University) with a Gansu greyhound they called 'Gobi'. They relished living in a city that was both a treasury of art and 'as far from the rat race as you could get in physical and spiritual terms while still feeling you were at the heart of civilisation'. Among Snow's students of journalism was the Young Marshal, Zhang Xueliang, son of the Manchurian warlord Zhang Zuolin.[1]

It was a small world, where everyone knew everyone else. They gathered in literary salons; perhaps the most famous was hosted by Lin Huiyin, a fashionable and cosmopolitan writer, who later married

Liang Sicheng (see Chapter 12); the pair met while studying at the University of Pennsylvania. I found her house, or what remained of the old courtyard dwelling, just before its demolition in 2003. It stood near Bei Zhonghu Hutong, not far from the minister Cao Wulin's house, where the May Fourth students gathered, and a few streets away from Zhihua Temple, the Ming dynasty eunuchs' home. By the time I found it, the courtyard and surrounding buildings had been daubed with the character *chai*, signifying that they were about to be demolished. A generation of brilliant writers assembled there, including Lin's lover, the poet Xu Zhimou, who modelled himself on Shelley and Keats. Xu Zhimou had studied in America, London and Cambridge, where, despite being married and the father of a child, he fell in love with Lin Huiyin, then just 16 and the daughter of Lin Changmin, director of the Chinese League of Nations Association. Xu was convinced she was his soulmate, the second Katherine Mansfield he dreamed of finding. The two embarked on an affair that continued even after Lin Huiyin returned to China and became a writer herself. Next Xu fell for Lu Xiaoman, wife of the police chief of Manchuria, a famous beauty, painter and singer. They married in 1926, though the engagement party – a grand affair with more than a hundred guests – was marred when Liang Qichao, father of Liang Sicheng, declared that a marriage between two recently divorced people was immoral. In 1931 Xu Zhimou, by then China's most famous poet and only 34 years old, died in a plane crash. As he had always hoped, his short tempestuous life became a romantic work of art.

These glamorous and intellectual people belonged to a loose clique who called themselves the Crescent Moon Society, though they espoused no particular 'ism'. Some were aesthetes, some traditionalists, others sought to create a fusion of Chinese and Western styles, to integrate modernism into Chinese ways. Together they created the best modern literature and art that China produced in the twentieth century. The left-wing writers tended to gravitate to Shanghai and preferred to cultivate ties with Soviet mentors like Maxim Gorky. Some writers, such as Ba Jin, moved between the two groups. In his autobiography, *Traveller without a Map*, Xiao Qian reminisced about those exciting days. Like Lao She, his father was a Manchu bannerman and he grew up in Goatsherd Lane without toys or books. Between herding a flock of Swiss goats near the moat outside Andingmen Gate and attending a Presbyterian church called Truth Hall, he learned English and plunged himself into the new exciting world of modern literature. Later he had a room to himself opposite the red-brick building of Beijing University. He started as an apprentice at the Beixin Book Company in Azure Lane, run by the revered Lu Xun and his younger brother, Zhou Zuoren. It published all kinds of books, magazines and translations. One day I managed to find its offices, just to the north of the Forbidden City. I squeezed through a labyrinth of narrow passages to find a small courtyard house. The residents had no idea of its history.

In 1925, as a member of the Communist Youth League, Xiao Qian found himself in jail after Marshal Zhang Zuolin's men arrested him for taking part in a protest. He was detained in Baofang Lane (*bao* is the Chinese word for leopard), where in the Ming dynasty leopards had been kept in a kennel. That, too, was still there in the 1990s, marked by a corner watchtower. At the Crescent Moon Society gatherings, Xiao met Ba Jin and the equally famous Shen Congwen, as well as the founders of the Communist movement like Qiu Bai. 'I felt myself lucky to have begun my literary career at a time when the Peking and Shanghai schools had merged their difference in the common goal of resisting Japan,' Xiao Qian wrote.[2] Many years later I came to know him slightly and he still had that jesting, playful Manchu bannerman spirit. He had finished translating James Joyce's *Ulysses*, which unexpectedly became a bestseller. Supporters of a rival translator accused him of plagiarism, but in his still fluent English he made fun of the incident.

The left-wing writers went to Moscow for their study tours and returned to form the much more disciplined Creation Society. Both groups came under increasing pressure from the KMT as the Nationalists sought to tighten their grip on the country and re-establish the traditional censorship which the imperial Chinese state wielded over the arts and education.

When Lao She returned from England, he taught in Shandong province while writing books and essays. At that time, he was unafraid of voicing contempt for the Communists and other ideologues. In 1933 he wrote a biting satire about an imaginary country, called *Cat*

Country, which ridiculed the devotion to all the fashionable 'isms', especially the belief in 'Everybody Share-skyism'. Lao She soon left teaching and, after trying his hand as a freelance writer in Shanghai, wrote his first major novel – *Rickshaw*, also called *Camel Xiangzi* – which he set in Beijing. It is an affectionate but pessimistic portrait of the city, its customs and its changing moods and seasons.

'It was filthy, beautiful, decadent, bustling, chaotic, idle, lovable; it was the great Peking of early summer,' he wrote, and in another passage described it as a city that 'paid no attention to death, paid no attention to disaster, paid no attention to poverty. It simply put forth its powers when the time came and hypnotized a million people, and they, as if in a dream, chanted poems in praise of its beauty.' The book tells the story of a strong young boy, nicknamed Xiangzi. He starts off full of optimism, pulling a rented rickshaw and dreaming of owning his own, but is met by a succession of disasters, making it partly an allegory on the fate of China. His rickshaw is stolen by warlord soldiers as he takes a passenger to Qinghua University. He acquires some abandoned camels and the name Camel Xiangzi, but then falls sick. Next he falls prey to a detective and becomes an informer. Then his wife dies. When he sets out to seek the woman he really loves, a girl called Joy, he discovers she has become a prostitute. He goes out to find her and the novel ends when he discovers too late that she has hung herself from a tree: 'Why hope any more? Watching a skinny stray dog waiting by the sweet-potato vendor's carrying pole for some peel and rootlets, he knew he was just like this dog, struggling for some scraps to eat. As long as he managed to keep alive, why think of anything else?'[3]

By the time Lao She was enjoying the success of his books Beijing's days of intellectual freedom were drawing to an end. Japan was moving to take control over northern China and was poised to occupy Beijing. Students mounted demonstrations calling for organized resistance to the Japanese. More than a hundred were killed, shot by the police. Everyone now had to take sides. At Yenching University, the American journalist Edgar Snow helped students and professors on the blacklist flee Beijing disguised as coolies, beggars or merchants. Some of his former students joined guerrilla organizations outside the city, and he allowed some to operate secret radio transmitters from his house. Among those the Snows helped was the lover of Jiang Qing, Mao's future wife. Beijing's artists now faced the choice of either fleeing to Chongqing and joining the KMT's government there, or trekking into the wastelands of Yan'an, where the Communists had established their rival headquarters. Lao She chose to go to Chongqing in 1938, where he continued writing poems, plays, articles and stories.

Perhaps because of its gloomy message, *Rickshaw* attracted the attention of the League of Left-Wing Writers, which was attempting to unite China's leading writers under the Communist Party's control. In 1938 Zhou Enlai, Mao's right-hand man, was representing the Communists in Chongqing after they had formed a common front with the Nationalists to resist Japan. There, Zhou Enlai established the All-China National Association of Literati against Japanese Aggression, which became a new vehicle to bring all writers and artists under one umbrella. Lao She joined and was elected a member of its standing committee. From then on he became increasingly drawn into writing propaganda with a marked left-wing bent. His characters became victims of their environment and class rather than individuals. One story, *Crescent Moon*, tells the sad story of a mother and daughter who are led by poverty and misfortune into a life of prostitution which had become a symbol of all that was wrong with China. 'Lao She had changed from an author bent on literary creation and aloof from political struggles to an organizer of the literary world, a social activist, and a conscious soldier in the resistance against Japan and in the struggle for democracy,' notes the scholar Fan Jun approvingly in the introduction to Lao She's collected works.[4]

Even in Chongqing and later in Kunming, Lao She continued writing about Beijing, describing the fate of the inhabitants of one hutong in *Four Generations under One Roof*, published in English as *The Yellow Storm*. It described how the collaborators prospered and those who resisted the Japanese lost everything. It is a patriotic book but behind the propaganda is an underlying cynicism. The Japanese project was to change all Beijingers, to force them to abandon their culture and language and become loyal servants of the emperor. Substitute the Japanese for the Nationalists, or the Japanese for the Communists and the emperor for the Chairman, and the story could be the same. What actually happened under the Japanese during their eight-year occupation of Beijing is never mentioned or recalled in Chinese publications today. It as if France had chosen to bury the story of its occupation by the Nazis. One reason is that the liberation of Beijing at the end of the Second World War was the work, not of the Communists, but of the Nationalists, with some American help. Beijing's post-war history begins with its 'liberation' in 1949.

The Japanese treated the inhabitants poorly but notably wanted to preserve the city's architecture, and they prepared to build a new administrative centre outside the walls. A grid of roads was laid out in Gongzhufen to the west of the city and, had the war not come to a sudden end in 1945, this is where a new central government administrative complex would have been built. The buildings of the complex might have been similar to those built in Changchun, the capital of Manchuguo.

Just what happened when the Japanese surrendered and Beijing was liberated in August 1945, I could not easily discover. According to official history, it was the Communist guerrillas who defeated the Japanese, not the Americans and certainly not their Nationalist allies. The real events have been blanked out in the history books. A force of US marines arrived from Tianjin and the KMT established a new administration in the city. The UN and American officials created an officers' club out of the former Italian Legation. Beijing, or Peiping as it was then called, became once more a place buzzing with parties. Some foreigners thought it was 'a gilded lotus land', a place that seemed to run on a different time and attracted free spirits, a place where, as one American, Arch Steele, said: 'You could do what you pleased for very little money. No one who's lived there for any length of time can ever be as happy or content or interested in life anywhere else. It was contentment in itself, it had everything.'[5]

Lao She moved to America in 1946 as the civil war between the Communists and Nationalists broke out, and he might well have stayed there. *Rickshaw* was a great success in America when it was translated into English and a successful film, *Rickshaw Boy*, was made. His American publishers, however, insisted that he change much of the book and introduce an upbeat ending. At the end, the rickshaw-puller rescues Joy from the brothel and they both escape to start a new life together. Lao She was persuaded to return to China by an attractive actress and Peking Opera star, Wang Ying, whom he met in America. Zhou Enlai had sent her to America to work as an undercover agent and in 1943 she was even invited to the White House to put on a performance of anti-Japanese resistance songs. She would eventually return to China herself and bitterly regret her choice.

When Lao She arrived back in Beijing a few months after Mao Zedong declared the founding of the People's Republic on 1 October 1949, he and his family were given a handsome courtyard house in Fengfu Hutong near Wangfujing. For his loyalty, he was also rewarded with a series of grand titles: member of the Cultural and Educational Committee in the Government Administration Council, deputy to the National People's Congress, member of the standing committee of the Chinese People's Political Consultative Conference, vice-chairman of the All-China Federation of Literature and Art, vice-chairman of the Union of Chinese Writers, and Chairman of the Beijing Federation of Literature and Art, as well as 'People's Artist' and 'Great Master of Language'. By choosing to return to Beijing, he must have realized that he had officially become 'an engineer of the human soul', as the party defined writers. He was soon dutifully churning out articles like 'I Love the New Peking'. Then in 1951 he wrote 'The New Society is a Big School', praising the new established institution of the political struggle session. In a new play, *Dragon Beard's Ditch*, he praised the remarkable improvements to the daily life of ordinary Beijingers.

It was Lao She who polished Henry Pu Yi's autobiography, *From Emperor to Citizen*, and he rewrote *Rickshaw* for the third time so it became a properly Marxist piece of literature. All its characters became victims of society, personifications of economic categories and embodiments of particular class relations and class interests. In this new version, the hero Camel Xiangzi ends up as an opportunist, a police informer, who survives by hiring himself out to march in processions or demonstrations, and who dies sick and alone. 'Handsome, ambitious, dreamer of fine dreams, selfish, individualistic, sturdy, great Xiangzi. No one knows how many funerals he marched in, and no one knows when or where he was able to get himself buried, that degenerate, selfish, unlucky offspring of society's diseased womb, a ghost caught in Individualism's Blind Alley.'

Lao She soon found himself an informer, caught up in political demonstrations, just like his character, as the party targeted every section of the population, including the intelligentsia, in succeeding political campaigns. Writers were increasingly restrained by a tight ideological straitjacket, yet two of his former colleagues, the writers Hu Feng and Feng Xuefeng, together composed a 60,000-character-long essay defending the need for artistic freedom. Once an underground Communist, Hu Feng had served as the head of research for the All-China National Association of Literati against Japanese Aggression when Lao She was its chairman. With Zhou Enlai's encouragement, Hu Feng then joined the KMT's Propaganda Ministry to work as a special contributor to Chiang Kai-shek's 'Cultural Movement Committee'. After 1949 Hu Feng had tried to stay clear of the party by declining all official posts, but soon found himself the object of a monstrous political campaign. Accused of being a KMT agent and a counter-revolutionary, Hu was revealed to be the head of a 'secret anti-party clique' and imprisoned for decades. In the campaign to criticize Hu Feng, the party forced all of his colleagues and friends to join in the public attacks against him; some of them even produced private letters or statements with comments that Hu had made in private conversations. Lao She, who had been a good friend of Hu Feng during the 1930s, was one of those who joined in and betrayed him.

In this way Lao She managed to survive. After Stalin's death in 1953 the party launched a 'Let One Hundred Flowers Bloom' campaign, calling on people to speak out freely. Lao She then wrote one of his best works, *The Tea House*. The play begins in 1898 just after the '100 Days Reform' and the execution of Tan Sitong, and ends in 1948. It follows the stories of sixty characters, such as Eunuch Pang, who wishes to take a young girl for a wife, Tubby Huang, the underworld boss, and Pockmark Liu, the pimp. Wang Lifa, the tea house owner, puts up a sign on the wall warning customers: 'DO NOT DISCUSS AFFAIRS OF STATE'. In each succeeding act the sign gets larger and larger. The play wittily shows how the tea house moves with the times, changing in each act as the inhabitants adapt to the changing political environment. Yet for all the great political upheavals that take place outside, life for those in the tea house seems curiously to continue in the same way. The characters die but their sons appear in the next act behaving as they did, in the same professions. This unchanging world is full of police informers, crooks and thugs, where people can disappear for airing private doubts about the government's stability or on the basis of anonymous tips and false accusations.

'In retrospect this was a most unfortunate choice and one which required some courage at the time,' the actor Ying Ruocheng commented many years later. It is not hard to read the play as a criticism of the Communist regime. The Hundred Flowers Campaign was quickly followed by a new purge, the Anti-Rightist Campaign. Over 500,000 intellectuals, including Ying Ruocheng, were sent to the labour camps, accused of disloyalty on the basis of false accusations and fabricated allegations. A great many of them would not return to their homes and jobs for another twenty years. Lao She was lucky to survive this purge, but he would have been wiser to have stopped writing. Many of the writers from the Crescent Moon group did so, like Shen Congwen, the author of lyrical works on life in Hunan province. He realized it would never be possible to write freely under the Communists. He tried to commit suicide but survived, and then worked as a clerk in the Forbidden City. There his job was to look after the textiles found in the Ming emperor Wan Li's tomb. Later he wrote a history of Chinese costume. In the Cultural Revolution, he was tortured, beaten and forced to clean toilets near Tiananmen Square, but survived.

Another literary giant who found a way to survive by keeping quiet was Qian Zhongshu, a cosmopolitan figure who had been a pupil of Sir Reginald Johnson, Henry Pu Yi's Scottish tutor. He, too, was considered a candidate for the Nobel Prize for Literature on the strength of just one major work of fiction, *Fortress Besieged* (*Wei Cheng*), a wry and humorous look at married life among the Chinese intellectuals who fled the Japanese invasion to Chongqing. He did not write another novel and after 1949 became a recluse with his wife, Yang Jiang, also a well-known writer and translator. As the endless political campaigns raged outside, they lived and worked in a single room. In the daytime they worked at a table, and at night the table was turned into a bed. To keep up their spirits, they spoke to each other in English, French and other languages. Even after 1979 they carefully avoided anything that might attract attention and turned down offers of scholarships and teaching posts from universities in America and elsewhere.

Qian Zhongshu was employed by the Literature Research Institute and during the Cultural Revolution was attacked in posters for being an anti-Mao 'element', but not actually assaulted. Red Guards subjected his colleagues to brutal struggle sessions seizing men like He Qifang, a poet who was the Institute's director, and Pu Pingbo, a famous expert on the classic Qing novel *The Dream of the Red Chamber*. 'Our only boldness was a lack of enthusiasm for the endless movements and struggles in which we participated,' Qian noted laconically in a later essay.[6] Qian spent most of his time working on an obscure work of scholarship, *Guan Zhui Bian*, which ran to five volumes. It seems to have been deliberately written in the classical Chinese used by the Confucian scholar-officials in order to stop ignorant party cadres from being able to read or understand it. In the work, Qian ranges through both China's literary heritage and the Western literary canon in an attempt to show the common ground between Western and Chinese culture. It is studded with quotations from classical Chinese as well as Greek, Latin and medieval and modern European works. The footnotes alone for *Guan Zhui Bian* run to hundreds of pages, with citations in Latin, English, French and Spanish from more than 2,000 works. Even though his books were burnt and all libraries were closed, Qian managed to do this, thanks to a photographic memory and the prodigious scholarship of his wife, a translator of *Don Quixote*, *Gil Blas* and other classics.

This erudite couple may also have survived due to the protection of Hu Qiaomu, a classmate of Qian, who became Mao's chief tool in carrying out his purges of Chinese artists. Hu began organizing such purges in the early 1940s, when a number of prominent intellectuals were executed. He was also a talented writer and, as one of Mao's secretaries, is suspected of having ghost-written some of his works, including his poems. Hu certainly relied on Qian's genius to help with the editing and translation into English of Mao's works. As Mao grew older, he became incapable of organizing his thoughts and would ramble on in a confusing way. Some believe that many of the essays and poems attributed to his genius were not written by Mao at all.

Perhaps Qian Zhongshu did far more than edit Mao's works. What-ever the case, when Qian died at the age of 88 in 1998 he took his secrets with him to the grave.

It is a curious fact that writers like Hu Feng, who in the 1950s were among the first to be targeted for persecution, or others who had held their tongues right from the beginning, did survive the Cultural Revolution, yet those like Lao She, who did their utmost to col-laborate, became the Cultural Revolution's first victims. Lao She made repeated and fruitless attempts to join the Communist Party. His wife, the painter Hu Jieqing, later recalled that Zhou Enlai came to his home to explain why, in the current difficult international situation, when China was isolated by reactionary forces, it was more useful for him not to have joined the party because what he said would then carry more weight abroad.

Although Lao She knew that millions were dying of hunger during the famine of the Great Leap Forward (1958–62), he stayed quiet or dutifully endorsed Mao's mad schemes with works celebrating the achievements of pig farmers in the People's Communes. When he was asked to rewrite *Rickshaw* for the third time, he agreed. Officials considered that the book gave the proletariat a negative image and wanted the rickshaw-puller portrayed positively as a hero. In the post-1961 thaw, when moderates in the leadership took charge and Mao was in retreat, Lao She embarked on another work about Beijing. At a meeting of writers in 1962, he announced his intention to write a trilogy of novels, all set in old Beijing. The first part, *Under the Red Banner*, was largely completed but never published in his lifetime. The title does not refer to the Communist banner but to the colour of the Manchu banner to which his father belonged. It is a largely autobiographical work, describing his family after the Boxer Rebellion and when it was published after 1978 many hailed it as his best work. He intended to set the second part in the brothels of the Bada Hutongs, and to describe the tragic stories of girls kidnapped in Suzhou and Yangzhou and sold as prostitutes. The last part of the trilogy was intended to present the idle life of Manchu princes and their obses-sions, such as cricket fighting and other 'small games'. These latter two books were never written.

Meanwhile, Mao was plotting his return to power and targeting a 'black gang' in the world of arts and literature, whom he suspected of disloyalty. Lao She was not originally on this list of enemies who were seized and brought to the Imperial Academy. He was only brought along as an afterthought, and those who took part in the beatings later confessed that they had no idea who Lao She was or why he might belong to any 'black gang'. The Red Guards were led by students from a printers' school attached to the Imperial Academy and they had to be told who these 'criminals' were and what insults to yell at them. It was a colleague of Lao She, a woman writer called Cao Ming, who came forward and told the crowd that Lao She was a traitor who had gone to America and published books, and was now hiding dirty American dollars. After three hours of humiliation, his tormentors brought Lao She to the Beijing Bureau of Culture, which occupied a beautiful courtyard mansion. There the beatings and attacks continued throughout the evening. When a car arrived and tried to take him to safety in a nearby police station, it was attacked by a furious mob. The crowd climbed over the walls of the Bureau of Culture and continued beating him in shifts until midnight. Finally, the police intervened and telephoned his wife, asking her to come and collect him. She struggled to find someone willing to help until, of all people, she located one of Beijing's last rickshaw-drivers, who agreed to help.

Back in the sanctuary of his modest courtyard house, Lao She rested but knew he had to return the next day. On the wall of his home, he read a poster which said: 'Since You Have Eaten the Bread of the People: Why Did You Return Home?' Early next morning he left his home, taking special care to bid farewell to his 4-year-old grand-daughter. He carried with him a volume of Mao's poetry and the placard identifying him as an enemy of the people. He never returned to the Bureau of Culture, where Red Guards were waiting to deliver another beating. Instead, he walked through the city he loved to Taiping Lake, just north of the city walls. There he lingered around the lake for half a day until eventually he loaded his pockets with stones, waded out into the lake and drowned himself. No witnesses to the alleged suicide have ever come forward and Taiping Lake no longer exists. The pond was part of a chain stretching north of the Forbidden City. Now one has to cross the second ring road, an ugly belt of flyovers and traffic jams, only to find in its place some residential high-rises.

His body was not found until the next day. Before dying he had carefully hung his jacket on a tree with his identity card inside. There was no autopsy or police report and his body was taken straight to Babaoshan cemetery. On the day his body was found, Red Guards attacked and killed 86 people in Beijing and the next day killed 125. The corpses were cremated without delay or ceremony. Lao She's widow and his son, Shu Yi, went to the crematorium and tried to obtain his ashes. Two girls manning the counter rejected their demand, saying they had received instructions from above that this was not possible: Lao She was a counter-revolutionary who had killed himself to escape revolutionary justice. They ordered the family to pay 28 yuan for all the costs associated with the disposal of his body. Perhaps if Lao She had not died, he would have been imprisoned for many years. Soon after Wang Ying, the actress and agent who had persuaded Lao She to return to the United States, arrived back in China she fell victim to the Anti-Rightist Movement. She had only left America to escape Senator McCarthy's anti-Communist witch-hunts. In China, she spent eight years in solitary confinement before dying in 1974. She was buried in secrecy, identified only as prisoner 6742. Among those persecuted alongside Lao She was the Peking Opera star Xun Huisheng, who died in the next phase of the Cultural Revolution, and Wu Han, who died in prison in 1969 after considerable torment.

Following Mao's death in 1976, Lao She's reputation was rehabilitated, but when his family prepared to honour his death with a memorial ceremony, all they had to place in his urn was a pen and a pair of spectacles. Leading members of the Beijing Writers' Association who organized the terror campaign – Hao Ran, Hou Wenjun and Cao Ming – all writers who had gone to Yan'an in the 1930s, continued their careers. Cao Ming went on to hold high posts in the All-China Writers' Association, right up to her retirement. The details surrounding Lao She's death began to emerge only many years later after these writers retired. Even as the party rehabilitated his works, the 'filthy, beautiful, decadent, bustling, chaotic, idle, lovable city' which he loved was being bulldozed into rubble. His home and those of other loyal writers have been preserved but many others, including those of the leading lights of the Crescent Moon Society, have gone for ever. And Beijing has never regained the role it once held as a home for writers and the birthplace of many loved works of literature.

I went to Beijing's Municipal Archives to see what could be discovered in the file on Lao She. They are housed in a new and grandiose edifice topped by a green pagoda roof. On the ground floor is a reading room where the public are free to use computers for their search. When I visited nobody was there and a thin film of dust covered the rows and rows of blank computer screens. The director, Mr Liu, a lanky figure in a grey suit with a knowing smile, was proud to show me around. 'We have files on everything, even some from the Qing and the Ming, but the ones here are documents from the Republic era,' he said. The archives housed 1.5 million documents and he showed me row after row of brown folders stacked along the shelves that could be pulled out on silent little wheels.

In the brief *glasnost* of the late 1980s, the party leaders approved modern China's first law on archives, a sort of Freedom of Information Act. It gave citizens the right to access public records that are more than thirty years old, and for the first time it gave them the right to see their own personal files or *dang'an* (archive, dossier). Everyone in China, at least in urban China, had a file that followed him wherever he went. 'We are gradually putting it all on digital data banks so anyone can access it,' Mr Liu went on, giving his smile again. 'Of course, they contain the secrets of many high-ranking leaders, and even those that are still alive. What they did and what others did to them cannot be revealed for the sake of social stability . . . or there would be a lot of divorces,' he added with a smile, as if he realized this sounded too sinister.

A personal file listed a person's class background, any links to the Japanese or the KMT and confessions made at political-education classes and self-criticism sessions. It would include reports by secret police agents or informers and an assessment of an individual's political reliability. During the Cultural Revolution people had been prepared to commit murder to seize control of such files. In government offices across Beijing, rival factions fought pitched battles at key ministries for them. Mao's henchmen used the files to extract confessions and to settle scores with his enemies, so access to the archives was a vital tool. When Red Guards rampaged through the homes of senior leaders, they were often hunting for any incriminating records that the victims might have tried to hide.

Chinese rulers began collecting written records even before the invention of paper by scratching characters on tortoise shells, sheep and ox scapulae – the so-called 'oracle bones'. They also recorded information on bronze and stone, and in tombs archaeologists are still unearthing records written on bamboo and wooden slips that reveal a habit of meticulous record-keeping. As the capital of so many dynasties, Beijing had long been the centre of the state archives: the repository of the state's official memory. Cycling down Nanchizi one day, I suddenly noticed a new plaque set above a large gate. The street runs parallel to the eastern wall of the Forbidden City and the high red ochre walls indicated an imperial building. Inside was a complex, the Huang Sicheng, which had once housed the Ming dynasty state archives. Inside it seemed deserted except for a doorkeeper. A huge courtyard of large white marble flagstones was overgrown with grass, and once inside the noise of the outside world faded, leaving me alone with the twittering of swallows nesting under the eaves. The repository itself is a rather imposing edifice with two flanking buildings and a bell tower dating from the end of the Ming dynasty (sixteenth century). Made entirely of stone, the 18-foot-thick walls keep a constant temperature and humidity throughout the year. The roof was made from stone to prevent fires and had the appearance of carved wooden beams.

As with so many ancient buildings in China, the Huang Sicheng produced a strong feeling of having been stripped bare. Inside the interior hall, rows of empty chests stood, smelling of camphor wood. Each glowed faintly in the dim light that filtered from high windows and reflected off the gold and copper panels of outstretched imperial dragons. New dynasties in China often destroyed the archives of their predecessors and desecrated the tombs of past rulers. The Manchus burnt all but 3,000 documents when they conquered Beijing, about a century after the building opened. The Qing dynasty left behind no fewer than 14 million documents, an extraordinary treasurehouse of information. For 360 years, its officials kept a daily record of everything the emperor did or said. Many were employed in an enormous effort to compile huge encyclopedias, an attempt to fix for ever knowledge about almost everything in the past and present. Some of the Qing archives are still state secrets, including maps and treaties that might contradict the current government's territorial claims. The Communists vastly expanded the Qing archive system. Under Mao, the state kept a file on every urban resident, some 200 million people, an endeavour that employed a million archivists. The peasants were considered too insignificant to merit such attention, but every resident foreigner has a file. In some archive somewhere must be my own file, listing all the friends and contacts I have ever met with, and preserving the weekly reports on my activities collected from cooks, drivers, translators, cleaners and watchmen.

The three years of the Cultural Revolution from 1966 to 1969 were therefore a rare moment in Chinese history when the state lost control over the official memory. The Red Guards made use of the freedom to say and write what they wanted by printing damaging details about top leaders and even state secrets, like a list of Communist agents in Taiwan. The KMT government subsequently hunted down and perhaps executed those on the list. This freedom came to an end in Beijing when troops arrived to occupy the archives in 1967. Many files were burnt by officials in the early 1970s as the party prepared to evacuate ahead of an expected Soviet invasion. The rest were hidden in underground caves along with many museum collections to protect them in case of a Soviet nuclear attack. In rural China, many files were lost or deliberately destroyed and most county-level archive offices were not reopened until 1980. The Cultural Revolution was also unique because every individual was pressured into informing not only on their colleagues but on family members too – children had to inform on their parents, wives on their husbands – and all this went into their *dang'an*. I was certain Lao She's dossier would therefore reveal the nature and reasons for his death.

'Yes, yes, I remember seeing some reports written by eyewitnesses who discovered Lao She's corpse in Taiping Lake,' Mr Liu said. 'but where they are now, I don't know. Try Mr Wang downstairs.'

Mr Wang helpfully looked through the index and turned up a speech that Lao She had made at a meeting of artists and writers in

1952 and something he had written in 1954. There was nothing after that date.

'What about his political struggle session? There must be some records here about what happened in 1966 and who gave the orders for his arrest,' I asked. Despite the law on archives, files later than the 1950s were hard to obtain because of the many damaging charges members of a family had levelled against one another. Lao She may have killed himself because, during his struggle session, he was shaken to discover that his wife or children had informed against him.

'Perhaps his real *dang'an* is not here and is still being kept somewhere else, perhaps at his old work unit,' Mr Wang suggested helpfully.

The Communist Party keeps its own archives at Wenquan, a small town about an hour's drive north of Beijing. Armed soldiers stand in front of an obscure prison-like complex which is said to hold 660,000 files and 8 million documents. Mao's personal doctor, Li Zhisui, reports in his memoirs how his followers bugged his bedroom and his railway carriage to ensure that his every utterance was recorded. No foreigner has been allowed to peruse the Communist Party archives, but perhaps the files will one day reveal just what Chairman Mao had for breakfast, or which girls he slept with on which day, the sort of details provided by the Qing archives. The only alternative was to take Mr Wang's advice, so I tried the Museum of Modern Chinese Literature, which was being run by Lao She's son, Shu Yi. He seemed bigger and stouter than I remembered but a little sad, the way people sometimes are when they get what they want. From around 1985 he began assembling an archive in cramped offices inside the Wanshou Temple. He started out with material donated by the Shanghai writer Ba Jin and used his own money to collect the manuscripts of many leading modern writers, as well as letters, magazines and photographs. In the 1990s Ba Jin had written an essay calling on the party to open a museum about the Cultural Revolution, an event he compared to the Holocaust. The purpose of the museum would be to ensure that, like the Holocaust, such an event could never happen again. The party never endorsed Ba Jin's plan and when his essay appeared on a website in 2004 it was blocked. Yet after years of lobbying, it had given Shu Yi over US$ 20 million and had created a new temple of literature complete with stained-glass windows, frescos and a portico with Greek pillars. Now Shu Yi sat behind a large desk in an office bigger than his old flat. 'Not many museums in the world have had this kind of luck,' he noted proudly. 'Only five other countries in the world have built this kind of museum to writers.'

'We now have almost everything that people need in order to know about modern Chinese culture over the past century,' he continued. The Museum of Modern Chinese Literature had a staff of 140 and the complex included a library, an archive, a research centre and a museum. The handles on the entrance doors were made from a bronze cast of Ba Jin's palm prints. A life-size bronze statue of Ba Jin stood in the museum garden along with icons from the 1930s. There was Lao She, of course, and the left-wing essayist Lu Xun, the playwright Cao Yu, the novelist Mao Dun, Mao's secretary Guo Moruo, and the woman writer Bing Xin, famous for translating children's literature. All were noted for their steadfast loyalty to the Communist Party, even Bing Xin. In 1989 she had voiced support for the student democracy protests but before her death was persuaded to recant.

Upstairs is a permanent exhibition hall. Preserved under glass, like holy relics, I found the gas mask that Xiao Qian had owned when he reported on the London Blitz. Rows of glass cabinets protected the old bicycles, typewriters, desks and chairs of other famous writers. Lao She had his own little shrine. I peered at a folded shirt, a straw hat and what looked like an old gardening trowel preserved under glass at a controlled temperature. Around it, the museum curators had hung photos of actors performing his plays and black-and-white images of old Beijing chosen at random.

For the troops of schoolchildren brought here to learn the history of modern Chinese literature, this was an exhibition that offered no insight or lessons. The government could change the meaning at will. It gave space to Hu Feng, almost the only modern writer to have openly stood up for freedom of expression and kept his integrity, but this is not explained anywhere. He became mentally deranged after twenty years in prison and on release talked of receiving messages through the air sent by Deng Xiaoping. He tried to jump out of a third-floor window and was then kept in the psychiatric wing of Beijing Number 3 hospital which was filled with 'untold numbers of prominent senior party cadres'. Lu Ling, another writer who was targeted along with Hu Feng and released after years of solitary confinement, was for long in a catatonic post-traumatic stress state but then began writing long and crazed letters to the leadership. So he was sent back to Qingcheng prison and held there until he lost all sign of sanity. The Museum gives equal space to the careers of Hao Ran, Hou Wenjun and Cao Ming, the writers who had persecuted Lao She. After the Museum of Modern Chinese Literature opened, the city announced a plan to allocate US$ 876 million and build another 150 museums, which would be ready in time for the Olympic Games.

14

The Red Maid's Tale

Madame Sun was in her sixties but she could still play a young coquette when she wanted. She was wearing a cardigan decorated with bright red peonies that not only matched her hair, dyed a darkish henna red, but also her red lips and scarlet fingernails. She moved awkwardly, even stiffly, and when she stood up my eyes kept being drawn to her legs and their thickened and twisted ankles. Then she did a little haughty flounce to show a student how it's done. Gaily humming a snatch of an aria, she suddenly became a graceful flighty thing, tossing her head back and neatly turning on her heel, as supple as a willow branch. Then she was back to herself, a tough and mature woman with too much mascara, her misshapen legs tucked underneath the sofa. Madame Sun ran a famous school for Peking Opera in Beijing and as I asked about the twisted history of opera under the Communists, a wary look came into her eyes.

She had studied Peking Opera under Xun Huisheng, one of the four great female impersonators of the time. A male taking on female roles is known as *dan* and Xun was especially famous for taking on the roles of *huadan*, or young coquettish girls. The empress dowager started the great vogue for female impersonators. During her long rule opera troupes naturally sought to win her patronage by putting on as many plays as they could that had legendary and patriotic heroines in the leading role. In operas like *Hua Mulan Joins the Army*, *Mu Guiying Takes Command* and *Women Generals of the Yang Family*, a female takes the lead from the menfolk and bravely and competently defends the country from barbarian invaders. The empress dowager had naturally regarded herself playing this role ever since Emperor Xianfeng fled the Summer Palace as British and French troops advanced in 1860.

This was also the role that Jiang Qing, wife of Chairman Mao, preferred to see herself playing. She too started life as a coquette, an actress with small roles in the Shanghai film industry during its heyday in the 1930s. From there she went to join the Communists in Yan'an, where she met and seduced Mao. Many writers and artists flocked to Yan'an in north-east China, and Mao seized the opportunity to lay down a new set of rules on art and literature. When the moment came, Jiang Qing eagerly grasped the opportunity to play a political role as China's cultural commissar and threw herself into the task of modernizing Peking Opera.

'We all still hate her,' Madame Sun said with unusual bluntness. 'She was a bad person, a second-rate actress. She was not even beautiful. In fact, she couldn't act at all. I think Mao became very confused under her influence.'

Her name and deeds have been almost erased from China's historical record so it is probably safe to say that she is most often called to mind in acting circles. Yet after Mao died in 1976, she and her followers, the so-called Gang of Four, were poised to win power. Had she succeeded, Jiang Qing would have become only the third female ruler in China; the first being the Tang dynasty empress Wu Zetian. In a way, the fate of Peking Opera has been closely bound up with feminism and the proper role of women both on and off the stage. Women were forbidden from acting and Madame Sun had been a pioneer in taking over the roles once played by men. Now she has risen to become head of the Beijing Performing Arts School and devoted herself to saving the great tradition of Peking Opera, a role for which she has paid a bitter price.

Officially, Peking Opera is still patronized by the state and presented as a national treasure. It features heavily in every tourist promotion but in reality it is a dying art. The Chinese public no longer cares to buy tickets and the handful of remaining theatres are kept afloat only with subsidies and the revenues from foreign tourists who can barely understand its subtleties. Generations have grown up ignorant of both the art and the culture from which it sprang. The slow-moving plots of Peking Opera hold little attraction for Chinese ignorant of the intrigues of the Han dynasty. There are hundreds – some say 6,000 – opera scripts, which draw on what was once a shared knowledge of

Chinese history and religion. The operas were once the chief mechanism by which a common history and culture were transmitted to a largely illiterate population. Travel through the poorer parts of China and you may still come across a stage pitched under a tent by the side of the road. The scene takes one back to the days of Shakespeare and the Rose Theatre on Cheapside. A crowd of brown-faced peasants wearing green or blue cotton sit watching the show, chewing watermelon seeds, completely entranced. The actors and actresses, dressed in the most fantastically gaudy Ming dynasty costumes, are often visible standing at the back, waiting their turn, drinking a Coca-Cola or taking a drag on a cigarette.

Peking Opera is only one out of hundreds of regional styles performed in dozens of different dialects. Its correct name is *Jingju* and it started after the Qing dynasty emperor Qianlong invited four troupes from Anhui province to come to the capital. They proved a great success and early in the eighteenth century the court set up a special training school which mainly recruited eunuchs and actors from the south. Thanks to this imperial patronage, mandarins and the idle Manchu bannermen also took up opera, writing and performing plays. Of all the Qing rulers, Yehonola, the empress dowager, was probably the most devoted opera fan and she was always hungry to see more performances. In 1884 she revived the idea of having one of these troupes perform Peking Opera in the court itself. She had a stage erected in her private quarters in the Forbidden City, as well as two large stages built at the new Summer Palace. There she and special guests could be entertained in style and comfort.

Beijing came to be dominated by opera dynasties, who maintained a tradition for generations. By the turn of the twentieth century, the famous actor-families were managing not only private theatres but also schools. These would train apprentices as young as 6 or 7 and later hire them out as performers in touring troupes. As the art evolved, the world of Peking Opera divided into rival schools; some specialized in training children to play particular roles: old men, young girls, clowns, warriors, and so on. By this time opera was so popular that Beijing supported forty theatres. Most of them were clustered in the Chinese city to the south of Tiananmen Square in the Dashalar area, close to the most famous brothels and tea houses. Beijing's pleasure-seekers would often leave the theatres and then pop in to a nearby restaurant or brothel to continue the fun. One of the handful that still survives is the Hu'an Guang Theatre, built by rich merchants from Hubei and Hunan provinces as part of their *huiguan* (guild hall) for members to use on their business trips to the capital. On festival days the members would invite an opera troupe to perform a favourite play. In 1912 Sun Yat-sen used the theatre for a meeting at which he announced his plan to replace the Qing dynasty. In the 1960s the site was being used as a warehouse and a factory for printing notebooks.

The 'floating world' of this entertainment district was notoriously amoral and sexually ambivalent. One of the early great Peking Opera singers, Wei Changsheng, is even supposed to have had an affair with He Shen, the handsome guardsman whom the Emperor Qianlong elevated to prime minister. Writing in the 1930s, John Blofeld describes in his autobiographical book, *Peking: City of Lingering Splendour*, how one night he went backstage after seeing a famous *dan* perform the role of a young maiden. There he encountered the middle-aged man lying on a couch, smoking opium, with a 14-year old apprentice. Great actors, Blofeld noted, often had the morals of a rabbit. Why the ban on female performers ever started is not clear; the Manchus were hardly puritans, after all. The explanation may be prosaic. No one wanted to invest years on training a pretty girl who would leave as soon as the first wealthy suitor came along. The popularity of female impersonators coincided with a new phenom-enon in Chinese society, the courtesan. Starting in Shanghai, famous courtesans, like geishas in Japan, became celebrities in their own right, leaders of style and fashion. They became the first modern independent women in China, unafraid of showing themselves in public and free to pick and chose their wealthy lovers. Newspapers invited readers to vote for the most beautiful and gifted courtesans. Actors, like court-esans, had once been allocated a very low social rank, but in the new society that sprang up in Shanghai, they became similar to Hollywood stars. In the new Republic, women started going to the theatre in ever greater numbers and playwrights began writing works to appeal to their new audiences. A hit in the mid-1930s by Xia Yan was about Beijing's most famous courtesan, Cai Jinhua, the Golden Flower.

Quite why Chinese continued to be fascinated by female impersonators, especially by their technical artistry, while Shanghai's growing film industry created real and glamorous female stars, seems odd. Yet in the 1930s readers of a popular magazine voted on who were the top female impersonators. The four winners, Mei Lanfang, Xun Huisheng (Madame Sun's teacher), Shang Xiaoyun and Cheng Yanqiu, can be seen in a photograph standing together in Western business suits. Like many opera stars, Xun Huisheng had joined an opera school, the Yi Shun He Clapper Opera Company, at the age of 8. To succeed, a student had to train from early childhood, standing on tiptoe for long hours and wearing stilted shoes so he could convincingly imitate the gait of a young and coquettish girl. A *huadan* played young girls and needed a sweet and resonant voice, and also had to learn how to use his eyes and hands so that the audience could read the character's changing moods from his gestures. Xun's greatest success was playing the 'Red Maid', a play written as long ago as the Jin dynasty (1125–1234) and based on an even earlier novel, *The Romance of the West Chamber*.

The heroine is a servant girl who plays matchmaker to her mistress. The latter is being courted by a handsome young scholar and their mutual happiness is thwarted by the lady's mother. The opera opens with the old lady, the widow of a prime minister, escorting his coffin back to his home town accompanied by her 20-year-old daughter. They take refuge in a temple because bandits are terrorizing the district. A young scholar on the way to the annual civil service examination chances to arrive at the same temple and the two fall in love. The Red Maid acts as the go-between as the lovers meet in secret every night in the West Chamber. On one of her missions, she sings this aria:

> A letter has become the very evidence of the match;
> Commanded by the Lady, I am on my way to the West Chamber.
> In the early morning with a little sunshine and a cold spring breeze,
>   silence reigns supreme;
> Let me, the Red Maid, have a little cough outside to give a little hint.

When the girl's mother gets wind of the affair, she resolves to flog the maid to force a confession, but the heroine talks her way out of it. She is determined to be a matchmaker.

My mistress, you are so charming and elegant;
Mr Zhang, you are so talented and well-learned,
But neither wealth nor talents will get you love;
Satisfied as you are tonight, a wonderful pair of lovers,
She is on her way although the moonlight shines on the flowers.
The Old Lady has gone back on her words and forbidden the marriage;
A good match is cruelly ruined.
Look, my poor mistress frowns her beautiful eyebrows every day;
And the young man is sick and skinny.
Despite the harsh punishments that the Old Lady threatens;
I, the little Red Maid, will help make their dream come true.[1]

Various complications involving the bandit chief and the old lady ensue, but thanks to the heroine's intrigues, the old lady finally gives her consent to the marriage on the condition that the young gentleman comes top in the examinations. He does so, and all's well that ends well.

Another of the four great *dans* was Mei Lanfang; he became the first Chinese stage artiste to transcend the closed world of traditional Chinese culture. He toured the world and elevated Peking Opera to a worldwide cultural phenomenon. In Hollywood, he was the guest of Mary Pickford and Douglas Fairbanks, who cast him in a few small film roles. Western audiences responded to the sheer exoticism of the bright costumes, the odd music and the stylized images of oriental women played by men. From Moscow, he returned with a bust of Lenin after his performances won the admiration of both Sergei Eisenstein, the great Russian film director, and the German playwright Bertolt Brecht.

One of the curious ironies of Jiang Qing's desire to modernize Peking Opera was that Bertolt Brecht decided to create a new and modern style of drama by importing many of its techniques. When Brecht, who was living in Moscow in exile, saw Mei Lanfang play the fisherman's daughter in *The Fishermen's Revenge* and the title role in *The Goddess of the River Luo*, he completely misunderstood the art form. He thought the heavily stylized stagecraft, the patently unrealistic gestures that actors used to signal things like riding a horse or walking, was a deliberate effort to destroy any sense of illusion or escapism. He developed a new theory of drama based on what he called this *Verfremdungseffekt*, or 'alienation effect'. As a Marxist, he wanted the theatre to serve as a propaganda tool so he tried to find ways that would make the audience think about the political message of the plot. A theatre to which the audience came to escape the everyday world was bourgeois. Actors, he argued, should not identify with the characters they portray but should rather clearly be seen to be standing outside them. 'This way of acting is healthier and (in our opinion) worthier of a rational being,' he said. He wanted to help the audience enter into a state of critical detachment rather than a place of magical enchantment. He was so taken by Chinese themes that he wrote plays like *The Good Woman of Sichuan* and *The Measures Taken*, the latter about the sacrifices made by Chinese Communist revolutionaries, all set in China.

Brecht's ideas ran contrary to the Stanislavsky method, which requires an actor to lose himself in the identity of the character he is playing. Stanislavsky argued that an actor's main task is to be believed, rather than recognized or understood. To reach this 'believable truth', Stanislavsky employed techniques such as creating an 'emotional memory'. To show fear, an actor must remember something frightening.

The techniques of Peking Opera were explained to me one day by Ghaffar Pourazar, an Anglo-Iranian who had arrived at Madame Sun's school in 1993 and became the first foreigner to complete the arduous five-year course. The school, which lies off the third ring road in the southern side of the city, is a collection of drab prefabricated blocks that could just as well have been a hospital, a factory or a prison. As we walked around, he talked about what he had learned. Seven days a week Ghaffar got up at dawn to exercise and train in order to achieve the suppleness necessary just to start learning the roles. 'For the first two years, I was sick or in pain continuously,' he said. 'I immediately fell ill and didn't get out of bed for two weeks. It was partly the food and mostly the air, the dust and the germs that hit me.' In one room, we stopped to look at two boys who were hurling themselves on mats, rehearsing the kung fu fighting parts, under the eyes of a middle-aged man in a brown pullover. Performing Peking Opera involves a degree of endurance and athleticism demanded by few other arts, and pupils must master an extraordinary range of skills. Ghaffar was 31 when he started, really too old for an art where most begin training at the age of 8, but he managed it.

In another classroom, other kids with pinched, earnest expressions were being coached to sing in a distinctive half-screech, half-warbling falsetto style of a eunuch. Others were clashing brass cymbals together or laughing as they smeared make-up on one another's faces.

Ghaffar had developed the strong balanced posture of an acrobat and the explosive strength of a sprinter or pole-vaulter, which showed when he picked up a spear or halberd and deftly twirled it around his back, demonstrating a few moves. He now specialized in performing the title role of *The Monkey King*, about the mischievous spirit who guides a Buddhist monk on his pilgrimage to India in search of scriptures to bring back to China. The Monkey King has two companions to help him and a magical staff with which he battles demons and witches, mostly disguised as Daoist priests, as the Daoists and Buddhists were great rivals in China

'The thing about Peking Opera', he explained, 'is that it's all about precision. The Chinese cut everything into pieces again and again – compartmentalize, categorize every part of the arts. I like that. It is very structured, with a very big concentration on technique. You practise every little movement so hard you can do it in your sleep. When your conscious mind is not engaged in what you are doing, then you are free to find the character you are playing.' Peking Opera actors therefore never immerse themselves in their roles as Stanislavsky actors are supposed to, nor do they attempt to create emotional distance, as Brecht imagined. Instead, the actors created an art form that simply pulled together all the various elements of traditional Chinese folk arts to tell a story and to entertain.

The Chinese Communists were themselves very much preoccupied with adapting traditional art forms, like Peking Opera or folk dances, to propagate their message among the peasants. Intellectuals from Shanghai who travelled to Mao's headquarters in rural Yan'an worked at the Lu Xun Arts Academy and soon experimented with creating new hybrid forms of drama, song and music. The goal was not entertainment. Mao issued instructions that art should exist only to serve the Communist Party's goals and propagate its message. His instructions became national policy after 1949, although at first it seemed as if the Communists were committed to preserving Peking Opera. Mei Lanfang was hailed as a patriot because he had grown a beard rather than perform for the Japanese. He was allowed to keep his own troupe but this was an exception in the post-1949 arena of the arts. The thousands of private opera troupes across the country were all disbanded and the actors brought under party control. The institution of the *dans* was attacked and the party insisted that female roles should only be played by women. Premier Zhou Enlai formally told Mei Lanfang that it was not proper for men to play women or women to play men, and that he hoped this would not continue. The party wanted plays featuring proletarians in heroic roles, as in the opera *A Bucket of Manure*, which is about a woman who wants to carry manure to her private plot but is persuaded by her husband to take it to the commune field. The heroine sings an aria about how a commune's cows had produced more milk since Liberation. It did not go down well with audiences. The fun of an opera house was gone. There were no more spontaneous shouts of applause at a great aria, or the simple happiness of vendors walking down the aisles offering hot towels or peanuts. And what was the fun of seeing a woman playing a woman?

Madame Sun's star began to rise as that of her teacher, Xun Huisheng, began to fall. She became a prominent actress in a state opera troupe and found herself wooed by a handsome and wealthy Hong Kong businessman who shared her love for opera. The world seemed to be at her feet, but she was soon caught up in the storm about to engulf Peking Opera. After tens of millions starved to death in the Great Leap Forward, Wu Han, the deputy mayor of Peking and an expert on Ming history, rewrote an old Peking opera, *Hai Rui Dismissed from Office*. In the traditional version, *Hai Rui Ba Guan*, the upright Ming mandarin resolves a tricky court case and demonstrates his honesty. Wu Han refashioned the text into a thinly veiled attack on Mao and a defence of Marshal Peng Dehuai, who had dared criticize Mao's agricultural policies and was then banished.

When Mao wanted to stage a comeback, this opera began a political battle. In 1963 Jiang Qing circulated a memorandum attacking traditional 'ghost plays' and demanding that all plays be purged not only of spirits but of emperors, princes, ministers and generals, too. She even printed and distributed a book, *How Not to be Afraid of Ghosts*. The next year she organized a festival of Peking Opera entirely devoted to revolutionary and contemporary themes. As Mei Lanfang was dead by this time, other leading opera stars like Xun bore the brunt of the attack. They had been buoyed up by a revival in traditional arts after Mao's setbacks, but now Jiang Qing led a counter-attack whose ferocity took its victims by surprise.

She and her cronies launched the Cultural Revolution in February 1966 with a blistering attack on the new Hai Rui opera, which was damned as a 'reactionary poisonous weed'. Then she set about burying Peking Opera for good, taking control of the arts and banning performances of all old operas. She even set out to wipe away the memory of Peking Opera by destroying all recordings and burning any books which contained the scripts of traditional operas. Students at the state opera schools set about beating, and sometimes killing, their teachers. In August 1966 Xun Huisheng was among the twenty-eight figures from the arts beaten by Red Guards at the Imperial Academy, next to the Temple of Confucius (see Chapter 13). Other gangs of Red Guards ransacked Mei Lanfang's house, covered the walls with posters, attacked his widow and even smashed his famous bust of Lenin.

Some believed Jiang Qing also wanted to settle scores from her days as a starlet on the fringes of Shanghai's theatre and film world. Her American biographer, Roxane Witke, records that there was no one she despised more than Xia Yan, a leading cineaste and left-wing dramatist in the 1930s who was once her patron in Shanghai. Also, there was no figure in modern Chinese history she hated more than Cai Jinhua, the courtesan heroine of one of Xia's most successful works.[2] In an essay, 'On the Reactionary Thought of the Play *Sai Jinhua*', one of Jiang Qing's pet critics, Mu Xin, claimed that Xia Yan was 'fawning upon foreigners' and his heroine was a 'secondary foreign devil'. And the Boxers were belittled when they should have been praised as revolutionaries. The essay said that Xia Yan had revealed 'a national inferiority complex' and made Western civilization look far too good by revealing that ordinary Chinese people were prostitutes, opium smokers, jugglers and women with bound feet.

On 12 December 1966, soon after this article appeared, Xia Yan was taken under military escort to the Workers' Stadium where 10,000 Red Guards were waiting to 'struggle' him. On the stage, he joined Tian Han, a playwright whose work about the Tang dynasty empress Wu Zetian, the only woman to rule China before Yehonola, had also drawn Jiang Qing's wrath. Tian Han, Wu Han and many of Jiang Qing's enemies lost their lives between 1966 and 1968. Xia Yan survived eight years of imprisonment and died in 1996 at the age of 94. Meanwhile, Madame Sun's life swiftly took a turn for the worse. Her affair with the Hong Kong businessman had put her under a political cloud and as a punishment she was sent to Zhengzhou, capital of Henan province, to work in a provincial troupe. Three days after she arrived the Cultural Revolution started in earnest and posters went up attacking her. She fled back to Beijing, thinking it would be safer in the capital, only to discover that her teachers and colleagues had committed suicide or were under attack. She returned to Zhengzhou and started acting in the new revolutionary model operas that Jiang Qing had invented.

Her troubles started again in the winter of 1968 when another political campaign, the 'Cleanse the Ranks Movement', commenced. She was dragged off to the local party school where posters accused her of being a traitor, and locked in a room for weeks writing self-criticism. Her tormentors had dug up her files and discovered the report about her love affair with the Hong Kong capitalist, and had become convinced she was also a spy. She was interrogated in shifts, day and night. 'They said he was a foreigner and I was a spy. They said I had a secret radio hidden somewhere. They kept asking me to reveal the secret codes,' she said. 'Then they came to me and said that if I did not confess, then I would be taken before another mass meeting.'

Madame Sun had not slept for many days and, in despair, decided to take her life. She jumped out of a window on the third floor and fell 40 feet. The impact smashed her heels and broke her back. She woke up in hospital, unable to move. As a criminal whose suicide attempt was an admission of guilt, she might have been left to die but the doctors helped her survive. For years afterwards she dragged herself around on crutches and slowly recovered with the help of blind masseurs. 'I still can't walk properly now. Underneath these socks my legs are a mass of scars,' she said. 'But after a few years, I began practising Peking Opera again, and I just kept practising again and again.'

Xun Huisheng was killed by Red Guards in the Cultural Revolution and Madame Sun stayed in Zhengzhou. Instead of a wealthy businessman, she was forced to marry an ordinary factory worker, with whom she had two children. She got up and showed me her family photographs, with her husband in a French beret and two handsome, grown-up children.

Jiang Qing tried to modernize Peking Opera by adding Western ballet sequences to the precise stylized gestures and a Western-style pit orchestra that played rousing and hummable tunes instead of the clashing cymbals. In the eight model operas that Jiang Qing created, Chinese women were cast not as simpering courtesans, scheming empresses or mincing girls but as liberated muscular women who fought the Japanese as equals to their men. Her American biographer records how once she went to Tianqiao Theatre with Jiang Qing and saw that the audience 'broke into thunderous applause' as she entered an hour late. As the character Granny Li sings of her sufferings at the hands of the Japanese invaders in *Raise the Red Lantern*, Witke turned to see how 'tears welled in Jiang Qing's eyes and coursed down her cheeks'. In 1972 she even brought President Richard Nixon to see the play *Red Detachment of Women*, about the guerrillas in subtropical Hainan Island, which features young women in Bermuda shorts dancing and fighting acrobatically. Henry Kissinger found it 'stupefying' but Nixon liked it. 'I had not been particularly looking forward to this ballet but after a few minutes I was impressed by its dazzling technical and theatrical virtuosity,' he wrote. 'Jiang Qing had been undeniably successful in her attempt to create a consciously propagandistic theatre piece that would both entertain and inspire its audience.'

In a way, Nixon was right; the plays were an artistic triumph but for ten years they were the only form of entertainment that the Chinese saw. Although Peking Opera was elevated to an unparalleled importance, the whole country was heartily sick of the eight operas by the time Jiang Qing was overthrown in 1976. Then all performances abruptly ceased. Meanwhile, in Beijing itself, events unfolded as dramatically as in any Peking Opera. After Mao died in 1976 Jiang Qing was quickly arrested in a military *coup d'état* by Deng Xiaoping, backed by a group of elderly generals. In street protests against her rule, cartoons mocked Jiang Qing as another Empress Wu Zetian or as the empress dowager. Had she been quick to take up arms and fight for power, then perhaps she might have ruled China like a second Wu Zetian.

In early 1978 Deng Xiaoping visited his home province of Sichuan for the Spring Festival and was asked if he approved of the revival of traditional operas. He replied 'yes'. Immediately people all over China started putting on the old operas, especially those featuring ghosts of revengeful spouses. Madame Sun acted quickly. She immediately got permission to travel to Beijing and sought out old contacts. Through the daughter of a senior party official who loved traditional opera, she managed to get permission to rejoin an opera troupe on the strength of her performance as the Red Maid. How she managed to play the part of a carefree girl – so different from her own life and times – I could not imagine. Yet for the next thirteen years, she established a new career based on playing the same role. In 1989 she joined the Communist Party and shortly afterwards was appointed director of the school.

'When I came here wages were just 204 yuan a month. Now they are close to 2,500 yuan,' she said. On many occasions, the school nearly went bankrupt but she managed to persuade Beijing's party secretary, Chen Xitong, to give her 5 million yuan to renovate the buildings. 'This was just a big toilet when I arrived – filthy dirty, with broken windows – and now she drives around in a big car and wears fur coats,' Ghaffar Pourazar recalled, adding that he thought her a tough bitch who cared little for the children under her care. 'I have had to develop the right political skills to survive,' Madame Sun told me. She doggedly cultivated connections with the senior leadership. A senior official in the municipal government helped her sell a plot of land to put up a twenty-storey office building to rent out. She also tried to make money in other ways, often hiring out the students to perform in shows or in films and advertisements. It helped that a few of the top Chinese leaders continued to demand private performances of Peking Opera, and some performers found good money in training officials who were passionate amateurs.

After leaving the opera school, Ghaffar struggled to find work. Almost all of Beijing's forty theatres were by then derelict. One of the ruined theatres is the Zheng Yici, built in 1830 by merchants from the port of Ningbo in Zhejiang province, south of Shanghai. It was renovated by a Chinese businessman, Wang Yumin, who also hails from Zhejiang. 'One day I was walking past here and I noticed this odd-looking building which had the character *chai* ['destroy'] painted on it,' Wang said. 'The local government was about to bulldoze it in order to widen the road, but I became curious and in the rubbish at the back I found an old wooden tablet with the name "Zheng Yici Theatre" carved on it.'

At some stage, the theatre had become the property of the local Xuanwumen government education commission, which turned it into a staff dormitory. Residents hung their underwear from the balconies to dry, cooked their meals on the stage and slept in bunk beds packed into the former boxes. 'By then everyone had forgotten what it was. They thought it had been a brothel,' Wang explained. It did bear a passing resemblance to the famous brothel nearby, the Xi Xiangyuan, as both had balconies and rooms overlooking a central courtyard. Now the private boxes looked down on a square stage that jutted into a covered courtyard filled with square, black, lacquered tables. The stage was a magnificent sight with a canopy held up by red posts, richly gilded and carved. 'The great, great Mei Lanfang performed on this very stage,' Wang told me in the hushed, reverential tones previously reserved for Chairman Mao. I could just picture the famous female impersonator tottering across the stage, playing the seductive courtesan in *Drunken Beauty* while the audience shouted '*hao, hao!*', sipped tea and mopped their brows with hot towels. A plump figure in black leather jacket and glasses, Wang was still only in his mid-thirties and justly proud of what he had achieved. The former soldier had made a pile by running a special hotel for People's Liberation Army officers coming up to the capital in search of a good time, and thought he saw a good business opportunity. As Wang described how he had evicted the residents and found craftsmen to restore the theatre to its former glory, I began to warm to him. Only a romantic who had succumbed to an ill-advised passion for the stage would have done this.

By the time Wang invited me and other foreign journalists to write about the theatre, he had begun to grasp that if even Beijing's diehard opera fans could not afford to pay enough, then he would have to look elsewhere. And that was where Ghaffar came in. The only people who could afford to pay enough for a ticket and allow the theatre to turn a profit were foreigners – though they were largely incapable of appreciating the art. Ghaffar was hired to help. One of his jobs was to stand on stage and translate into English what was happening, but this was not enough to make the theatre pay for itself. 'We tried to put on every kind of show: acrobatics, slapstick comedy, Mongolian dancing, Northern operas and Southern Yue operas performed by an all-female cast,' Ghaffar told me. Yue Opera is *Jingju* (Peking Opera) in reverse because there are no men allowed on stage and it's the actresses who put on moustaches and strut around as generals or young scholars. 'Wang even started a restaurant in the courtyard so he could entertain people like government officials at lunch. And day after day, he was in meetings trying to think of ideas of how to make it profitable.'

They resorted to dressing up the audience in costumes and painting their faces. He got the actors to go among the audience hawking souvenirs such as opera masks, musical instruments and T-shirts. They tried attracting tourists on bicycle tours of the hutongs to stop by to take tea. They rented out the rooms as an art gallery and even attempted to make money by selling paintings directly to the audiences. 'Wang Yumin was always sitting around with friends making big plans, talking on the phone, wheeling and dealing,' Ghaffar said. 'There were also a lot of friends, actually most of them were really parasites and they treated him like a big boss – but he enjoyed it.'

'Almost all of these things turned out to be failures,' Ghaffar admitted. 'We made money, especially from conferences, but never quite enough.' They even hosted the duke and duchess of Gloucester and, almost, President Clinton on his state visit in 1998, but on returning from the Great Wall he was held up by traffic for so long that he missed the show. 'The foreigners liked the setting but Chinese always preferred to go to the Hilton. They liked all that steel and glass and thought that was modern,' he said. 'Sometimes we let old people in for free just to fill the seats but they turned their noses up at the sort of thing we put on. To save money, we did the minimum so the standard was very low. In the end we were just dishing up a poor imitation of the real thing.'

The building still belonged to the government, which demanded a hefty rent. By 1998 matters came to a showdown between Wang and the Xuanwumen Education Commission. Wang insisted that he couldn't and wouldn't pay their extortionate rent any more. The local Bureau of Culture also tried to extort money from him, and when he refused to pay he found rubbish piled outside the entrance. The dispute went to the courts and Wang lost the first round in the intermediate court, but appealed. When he lost again, the Xuanwumen authorities called in a detachment of the People's Armed Police. 'They came into the building with machine guns and confiscated everything,' Ghaffar recalled. 'It took me months before I could reclaim my stuff from the police.'

Wang Yumin disappeared and went off to try his luck in Shanghai. The theatre he had saved was sold. When I happened to pass by some years later it was empty and abandoned. In the meantime the Beijing government proudly announced it had spent money restoring the homes of Mei Lanfang, Xun Huisheng, Xia Yan and Tian Han as museums. The rest of the theatres in Dashalar were demolished. In their place the government invested billions on a new Grand National Theatre, a huge egg-shaped edifice designed by a French architect.

Somehow, Madame Sun succeeded where Wang Yumin had failed. She kept the school going even though her pupils struggled to make a living after they graduated. Most of the state opera troupes, faced with shrinking audiences and declining state subsidies, gradually went bust. Yet she succeeded by meeting a demand for parents who wanted their daughters to study Western ballet. No one trains to become a *dan* any more. The great tradition is dead. Jiang Qing ended her life after twenty years in prison by hanging herself with a white silk scarf. In the opera *Nixon in China* by the American composer John Adams, there is a scene in which Nixon is watching *Red Detachment of*

Women. Jiang Qing interrupts the ballet and angrily shouts orders at the dancers. Then she sings the aria 'I am the wife of Mao Zedong', revealing her frustrated hunger for power. Jiang Qing died as an actress who was unable to take on a man's role and become the emperor.

15

The Last Playboy of Beijing

The most magnificent collection of Ming dynasty furniture to be seen
in China is on display in the Shanghai Museum and it has a curious
story. The odd-looking building is made of concrete but shaped like
an ancient bronze vessel, a *ding*. It squats near the old racecourse
opposite the new seat of the Shanghai government, and was built in
the 1990s to display the city's collection of antiquities that survived
the Cultural Revolution. This occurred largely thanks to the efforts
of its curator, Ma Chengyuan, by then a small, dignified man in his
seventies. Ma was a crafty survivor and told me how in 1966, before
Red Guards stormed his museum with the intention of smashing up
the collection, he dressed up his own staff in Red Guard uniforms and
daubed Maoist slogans over all the cupboards and display cases.
When real Red Guards arrived, he turned them away saying they were
too late.

Later his staff split into two rival groups of Red Guards and he
nearly died when the radical faction seized him and other senior staff.
They were held in a former bank and several victims died after the
radicals beat their heads against the bank's marble floors during
interrogation sessions. When Shanghai was rebuilt in the early 1990s,
Ma helped persuade the authorities to build a new museum. He
cajoled wealthy members of the Shanghai diaspora to help fund the
new museum, and with their donations he was able to enlarge the
collection. Shanghai, once the richest city in Asia, had the largest
antiques market and this was where Shanghai's wealthy industrialists
built up great private collections. After 1949 they were forced to
donate these works of art to the Shanghai Museum; now the clock
was being turned back.

By the 1990s Ming furniture had suddenly become very fashionable; it was often made of hard, dense tropical woods that allowed sophisticated carpentry techniques. Its plain and straight minimalist lines, free of the ornamental clutter of the later Qing designs, appealed to contemporary designers. Ma Chengyuan knew that his Shanghai Museum lacked a collection of Ming furniture and he had his eye on the only collection left in China. He persuaded one of Shanghai's wealthy shipping dynasties, the Zhuangs, who had fled to Hong Kong before 1949 and subsequently rebuilt their fortune, to open their wallets and acquire it. The collection of seventy-nine pieces, which visitors can see on display in the Zhuang Gallery, was then owned by a remarkable man called Wang Shixiang. In almost every respect, Wang Shixiang was the opposite of Ma Chengyuan. While Ma had loyally served the Communist Party after 1949, diligently carrying out all its orders, Wang Shixiang had always remained true to himself and his own passions. Somehow, amid the whirlwind of Mao's rule, he had managed to save from each wave of destruction and confiscation enough to build up an extensive private collection of art. Wang Shixiang was not just an obsessive collector prepared to risk his life for his collection, but a scholar who found time in his long life to write many studies of Chinese arts, including the hallmark work *Classical Chinese Furniture: Ming and Early Qing*, now the bible of collectors around the world.

As I soon discovered, Wang was still publishing new books in his eighties and the latest opus was a delightful treatise on pigeon whistles.[1] Beijing once had many pigeon lovers and was home to a special breed of birds. The pigeon fanciers would buy finely carved whistles to attach to the tails of the birds so that when they were released, the birds flew around producing a haunting flute-like sound. 'It is the divine music played in heaven that exhilarates the mind and delights the spirit,' as Mr Wang puts it in the preface. A call to the publisher of this work produced his telephone number and Wang kindly agreed to visit me in my office. He now sat there like a pixie chortling in near flawless English, 'All work and no play makes Johnny a dull boy.' Then with a laugh he added, 'I like saying this very much.'

He had learned his English in the Beijing American School more than eighty years earlier and remembered his schooldays with affection. 'I was a sort of playboy at school and I suppose I still am,' he said. 'In high school we were supposed to write a composition a week. For four weeks in a row, all my compositions were concerned with pigeons. Our teacher was so exasperated he said, "If you write another composition on pigeons, I'll give you a P, for poor, no matter how well you write."' Wang Shixiang was a product of Beijing's old Manchu culture, where princes and bannermen frittered away their time on 'small games'. As a boy, he hunted rabbits outside Beijing with falcons and liked badger hunting and cricket fighting too.

'All these years and I suppose I am still wasting my time on useless things,' he said cheerfully. Over the past decade he had written about making musical instruments from gourds, carving bamboo, playing ancient Chinese music, painting lacquerware and building traditional wooden furniture. The art of carving pigeon whistles was just one of many handicrafts that he was almost single-handedly trying to preserve.

Wang grew up in the heyday of sinology, when the first proper studies of Chinese art history were made by men such as Dr Osvald Sirén, the Swedish scholar. Elsewhere, archaeologists excavated Shang dynasty (seventeenth to eleventh centuries BC) palaces and discovered bronzes and tortoise shells that revealed the origins of Chinese writing. It was not just Chinese culture that suddenly came to light but a host of unknown civilizations, languages and cultures. Some were discovered along the Silk Road in a multinational scramble led by Sven Hedin of Sweden, Sir Aurel Stein on behalf of the Indian government, Count Otani of Japan, Albert von Le Coq of Germany and Paul Pelliot of France. They explored forgotten cities, ancient tombs and caves filled with paintings and ancient manuscripts in places like Dunhuang in Gansu province, all of which opened astonishing new vistas. Archaeologists began to grasp that in early times China had been home to not one but many cultures. When the first emperor of all China, Qin Shi Huangdi, conquered his neighbours two thousand years ago, he methodically and deliberately erased traces of other cultures, and the past was later blanketed under a uniform Confucianism. Much still remains to be discovered. What these foreign explorers did was sometimes illegal, yet most of their activities were carried out with the approval of the Chinese authorities. The officials of the new Republic of China believed that the accumulated weight of this moribund civilization was holding the nation back. The Chinese were anxious to jettison their past as quickly as possible in the rush to embrace modern art and technology. As warlords marched their armies in and out of Beijing, few Chinese intellectuals or officials cared what became of the relics from a discredited culture. China emptied its attic room of ideas and objects from the past, but wealthy industrialists in America, Europe and Japan snapped up China's great heritage at rock-bottom prices. Even those with relatively little money, like Herbert Squiers, first secretary at the US Legation, could accumulate a great collection of Chinese ceramics which is now in the Philadelphia Museum of Art.

Some imperial treasures had already disappeared after the sacking of the Yuanming Yuan in 1860 and at the end of the Boxer Rebellion, when Beijing was ransacked by the eight invading armies. Many treasures ended up being sold in shops in Beijing's antique market at Liuli Chang, not far from the Bada Hutongs. Originally a street of tile-makers, its heyday was during the painful last years of the Qing, when the Manchu aristocracy sold off their collections to escape poverty. Even Henry Pu Yi, locked up inside the half-deserted Forbidden City with the world's greatest art collection, did the same. After four hundred years not even his own servants seemed to have any idea how much was there. In *Laughing Diplomat*, Italian diplomat Daniele Vare describes joining Kung Pa King, a curator for the new Museum of Chinese Art, on a trip to the Forbidden City in 1914. Under the overhanging roof of a doorway, they found bales of sackcloth with odd looking seals:

I bent down to examine the seals, and exclaimed in genuine astonishment: 'But these are the lilies of France!'

'You mean the arms of the French royal family?'

'Yes. Of the Bourbons . . . That means that the bales have never been opened.'

'Evidently not.'

'And are you going to open them now?'

'If you like.'

Twenty minutes later, the contents were spread out. They were pieces of Gobelin tapestry, representing birds, larger than life size: a present from Louis XV.

'I have no doubt you are right. And nobody took the trouble to see what the bales contained. Possibly the Emperor never even heard of their arrival. Perhaps one of the bales *was* opened and the contents were considered of no interest ... The gift was taken as an insignificant offering from some vassal state, and put aside and forgotten.'

And so it happened I had the unusual experience of being present in Peking at the opening of a parcel that had been done up in France in the eighteenth century.[2]

All sorts of treasures turned up in Liuli Chang, such as 'The Complete Map of the World', the very map that Matteo Ricci had produced to astonish the Ming court because it did not show China to be at the centre of the world. The map was then bought by the former History Museum of Beijing in 1923 and later lost when the entire collection was sent south in 1933. During the Japanese invasion, some private collections, like the ancient books collected by Weng Tonghe, former tutor to the Emperor Guangxu, were taken abroad for safety. In 2000 they were in New York at the Metropolitan Museum of Art, until Weng's grandson agreed to send them back to Shanghai. Most great American business dynasties, like the Rockefellers, Gettys and Eli Lilly, built up fabulous collections quite legitimately. The result is that America now boasts some of the largest and best collections of Chinese art in the world. Charles Lang Freer (1854–1919), a railroad-car manufacturer from Detroit, built a collection famous for its Zhou dynasty (1027–221 BC) bronzes, so big that it is now spread between four museums. Collectors like Freer never came to China at all but acquired everything from dealers in New York. Dr Arthur M. Sackler (1913–87), a Jewish doctor and medical publisher from New York City, created another great collection which is now housed in the Smithsonian Institution, Harvard University and Beijing University. Others, like William Rockhill Nelson, the founder of the *Kansas City Star*, and the Nelson-Atkins Museum in Missouri, sent agents to China. Backed by a fund of US$11 million, Langdon Warner and Lawrence Sickman flew around China in a private plane. They bought paintings directly from Henry Pu Yi, who, according to Sickman, seemed more interested in his new Japanese motorcycle than in art. Sickman was left alone to pick the works he wanted. Various impoverished but anonymous aristocrats would also show up late at night to offer masterpieces by the likes of the eleventh-century Song artist, Xu Daoning, for next to nothing.

Outside China, Chinese art became so admired that every great city with a museum felt it had to have its own extensive collection. London now has the Sir David Percival collection of ceramics, the T. T. Tsui Gallery of Chinese Art in the Victoria and Albert Museum and a vast store of nearly everything in the British Museum. Stockholm has the East Asian Art Museum with 100,000 pieces. Berlin has its own East Asian Art Museum. Paris has the Musée National des Arts Asiatiques-Guimet, with the best collection of porcelain, and another almost as large at the Musée Cernuschi. Japan has the largest collection of ancient inscriptions on tortoise shells. In the past, wealthy Chinese had always collected antiquities and they continued to do so in cities like Shanghai. The Republican government took great care to spirit the imperial collection out of Beijing to prevent it from falling into Japanese hands, but even so, by the end of the 1930s there were better and bigger collections outside China than inside. In view of what was to happen later during the Cultural Revolution (1966–76), this may be considered fortunate.

While Wang Shixiang devoted himself to his playboy interests, Beijing attracted artists interested in fusing Western and Chinese artistic traditions. Artists had always flocked to Beijing in search of patrons and they became known as *mo ke*, or 'ink guests'. The Chinese have always shown an aptitude for painting nature and animals. One Beijing museum devoted to painters is the former home of Qi Baishi, whose paintings of crickets, tadpoles, fish, crayfish, crabs and the like had a broad and lasting appeal. His artistry draws on the Chinese tradition of repeatedly practising the same movements to achieve perfection and spontaneity by the development of the artist's inner *qi*.

Beijing also has museums dedicated to the memory of painters such as Xu Beihong, who, in the 1920s, went abroad to study Western painting. Xu Beihong's ink wash of a running stallion, with simple brushstrokes that expressed life and a vivid fluid motion, became a popular print all over the world. Many painters who became famous at that time also embraced Zen Buddhism, a Chinese sect originally known as Chan. In the nationalistic spirit of the 1930s and 1940s, artists like Zhang Daqian discovered a renewed interest in China's artistic heritage. He went off to study and then to copy the Tang dynasty wall paintings that had been discovered preserved in grottoes in Dunhuang, a Silk Road oasis in Gansu province. Just as Liang Sicheng had been inspired by the richness of China's architectural heritage, Zhang Daqian felt moved to reinvigorate ancient painting traditions.

After Japan's defeat in 1945, Wang Shixiang's vast knowledge was put to use in helping the government trace and recover many ancient books and works of art that Japan had taken as war booty. He and his wife, an expert in ancient music and instruments, continued to add to their private collection as the civil war spread, inflation devastated savings and the wealthy began to sell off their collections to survive. Many escaped from Beijing or Shanghai, taking their most precious and valuable items with them which they sold in Hong Kong to finance their new life. Hong Kong became the new market for Chinese works of art.

After 1949 the new Communist state employed experts at the Cultural Relics Bureau, like Ma Chengyuan, whose job was to go around the homes of noted collectors and to insist they voluntarily donate their treasures to the state. Invariably, the terrified owners complied. These items were carefully inventoried and stored in warehouses. During these years, the Chinese government sold off as many of these confiscated artefacts as it could to raise foreign currency. Foreign art dealers were either invited to tour the warehouses in Beijing or made their purchases at the annual Canton (Guangzhou) trade fair. Americans, as enemy nationals, were excluded and most of the dealers came from Hong Kong, London or Paris.

Jacques Marcuse, an acerbic French correspondent, described in *The Peking Papers* how he would occasionally run into these dealers. The Chinese authorities insisted on being paid in dollars and Marcuse wryly noted they asked only one-tenth of the market price because they were so ignorant of art. The real experts were either dead or working in the countryside in re-education camps. Wang Shixiang was jailed in 1952, accused of stealing from the Palace Museum, and five years later fell victim to the Anti-Rightist Movement. He narrowly escaped being sent to the Great Northern Wilderness in Manchuria, where many of his colleagues were worked to death draining swamps.

From the 1950s onwards the Communists urged people to destroy all their possessions from the old society. People even dragged their old wooden furniture outside and burned it in a bonfire in their courtyards to show commitment to the new order. The American writer David Kidd recalls in *Peking Story* how his in-laws, the Yu family, took their Ming furniture to the market, where it was bought as firewood and priced according to its weight. Wang Shixiang remembers this, too: 'Furniture was worth nothing in those days. People had to get rid of their old furniture but I thought it a pity to see so much destroyed. Every time I could, I would bicycle to the countryside and go to well-known families to see their pieces. If I could afford it, I would buy them,' he said. Often he bought parts of furniture, which he learned to repair by studying recently discovered Ming manuals on furniture-making, just as his friend Liang Sicheng had used manuals on architecture.

Everyone in Beijing received orders to bring their old belongings to state-run collection points called *feipin zhan* or 'useless objects stations' – to earn a few yuan from their value as firewood or scrap metal. Anything made from metal was melted down. The campaign took on an even greater intensity during the Great Leap Forward campaign that started in 1958 and included a frenzied effort to make steel in backyard furnaces. In many parts of the countryside, peasants went around digging up tombs to find bronze and copper relics so they could sell them. Lei Yuqi, a worker at the copper smelting works in Taiyuan, Shanxi province, whom I once interviewed, decided to save some of the objects that had been brought in. By the end of the 1970s he had stored 5 tons of bronzes, which required eight trucks to move when he finally gave his collection to the local museum. He was rewarded with a television set. In another case, peasants discovered a hidden cache of 11 tons of coins in Xianyang, Hubei province, and all except three sets were melted down.

Later all this destruction was blamed on the 'chaos' of the Cultural Revolution, but in fact it started well before 1966. Far from being unplanned, it was a deliberate and systematically organized programme. Ma Chengyuan told me how in 1958 he was a member of a team that destroyed Tibet's cultural legacy. Soon after the conquest of Tibet, the Communist Party decided that if Tibet was to be modernized, its entire religious and cultural inheritance must go. Ma was ordered to join a mission of Chinese experts who toured the newly conquered Tibetan lands for six months, selecting representative pieces of the best Tibetan art and culture to hold in Chinese museums; the rest was destroyed.[3] Thanks to its remoteness and physical inaccessibility, the wealth of Tibet had accumulated untouched for longer than anywhere else in the world. The pious Tibetans, rich and poor, had always given generously to monks and lamas so their monasteries were far wealthier than their kings and princes. Until the People's Liberation Army invaded in 1951, it had piled up in monasteries untouched since the seventh century. The troops melted down statues and other treasures into gold or silver bullion. At a time when the entire nation was gripped by a devastating famine and the economy had come to standstill, this bullion, worth billions of dollars, may have made a crucial difference to the party's survival.

After Ma and the other experts finished their survey, the destruction of the monasteries began. Party officials burnt *thankas* (religious paintings) and books on the spot inside temple courtyards, blew up statues or more often loaded them onto trucks which transported them to China. The metal objects were brought to foundries as far away as Shenyang in Liaoning province, where the curators at the provincial museum found it a pity to destroy so much and saved about 2,000 pieces. Another 26 tons of statues ended up in a warehouse in the Forbidden City and were found after 1979. Six hundred tons of Tibetan artwork ended up in Beijing, where it was all melted down.[4] It was not just monasteries that were plundered, but also the homes of ordinary people. All their carpets, tapestries, small bronzes, silk garments, swords, knives, belts, bells, buckles, pipes, lamps, coral necklaces, gold and silver jewellery were confiscated too. Even when they were not immediately destroyed, fragile artefacts like books, carpets or paintings were left out in the rain for long periods or piled up in leaky buildings. The Johkang Temple, the most important structure in Lhasa apart from the Potala Palace, was turned into a warehouse for relics seized from other monasteries.[5]

This unprovoked assault led to a Tibetan uprising in areas like Qinghai, and when refugees fled to Lhasa to seek the protection of the Dalai Lama, the conflict came to a head. In 1959 the Dalai Lama fled to India with many followers. The destruction of Tibetan culture resumed in 1966. Hundreds of Red Guards arrived at the Johkang Temple to destroy whatever had been collected there. Some Red Guards were local children but many were ethnic Chinese who arrived from Shanghai or other cities in the interior. There was still so much left that it took them a week to complete the task; however, before they started officials from the Cultural Relics Bureau sifted through the stuff, selecting anything that might be wanted for state museum collections.[6] Some monks and laymen tried to hide the best pieces. At Ngor Monastery near Shigatse, the lamas gave about a hundred bronzes to the villagers, who buried them. Many were returned to the monastery after 1979 but others were kept and sold to dealers in the 1980s. Mostly, objects of metal survived. Antique dealers in the 1980s were brought to see two warehouses in Lhasa full of bronzes that had lost their arms and had holes where gold or precious stones had been stripped away. Even now experts are still astonished by the sheer quantity of what did survive. The Jokhang Temple still holds 10,000 *thankas*, more art than any scholar could examine in a lifetime. The vast rambling rooms of the Potala Palace, the home to thirteen reincarnations of the Dalai Lama, still holds 600,000 objects, most of which have never been seen or studied.

Meanwhile in Beijing, Wang Shixiang found this whirlwind of destruction an irresistible opportunity to augment his collection, which he kept in the yard of his courtyard house. He was not the only collector. The canniest buyers were top party revolutionaries who would go to the *Wenwu Shangdian* or 'cultural relics shops' that, like the Friendship Stores, were open only to foreigners. They would be taken to a back room and shown a special selection for sale at special prices.

It can be hard to grasp how for everyone else art became a matter of life and death in Mao's China. Like all previous dynasties, the Communist Party established a Central Academy of Arts, which copied the Soviet Union in rejecting the decadency of Picasso and all the other modernist artists. Art had to be heavily politicized propaganda that the masses could understand. Over the centuries, many famous literati had fallen foul of various Yuan or Ming dynasty emperors for allegedly using painting to send out covert messages, encourage resistance or voice protest. The first Ming emperor, Zhu Yuanzhang, had a number of artists executed because he thought they had expressed their dissatisfaction with his government in their works. Mao, however, was the first to attempt to wipe out the great tradition of Chinese painting itself along with anyone who objected to his grand plan.

A resident Canadian journalist, Charles Taylor, described in *Reporter in Red China* what happened to artist Li Zehao. In 1964 he exhibited an oil painting of cheerful, smiling young peasants surging through a wheat field and bringing in the harvest, titled *You Lead, I Follow*. Then a year later the highly praised work was revealed to contain hidden messages. Censors identified characters in the work that spelt out 'Long Live Chiang Kai-shek' and 'Kill the Communists'. The smiling peasants were actually found to be trampling images of Lenin and Mao into the dust. Every copy of the magazine *China Youth* which had carried the work was recalled from every school library and home, and the painter himself disappeared.[7]

The strangest tale to emerge from those years concerns a giant painting, *Shifting to Fight in North Shaanxi*, which features prominently in the Museum of Revolutionary History that sits across from the Great Hall of the People on Tiananmen Square. The two buildings belong to the ten great edifices thrown up in a great rush before 1959, the tenth anniversary of the 1949 victory. The museum is a rather empty, bleak sort of place, built around two courtyards; its architectural purpose is to counterbalance the vast weight of the Great Hall on the other side. This painting was the work of a leading painter at Mao's court, a devoted Communist called Shi Lu (1919–82). Shi Lu, a short, slender, intense man, had joined Mao in Yan'an, where he developed his own 'North-west school' of Revolutionary painting. With the party's backing, he acquired a following and artists everywhere tried to imitate the style and content of works like *Down with Feudalism* (1949). This painting in the Museum of Revolutionary

History shows Mao as a small figure on a horse with two aides standing on a cliff, gazing out at the yellow hills of the Loess Plateau at a critical point in his revolutionary career. Trouble began a year later when Shi Lu took the brave and reckless step of disowning his own school and the whole theory of 'socialist realism'. Instead, he began to go about saying that rather than sticking to Revolutionary styles, a painter must 'grasp tradition in one hand and grasp life in the other'. So from 1960 onwards he began to paint solely in the Chinese tradition, using brush and ink to evoke the half-imaginary landscapes that the Chinese call 'mountains and water'. To paint in this style requires a more sophisticated and delicate technique than the Soviet style.[8]

As soon as the Cultural Revolution was launched, Mao's followers began to exact a terrible retribution on Shi Lu, who became one of the targeted 'black artists'. Art students at the Central Academy of Fine Arts murdered some of their professors and forced others to commit suicide. As Shi Lu came under heavy attack, *Shifting to Fight in North Shaanxi* was removed from the museum. He was accused of depicting Mao in a hopeless position because, by showing him too close to a cliff, the painter seemed to want him to fall off. The style was condemned as 'wild, weird, disorderly and black'.

In these paranoid and violent times, Shi Lu wisely took refuge in a lunatic asylum but he was later found, dragged out by Red Guards, locked up in a room and forced to write confessions. He was suspected of faking his madness by accusers, who said he was far too logical to be genuinely mad. At a second trial, it was decided that he was not a 'past counter-revolutionary' but a 'current counter-revolutionary', a far more dangerous label. He was again locked in a makeshift jail, a so-called cowshed, next to the Shaanxi provincial Office for Literature and Art. Inside, Shi Lu performed exercises to develop his *qi* and scribbled poems ridiculing Jiang Qing. His interrogators then found a drawing of someone who looked like Chairman Mao next to a prediction that 'in the twentieth century this thing is certain to blow up'. This constituted a 'grievous crime' and Shi Lu was sentenced to death. Before the sentence was carried out, his wife successfully pleaded for his life by arguing that he was simply mad. Shi Lu was again sectioned as insane and eventually allowed to go home. The party believed that the insane were not sick but victims of their 'backward' or 'reactionary ideology'. Many people were sent to asylums for shouting anti-Mao slogans but sometimes the authorities decided that inmates were only pretending to be mad to escape being shot or imprisoned for counter-revolutionary thoughts and actions. By 1967 such people were being dragged out of mental asylums and brutally coerced into 'confessing' they had been sane all along. However, if they were reclassified as counter-revolutionaries they could be jailed or summarily executed. Whether Shi Lu truly faked his madness or was really a mad genius depends on who you talk to. His son, Shu Guo, claims that he had been diagnosed with schizophrenia even before the Cultural Revolution but agrees that he was lucky to escape with his life.

The following years were among Shi Lu's most productive, but by the mid-1970s he was in trouble again. He was dragged out and 'struggled' against by members of the then powerful School of Peasant Painters. This school of painting was another of Jiang Qing's creations like the model operas. The colourful, naive paintings produced by untutored peasants supposedly expressed the pent-up creativity of the lower classes. In reality, the whole phenomenon was the work of professional artists in Beijing. Shi Lu drank himself to death in the early 1980s, but since then his reputation has grown and grown. His paintings now fetch huge sums at international auctions, where he is hailed as China's Van Gogh.

When the Cultural Revolution started in Beijing and Red Guards went from house to house searching for objects to destroy, Wang Shixiang acted quickly. He telephoned the Cultural Relics Bureau and appealed for help. Soon a truck arrived and took the whole collection for safe storage in the Temple of Confucius, next door to where Lao She and other intellectuals were tormented. Wang was then brought to Beijing University and held there as he wrote one self-confession after another. Next, Wang and his wife were sent to a cadre thought-reform camp in the countryside where for three years they tended water buffalo and planted rice. 'I was happy wherever I found myself,' was all that he would say about those years. When pressed, Wang never wanted to reveal to me just how he, unlike many of his friends, survived those years of madness, and held on to his collection.

The authorities sent troops to protect designated key cultural sites, such as the Forbidden City, from the Red Guards. Paper strips were stuck on some objects, like the bronze lions at the Summer Palace, warning the Red Guards not to harm them – instructions which they obeyed. In Tibet, the Potala Palace and a dozen other sites came under similar protection. Not everything that the Red Guards seized was instantly destroyed. Anything that looked valuable was taken away, often after an official receipt was issued, and transported to vast warehouses on the outskirts, where it was sorted and slowly sold off. The leaders of the Cultural Revolution continued to amass fine private collections. Marshal Lin Biao, Jiang Qing and Chen Boda, who was the top theorist behind the Cultural Revolution, each assembled thousands of pieces, often the kind of items that Confucian literati have always liked to collect and show off to friends over a cup of rare green tea. One of Mao's secretaries, Jian Jiaying, collected ink tablets, used for mixing the ink and water and an essential accoutrement of the study. Kang Sheng, the vile mastermind of Mao's brutal purges, liked seals – the carved chops made of precious stone or metal, which are often miniature works of art.[9]

During the 1960s and 1970s China continued to export these confiscated wares. At the 'Friendship Stores' in major cities, foreigners with dollars, such as George Bush, the unofficial ambassador to Beijing in 1974, could pick up things like a Cartier bracelet or Fabergé candlesticks for a few dollars. Premier Zhou Enlai himself became concerned and issued instructions limiting sales because he feared that China was flooding the market with too much art and therefore prices were dropping. After 1979 the Communist Party established a 'Bureau of Returning Looted Goods'. People could try to reclaim their possessions if they could provide a receipt issued by the Red Guards. Nien Cheng, in her bestselling memoir, *Life and Death in Shanghai*, recounts how she recovered her porcelain collection. She arrived at a vast underground storeroom filled with objects covered by thick dust. When she found her own collection, it still included a Ming celadon plate. A receipt stuck to it, written by a Red Guard, noted that all collectors are 'bloodsuckers'. Even though she got the collection back, party officials immediately afterwards insisted that she voluntarily consent to hand over her finest pieces to the Shanghai Museum.[10]

Wang Shixiang and his wife got their furniture back as well. When an American friend visited them in 1981, he found the couple living in a courtyard house where the Empress Dowager Cixi had been born. 'It was freezing and there was no hot water. He sat with a bowl of tea by him, and he had put his crickets near the stove, and occasionally he would feed them with honey.'

At the start of Deng Xiaoping's 1979 economic reforms China needed hard currency to begin reinvigorating the economy. The Ministry of Foreign Trade was instructed to sell off valuable cultural relics as quickly as possible to pay for imports of fertilizer, cement and steel. So much had been confiscated, and so little reclaimed, that China was still left with vast quantities of valuables. 'It was staggering to see,' recalled the American dealer Robert Ellsworth, who came to Beijing in 1980 and was taken to a place an hour's drive from the centre. 'The warehouses were specially built and looked a bit like Connecticut tobacco barns. You would wait in this hall heated by one stove, and then they would bring out the paintings. I saw things you have never seen in the West. The Chinese didn't really know what they had and they sold things in lots. You had to buy the whole batch.'

One American lawyer recalled that when she accompanied an American magnate on a business trip to Beijing, she saw him sign a cheque for US$5 million for antiques to decorate the garden of his private island in Hawaii. In Hong Kong, rows of new antique shops opened on Hollywood Road. The stuff arrived from the mainland in railcars filled with anything from life-size pottery horses dating back to the Han dynasty to snuff bottles. Over a million snuff bottles were exported during this period. The Cultural Relics Bureau even complained to the State Council in 1982 that when the Ministry of Foreign Trade sold antiques by weight, it depressed prices. When word spread about the easy profits to be made from antiques, organizations without access to the warehouses, like the Beijing Arts and Crafts Company, sent agents into the countryside. When they couldn't find anything, they asked village heads to dig stuff out of tombs. In places like Houma in Shanxi province, home to many dynasties, experts reckon that 40,000 tombs were robbed in China between 1978 and 1998.

In the early 1980s the antiques market inside the country revived slowly. Buyers and sellers met furtively, shifting the market from place to place, keeping one step ahead of the police. There were few buyers because it was strictly forbidden to take antiques out of the country. Anything made before 1840 was designated an ancient relic and the authorities were particularly sharp on preventing religious relics, like bronze Tibetan Buddhas, from leaving the motherland. Later a few antique shops opened on the banks of Beihai Lake, north of the Forbidden City, and then in Liuli Chang, mainly for the tourist trade. Wang did his best to stop the best pieces from leaving the country, sometimes charging into shops in Liuli Chang terrorizing the shop-keepers in the hope of shaming them. However, by the end of the 1980s, when the Cultural Relics Bureau managed to wrest back control over the trade in antiques, it was too late. The warehouses were empty and an industry that systematically plundered tombs and smuggled out relics was thriving. Even if the honesty of the badly paid officials employed by the Cultural Relics Bureau could be trusted, most of the staff were poorly educated demobilized soldiers and non-commissioned officers. What was easier than thieving from the vast pile of uninventoried relics that every local museum possessed? And what customs official could tell Ming furniture from a heap of old lumber?

Wang's treatise on Ming furniture made him a respected figure and earned him the epithet 'father of Ming furniture', but in the 1980s nobody wanted any of it, least of all the Chinese; nobody but the small community of foreigners ever visited the warehouses stacked high with old wooden furniture near the Jianguomenwai diplomatic district. Many of the pieces were in bad condition and needed repair but there seemed to be an endless supply. Bored saleswomen sat knitting and were deliberately vague when asked where the stuff came from, though the best pieces originated in the mansions of once-wealthy merchants in Shanxi province, especially those around the walled city of Pingyao, which had been China's financial centre in the Qing dynasty. Buyer agents now scoured the country, looking for remote towns where peasants were only too happy to jettison their furniture or fish it out of a rubbish dump. Hand-carved doors, windows, beds and even wooden tools, began to be exported in bulk, ending up in street markets as far away as New York. By the time

China's economy really started booming in the late 1990s, the world's biggest garbage sale was over. China had been cleared out of five thousand years of art, leaving buildings, empty of the accumulated artworks that give any temple, palace or house its irreplaceable patina.

Liuli Chang was rebuilt from scratch. Tourist buses now empty out in front of rows of newly built Ming houses to scour antique shops that sell nothing but imitations. The main market has shifted to Panjiayuan in another corner of the city. Early one morning Han Zhihua, a dealer in Chinese relics, took me around the market. 'Look at this!' he said abruptly, stopping in front of a display of clay figures wrapped in straw and pointing at one. I looked at the plump dancing girl. It was about 9 inches high and her eyes disappeared into smiling cheeks that had Tang dynasty written all over them. 'It's a fake,' he expostulated with a sweep of his hand. 'They are all fake.' No matter whether we passed lines of stallholders selling old gramophones and Singer sewing machines or ancient peasants with the wispy white beard of a sage displaying some crudely painted neolithic pots on a cloth laid out on the pavement, Mr Han said the same thing: 'Fake! Fake! Fake!'

I was disappointed and sometimes dared to voice a protest. Surely these pots had been dug up in their very own dusty fields in Gansu province, and who could possibly doubt the honesty shining out of the eyes of this horny-handed tiller of the soil? Mr Han only sniffed at my innocence. These days you had to get here at 4 a.m. and meet the dealers secretly in their hotel rooms if you wanted a genuine find. Even then, he hinted darkly, they had many tricks. Some counterfeiters had become so ingenious they made forgeries using clay scraped off ancient kilns so they could defeat laboratory tests using sophisticated radiocarbon-dating technology. I had been introduced to Mr Han by a colleague whose wife, a Taiwanese, was an avid collector of Chinese porcelain and who belonged to a group of like-minded Taiwanese ladies. They laughingly dubbed themselves the 'Taiwan Triad' and after the tour, as we sat together in a local restaurant having lunch, they hung on Mr Han's words like adoring groupies. Only someone with his eagle eye could help them spot the real thing and strike a bargain. By the time the first dim sum arrived, Mr Han was holding forth about his early days in the antiques business, when it was still highly illegal. 'In those days, you could buy real Ming furniture for a bowl of soup. A winter's supply of winter cabbage ration tickets would do,' he said. 'Now, you couldn't buy a *zitan* [red sandalwood] wood chair for less than US$100,000; some people even pay a million dollars.' The Taiwan Triad ladies tittered, thrilled by the mere thought of such missed bargains.

'Now, ladies, let's look at what you've got and see whether it's worth anything,' he said graciously, and the Taiwan Gang squealed delightedly and began opening packages and thrusting their purchases in front of him.

As mainland Chinese began to travel abroad, they noticed that the finest collections of porcelain, painting, sculpture, embroidery and carving were now to be found in foreign museums. The government responded by creating a China Cultural Relics Recovery Programme, funded by an obscure group called the China Foundation for the Development of Folklore Culture. Its declared mission is to get back items that were stolen, excavated or looted and trafficked abroad between 1840 and 1949. It claims that there are 1.6 million 'looted' Chinese cultural relics found in 200 museums in 47 countries. The *People's Daily* quoted Xie Chensheng, an adviser to the Cultural Relics Bureau, asserting that 'most were either stolen by invading nations, stolen by foreigners or purchased by foreigners at extremely low prices from Chinese warlords and smuggled abroad'.[11]

In Hong Kong, the august British auction houses Sotheby's and Christie's found themselves targeted at their summer auctions in 2000. A group of eight protesters with banners appeared outside the hotel and scuffled with guards. 'If you were Chinese, wouldn't you want to stop the sale, as these pieces are our cultural heritage and must be returned to our motherland?' one of the protestors yelled. The next day another man forced his way into the bidding, indignantly shouting: 'Stop selling looted goods. Return them to the motherland!' The auction houses were actually offering objects made by the Jesuit priests for the Yuanming Yuan, including several waterspouts from one of Father Benoît's magnificent fountains. Although such items barely qualify as either Chinese or antiques, Poly Investments Holdings Ltd, a commercial arm of the PLA, bought the waterspouts and returned them to China in triumph.

As China grew richer, many individuals also wanted to invest in art and antiques and some even started their own private collections, bidding up prices to record levels. The children of several top officials set up their own auction houses and used their connections to bring the private collections of retired generals and cadres to the market. Quite a few rare pieces belonged to families who had acquired them in the Cultural Revolution. Good pieces are so rare that they fetch high prices. Ma Chengyuan persuaded Wang Shixiang to sell his Ming furniture collection to the Shanghai Museum, but for a fraction of its real worth, some hundreds of millions of dollars by then. Yet it was enough money for Wang to move out of his hutong house and to buy a modern apartment. The seventy-nine pieces are now in the Zhuang Gallery. I could find no mention of Wang at all.

One day, however, I heard that Wang Shixiang had put up the last of his great collection for auction. The sale took place in one of Beijing's new concrete-and-glass hotels and generated a wave of excitement. After his wife died he thought he might as well sell her collection of ancient instruments. Lot 1223, for instance, was a lacquered *qin*, a six-stringed instrument that dated back to the Tang dynasty, making it more than 1,200 years old. It was so rare as to be virtually priceless. Some plump Tang lady would have once plucked at it, smiling and seated at an elegant low table. He had bought it for a song in 1945 from his wife's old teacher and couldn't bear to watch the auction. The bidding reached $1 million before it was sold. Not long after the auction I visited Wang again in his new apartment. By then he was at least 90, but still sprightly and writing books. He let slip that Ma Chengyuan had killed himself. 'Jumped off a building, I heard,' he said with a flicker of satisfaction.

Wang was still his old self, gamely playing the playboy, but now with a tinge of regret as he looked back on his life. 'In a way, I am partly to blame,' he confessed. 'So much was smuggled out of the country and into foreign museums and private collections, but if I hadn't written about all those things, the craze would never have started. And there wouldn't be all these fakes and copies everywhere.' Before we parted he added vaguely, 'I suppose it is inevitable that it all had to disappear; it is true everywhere. The world changes but it is a pity all the same.'

16

The Protectress of Flowers

Like Sherlock Holmes hunting Moriarty, the supremely rational Professor He Zuoxiu dedicated himself to destroying Zhang Baosen, an elusive enemy with fabulous psychokinetic powers. The Master, as his followers called Zhang, had powerful protectors in the highest ranks of the People's Liberation Army, who sheltered him in top-secret laboratories hidden around Beijing. It required a lengthy courtship and careful preparation to see him, but finally I managed it. We would meet at the prestigious Diaoyutai Guest House, set in a park established by a Jin dynasty emperor who came here to fish, hence its name, the Fishing Pavilion.

As I waited in a private room, two of his followers gave me a breathless run-down on his great stature and powers. 'The Master has a direct line to President Jiang Zemin and to Premier Zhu Rongji,' boasted one of the women, a large-boned, middle-aged daughter of a PLA general resident in Zhongnanhai. Secretive and conspiratorial, she alone among my acquaintances possessed sufficient *guanxi* (connections) to set up the meeting. I had given her a code name – 'Mrs Y.' – and found her a little alarming. She talked in a brusque, barking fashion that brooked nothing but agreement from the listener.

'Once President Ronald Reagan said there is always a visa and welcome for him in the United States,' Mrs Y. asserted. Her companion, smaller and more accommodating, invariably chimed in with an explanatory attenuation. 'The Master is a state treasure, they can never let him out of the country. No one else has special powers like his,' agreed the companion, another frumpish creature, who fixed me with eyes that dared disbelief. 'His breath can raise the temperature by 3,000 degrees centigrade, he can cure anyone.'

'Master Zhang has been the guest of Deng Xiaoping, Hu Yaobang and Zhao Ziyang,' she said, listing further party bigwigs. With us sat another follower of the Master, a plump Chinese-American business-man involved in a chain of sandwich bars; he kept nodding and smiling broadly in an ingratiating fashion. 'I have seen with my own eyes the extraordinary power he can produce, on many occasions. He can move a car from one place to another, just by magic,' he whispered to me confidentially. 'That's why I want to persuade him to use his connections to help me.' 'I am sure the Master will help,' Mrs Y asserted confidently. 'The Master has the rank of a minister, wears an army uniform and works in a secret government research facility. He has one Lexus, one Mercedes Benz 600 and a BMW 3.5. The new model, you know.'

Professor He Zuoxiu owned nothing more splendid than a black bicycle but the expert in theoretical physics had a slight physique exploding with energy pent up over fifteen years. He was powered by anger and indignation against the forces of ignorance and superstition that had kept China poor and backward for centuries. He had tried again and again to corner his quarry and force his opponent to put his powers to a laboratory test. Yet the fame of his opponent continued to grow in a city gripped by an obsession with the supernatural. Zhang Baosen became a favourite in Zhongnanhai, where China's elderly and ailing rulers lived, a sort of Rasputin to the court who promised to deliver miraculous cures. Beijing attracted many others who claimed to possess powers derived from a mastery of ancient Chinese knowledge. Tens of thousands, perhaps millions, became devoted followers of Masters who manipulated cosmic forces unimagined by Newton or Einstein.

One of Mao's goals was the eradication of religion and feudal superstition from China. Beijing once had thousands of temples, more than any other city in Asia. Its fame as a holy city was such that tens of thousands of devout pilgrims went there every year from every part of the empire. Some spent months on their journey and as an act of penitence frequently stretched themselves full-length along the ground. In the hills all around Beijing are the remains of monasteries and nunneries that trace their history back more than thirteen hundred years. In a landmark 700-page study, *Peking Temples and City Life:*

1400–1900, the American scholar Professor Susan Naquin identified 2,500 religious sites in the city. She thinks she may have under-estimated this by at least a third. Beijing was a holy city, almost a Rome, not least because its emperors were divinities in their own right. The religious convictions of the imperial court in any dynasty varied from emperor to emperor, making Beijing tolerant and uniquely ecumenical. It had places of worship devoted to Buddhism, Sham-anism, Daoism, Islam and Christianity, plus the grand state temples devoted to the worship of heaven, earth, sun and moon, temples dedicated to the worship of imperial ancestors, and hundreds devoted to the pantheon of gods who make up China's complex folk religions.

In the 1990s the city's great legacy of temples was swept away, leaving only a few dozen that were to be preserved as tourist sites or token places of worship. One day I stumbled across the temple of the Beijing City God, hidden away behind a brand new Parsons depart-ment store and a newly constructed Financial Street, which was begin-ning to fill up with imposing bank buildings. I talked the doorman into letting me in and found myself in a courtyard littered with piles of lumber and rubbish. There had once been three halls, each with a roof made of layers of rafters arranged in the hip-gable style topped by black tiles – but now grass grew tall on the roof of the one re-maining hall. Peering through the windows I could see the halls littered with more piles of careless rubbish. The original entrance had been replaced by an iron door with a notice identifying the place as an 'important workshop ground'. Stepping inside one hall, I could see even in the darkness that it had once had beams and walls gaudily painted in bright colours. Now the paint had curled and mottled. Some tablets with chiselled inscriptions had been cemented into the wall of what was a storehouse. On a marble stela covered by a pile of timber and scrap metal, I could still read a fragment of an inscription which promised that such-and-such place's 'fragrant reputation will be handed down for a hundred generations'.

Soon after 1949 this temple, like most of the others, had been closed and turned into a factory, a school or a warehouse – in this case the Hydro-Energy Publishing House. Yet it had always perplexed me how it was possible for the Communist Party to eradicate beliefs and customs that had put down roots over thousands of years. The party appeared to be building a new city entirely devoted to the gods of commerce and consumption, but then I began to grasp that inside the walls of plate glass that fronted the new shopping malls, offices and apartment complexes, something else was going on. The seemingly contented people and rulers were locked in a continuous but silent struggle. A strong tide of irrational beliefs ebbed and flowed through the city. The party wanted the people to believe in a rational universe – across the city it constructed public monuments devoted to geometry, sculptures of globes, triangles and cubes. Across one new street over-pass, the party even put up Einstein's formula $e = mc^2$, as if it were a reassuring citation from sacred scripture. Yet there was little comfort or fellowship to be derived from such symbols. Most people seemed desperate to find something else to fill their lives.

One day I got up before dawn to visit the Altar of the Sun near the diplomatic district and found that a crowd of silver-haired men and women had gathered, fidgeting outside the gates, impatiently grasping glittering broadswords, red-tasselled spears and halberds. The Altar of the Sun is now a public park but was one of nine major religious complexes, including the Temple of Heaven, built in the Ming dynasty. The court with its rituals imposed a comforting timetable on Beijing life. As the Sons of Heaven, the emperors came to worship the earth, the heavens, the sun, the moon and the spirits of their own ancestors and those of all previous emperors. A ninth temple was built exclu-sively for the empresses to spin silk ceremonially. Until 1911 it was the emperor's duty to plough the first furrow at the Temple of Agricul-ture, a symbolic gesture to mark the start of the new agricultural year. At year end the chief of state had to inspect weapons and strengthen city walls. Then, at the winter solstice, the emperor would give thanks to the earth and sky and honour his ancestors by offering sacrificial balls of dough.

When the park gates opened at 6 a.m., the crowd stormed in like an avenging army, issuing wild yells and hoarse challenges to the rising sun and dispersed among the trees. 'He-he-heee! Ha-ha-hee!' bellowed one woman, lifting up her chin and spreading her arms out wide at the silvery disc, like some defiant warrior queen. I noticed five or six others join her short and plump frame on the topmost rock, yelling and shouting. Some slapped themselves from side to side as if possessed by a dangerous spirit. These veterans in baggy shorts and shapeless white vests stretched and pushed against ancient gnarled pines with creaking knee joints and backbones. In quiet glades and rookeries, squads of dedicated geriatrics rehearsed the feints and lunges of shadow-boxing or wielded their bright swords to thrust and parry imaginary enemies.

Under the floating eaves of a pagoda, *erhu* players practised Peking Opera arias and the 'piddle-piddle-ping' of the *erhu* strings was interspersed by the clash of brass cymbals. Everyone seemed to be in training, no matter how flabby their pale flesh, for some impending trial of strength, some epic and final battle before the long-vanished walls of Beijing. When night fell over the surrounding streets, I could hear from the nearby diplomatic compound where I lived an insistent 'dum-dum dum' of drums and the jangle-jangle clash of bells, as troupes of dancers dressed in red-silk costumes performed the *yangge*, a peasant planting dance invented and then introduced by the Communists after they arrived from Manchuria. These tom-toms sounded menacing, as if the restless natives might at any moment attack. At other times the park would be filled with couples lining up to do the cha-cha-cha – quick step, slow step, quick step – on the floor of the dodgems ring erected in Ritan Park for children. In another corner, the pensioners could be seen waggling their bottoms, getting down to the beat of funky disco. Some preferred country dancing and once I heard the familiar rhythms of 'Marie's Wedding'.

These social gatherings which take place in public spaces all over China seem to have filled the gaps left by such institutions as the family clan or artisan guild in the old society. Formerly, most ordinary people's lives revolved around the activities organized by local guilds. There were hundreds of guilds for every occupation and each had its own temple. The Temple of Joy, for instance, was patronized by people in the entertainment business and was decorated with the names of famous opera singers. In addition, Beijing had many *huiguan*, hostels catering to visitors from distant provinces. The more important guilds and *huiguan* organized charities, schools, medical services and other social services.

Some gods had many temples serving them, like Guandi, the God of War, but Beijing became populated by many other intriguing deities.

There was the God of Literature who governed the luck of scholars attending the imperial exams, the God of Rheumatism for those suffering from fever, colic, consumption and stubborn coughs. Traders from Shanxi province erected a temple to the God of Horses and there were gods who looked after granaries, kilns and even city gates. The Manchu bannermen paid homage to the God of Cannon. I once ran across a Tang dynasty temple dedicated to Er Lang, nephew of the King of Heaven, and his dog, to whom those with sick pets would come and pray. The largest temples had their own fairs, some lasting as long as a month, so at any time of the year there was a fair going on somewhere in the city. Almost every day had significance and was marked by some ritual, festival or market in one or other quarter. The worship of the metropolitan city gods became particularly important during the Ming dynasty and the birthday of Beijing's City God was marked by huge processions, festivals and sacrifices.

Though people belonged to guilds, their strongest allegiances were to their large sprawling families. Most people lived or worked in large households where life was minutely regulated by the so-called 'three thousand rules of behaviour' and the calendar. My Chinese teacher, Mr Liu, an imperturbable Jeeves-like figure with a taste for chocolate digestive biscuits, grew up in his grandfather's house in Tianjin, and his household of a hundred people, including the servants, would celebrate feast days together. His grandfather, a deputy commissioner in charge of the imperial salt monopoly, lived with four generations in numerous courtyards behind high walls. Liu's own children, cleaners and mechanics who had missed any education thanks to the Cultural Revolution and their class background, now lived alone. At midnight on New Year's Eve it was the custom for all family members to line up and *ke tou* (prostrate) before the master and mistress of the house, who would be sitting as rigid as statues on two stiff chairs. Then, during the Hour of the Tiger, between 3 and 5 a.m., the household performed the triple rites in honour of Heaven and Earth and the ancestors. Every day over the next two weeks they would be offered food and drink as if they were mortal guests. After a twenty-four-hour fast interrupted by a vegetarian meal, the household sat down to a grand New Year's banquet. The second day was devoted to worshipping the God of Wealth (Cai Shen), when his picture was burned and replaced by a new one. Poor children ran from house to house crying 'We have brought you a new Cai Shen! Here he is under his money tree, whose fruits are gold, whose branches drip with coins!'

There were other festivals throughout the year: Qing Ming, when, in the spring, people went out to sweep their ancestors' graves; Zhongqiu Jie, the autumn moon festival when people would watch the moon and sip chrysanthemum wine; and the festival of hungry ghosts, when people would light tapers on the streets for the souls of the dead in purgatory. The calendar minutely regulated life in a world where everyone knew his place and even knew what the weather would be. China's traditional calendar is divided into twenty-four solar terms of fifteen days. When it came to forecasting changes in the weather, it seemed as reliable as a railway timetable. 'Tomorrow, you will sleep better, it is start of the "limit of heat",' Teacher Liu would say confidently in August. Sure enough, the fourteenth solar term would be cooler. Or in winter he would forecast, 'There may be snow soon, tomorrow begins the small snow,' and there would indeed be a slight snowfall decking the Great Wall or the Forbidden City in a fairy-tale frosting. However, the religious calendar and seasons always seemed out of joint. The first day of spring finds Beijing still in the depths of winter, much as the first day of the autumn arrives in the stifling heat of August. Although one period was called 'the waking of insects', little stirs in the brown and bare fields around Beijing for another month. Beijing's winter really ends in March, when catkins first appear on the willows.

Spring weather lasts only a few weeks before the temperatures rise and it is summer. The clear, warm days are all too brief and the monsoon clouds gather above the city, bringing a stifling, oppressive humidity. In imperial days the court left free jars of cool water around the city in the fifth moon, with the inscription 'The Imperial Mercy is All-Embracing'. Beijing legend claims that the rains come when the Dragon King celebrates his birthday in the thirteenth of the sixth moon. The city is actually guarded by four dragons: one in the Summer Palace Lake, the black dragon in the Heilong Lake in the Western Hills, another who resides in the Jade Spring, which provides the imperial water supply, and a white dragon under Lake Miyun. Still, the violent thunderstorms start well before the dragon's birthday. The court also influenced the calendar, decreeing on which days attendants could change from fur-lined robes with ear-covers into silk gowns, or when they could wear lightweight gauze in the hot summer. The regulations even specified when flowers could be taken out of winter storage, when leaves should be raked and ditches dredged.

In Beijing, the capital of many dynasties, the court also marked the calendar with many imperial celebrations, like those held in Ritan Park, the Temple of Heaven and the Temple of Confucius. In addition, many Jin, Mongol and Manchu emperors converted to Buddhism, although some continued to practise shamanistic rituals and divination in a handful of now vanished shrines. Over the centuries, Beijing became a significant centre for Tibetan Buddhism. The Mongol khans inaugurated a tradition by appointing various Dalai Lamas and Panchen Lamas as their personal spiritual gurus. Beijing has two celebrated white stupas: the 150-foot White Pagoda Temple, off Fuchengmennei Dajie in the north-west, and another one in Beihai Park north of the Forbidden City, dating back to the time of Khublai Khan (thirteenth century). Various Panchen and Dalai Lamas, notably the great fifth Dalai Lama (d. 1682) came on pilgrimage, journeys that could take several years to complete; such visits were marked by the erection of stupas. The sixth Panchen Lama, who came in 1780 for the birthday of the Emperor Qianlong, died in Beijing. Mongols came to believe that Beijing was actually the home of Vairochana, the transcendent Buddha and incarnation of the Law (*dharma*). The city became integrated into the esoteric world of Tantric Buddhism and the Tibetans thought the city was modelled on a *thanka* of the terrible underworld god Yamantaka.

The Manchu emperors were especially eager to cultivate powerful lamas as they sought to project themselves as the legitimate rulers of the Mongols and Tibetans. The Emperor Qianlong presented himself as the incarnation of Manjushri, the Bodhisattva Wisdom, and visited his temples at the holy mountain of Wutai in Shanxi province. In the hopes of pacifying the warlike nomads, the Qing dynasty fostered Buddhism by naming new living Buddhas (that is, child-monks who had been recognized as reincarnations) and by founding new monasteries, so Beijing became home to many communities of monks and lamas; palaces reserved for living Buddhas; and printing houses for sacred texts. Many of these places are now hard to identify, such as the seventeenth-century Lofty Blessings Monastery, which printed Buddhist scriptures but later became a television factory. Only the magnificent Yong He Gong, the Lama Temple, is now open to the public as a tourist destination. Once the palace of a Qing prince who became the Emperor Yong Zheng, it later served to house several great lamas.

The emperors in Beijing considered themselves to be the patrons of all religions, so they not only visited the Temple of Confucius but also attended the city's great Buddhist and Daoist institutions on important days. Daoism's history in the city dates back to before the Jin dynasty, when two rival sects each had a major temple complex. One is the Bai Yun Guan or White Cloud Temple,[1] founded, it is said, in the eighth century AD, which follows the teachings of the Quanzhen (Complete Perfection or Complete Truth Sect). Quanzhen Daoist priests practise celibacy and keep their hair tied in a topknot. When its abbot, Qiu Chuji, known as the 'Perfect Man', went to meet Genghis Khan in 1124 while he was attacking the Jin kingdom, this Daoist sect switched loyalties. So when the Mongols became the rulers of Beijing, the sect and its temple flourished and expanded. The abbot was buried in the White Cloud Temple and his remains are in the Hall of the Patriarch Qiu. The White Cloud Temple was the only Daoist temple to reopen after 1979 and is now the headquarters of the Communist-run All-China Daoist Federation.

The Dongyue Miao, Temple of the Zhengyi or Righteous Sect, on the other side of the city, is its great rival. Its origins lie in the thirteenth century when a Daoist Master called Zhang Liusun started worshipping the spirit of Mount Tai in Shandong province near the birthplace of Confucius. The Dongyue or Eastern Peak Temple is dedicated to the God of Mount Tai and for generations a direct descendant of Zhang was its master. The Eastern Peak Temple, however, was regarded as the greatest centre for Daoism in north China. It is enormous, with 376 rooms covering 11.6 acres, filled with stone stelae, ancient pines and cypresses. Lining the edge of the courtyards are seventy-two cells, each with a wax tableau showing the magistrates of hell and heaven meting out judgement to penitents and sinners. In one room sits a life-size clay statue of Zhang Liusun, dressed in his red robes and with a long white beard. In another cell is the Department of Rain and Earth, run by a fierce deity baring savage white teeth and dressed in an emperor's dragon robe, with a flat black hat and beaded fringe. On either hand wait both human supplicants and strange creatures with heads of frogs or snakes. Daoists believed that the God of Mount Tai determines the span of each human life, judges the deeds of each person after his death and orders his rebirth. This vast administrative task required the aid of an extensive supernatural bureaucracy as confusingly reduplicative as the one on earth. It even had a department of official titles where mandarins lined up before a god to receive their buttons, titles and seals of office.

Beijingers used to come here to pray during the second moon on the anniversary of Qing Kuang, a king who ruled the first of the ten Daoist hells. These were divided into sixteen wards and the tableaux were intended to warn ordinary people. In the First Court, they were shown how their deeds, good and bad, were inscribed into the Book of Life and Death, and how grinning devils dragged the wicked up to the Evil Mirror Tower where a large mirror revealed their past. Each officer of hell had jurisdiction over a particular kind of soul. One magistrate specialized in those who died prematurely, another judged only thieves and robbers. Tableaux showed the officials at work: seizing unfilial sons, disobedient slaves, rebellious soldiers and even disloyal ministers, interrogating them or affixing seals on documents. Just as in a real-life *yamen*, each magistrate had a staff of recorders, lectors and executioners to help.

On the third moon the temple would be bustling with all kinds of other pilgrims. Lovers came here to pray that the 'Old Man of the Moon' would help them. Debtors came to settle disputed accounts with the aid of a magical abacus that hung on the wall just inside the gate. Invalids came to touch a famous bronze mule – still there – which supposedly could cure all maladies. Scholars came to worship the God of Literature, Wen Chang, bringing him pen brushes, ink slabs and writing paper. Tens of thousands of people would throng the courtyards burning incense and praying. Markets sprang up around the temple and many came to discus business, eat and drink.

These and other festivals made the Dongyue Miao immensely rich, but its grandeur has been diminished by the huge concrete buildings that now tower over it on every side. The grand entrance, a triple arched *pai lou*, was severed from the temple by an eight-lane expressway. Inside, it now seems a forlorn empty shell. For fifty years the Ministry of Public Security used the site as a police training academy before turning it over to the tourist department, who made it a museum of Beijing traditional folk culture. At the back there was a pathetic collection of items one could come across on a country walk: a basket of maize cobs, a thresher, hoes and shovels, wooden ploughs, grindstones and even a well. A brochure asserts that the museum's purpose 'is to help in socialist construction' by 'improving the moral thinking of the People's Republic of China' and 'to unite the people and to keep social order'. The real intention seems to be to demonstrate how this medieval world has been thoroughly destroyed.

It is difficult to convey in a few words the rich and satisfying complexity of this Chinese world of belief, which only survives in some form in villages and in a few places like Macao or Hong Kong where foreign governments largely left people to follow their traditions. One day I was intrigued to read in a newspaper that in the fourth moon, that is, in May, one could once again go to Miaofeng Shan, a mountain about fifty miles west of Beijing. This had been the greatest pilgrimage centre in northern China and its history dated back at least a thousand years to the Liao dynasty. During the Ming, the temples on this 4,000-foot-high peak had become even more famous, and even in the 1930s the annual festivals were still attracting hundreds of thousands of worshippers.

On the spur of the moment, I invited Teacher Liu to join me and to my surprise he agreed. We drove out one Sunday morning, grumbling about the thick traffic clogging the city centre, and soon became lost in the unfamiliar suburbs. Much of Beijing's industry is concentrated in the western side of the city. The road passes through the choked industrial suburb of Shijing Shan, home to the belching chimneys of the Capital Iron and Steelworks. Nearby was a huge power station and dense clusters of cement works and chemical factories. Dump trucks hauling river gravel bowled along, lost in their own cloud of dust in the dried-out river beds of the Yongding River and another large river whose name I missed. Soon, though, the road began winding through a narrow gorge, leaving the coking plants and cement factories behind. It was the birthday of Wei Shen, protectress of flowers, and as we left the dust and pollution behind, it turned out to be a fine May day. Nothing is prettier than the hills around Beijing during its brief spring. The first pink-and-white blossoms on the apple and peach trees appear on the dry limestone hills, followed by flowers from the wild jujube and walnut trees scattered among the rocks and crags.

Popular religion and folk culture in China are related to but distinct from the high culture with its difficult Confucian texts and allusive Tang dynasty poetry. The gatherings at Miaofeng Shan were a celebration of a living tradition that developed independently of the court and its refined mandarins. Like most of Beijing's religious traditions, the festival seemed to be a mixture of Buddhist and Daoist folklore. The mountain pilgrimage had started off as an offshoot of the Daoist worship of Mount Taishan in Shandong province and was devoted to veneration of the Jade Maiden of Divine Immortality, Bixia. Just who she is, is not clear; some say the daughter of the legendary Yellow Emperor. Gradually the cult became mixed up with all kinds of other worship and as the festival developed it spread to eight other peaks in neighbouring counties. The Emperor Qianlong decreed that Miaofeng Shan and the Bixia Goddess were the most prominent. Women in particular came here to entreat her blessing if they wanted children, or to avoid a difficult childbirth.

After a gap of nearly sixty years, the festival has been cautiously revived. In the 1930s, pilgrims would set out early in the morning from Xizhimen Gate, and every guild set up shelters along the way offering free hot porridge, steamed bread, tea, lodgings or free services. The shoemakers repaired shoes for free but many penitent pilgrims would kneel down every three steps and prostrate themselves every nine steps. Such a journey might take weeks or months, with overnight stops at one of the many temples along the way. On key festivals, pilgrims took part in a torch procession that travelled up to the peak, where stilt walkers, actors, dancers and opera singers performed at the temples.

These days the new pilgrim road to Miaofeng Shan ends in a car park at the bottom of a small hill in a remote, poor village. A newly paved road has just been built leading right to the summit, so the lazy visitor can entirely avoid having to walk up. The pilgrimage route has been shortened and a few families were walking up the path with its cracked stones. Teacher Liu began to enjoy himself.

The state started to rebuild the three main temples at the summit only in 1990. Three years later the first temple fair was officially reopened. Now the local authorities were trying to establish it as a tourist attraction and here was even a museum with maps showing the old pilgrim routes and references to Professor Naquin's research. Yet it was a pale shadow of what it had once been. The visitor had to buy a ticket to enter the Jade Maiden's Temple and the seller told me that just a couple of thousand people now attended. Still, the temples and shrines were not empty. Many visitors drove up by car and admired the views, munched some snacks while browsing through the goods on sale, the calendars and almanacs, toys and firecrackers. Before the Jade Maiden's altar, some people stood bowing their heads and burning incense. Hopeful women had covered the altar with stuffed toy animals. 'This is dedicated to obstetrics,' a friendly caretaker explained and presented me with an apple to eat.

'It is not really like it used to be,' Teacher Liu said at last. 'There are no priests or fortune tellers. And where are the travelling performers?' As we walked back down the hill exchanging greetings with those climbing up in excitement, he seemed gently surprised that anything had survived at all. The government still harshly enforced a ban on fortune telling and geomancy, although I found in Beijing that a few people still secretly earned their living by performing these services. As in the French Revolution, when Robespierre banned all Christian festivals, created a new calendar, renamed the months of the year and introduced new festivals honouring the Supreme Being, the Chinese revolutionaries also tried to create new rituals and traditions.

On the first day of the new year (according to the Western calendar) it is the duty of the general secretary of the party to visit the home of a worker, often one who has been laid off. And at spring festival (the Chinese New Year), the premier visits the home of a farmer somewhere outside Beijing, where he folds two dumplings, the traditional festival delicacy. Like the imperial court before it, the party also used to manipulate the arrival of cooler weather. It alone decided when winter began and hence when the central heating could be turned on. Just as the court ruled when officials could change into their fur-lined robes, the heating could stay off in freezing temperatures or, more usually, go on when it was fine and sunny. That meant on many a fine autumn day all the windows had to be opened to keep the temperature bearable. At spring festival, the state now entertains the populace with a television gala variety show filled with soldiers singing patriotic songs like 'I love you, China'. Many acts look like folk art performances, since the Communist Party appropriated the styles of folk art for their own propaganda, so one can watch north China dancers and drummers performing numbers like: 'Sing about the spirit of the fifteenth Party Congress, the glorious return of Hong Kong, sing loudly about coal delivered to new electric power stations.' The next political celebration takes place in March, when Beijing is spruced up for the first big political meeting, the National People's Congress. Squads of citizen-volunteers can be seen wiping down the railings and lamp-posts with buckets of soap and water.

By the 1970s it was considered to be revolutionary not to celebrate spring festival at all in the spirit of being selfless and austere. Instead, the calendar became crowded by new festivals dedicated to honour anonymous social groups – workers, teachers, soldiers and women. But there was no fun, nor much meaning in any of these artificial 'events'. All life had been bleached away from this once great city by the time I arrived in 1985. The populace still spent part of nearly every day attending ideological indoctrination classes. The worship of Mao and his little red book of sayings had become a quasi-religion and those who relied on his doctrine were reported to be able to perform medical miracles. The sick could be cured of cancer and doctors were able to perform surgery without anaesthetics.

After 1979 the party cautiously allowed a revival of some old Beijing traditions, admitting it had made some 'mistakes' during the Cultural Revolution. I was among the thousands who flocked to the Great Bell Temple when it held its first temple fair in over thirty years. People loved the performances by strolling players, storytellers, acrobats and qigong strongmen who would smash a sledgehammer onto a stone slab laid across the chest of another. Old customs like dressing up small children in red to protect them from evil sprits re-emerged. Children bought spinning tops, gaily painted wind wheels, or figurines made of painted dough modelled on legendary characters. In the temple precincts, stalls sold toffee crab apples, steaming broths, spicy noodles, grilled lamb and bean porridge – a special concoction called *la ba er* made of whole grains, old rice, nuts, beans and fruit. Outside there were scenes like a Chinese Brueghel: skaters gliding on the frozen moat of the Forbidden City while children pushed themselves along the canals, kneeling on little sledges and grasping sticks in either hand.

The state allowed the reopening of one church or temple for each of the five recognized faiths. Before 1949 Beijing had sixty Protestant churches but only one of these was permitted to hold regular services. The state kept the property of other places of worship. The surviving temple buildings had been put under the protection of the Beijing Municipal Office for the Administration of Cultural Properties in 1984, but they remained, like most of the city, in state of shabby neglect. Once I came across some peasants camped out in the Temple of the Earth (Ditan). In the sacrificial halls, they had strung up their washing and planted bitter gourds, which hung like bells from the porticoes. They seemed to be like Visigoths after the sack of Rome. With the vast majority of temples and churches closed and the state nervous that any kind of civic organization could turn into a political opposition movement, people began to congregate in parks and any other public space. The only permitted excuse for any small public gathering was for dancing and exercising, especially *qigong* breathing exercises. *Qigong* dates back to the harmless exercises that Indian yogis brought to China as early as the fifth century AD. By practising these exercises, Daoist masters like Zhang Liusun, who founded the Eastern Peak Temple, began to claim that they could acquire super-human powers. They claimed to be able to do anything, even to fly through space and time. To obtain the patronage of rulers like Genghis Khan, they offered to put their powers at the service of the state. A body of medical learning also evolved called *Ren Ti Ke*, which enabled the masters of *qigong* to cure the sick, and this became part of traditional Chinese medical practice.

The fascination with *qigong* medicine began in the 1970s when a girl in Sichuan claimed she could read with her ear and a local party cadre won promotion by sponsoring her rise to national fame. Soon, people with special powers were discovered all over China and brought to Beijing to be studied, often at special military research institutes. The capital's top hospitals are run by the military and soon they, too, were employing *qigong* doctors and girls like Zheng Xiangliang, who claimed to use X-ray vision to look at internal organs and see cancers, and converse with extra-terrestrials. The head of the 301 PLA Hospital in Beijing, where Deng Xiaoping himself would eventually die in 1998, was a particularly fervent believer in *qigong*'s power to cure cancer and even Aids. Scientific credibility to these claims was given by Qian Xuesen, the father of China's atomic bomb. He had defected from the United States in the 1950s and helped the Communists to design and launch their first rockets before taking the world by surprise with the testing of an atomic bomb in 1964. He then endorsed Mao's absurd beliefs, made during the Great Leap Forward in 1958, that China could quadruple its grain harvests over-night using special agricultural techniques, like planting seeds close together. As a result, some 30 million starved to death. After Mao's death Qian found himself in a difficult position. Deng Xiaoping was now in charge and held him partly responsible for this catastrophe. Qian returned to favour in the 1980s by strongly promoting the study of *qigong*. If China could understand and harness these forces, he promised a revolution in science, greater than the theory of relativity. With Professor Qian's backing, more and more people with special powers turned up. In addition to Miss Zheng Xiangling, who could not only converse with extra-terrestrials but cure any kind of disease, there was Mr Yan Xin, whose psychokinetic powers enabled him to direct the weather and put out forest fires, and Mr Wang Hongcheng, who had a 'secret formula' to change the molecular structure of water into that of petrol and thus solve China's energy shortage at a stroke.

Under Professor Qian's guidance, researchers at Qinghua University published papers in 1987 and 1988 with evidence from scientific experiments that supposedly proved how *qi* could be directed to strike objects 1,240 miles away. At the time both the Russians and the Americans were also working on secret programmes to employ people with paranormal powers to find and destroy hidden nuclear missile bases. One of those who could help China deploy such weapons was

Zhang Baosen, who became the focus of a top-secret military research project into paranormal powers.

According to his biography, *Superman Zhang Baosen*, he was an ordinary teenager growing up in Benxi, a dismal steel town in Liaoning province, when he discovered an uncanny ability to read love letters which a classmate held unopened in his hands. Inevitably, the local branch of the Anquan Bu, China's secret police, was anxious to employ his talents. Soon he was on his way to work for the secret police in Beijing. Zhang arrived in the capital in 1983 and came to the attention of Marshal Ye Jianying, a powerful figure who had ordered the arrest of the Gang of Four and helped Deng Xiaoping into power. By then, Marshal Ye was 85 and had been ill for a long time. He tested Zhang's powers by writing three characters on a piece of paper, which he sealed in an envelope. To the great marshal's astonishment, Zhang was able to read what he had written by using his nose, and this gave him confidence in Zhang's miraculous powers. More of the country's top military leaders became convinced that with talents like those of Master Zhang, China could use such mastery of *qi* and 'cosmic forces' to become invincible. One of Master Zhang's most powerful patrons was Major-General Wu Shaozu, son of Long March general Wu Xiuquan, who had studied nuclear physics in Qinghua University. In the 1980s he had run the PLA's research programme and after 1990 he headed the National Sports Commission, which supervised all *qigong* sects.

By now, the party was phasing out the endless political indoctrination sessions and people had more and more private leisure time to fill. With established religions so constrained by the state, people gravitated to these cult leaders who offered their followers miraculous cures for cancer and other problems. More and more sects sprang up all over the country and there were groups of people who gathered in parks and public spaces to perform *qigong* exercises. One, with the delightful name of the 'Fragrant Sect', claimed that with the right training its followers could always release the smell of fragrant flowers into the air. Another was called Falun Gong; it was founded by a postal clerk from Liaoning province called Li Hongzhi, who borrowed elements from traditional *qigong* breathing practices and mixed them with Buddhist thought and his own peculiar notions of the universe.

Li Hongzhi believed that the human race, or at least the Chinese race, was created by aliens from outer space.

In the meantime Professor He Zuoxiu used his position as director of the Chinese Institute of Theoretical Physics to challenge this wave of superstition. He demanded that Zhang's claims should be put to the test. The first time was in May 1988 and the entire politburo of the Communist Party attended, along with Dr Paul Kurtz, an American who was then chairman of the Committee for the Scientific Investigation of Claims of the Paranormal. Under laboratory conditions, Professor He demonstrated that Master Zhang could not genuinely twist forks, remove tablets from bottles or read documents in sealed envelopes with X-ray vision. To Professor He's dismay, this trial was to no avail and no reports of the experiments were published. Zhang continued to enjoy the patronage of top party leaders and live a life of luxury in the People's Liberation Army's Space Research Centre. By the early 1990s *qigong* was close to becoming China's unofficial state religion.

When I met Professor He in the cramped study of his apartment he explained why such cults had become so popular. 'So many people still believe,' he said. 'They want to believe that we Chinese possess special abilities – just like the Empress Dowager Cixi believed the claims of the Boxers.' Before the siege of the Legations in 1900 she had invited Boxers to give demonstrations of their special power in the Forbidden City and became convinced they could stop bullets and so easily defeat the foreigners. Then she ordered those *qigong* demonstrators to attack the German delegation and kill its minister. She believed their magic powers to deflect bullets would defeat the foreign enemy.

Professor He believed that, like the Boxers, Zhang performed simple conjuring tricks. 'Zhang relies on sleight of hand and the credulity of his audience,' he explained. He tried again and again to disprove Zhang's claims. On one occasion, Jia Chunwang, the Minister of Public Security, agreed to be the adjudicator. Professor He methodically set out to disprove Zhang's five tricks: bending forks, shaking pills out of a medicine bottle, setting clothes on fire, restoring a name card that had been torn to pieces and using X-ray vision to read letters. To test the latter, Professor He wrote something down on a piece of brown paper and folded it in an envelope. 'Zhang tried but failed to read what was written down. Then he said my body had a strong magnetic field, so he could not perform normally,' Professor He said gleefully. 'So we organized another experiment.' A text was once again placed in a sealed envelope and while Zhang was told to leave the room, the envelope stayed put. While Zhang was out of the room demonstrating his X-ray vision, the minister opened the envelope. 'We found he had switched the envelopes – so that trick was exposed in public.' The professor laughed triumphantly. Next he exposed the bottle and pill trick. They took a glass bottle from their laboratory and marked it with a fingerprint, put pills inside, each identified by a number, then sealed the bottle with 501 Superglue. 'After four hours of shaking the bottle, not a single pill came out,' the Professor chortled again.

Then in March 1999 an altogether different phenomenon occurred which was responsible for Professor He's greatest victory over Zhang. One Sunday morning around 15,000 peasants mysteriously, almost magically, appeared out of nowhere and surrounded Zhongnanhai. They sat humbly on sheets of newspaper, each person equipped with a bag of provisions, outside the high red walls of the old imperial gardens, ostentatiously praying and studying one or another book produced by the Falun Gong sect. There they stayed for twelve hours and then quietly dispersed while the paralysed government wondered what to do. No one had ever mounted such an audacious protest before. It took the party's famed security apparatus completely by surprise and the punishment that followed was massive and sweeping. Tens of thousands were arrested and many ended up being beaten to death in prison cells when they refused to recant their beliefs. Some believers even set themselves on fire in Tiananmen Square. Li Hongzhi himself fled abroad. The investigations that followed revealed that Li Hongzhi had created a nationwide organization around his cult, whose members included senior party officials up and down the country. The party could no longer even rely on its own members to remain true to its values and belief.

All the *qigong* sects came under scrutiny and had to disband. In Ritan Park, I no longer saw large groups practising the exercises or listening to lectures. The revival of Miaofeng Shan stopped and the

number of visitors fell. Even so, Zhang Baosen was not entirely dis-
graced although his powerful patrons in the military lost their posts.
Professor He's triumph was not complete and Zhang was still in
business.

When he finally slipped into the room, we all fell silent and waited
expectantly. The Master looked outwardly rather dull. Of average
height, with a smooth, tanned skin, he wore a sawtooth sports jacket
over a stripy casual shirt that suggested a salesman. He sat down at
the table without a greeting and maintained a distant, preoccupied air
that said 'what-am-I-doing-here, you-are-not-going-to-buy-anything-
anyway'. As the waitress came and went, delivering a succession of
tiny plates decked with sea slugs, chicken claws and abalone, Zhang
ate nothing and said nothing. He kept a poker-face as I peppered him
with questions.

'Have you really met Jiang Zemin?' Silence.

'Did you really cure Zhao Ziyang's medical condition?' Silence.

Under the table, I could feel his feet jigging up and down. From
time to time, he abruptly stood up, went to a corner, flipped open a
mobile phone and mumbled something. Then he sat down again, then
up he went to a hotel telephone for another urgent conversation. Or
else he would simply get up and leave the room without explanation.

'Jiang is angry with him because he is too friendly with Zhao,'
explained Mrs Y, referring to the former party chief who had been
under close house arrest ever since Jiang Zemin had replaced him.
'Because of his powers, the Master sometimes behaves quite childishly.
Sometimes he is happy one moment, unhappy another,' her companion added helpfully. At that, he suddenly stood up, picked up a
dumpling between his chopsticks, thrust it into her face, laughed, and
walked out.

'You see, he has never given an interview to a foreigner,' Mrs Y
added in her loud peremptory way. As we picked at the food, a stream
of people, often diners from other rooms or guests in the hotel, kept
coming into the room to greet him, bowing low and proffering their
name cards, excited by the chance to encounter such a famous and
gifted person. Mr Zhang, as a look of intense concentration gripped
his face, stroked three forks, then with a flourish displayed them, all
twisted together by some superhuman force. Next, he took a little

medicine bottle and, appearing to rub the bottom with his index finger, shifted it to his other hand. Suddenly he dropped white aspirin tablets onto my hand so it looked as if the tablets had materialized through the solid glass. Then I noticed that my mobile phone, which I had left on the table, was in his possession. He managed to make the SIM card from the phone disappear and then re-materialize inside the empty medicine bottle. When we opened the bottle and put it back in the phone, there was no doubt that it was my SIM card. Lastly, he asked for someone to volunteer their clothing, specifying that it had to be clothing made from chemical fibres. This he 'set on fire' by passing his hands across the clothing, leaving two streaks of melted polyester fabric.

Then it was all over and without taking any further questions about his feats, the Master was ready to go. As we got our coats, he gave me a Parthian shot, touching my back and giving me a jolt of *qi* energy that shot up my spine like an electric shock. Zhang left the hotel, sitting calmly in the back seat of a black Audi without number plates. Finally the hotel manager appeared and presented me with a bill for US$1,000. After paying up with some reluctance, I drove back through the city and pondered the significance of what I had seen. Professor He was right: Zhang was just a crude charlatan, but people wanted to believe in him, even dedicated Marxists. After the 1999 crackdown against Falun Gong, the destruction of old Beijing intensified. Yet all the huge modern buildings going up now seemed to me to be totems, erected to exhibit China's devout faith in modernism. However high and imposing these edifices might be, they seemed matched by the hidden forces of irrationalism coiled beneath the office blocks and shopping malls. No matter how modern Beijing looked, these destructive forces might still burst forth at any time and overwhelm the project to modernize China.

17

Radiant City of the Future

When Liang Sicheng was in New York in 1946, he met the Swiss-born architect Le Corbusier, the godfather of modern cities. As prestigious architects with an international reputation, they had both been invited to present designs for the headquarters of the newly established United Nations. An intriguing photo from the time shows them together, along with a group of other eminent architects, in front of an architectural model. Liang looks dapper and is smiling in an upbeat way, but Le Corbusier wears a slightly sardonic smile. Liang had put forward designs that drew on his knowledge of traditional Chinese architecture, but his ideas were rejected out of hand in favour of those of the Swiss. The UN headquarters became what they are today, a series of unadorned and uncompromising geometrical blocks and slabs. In retrospect, Le Corbusier's triumph over Liang presaged the latter's ultimate defeat over the creation of the new Beijing. It incorporates almost all of Le Corbusier's vision of what a modern city should be and none of Liang's.

Le Corbusier, whose real name was Charles Édouard Jeanneret, rejected everything from the past and sought to use architecture and town planning as instruments for grand social engineering, which would transform the lives of everyone: 'Modern life demands, and is waiting for, a new kind of plan, both for the house and for the city,' Le Corbusier claimed in his manifesto *Towards a New Architecture*. 'We must build places where mankind will be reborn', where he promised that 'each man will live in an ordered relation to the whole'.

Le Corbusier was thwarted in his ambitions to rebuild Paris when, in the 1920s, he put forward his Voisin Plan for Paris. The elegant city designed by Baron Haussmanu only eighty years earlier was, he believed, no longer modern enough for the new machine age. So he proposed rebuilding the centre of Paris, demolishing entire neighbour-hoods of low-rise buildings and replacing the neo-classical architec-ture with huge blocks cast in concrete. The mammoth structures, ten times taller and several hundred times larger than anything that existed, should each stand isolated in green parklands linked by high-ways and pedestrian walkways. In the Radiant City of the Future everyone would have a car and speed along a grid of broad, straight motorways. The new Beijing is an attempt to realize Le Corbusier's dreams. The historic city with its small-scale buildings has been demol-ished to make way for gigantic edifices that dwarf any pedestrian struggling to cross multi-lane highways. Just as Le Corbusier wished, the inhabitants no longer live in individual houses with private court-yards but in immense collective housing projects.

Liang Sicheng had dreamed that old Beijing would be saved and the city become a sort of Washington DC, a modest government centre with beautiful and elegant buildings, full of history and charm. Yet Le Corbusier belonged to the wave of German, Dutch and other European modernists who, after the horrors of the First World War, believed European society required an entirely fresh beginning. Archi-tects like Walter Gropius of the Bauhaus in Germany wrote manifestos and set up schools whose ideas found a warm welcome among socialist parties.

The dictators of Europe all set about tearing down their capitals to build for the future. Benito Mussolini drew up plans for Rome and intended to build the world's tallest skyscraper, with a hundred storeys, as headquarters for the Fascists. Stalin ripped out the heart of old Moscow, destroying many of its most famous old churches. He encouraged many public buildings to be constructed in a pseudo-classical style with a great deal of decoration in the manner of Man-hattan Gothic. For the proletariat, however, the new housing was in the Bauhaus spirit. Adolf Hitler was determined to rebuild the old Prussian capital of Berlin on a grand scale, and all these projects had to be completed in a great hurry to show that the future could not wait. Albert Speer, Hitler's architect, was ordered to build the vast Olympic Stadium in just 940 days, in time for the 1936 Berlin Olympics. The project was designed to showcase Germany's new power, its mastery of technology and the power of the masses mobilized by National Socialism. Next Speer was given the project of 'Reconstruction for Berlin', to create a new capital for a thousand-year Reich. Hitler took a huge interest in culture but rejected both Germany's new Bauhaus movement and the entire modern art movement, preferring a sort of pastiche neo-classical style. Speer intended to create an axis that ran for 30 miles from east to west and 25 miles from north to south. At the centre, Hitler wanted a huge triumphal arch, as high as the Eiffel Tower, and a giant assembly hall. The demolition of large parts of old Berlin began on schedule but the work was interrupted by the invasion of the Soviet Union.

The Bauhaus architectural philosophy was taken up all over postwar Europe and later in America, where it was known as the 'international style'. The destruction of so many cities during the Second World War encouraged architects to put forward designs for new housing that were simple and cheap to build. In Warsaw, however, the Poles rebuilt the old city brick by brick, copying every detail from photographs and maps. It was a defiant act which said that although the Germans had promised to utterly destroy the Poles as a nation, they had failed despite the total destruction of Warsaw after the uprising.

Fighting (and fires) in Asia also destroyed much of Tokyo, not to mention Hiroshima and Nagasaki, and later the Korean cities of Seoul and Pyongyang were levelled in the 1950s. However, when Mao Zedong chose Beijing to be the capital of his new state, he inherited a city that had been preserved almost by a miracle from serious damage. The few modern buildings of note, such as those on the campuses of Qinghua and Beijing universities and the Beijing Union Medical Hospital, successfully incorporate key elements of Chinese architecture, the courtyards and the tiled saddleback roofs with floating eaves. Mao first set about engaging Soviet architects to help plan the new city and pushed them to create a copy of Red Square in front of the Forbidden City. The Soviets also designed the public buildings that made up the 'ten great projects', which were completed in a great rush in time for the tenth anniversary of the Communist victory. These include the Great Hall of the People and the Museum of Revolutionary History, which flanked the new square. Some of these adopted the pseudo-classical style favoured by Stalin, but not all. When designing Beijing's new railway station the Soviet architects deliberately tried to add a few Chinese touches, some decorative pagodas on the roof, for example, to give it a local feeling.

Mao's plans to demolish the old capital entirely met with resistance from many sides, including Liang Sicheng, but in the 1950s he pushed ahead with his desire to transform Beijing into a major industrial city. It was quite unsuitable for this role because, without a river, there was no adequate water supply, nor were there natural resources like coal or iron ore to fuel large-scale iron- and steelworks. Coal was still being brought into Beijing by camel caravan at the start of the 1950s. Large reservoirs had to be built and water brought in by diverting distant rivers, or pumped from subterranean aquifers. By the mid-1990s it was probably the world's most polluted city. Every waterway, river, canal and lake stank. Only a quarter of the city's urban and industrial wastewater was treated. Surface water was covered by algae and the bed of the Wenyu River and others was so toxic that they could only be cleaned by dredging and removing the mud. My house was near the banks of the Wenyu River and in the summer it stank so badly it was impossible to sit outside. The capital only began collecting air quality data in 1981, but it was more than fifteen years before it dared to release the data. Beijing was the last major Chinese city to make public an air pollution index, and it ranked last on the list of China's eighteen major cities. The awful mess that the Communists had made of Beijing was hidden behind a veil of secrecy. One day the *China Environment News* admitted as much. 'We should not publish our environment report if it is bad. As an ugly bride dare not show her face to her parents-in-law, so the facts should be covered by a veil,' a certain unnamed leader was quoted as saying.

Le Corbusier thought that the inhabitants of his new radiant city did not need private gardens because there would be public parks, and they no longer needed individual kitchens in their apartments because everyone would eat in communal dining halls. Children would no longer be raised by their families but by the state, and when their parents went out to work, they would attend communal and compulsory pre-school kindergartens. Before the Chinese economy collapsed during Mao's disastrous Great Leap Forward, the Chinese

Communists began preparing to divide the population into urban communes and to house them in a new type of building, known as a 'Communist Mansion'. Some prototypes were built around a twelfth-century pagoda near a hutong called Gongmen Kou Heng. Just as Le Corbusier had dreamed, they were designed for communal living so none of the flats had a kitchen. Instead, each housing block included communal dining rooms in the basement, plus a barber shop, a communal tailor, a communal nursery, a common laundry, a communal bathhouse and a recreation room. Once I found such a building. Residents told me that eating in the communal kitchens had only lasted two years because there was nothing to eat, and by then most people who could had moved out. Le Corbusier's ideas on mass housing for the new socialist man became widely adopted throughout China by way of the standard designs that the Soviet experts left behind after 1959, when they returned home. Le Corbusier rejected everything bourgeois or that smacked of the past. 'Architecture is stifled by custom,' he stated, and demanded that we 'eliminate from our hearts and minds all dead concepts' and embrace 'the mass production spirit'. He thought the house should be a machine for living, designed by engineers and mass produced. All houses should be made from standardized units and created out of the new materials of steel, reinforced concrete and glass. His favourite images were of giant modern constructions, grain elevators and ocean liners. In this brave new world, there was no need for architects or even for design because everything would be made from standardized and mass-produced units. Like other machines, such as cars, aeroplanes and ships, every building should be designed by engineers.

The Chinese tried to implement Corbusier's ideas with a greater thoroughness than anyone else. After the Soviet architects departed, there was no real architecture to speak of and most trained architects were undergoing thought-reform. Everything was indeed built directly by engineers, just as Le Corbusier had dreamed. They started by using fifty standard Soviet blueprints to meet the requirement of every kind of building. Government engineers followed exact specifications for every detail, but there were variations. The higher an individual's position in a society divided into twenty-four ranks, the more generous the specifications. The Communist elite in Beijing continued, however, to live in comfort in the imperial-era *wangfu*, surrounded by servants. In the ultra-egalitarianism of the Cultural Revolution, the number of designs was reduced to just four, and by the 1970s Chinese engineers used just two designs to build new apartment blocks. Everything was entirely made from standardized fittings and there was just one size for every door – 5 feet 11 inches by 2 feet 11 inches.

China became a country where every hospital, school, factory, prison, residential block and office seemed indistinguishable from every other building. Most places looked like prisons. Each work unit had its guards and high walls, and inhabitants lived in sparse rooms lit by 15-watt bare light bulbs, and where the lifts, if there were any, closed at 10 p.m. Much of the construction was done in grey concrete of such poor quality that one could crumble it with one's hand.

During the Cultural Revolution the war against 'bourgeois ornamentation' was taken to extremes only dreamed of by the authors of those 1920s architectural manifestos. The Red Guards went around searching offices to make sure no one was hiding any trinkets or ornaments. They told barbers not to give any fancy hairstyles, and tailors not to cut any fashionably narrow trousers. They stormed into curio shops telling the shopkeepers they had been serving the bourgeoisie. All neon lights were destroyed and some owners did the work themselves, using long sticks, so that for days shopping streets were strewn with broken glass. They marched through the streets with hammers smashing all the ornaments and stone lions, attacking the façades of old houses and painting the frames and doors of windows plain red. The large lions in front of the Ministry of Foreign Affairs were removed by break-down lorries. At the Summer Palace, the paintings were covered by pink or white paint and the heads of stone turtles were knocked off.[1]

According to Le Corbusier's theories, Beijing's residents ought to have been very happy living in a world entirely free of bourgeois ornamentation. By the 1980s most people lived in bare, whitewashed, box-like rooms, wore shapeless blue or green unisex uniforms and rode to work on black bicycles or in crowded unlit buses. Instead, Beijingers looked tired and depressed. It all created a feeling of sensory deprivation. Many inhabitants also lived cramped in an average of 20 square feet per person. Streets and courtyard houses were cluttered with thousands of crude homemade shacks, which the residents had erected to create more living space. Beijing was such a slum that in 1992, the party secretary, Chen Xitong, who led the first bid to host the Olympic Games, tried to hide them from inspectors by erecting huge boards painted with big new modern buildings. Even so, the 1993 Olympic bid failed by two votes and the games went to Sydney.

The party still frowned upon modern art and design and considered them subversive. The Maoist art establishment was led by Li Qi, a painter who did the official portraits of Mao and Deng Xiaoping. An underground art movement sprang up, including a group known as the Stars, who risked imprisonment to stage unauthorized exhibitions. Li Qi firmly believed all this 'dissident' art was funded by the CIA. These New Wave artists held their first exhibition in 1979 and for the first time began displaying nudes and purely abstract paintings. Artists trawled through art history books to catch up on fauvism, Cubism, Impressionism, surrealism, Dada, expressionism, pop art and hyper-realism. Many artists could only exhibit in the homes of foreign journalists and diplomats. An artists' colony several hundred strong that sprang up near the Yuanming Yuan fell under suspicion and the police often raided it and sometimes imprisoned or expelled its members on flimsy pretexts.

Just before the Tiananmen democracy protests began in 1989, Beijing's avant-garde staged its largest exhibition ever at the National Art Gallery. Two artists, Tang Song and Xiao Lu, fired pistols at their own installation, shooting their own images in a mirror. Police arrived with machine guns to arrest them and close the show. Many of the works were political and nothing was sacred, not even the moderniz-ation project itself. In one piece of performance art staged in 1989, spectators watched a pig painted with Chinese characters mating with another pig, whose hide was inscribed with Western writing. All of Chinese culture, not just modern culture, was held up for ridicule. One artist who became famous, Wu Bing, created huge hanging texts written with thousands of invented and unfathomable characters. Others set out to shock by designing images or objects that mocked leaders like Mao or institutions like the Communist Party with gro-tesquely distorted images of cadres. After the 1989 Tiananmen mass-acre, many fled to Paris or New York, like Ai Weiwei, the son of Ai

Qing, a well-known poet who spent the 1960s and 1970s in political exile in Xinjiang province. Ai Weiwei ended up in Manhattan and did not return until the mid-1990s, after the fall of Chen Xitong in 1995.

Chen Xitong had wanted to preserve Beijing's cultural townscape, so it was ironic that the first sign of his downfall came when a controversy sprang up over a massive shopping and office development project. Chen had awarded a prime plot of land close to the Forbidden City to Li Ka-shing, whose investments in Hong Kong property had made him one of the world's richest tycoons. Li Ka-shing called the featureless wall of concrete and blue glass windows the Oriental Plaza, although there was nothing remotely oriental about it. He insisted it should be over 164 feet tall, five times higher than permitted under the zoning laws that Chen himself had introduced. In addition, UNESCO had just recognized the Forbidden City as a World Heritage site and the city was obliged to preserve the surrounding environment. As political infighting raged, work on the project was suspended, but after Chen's downfall it resumed. Chen was accused of accepting bribes from real-estate developers but these developers were never identified. Most intellectuals applauded his going, and not just because of the leading role he had played in ordering in the tanks in 1989. Chen Xitong had also poured billions into expanding Beijing's Capital Iron and Steelworks in a bid to create China's biggest industrial conglomerate. The steelworks ensured that industrial pollution steadily worsened during the 1990s.

Le Corbusier's dream of a society with no architects and only engineers had come true. 'The engineer, inspired by the Law of Economy and governed by mathematical calculation, puts us in accord with universal law. He achieves harmony,' he wrote. Anything built and designed by engineers, he insisted, was not only more practical, it was more beautiful, too. 'Working by calculation, engineers employ geometrical forms, satisfying our eyes by their geometry, and our understanding by their mathematics; their word is on the direct line of good art,' the visionary wrote in his *Towards a New Architecture*. Promoting architecture as geometry, he designed buildings in the form of 'pure' geometric shapes: rectangles, cubes, spheres and triangles. 'Primary forms are beautiful forms because they can be clearly appreciated,' he announced. This helped start an international fashion of erecting sculptures in public spaces that are no more than geometric shapes made of steel or concrete. Beijing has its fair share, too.

Chen Xitong, a traditionalist who disliked modern architecture, was ousted in the successful effort by President Jiang Zemin to establish his authority and assume control over the capital, destroying any possible rivals. Jiang had been appointed as general secretary of the party after 1989 by Deng Xiaoping, but only after the elderly Deng fell into a coma around 1995 was he able to consolidate his rule. A Shanghai-educated electronics graduate, Jiang brought in a team of engineers, promoted an electric power engineer, Jia Qinglin, to run Beijing, and gave Liu Qi, a graduate of the Beijing Institute of Iron and Steel Engineering, a career in steel-making. Nearly everyone in both the Beijing government and the top ranks of the party was an engineer. Jiang belonged to the 'third generation' of leaders, after Mao and Deng, and he surrounded himself with 'fourth-' and 'fifth-generation' engineers. Hu Jintao, who took over from Jiang Zemin in 2002, graduated in 1964 with a degree in hydropower engineering. Almost no one with a background in the humanities or law rose through the ranks. A large number of the fourth generation, including Hu Jintao, were educated at Qinghua University, the birthplace of the Red Guards – some of his Qinghua classmates played leading roles in the Cultural Revolution. By the late 1990s the core of the leadership included a group of forty former Red Guards from Qinghua who took part in the '100 days war' as leaders of the moderate April Fourteenth Faction. These include Jia Chunwang, a member of the Cultural Revolution Preparation Committee at Qinghua in 1966 and a leader of the April Fourteenth Faction, who had been captured by the Jinggangshan Regiment and tortured. He was appointed to run China's judiciary and police as Minister of Public Security, and the Minister of Justice was Zhang Fusen, another Qinghua militant. Ren Yansheng, one of the violent 'rods' during the 100 days war, served for a period as chancellor of Beijing University.[2]

The 'fifth generation' includes the children of top leaders who were in middle school in the 1960s and had taken part in the persecution of their school teachers. Among this group are the Minister of Commerce, Bo Xilai, son of veteran revolutionary Bo Yibo, and Deng Rong, daughter of Deng Xiaoping, who was a student at Beijing

Normal University Girls School when the headteacher was killed. After they spent from 1966 to 1969 spouting Maoist slogans and smashing up the 'Four Olds', Mao sent them to live in the countryside.

All power was concentrated in the hands of an elite who embodied Le Corbusier's ideal of engineers-as-architects and who were the product of Mao's programme to turn the Chinese into 'a blank sheet of paper'. Few members of this generation had studied or lived abroad and they were adrift, without firm roots in either Chinese or Western culture. They were open to taking any radical steps in the name of modernization. To this fatal mix was to be added yet another crucial factor, the Asian financial crisis of 1997. Economies across the region collapsed, causing political earthquakes in some countries. Student protests in Indonesia brought down the Suharto clan's thirty-year-long dictatorship. China's economy came to a standstill and, as 30 million jobs disappeared, its leaders feared a fresh wave of urban protests, like that of 1989. The state-owned enterprises were bankrupt and shedding millions of workers every year.

In order to restore growth and confidence in the country, the Communist Party grasped at a daring and ambitious plan – a 'New Deal' fiscal stimulus programme. Chinese leaders announced they would spend a trillion dollars on new infrastructure. At the core was a programme to create new housing for all 200 million urban Chinese and triple their average living space to 50 square feet. Chinese cities had been neglected by the state since 1958, while China's population had doubled. Now, the state would make up for lost time by launching another kind of 'great leap'. Jiang and his crusty premier, Zhu Rongji, started a frenzy of construction. In its scale the project dwarfed the reconstruction of Germany's bombed cities in the 1950s and mirrored Germany's Economic Miracle. It sucked in huge amounts of foreign investment and galvanized heavy industry. China needed ever greater quantities of concrete, steel, iron ore and power; these needs in turn drove up commodity prices worldwide. Soon China was consuming 40 per cent of the world's cement output and 35 per cent of the steel being forged. Before Premier Zhu stepped down, he declared that he had saved the country from collapse.

At last China's Communist rulers had both the opportunity and the means to create a new capital for their dynasty. Mao had wanted to level Beijing, including the Forbidden City, but his economic miracle in the Great Leap Forward had been a disaster and prevented the destruction. His successor, Jiang Zemin, could realize Mao's wish. The old plans to redevelop Beijing were thrown away. The biggest influence on the rebuilding plans was probably Deng Xiaoping, not Mao. He had died in 1997 at the age of 92, just over twenty years after launching the reforms. Although he never visited Hong Kong, he had consistently urged the Chinese to learn from the British colony and to 'Build more Hong Kongs'. Every city in China strove to implement this quasi-imperial edict as quickly as possible. Inevitably, Beijing's city planners began to refashion the city after Hong Kong's image. The offices of many municipal planning officials displayed an artist's impression of the city they wanted to administer. It was not Beijing at all, but a city night scene of illuminated office blocks set in a grid of streets. After 1949 Mao had wanted to turn Beijing into a 'city of production' – now 6,000 factories were closed or relocated. It was to become a city of high consumption, like Hong Kong, and powered by a service economy even though it lacked both a port and a stock exchange.

There was no public discussion or debate about the plan for Beijing; it seems to have been a decision taken in private by a handful of people. The 1997 plan was drawn up and implemented by unelected officials who had no ties either to the city or its people. First party secretary Jia Qinglin was born in Hebei province and had earlier run Fujian province. Liu Qi was a steel engineer from Jiangsu province who spent his career in Wuhan. Jia was replaced in 2003 by Wang Qishan, a banker from Shanxi province. Jia's deputy was Meng Xuenong from Shangdong province until a scandal over the severe acute respiratory syndrome (SARS) epidemic, when both men had tried to cover up the extent of the disease. Just before he was sacked, the official media portrayed Meng Xuenong as a popular 'man of the people'[3] who shared the hardships of ordinary citizens, but these leaders were remote figures, only glimpsed on television addressing meetings or seated on podiums. It was hard to tell them apart. You always saw a row of seated men of the same age, wearing the same suits, and with the same dyed black hair. You rarely heard them actually speaking; instead a voice-over invariably gave a summary of whatever decision had just been taken. They never appeared before crowds or answered media questions. No domestic media could openly criticize their plans, and sporadic public protests over land and compensation were quickly put down. After the uprising of 1989 was crushed no one dared organize any protests although most people opposed the massive relocation.

Exactly how many residents were forced out of their homes remains another secret, but at least a million have been removed from the area within the old city walls. In the late 1990s, the city planned to remove 2.4 million of the 6.5 million urban residents, a number that excluded the municipality's rural population. In old districts like Xuanwumen, only about 10 per cent of the original population was allowed to remain. Then in 2004 the city passed a blueprint which promised that the urban residents would fall to 1.93 million and 4 million people would be relocated to the suburbs. The government would speed up the construction of eleven new satellite towns to house them. People were dumped in bleak high-rise blocks thrown up around rural market towns like Tongxian or Changping before there were any services or even proper public transport links to the capital. A further 500,000 rural people would be moved from their homes in the surrounding mountains to help reduce the threat of sandstorms: to reverse the droughts and end the perennial sandstorms, the municipality embarked on another of its periodic afforestation projects, this time with the intention to cover half the municipality with trees.[4]

The pace and scope of the destruction took everyone by surprise, including its architects, most of whom continued to believe that the 26 square miles of the city would be spared. From 1998 onwards Beijing became a vast dusty construction site, perhaps similar to six hundred years ago when the Emperor Yong Le rebuilt the Mongol capital with 200,000 convicts and press-ganged peasants. Now there were 1.3 million peasants working on 7,000 construction sites and the dust was everywhere. The work went on in three shifts, day and night. If you lived anywhere near a building site, and nearly everyone did, it was impossible to sleep. Sometimes local residents, incensed by the incessant drilling and hammering, stormed out to attack the workmen, often with their own shovels and picks. The peasant labourers were treated little better than Yong Le's workforce. About 10,000 had died in accidents in the four years up to 2005 and they were lucky to get paid. In theory, they earned US$20 a month, but the authorities admitted in 2002 they were owed a staggering US$2.3 billion in back pay. They lived in crowded dormitories on site until the project was finished, but afterwards they were forbidden to actually live in Beijing and enjoy what they had helped build.[5]

The plan to rebuild involved much more than just rehousing residents. When China joined the World Trade Organization after 1999 it opened its markets, creating opportunities to redraw China's economic geography. Every major city in China sought to attract new industries. Beijing grabbed at anything and everything. It promoted itself as a centre for steel, petrochemicals, cars, a global logistics hub and an international convention and exhibition centre. It even fancied itself as an international harbour by touting the attractions of the transport opportunities provided by the old Grand Canal. The most lucrative opportunity lay in staking a claim as China's international financial centre. Beijing had the advantage of being home to the central bank and the financial regulatory bureaucracies. China already had two stock markets, in Shanghai and Shenzhen, and another in Hong Kong, but this did not stop the capital from making a play to become a financial centre. So the Xicheng district to the west of the centre knocked down 20,000 courtyard houses to build a Financial Street, which was trumpeted as another Wall Street. For a few years Beijing actually ran a commodity futures exchange, hoping to become the Chicago of China. However, the central government decided against permitting the city to become host to yet another financial marketplace and the commodity exchange closed down. Beijing might not become a rival to Tokyo, London or New York but it still decided to build a second central business district with a concentration of high-grade office buildings. In fact, every one of Beijing's core districts set about building its own business area. Chaoyang district, on the east side, had one with hundreds of skyscrapers; Xuanwu district to the south created another with an international media centre plus a hi-tech development zone; Haidian district to the north-east, which is full of universities, built one which aspired to be a second Silicon Valley, ready to incubate the next Microsoft Corporation.

After the Sydney Olympics of 2000, the International Olympic

Committee (IOC) felt it was China's turn and the country won its bid for the 2008 summer games. When IOC inspectors arrived in February 2001 the city sprayed dead grass with green paint on all open areas and produced an opinion survey showing that 97 per cent of the public supported the bid. The IOC delegates who voted in favour of Beijing believed it would strengthen China's modernization drive and stimulate faster political change. The immediate impact was exactly the reverse. Armed with an international mandate, the municipal government ruthlessly set about completing the demolition of the old city, evicting its residents, crushing opposition, confiscating land, and rebuilding at a helter-skelter pace. The government now had the perfect excuse to brush aside any objections to any or all of its schemes. Existing planning procedures could safely be ignored and some claim that a third of all urban projects approved after 1999 failed to comply with planning regulations.[6]

Projects that would take ten years to plan and build in the West were rushed through in a quarter of that time. The urgent task of building 'a world-class city' had to be finished in just seven years. A dizzying list of infrastructure projects was started almost at once: ten expressways, six ring roads, five new subway lines, several light rail links, a new airport, three large sewage works, a 700-mile natural was pipeline from Shaanxi province in western China to help switch from coal to gas, and the relocation of 1,100 factories. The number of hotels had to be doubled, buses had to be replaced, pedestrian crossings built, staff trained in English. A project to digitalize the city's communications alone was billed at US$3.6 billion.

This ambitious timescale was even reduced by two years so as to give enough time for the air quality to reach an acceptable level. Work on all new projects had to cease by mid-2006, a rule that was also ignored. In the winter of 1995 the levels of suspended particles in the air were six times higher than World Health Organization standards and double Chinese national standards. As more and more cars crowded onto the streets in the late 1990s, average concentrations of carbon monoxide and nitrogen oxide rose steeply. In the summer, when most of the rain falls, the city was covered by dense layers of rain clouds that trapped the smog for weeks on end, building up such noxious concentrations that the city government even advised people not to go to work but stay indoors. The average amount of dust kept rising, from 18.7 tons per square mile in 1991 to 20 tons in 1995, creating the worst possible environment to host the summer games.[7]

A habit of rushing important projects to meet arbitrary deadlines and brushing aside normal planning or consultation procedures is ingrained in China. The Great Hall of the People had to be designed and completed in just ten months, along with the other monumental constructions. Mao's ugly mausoleum had to be finished in just three months. Often the result was shoddy construction and flawed design. Beijing's new railway station on the western side of the city, billed as the largest in Asia, was, for instance, constructed in just two years, in time for the forty-sixth anniversary of the People's Republic in 1995. Afterwards it emerged that the pipes burst regularly, the concrete cracked and several platforms were too poorly made to be used. The biggest obstacle to Beijing's rapid expansion was the shortage of water. The city had never been able to support the demands of heavy industry, and by the 1990s its famous Jade Spring had dried up. The Miyun reservoir, built in the 1950s, was frequently no more than half full. Another major reservoir, Guanting, became so polluted its water was undrinkable. Farmers who ran short of water to irrigate their crops sank wells deeper and deeper until, by the 1990s, they were drilling down 1,000 feet.

All the rivers across north China were drying up and neighbouring Tianjin was in an even worse plight. Water had to be rationed and industrial waste used to water the city's market garden farms. As the subterranean aquifers were drained, Tianjin began to sink at an alarming rate and when subsidence brought it below sea level, the city was forced to protect itself by building sea dykes. The two cities had to reach further and further afield to find fresh sources of water. When even the Yellow River, the largest river system in the region, ran dry, the future of Beijing was in doubt. Many experts began to question whether it would not be wiser to relocate the capital to the Yangtze delta. It was clear, although the state did not readily admit it, that the crisis was caused by its own planning errors. The drought in the whole of the North China plain had begun forty years earlier when the Communists took over. They tripled the population and turned Beijing into a centre for heavy industry. In the early 1990s Beijing wanted a steel industry producing 10 million tons a year, more than either Britain or France produced. Finally, it was decided with great reluctance that the whole venture had to be abandoned and the Capital Iron and Steelworks should be relocated to the neighbouring Hebei province.

To save Beijing, China has had to embark on a massive engineering project equal to that of the Grand Canal. In imperial times it was food and other supplies that had to be shipped from the Yangtze, but now it was water. The solution, a south–north water diversion project, will cost at least US$50 billion when it is finished and require the relocation of some 400,000 people. Three routes are to be used, including one along the Grand Canal. As Liang Sicheng had concluded in the 1950s, Beijing's only natural role was to be the political and administrative capital of China. He had drawn up a neat plan that marshalled regular formations of ministries on either side of the State Council building, which was located outside the old city. The plan was rejected, and even in the 1990s many powerful officials at the State Council, the core of the government, still worked in courtyards dating back to the Ming dynasty. The municipal government, administering a population bigger than many European countries, was based in the old Legation Quarter.

As all these areas lay close to the Forbidden City, they could not easily be redeveloped. So even in the midst of the furious rebuilding that took place after 1998, no coherent design for an administrative centre ever emerged. Any planner or architect was immediately faced with sensitive and unresolved political issues. After the savage onslaught against the 1989 pro-democracy marchers, the Communist Party had ruled out any political reform. This implied that there would be no future separation between institutions of the Communist Party and those of the government, so they continued to share the same buildings. The party committee operating in a ministry did not need separate offices. It also meant that there would be no need for a parliament or offices of political parties. In the late 1980s, when political liberalization was in the air, a plot of land south-west of the Forbidden City was designated for the new parliament, with offices for the elected members. This was the site chosen ten years later to house the Grand National Theatre. The Communist Party membership continued to expand and, with some 70 million members, it needed more space to house its management and welfare operations. Because the party still maintained its status as a secret underground organization, new buildings were 'secret' in the sense that no plaque outside declared their purpose or function; only the presence of armed guards outside gave away their real nature.

As a centrally planned economy, China had more than a hundred ministries, but as the country moved towards a market economy, the number of ministries and their size fluctuated constantly. Every five years the government organization plan was comprehensively redrawn. The number of ministries fell to less than thirty by the end of the 1990s, but other bureaucratic institutions appeared or expanded. Without a permanent plan, each ministry acted as it thought best and commissioned buildings in a haphazard way. Many were granted plots along the Avenue of Eternal Peace (Chang'an Jie) and built lofty buildings that flouted the zoning law, which limited the height of buildings inside the old city walls. The Avenue of Eternal Peace became a huge valley of colossal buildings running east to west that competed with the imperial north–south axis. The unattractive avenue lacks both the grandeur that its name implies and the coherence of the Ming city design. The Beijing government then invited Germany's Albert Speer to design an expanded central north–south axis linking the Olympic Park with a newly developed district at the southern end. The choice of Albert Speer, the son of Hitler's chief architect, who had designed a similar axis for Berlin, who caused some controversy so the plan was dropped.

'The comparisons with my father are unfortunate but cannot be avoided,' the younger Speer said in an interview. 'What I am trying to do is to transport a 2,000-year-old city into the future. Berlin in the 1930s, that was just megalomania.'[8] The world's leading architects shuddered at the comparison with Hitler, but it was apt. Beijing promised the world a 'People's Olympics', but such vast changes to an ancient city could never have been done in anything but a totalitarian society. Imagine the residents of London or Paris voting for a mayor who promised to remove 4 million of them and to tear up every property deed that had ever been issued. China's leader, President Jiang, a portly and rather vain man, disliked being called a dictator and presented himself as a man of culture. A good amateur musician, Jiang Zemin would often take up the baton at state banquets and conduct the orchestra. He had a fine voice, too, and enjoyed nothing better than breaking down barriers by getting everyone to join in a singalong. Jiang often quoted Chinese poetry and loved showing off his knowledge of Western literature. In meetings with French President Jacques Chirac, he let slip how much he had enjoyed reading Victor Hugo. With Americans, he said how he liked Mark Twain and would even recite the Gettysburg Address. Compared with the upcoming Red Guard generation, he was genuinely cosmopolitan. Jiang had studied in the Soviet Union at the Stalin Automobile Works and could sing Russian songs, and later he had worked in Romania. He not only made sure everyone knew his taste for Western culture, but demonstrated a love for the arts by commissioning a new Grand National Theatre in 1997. Visiting Paris, he saw I. M. Pei's 'Pyramid' at the Louvre and decided he wanted something just as striking in his capital, a symbol of the new Beijing that would be as instantly recognizable as Sydney's Opera House.

President Jiang Zemin took the unusual step of holding an international competition for the best design. When forty-four of the best designs were put on display, a rare public debate sprang up on whether there should be anything Chinese in the new city. A joint petition by forty-nine members of the Chinese Academy of Science and the Academy of Engineering said that 'architecture demands a design that is practical, reasonable, is economically efficient and respects Chinese tradition and reality'. Among the Chinese architects who spoke out were some of Liang Sicheng's former disciples at Qinghua University's architectural department, such as Professor Wu Liangyong. He had designed the Ju'er Hutong in the late 1980s, the prototype for new low-level courtyard housing, and always tried to persuade the city government to adopt an organic approach to redeveloping Beijing. Professor Wu led a battle against the design of the Grand National Theatre, which became the key architectural battleground, a battle in which the traditionalists were completely routed.[9]

President Jiang Zemin ignored the protests and insisted that the winning design must be avant-garde and in no way traditional. He intervened to approve the design by Paul Andreu, a Frenchman with a successful record of designing airport halls for Nice, Jakarta, Cairo and the Charles de Gaulle Airport in Paris, the last of which subsequently collapsed, killing a number of Chinese passengers. In China, he had made a name by designing Shanghai's second airport in Pudong and an opera house for Guangzhou. Many of his innovative structures are of steel and glass with airy, light-filled interiors; the Grand National Theatre, his first attempt at designing a key civic building, was his best and most important work, he said. Its most striking features are the roof, made from translucent glass and titanium, and the entrance, a tunnel under a lake. Inside are four theatres, originally with seating for 6,000 but later cut back to 2,700. The site is opposite Zhongnanhai and behind the Great Hall of the People, at the centre of a rectangular lake; its height of 183 feet breaches regulations restricting tall buildings close to the Forbidden City. When the choice was announced, 108 Chinese architects signed another protest letter complaining that such an important building should not be the work of a foreigner who ignored or misunderstood Chinese traditions. In China, they pointed out, only a tomb would be entered by passing through such an underground tunnel. Locals thought it resembled a UFO and jokingly christened it 'The Alien's Egg' or simply 'The Big Turd'. Paul Andreu predictably argued that his design 'achieves harmony between tradition and modernity' because the round theatre sat in a square lake, a design often seen in China, such as temples where round altars, representing the heavens, are placed in square parks, representing the earth.

Le Corbusier's dream of levelling an ancient capital and replacing historic architecture with a series of gigantic buildings of geometric shapes had at last come true. A country ruled by engineers and devoted to modernity was perhaps the only place where it could have happened. After Paul Andreu's victory, the city quickly approved a string of daring buildings. A Swiss architectural firm, Herzog & de Meuron, designed an oval Olympic Stadium to sit next to a square National Swimming Centre, the 'Water Cube', designed by PTW of Australia and Ove Arup Engineering. Lord (Norman) Foster designed a third terminal at Capital Airport, Iraqi-born Zaha Hadid won a commission to design a complete urban residential and office complex, and Holland's Rem Koolhaas designed a huge trapezoidal tower to house the new headquarters for Chinese Central Television. Professor Wu fumed that China was being 'turned into a laboratory for foreign architects', but nobody was listening any more. President Jiang had made his wishes known.

By endorsing Andreu's design, President Jiang ended the party's rift with the progressive artists and architects. The younger generation of modern artists now found themselves sharing the same political platform with Jiang Zemin, as his favourite architect, Paul Andreu, explained. Echoing Le Corbusier, Andreu said that this design was born out of a desire to deliberately sever links with the past. 'The problem is that creation disturbs,' he wrote in defence of the Grand National Theatre design. 'It disturbs because it arises from new aspirations, and because creation, like life itself, is always linked to the present, not the past, to what we are, and to what we want to become, not what we were.'[10]

The party no longer seemed a stifling reactionary force dominated by old men who were stuck on fuddy-duddy styles, like socialist realism, or absurdly prudish about nudity and sex. Within three years, the Ministry of Culture was organizing exhibitions of New Wave art and selecting 'dissident artists' to attend the Venice Biennale, the world showcase for modern art. With the state once again the patron of 'progressive art', some artists began enthusiastically helping to design new buildings for the 2008 Olympics and finding they had plenty of commissions to put up geometric sculptures in public places all over China. Ai Weiwei, who had fled China in the 1980s and returned to set up his own studio and gallery, now had a commission to help with the 'birdcage' Olympic Stadium being built by Swiss architects Herzog & de Meuron.

A few 'dissident' artists did make works questioning the destruction of old Beijing. One was Zhang Dali who, over ten years, spray-painted graffiti on Beijing's buildings. Almost every night he would get on his bike after 11 p.m. and head off like an underground guerrilla. It took only a couple of seconds to spray the silhouette of a head and the letters AK47. Zhang Dali said he meant it as a protest against violence, dictatorship and state control, hence the AK47 (a Russian assault rifle), and to regain the walls for private expression. 'I wanted to establish a dialogue between the people and the city,' he said. As with so much modern art, Zhang found that his act of defiance was completely incomprehensible without an explanatory text. Even the police, when they came to arrest him in 1997, found its message baffling. They let him go, convinced he was not a member of a subversive organization after he showed them books about New York graffiti artists.[11] Beijing began to win itself a reputation as a centre for progressive art as the 'dissident artists' became accepted and their works fetched high prices. The artists' energy now went into preserving an abandoned set of factories known as 798, where many art galleries set up shop. They thought they should be preserved because they were built by East Germans and were a wonderful product of the Bauhaus design school. It left only a few old-school intellectuals like Shu Yi and Liang Congjie, the son of Liang Sicheng, to speak up for the cause of preserving old Beijing. Even Liang Congjie's hopes of establishing a memorial to his father failed.

The only outside voice raised in protest was that of UNESCO, which from 2002 repeatedly tried to persuade the Beijing government to protect the area around the Forbidden City, a World Heritage site, and to take the existing zoning regulations seriously. UNESCO reminded Mayor Meng Xuenong that 'the renovation of historic towns should take into account the urban project as a whole; the life in neighborhoods, their social and cultural identity; the participation and the implication of local people and, most importantly, the inhabitants' engagement in the elaboration and the management of the policies of renovation'.[12]

Many architects argued that it would be far too expensive and difficult to renovate the old city, although repairing old courtyard houses is simple and easy. There was no international campaign to save Beijing, like that for Venice, or a storm of protest, like that which greeted the destruction by the Taliban of the giant Buddhist statues at Bamiyan in Afghanistan. After the collapse of Communism nearly everywhere on earth, and the crushing of the democracy movement inside China, the party had trouble convincing the rest of the world that it had not become an anachronism, almost the last of a dying breed of Marxist-Leninist dictatorships. Now the high priests of international modernity, such as Paul Andreu and Rem Koolhaas, hailed Chinese leaders as modern and progressive.

Rem Koolhaas, founder of the Office for Metropolitan Architecture (OMA), had failed to persuade Berlin to accept his designs. After German unification, the city decided on a plan to limit the height of new buildings so they would be in harmony with the surviving classical and baroque architecture. Progress was slow as the rebuilding of the city was hotly debated and the government had to take note of the public mood. Koolhaas was also turned down by New York when he put forward designs for the new Twin Towers. In Beijing, however, he found a warm welcome and won a commission to build the new Chinese Central Television headquarters.

'It's the choice between associating yourself with a regime that is on the brink of opening up and propelling itself into a positive thinking future, or associating with another nation that is at the end of its height, propelling war plans into the world,' said Ole Scheeren, the OMA architect charged with seeing through the US$600 million project.[13] Twisted and looped like a double Z, the large, dramatic, cantilevered overhang, with a diamond-shaped façade, relies on construction techniques never attempted before. When completed, it will be among the largest buildings ever built, bigger even than the Sears Tower in Chicago. Among the forest of 300 skyscrapers in the Chaoyang central business district, the 750-foot tower will stand out. Covering the equivalent of forty football pitches, it will house 10,000 staff and the 2,000 visitors a day will rely on the largest elevator system for any building. 'It will be a huge hutong in the sky,' Ole said. Although Chinese Central Television had a record of putting out propaganda worthy of Goebbels, Ole was confident that China was changing and the new generation would be more open and democratic than the last. 'They want to be like the BBC,' he said. 'It is all about the future. It will be a vision of where they want to go.' For Koolhaas, the sheer size of the building was part of its beauty; such 'hyper-buildings' are the way of the future. Nowhere else but in China, he said, could architects hope to create the future of cities, testing out new construction in such a short time.[14]

Only in China could architects find such an enormously wealthy and politically powerful patron, the state – which ignored all official planning procedures and was able to afford such extravagant buildings. Beijing's first party secretary Liu Qi, who told IOC inspectors that the Olympics would be a 'People's Olympics' with an emphasis on 'individualism', also maintained that the goal was to 'integrate the 2008 Olympics with Chinese culture and spiritual civilization'.[15]

As a result, the world's leading architectural firms took part in an elaborate pretence. When they put forward designs, they claimed that they were at once pushing the boundaries of modern architecture and paying homage to Chinese history and culture. So when Australian architects Woodhead International put in a bid for a 2,800-room hotel in the Olympic Park, they declared that it was 'reflecting the Confucian philosophy used by the Ming emperors when they established Beijing in the fifteenth century'. Or when the American firm Johnson Fain Partners submitted a winning scheme to develop Chaoyang's Central Business District (CBD), it said: 'Our vision for the design of Beijing's new CBD is grounded in historic Chinese planning principles, including sun access and axial symmetry and at the same time is responsive to emerging global trends of the information age as well as conservation and sustainability.'[16]

The only internationally famous architect who repeatedly spoke out against the dangers of losing Beijing's magnificent legacy was the Chinese-American architect I. M. Pei. He even criticized the work of his sons, Lien Chung and Li Chung Pei, who designed the new Bank of China headquarters. They claimed that their concrete bunker design incorporated references to the courtyard houses demolished to make way for its construction, which meant that under the large atrium they included a goldfish pond and a rock garden. Pei senior complained that the design 'is not really right for such a location, so close to Tiananmen Square and the Forbidden City'.[17]

None of the world-famous architects, such as Zaha Hadid, Lord Foster, Pierre de Meuron, Jacques Herzog, and Rem Koolhaas, who flocked to Beijing (and the rest of China) ever spoke out in public to condemn Beijing's reconstruction, although they were often interviewed by the Chinese press. As laureates of architecture's most prestigious award, the Pritzker Architecture Prize, their words would have carried weight. While Beijing was being celebrated in the international architectural press, doubts began to creep in. It was evident that the new buildings were in many ways inferior to Ming design. In the summer, the strong sunlight reflected off the walls of glass from the high-rise office blocks heated up the expanses of concrete and asphalt, raising temperatures to a record 80 degrees centigrade. One spring, winds gusting along the valleys between the buildings reached typhoon speeds. In 2004 the gusts blew workers off a scaffolding, killing two and injuring hundreds. In the summer the combination of high temperatures, heavy rains and dust whirlwinds could create a deadly micro-climate. The old capital, with its canopy of trees and quiet courtyards which Lord Elgin had so admired in 1860, had never suffered such problems.[18]

The stress of constant change, the endless construction that has gone on day and night, the deadly dust and noise, has showed up in occasional reports on the health of Beijingers. They die, on average, fourteen years younger than in the rest of the country. A separate study has found that among those working in Zhongguancun, Beijing's would-be Silicon Valley, the average life expectancy was only fifty-three years – five years less than a decade earlier.

The massive motorway building programme, with six ring roads linked to broad highways that dissect the city, was supposed to speed drivers straight into the city. Little money went into creating a metro system and instead the car population grew from fewer than 500,000 to 3 million in just ten years. The city's streets rapidly became clogged and congested, compounding the pollution problem, especially during the overcast summer months. As the huge swathes of ramshackle housing and shops that had sprung up along many streets were demolished, the authorities tried to imitate the appearance of a European city by planting lawns. Since Beijing's climate is simply too dry to grow European grass, a special kind of hybrid desert grass had to be used that could survive the winter, provided it was fed copious amounts of water. These artificial lawns cover 299,000 square yards and give the appearance of open public spaces, although it is forbidden to walk or sit on this grass. No one can sit out in Tiananmen Square because the police are too nervous of public protests, nor near the Grand National Theatre. Articles appeared attacking the distressing minimalism of Andreu's designs for the theatre and its environs. At night, much of downtown Beijing feels like a deserted wasteland, with few pedestrians attempting the yawning distances between huge office complexes, department stores and hotels.

With the removal of the indigenous communities, much of old Beijing became inhabited by rich people from all over China and the rest of the world, because only they could afford the prices. They moved into new developments with names that were ostentatiously cosmopolitan. This meant one travelled from Upper Eastside to Palm Springs via Park Avenue, or went from Yosemite to Manhattan via Fifth Avenue. China's ruling class bought houses in Château Regalia, Merlin Champagne, Somerset House, attracted by sales material endorsed by pictures of Picasso, Beethoven and Pushkin. No Bauhaus for them. They wanted to live like French aristocrats. One developer even built his clients a copy of a seventeenth-century French chateau, Château Zhang Lafitte, as if to say that the revolution had now come full circle.

18

Destroy!

During the night, someone had painted the order 'Destroy' on the wall of Mr Du's house. He woke up to find the single character *chai* hastily daubed in white paint inside a circle. It was conspicuously large, like the sign of some malevolent secret society. Du Zhonglian did not seem the sort to be easily cowed. He wore a black leather coat with a sheepskin collar stretched across a barrel chest and his face had the tough broad look of a wrestler. 'Who did this?' he repeated in bewilderment, looking up and down the narrow hutong as if he might still catch an urchin fleeing with a pot of whitewash and a large brush. Then he laughed in the way some Chinese people do when they are angry or frightened. 'Of course, they only come at night.'

Signs like these appeared all over old Beijing in the months after the city was chosen to host the Olympic Games in July 2001. They seemed like a warning out of the Old Testament from an implacable deity notifying the inhabitants of Nineveh or Babylon of their impending destruction. Du Zhonglian's real name was Viktor Dubinin, the same as his ancestor, a Cossack born in Ukraine. He belonged to a small community of Russian Orthodox Christians, the descendants of five Cossacks, Romanov, Khabarov, Kristov, Jakovlev and Dubinin, who had been brought to Beijing in 1685 by the Manchu emperor Kangxi. As Mongol power waned across Asia in the seventeenth century, the Russian and Manchu empires steadily expanded into the vacuum, rapidly acquiring territory and moving steadily closer to each other. The tsarist and Manchu empires collided on the banks of the Amur River. The Manchu emperor had sent a force of 15,000 men to besiege 1,000 Cossacks in the Albazinian fortress north of the river, which the Chinese call Heilongjiang, the Black Dragon River. Du said the five Cossacks were emissaries who had been taken hostage and brought to Beijing early in the conflict. 'Kangxi admired them because they were so big and strong, so he saved them,' he said. According to legend, the Emperor Kangxi married off the five men to the widows of executed prisoners because no one else was willing to marry the foreigners. The Albazinians, as the community is called, hotly dispute this. 'We had a very high social status because we were made banner-men, members of the Embroidered Yellow Banner,' Du told me. This elevated his ancestors to the ranks of the Manchu aristocracy and they married high-born Mongol or Manchu women from the same banner. Du pulled out his wallet and showed me his identity card to prove that his nationality was listed as Mongol.

By becoming bannermen in the personal service of the emperor, they were permitted to live within the city walls, something no Chinese were allowed to do. Emperor Kangxi gave them a former temple to live in, a Guandi temple to the God of War, with extensive grounds. The Cossacks petitioned the court to be allowed to bring from Russia a priest so they could continue to practise their religion. Their wish was granted and for more than two hundred and fifty years the headquarters of the Russian Orthodox mission to China was based there. Du said that parts of the original temple still exist in the grounds of the Russian embassy, near to his house. 'About a thousand of us all lived in here in a self-sufficient community until 1955,' Du recalled. The community had a farm, orchards, a mill and an apiary. 'It was the largest farm in Beijing and I still remember we had black-and-white Swiss cows ... Now we are fighting to stay in our homes ... After three hundred years of history, what will be left of us? Look at my son,' he continued, nodding in the direction of a strapping 27-year-old. 'He cannot even understand the Slavonic church service because he cannot speak Russian. When we leave here and scatter across Beijing, the young will forget their heritage, the ties that bind us together will be gone. This land belongs to us but the authorities say we have no legal documents to prove it. But where can we get such documents?'[1]

When the first *chai* signs appeared, residents across Beijing knew they had just a month or so to organize their resistance. In parts of the city, local party officials spread the word that putting up posters would incur two years' imprisonment and that anyone trying to organize a street protest would disappear for four or five. Local party committees have the power to sentence troublemakers to a two- or three-year stretch in a labour camp. It is termed an administrative decision and a recommendation by a street committee can be enough – no trial or other judicial review is required. If the local officials wish, they have the power to extend a prison term in the same manner.

Sometimes desperate residents tried to band together and appeal to the courts, but the lower courts were often under the control of the same officials who ran the property development companies. Others sought to put pressure on the local government by appealing to foreigners to publicize the issue abroad, but that ran the risk of involving the much-feared Ministry of State Security. Its agents had been known to simply kidnap people from the street in broad daylight, and then the hapless homeowner would be untraceable for weeks.

Once the developers were ready to start demolishing an area, they hired a special 'demolition and removal office' called a *chai qian ban*. They never dealt directly with the residents. These were really a bunch of thugs who set up a temporary office on the site. They claimed they were acting in the name of the government, but they were actually working for the developer. Their job was to force people out, and they could earn extra bonuses if they persuaded people to leave quickly.

Residents said that a gang of big men, usually peasants from out of town, would come round at night. If the residents didn't take the government's offer, then the toughs would threaten them with the police or hint at beatings or arson. The thugs would offer people more money if they agreed to leave early. It was hard to keep up a united front, because some caved in quicker than others and moved out. Everyone knew that once the *chai* signs went up, the clock was already ticking. People like the Du family came under a lot of psychological pressure to settle. Yet across Beijing, many dared to take to the streets or gather outside party offices. It was a low-intensity war of small guerrilla actions, fought hand to hand in the trenches and worksites by ordinary people who had few weapons.

When I first arrived in Beijing, its 6 million inhabitants seemed a uniform mass, clad alike in drab Mao blue or green suits. I never suspected that there were still distinct communities who had survived intact through a century of turmoil and change. Some were older, far older, than the Albazinians. The Muslims of Beijing claim to have lived around the Temple of the Green Truth in Ox Bow Street without a break for a thousand years. The most famous mosque in the city lies in Beijing's oldest quarter, dating to 996 and the Liao dynasty, which first built a walled city. In design and layout, the mosque at Ox Bow Street looked exactly the same as any other kind of Chinese temple, but inside is a quotation from the Koran written using Chinese characters: 'In the name of Allah, the Beneficent, the Merciful. O Mankind! Lo! We have created you male and female, and have made you nations and tribes that ye may know one another.'

There were once around sixty mosques in Beijing, serving a population of some 250,000 Muslims. How they first came there nobody quite knows any more. Perhaps traders from Central Asia married local women. Members of this mixed race are now known as 'Hui' and their religion is called *qing zhen*, or 'green truth'. The green tile roofs of the Ox Bow mosque once peeked out at a shabby maze of streets and markets in Xuanwu district, famous for restaurants selling lamb dishes. White-capped men with hooked noses bought rich meaty broths, spicy kebabs and braised lamb hotpots, eaten with tiny white buns garnished with sesame seeds. Now they, too, were being forced to leave. The mosque was being carefully restored as a sort of museum and to showcase the government's respect for religious freedom. However, the rest of the neighbourhood was being torn down. The bulldozers were still at work demolishing the few remaining houses as I walked along ghostly alleys that wound amongst the piles of rubble. The land looked naked and indecent. A few women and children stooped down picking through the rubble, looking for wood, copper wiring and ironmongery.

A row of colonnaded shops had already gone up along a new road, which was wide and as straight as a ruler. The new buildings were made from concrete. The roofs were decorated with green tiles and had arabesque upper windows intended to give the impression of something out of the *Arabian Nights*. A few idle men clustered on the kerb smoking, but they hesitated to be drawn into conversation. One of them offered to sell me a green corroded copper coin he had found nearby. How old it was, he couldn't say, but it could be very, very old, dating back to the Mongols.

Some of Beijing's Muslims had been brought to the city by the Mongol khans to help rule China. Marco Polo had called them 'Saracens' in his *Travels*, educated men who were given important posts. Khublai Khan employed Muslim architects, including one listed in Chinese records as Yeh-Hei-tieh-erh, to help design the Mongol capital in the thirteenth century. Muslim and Persian doctors were hired to staff the newly founded hospitals and the Imperial Academy of Medicine. A Persian astronomer, Jamal Al-Adin, had been brought to the court in 1267 to run an Institute of Muslim Astronomy. Jamal Al-Adin brought with him diagrams of how to make an armillary sphere, sundials, an astrolabe and a terrestrial globe, and he produced a new and more accurate calendar, known as the *Wannian Li*, Ten Thousand Year Calendar. Now, after over seven hundred years, their descendants were being evicted and dispersed.

Digging was about to start for the foundations of new high-rise blocks, and there was already a huge trench for the natural gas and sewage pipelines. At one of the remaining houses, a lean man in a brown woollen jumper appeared at the door of his courtyard house and examined me cautiously from the shadows. He seemed willing to talk and his wife appeared briefly to inspect me and then disappeared. 'They've cut the water off so we will have to go soon,' said the owner curtly. 'We can't stay any more. It is only for the rich . . . That's what they will build for the rich outsiders,' he said and pointed to some twenty-storey high-rise buildings nearby.

His was a 'nail household', so called because the owners refused to be pulled up and displaced. Perhaps he was holding out in the hopes of extracting some better compensation deal. He smiled slyly and tapped his nose, which was more prominent and hooked than is common. 'You had better come in then. It is not safe to talk,' he said and held the door open a little wider. We sat down on a hard leather sofa and his wife brought eight-treasure tea, sweetened with rock sugar. As he talked, I looked at a woollen tapestry that hung on the wall showing golden minarets against a purple sky.

'Mecca?'

'The Dome of the Rock.'

Like many Chinese Muslims, he called himself Ma, short for Muhammad, and said his family had lived in this house since the

Ming dynasty. His ancestors had been poor people brought from Yunnan province far to the south to work in the city built by the Ming emperor Yong Le. Some Muslims rose to powerful positions in his army. One general, Chang Yuchun, had built a mosque in Li Bai Hutong (Prayer Hutong), which still exists. Another famous Hui was Zheng He, a eunuch from Yunnan province. A huge man nearly seven feet tall, he led seven maritime expeditions in the early fifteenth century and returned from Africa with China's first giraffes. Ma explained that their title to this land should have been beyond dispute. After 1949 the state issued new title deeds and each month landowners had to pay land taxes. During the Cultural Revolution, the government 'lost' their deeds of title and the owners had to accept new 'tenants'. All property was divided up and those without any moved into other people's property. When the Cultural Revolution was declared to be over, they were given back their title deeds after 1979, provided they did not chase off the new 'tenants'. The 'tenants' might be persuaded to leave but only if the owners provided them with satisfactory accommodation elsewhere. 'We could only get rid of these people by buying them new property, it could cost a lot of time and money to get them to leave,' Ma said.

Then in 1982 the state changed the law and formally amended the constitution. All urban land became the property of the state, as was the case in the countryside. The Ma family only had the right to use the land and as such could not sell or transfer it. In this way, Ma and other families actually only enjoyed legal rights to the possession of the bricks and mortar of the building and not to the land. If the state chose to demolish a building for the purpose of building a road, then it had only to compensate the owners for the cost of replacing the building material. Since most owners could not afford to get rid of their 'tenants' or renovate their houses after decades of neglect, the buildings became extremely dilapidated. In early 1992 the government then introduced fresh regulations for the 'reform of dangerous residential buildings', enabling them to order the demolition of any building considered old and dangerous. In this way a local government could decide to level an entire neighbourhood whenever it saw fit, simply by declaring it a slum.

'According to the law all these houses were too old and dangerous,'

Ma said. 'We went to the court. We signed petitions. We wrote letters and gathered outside the Xuanwu party headquarters, but they said we had to obey the law. That meant all you can do is fight for the best compensation but you couldn't do it as a community. That was not allowed.'

One man who tried was Feng Xiaonian. He collected 10,000 signatures for a petition and tried to fight the destruction through the courts but with little success; the courts are controlled by the party. He calculated that, from 1990 to 2000, Beijing government officials and developers had earned 126 billion yuan (US$15 billion) by acquiring the land cheaply and reselling it to developers and foreign investors. For a real-estate company, the temptation to bribe an official with cars, apartments and envelopes stuffed with cash was overwhelming.[2] A regulation issued in 1991 protected the homeowner to some extent by insisting that he must be compensated with a house of the same size, but there was nothing to stop the authorities from offering the displaced an apartment in a distant suburb.

In Xuanwu district, where Ma's house and the Ox Bow mosque are situated, the local government set up its own joint ventures with developers and simultaneously had the power to remove residents, determine their compensation, and construct and sell them the newly built property. All these activities were carried out by government officials operating through a series of shell companies, which made it hard to identify those responsible. Only in 2001 was a law passed giving residents the right to appeal to an independent appraiser to value the property, but by this time it was too late for Ma and everyone else. 'Really, they are all just a band of *tu fei*', Ma said, using an old-fashioned word for robber bands that prey on hapless peasants.

Sometimes, all the residents could glean about the new landlords was from a small bill poster pasted onto a wall at the entrance to an alleyway, which would inform them that the International Investment Corporation or another such anonymous company had acquired the land. It was such an easy risk-free way to make money that every department in the Xuanwu district government wanted to join the scramble. Even the Cultural Relics Bureau set up its own real-estate company that knocked down the listed properties it was supposed to be protecting. In the media, the hasty demolition of these ancient neighbourhoods was always presented as an urgent slum clearance, an expression of the government's benevolent and pressing desire to improve the living conditions of the inhabitants. The planning, however, neglected to include public transport from their new homes in satellite cities so the residents were effectively being expelled from Beijing to make a new life as exiles. The costs of renovating the old buildings and providing new sewage and water pipes were said to be prohibitively expensive for these poor people. 'We were actually quite rich once,' Ma remarked casually, 'but in the Cultural Revolution we lost all our family heirlooms. One thing I can never forget was this oil painting, a portrait of Jipar Han by this foreigner.'

Jipar Han was the real name of Xiang Fei, the Fragrant Concubine, a Turkish princess with whom the eighteenth-century emperor Qianlong had fallen hopelessly in love. He had ordered Jesuit priests who were living in his court to build a special palace for her in the Yuanming Yuan. After conquering eastern Turkestan, Qianlong had brought her, together with 800 Turkish families, including 300 musicians and acrobats, to Beijing. Some of the men were enrolled in the Red Banner and quartered in the south-west corner of the Forbidden City, near what was later the National Art Gallery. One of the captured Turks narrowly missed killing Qianlong when he took part in an archery contest held in Chengde, the summer hunting retreat north-east of the capital. The descendants of this group were still living in this same corner of the city in the 1980s, worshipping at a large mosque on Wangfujing, selling kebabs and whispering offers of hashish to any passing foreigner.

Jipar Han was so homesick in Beijing that she would stare blankly towards the north-west with tears running down her cheeks. Qianlong built her a tower, called Ladies' Gazing Tower, and a mosque, which stood opposite the southern entrance to Zhongnanhai (where Chinese leaders now live), and he ordered his guards to watch her night and day in case she committed suicide. Qianlong commissioned the Italian Jesuit, Giuseppe Castiglione, to present him with a portrait of the Turkish beauty. Castiglione painted Han in steely Italian armour so that, with her cascading hair and dark eyes beneath a helmet, she looks like a noble operatic heroine.

'My grandfather and father kept it in the house but in the Cultural

Revolution they got nervous about keeping something foreign. The Red Guards were searching every house,' Ma recalled. The imam of Ox Street mosque was beaten to death and many Hui were forced to eat pork. 'Anyway, they threw this thing away; it was wrapped up in a scroll, and I have never been able to find it again.' As Ma spoke, I racked my brains for Castiglione's Chinese name. It suddenly hit me. 'Do you mean you had the portrait of Jipar Han by Lang Shi-nong? If so, even a copy would be worth millions now.' 'Yes, that's the one,' he nodded with a smile.

Later I heard about one family whose resistance won them a partial victory. On a spring Sunday morning, which fell on the festival of Qing Ming, when it is the duty of every Chinese to sweep the graves of their ancestors and comfort the dead with offerings, I set off to find the new home of Mrs She Youzhe after she and her family had been forced out of their old home. They now lived in a flat near the Temple of Heaven, one of the great state temples whose round, tower-like hall with a roof of azure blue tiles makes it the most famous architectural landmark in China. Although I had often been there, I soon lost my way. The higgledy-piggledy juxtaposition of temples and factories, crooked alleys and ramshackle courtyard houses had gone. Now there were broad straight roads so wide they could only be crossed by footbridges. On either side marched rows of shopping malls, office tower blocks and residential housing developments. None of them had any features and the cheap hand-me-down modernism made me at first irritated and then indignant. Every new urban development in China was identical to this. Try as I might, I simply could no longer call to mind just what had been here and what it looked like before it had all been demolished. What was wrong with my memory?

In Beijing, it is easy enough to orient oneself. As befits a great imperial city, it had been aligned along a north–south axis and the principal streets made a grid. People would give directions by saying: 'Go north, then at the second street turn east, and then north again.' Eventually I found the apartment and Mrs She led me to her family shrine. Her story begins in the Ming dynasty, which after some two hundred and fifty years was in its final days when the last emperor, Chongzhen (r. 1628–44), heeded the advice of his eunuchs and ordered the execution of General Yuan Chonghuan for high treason. General

Yuan's sentence, an excruciating death by a thousand cuts, was announced at the Meridian Gate, the southern entrance to the Forbidden City. So on a summer morning in 1630 soldiers dragged the loyal general to a post where an executioner was waiting with a bright razor.

One night after the general's death, Mrs She's ancestor, the loyal soldier She Yishi, secretly crept to the execution ground where the general's body was being displayed, cut off his master's head and took it home. It was an audacious act of defiance which, if he had been caught, would have cost him his life. In the grounds of a hospice used by visitors and residents up from Guangdong, the family buried the head, hoping to hide it in a place full of corpses. No member of the family dared reveal the existence of this gruesome relic for 152 years, by which time the Ming dynasty was long gone. When the Manchu emperor Qianlong heard the story, he was so pleased by this example of loyalty and courage that he commissioned a shrine which would foster the general's virtues of bravery and honour. The She family stayed and looked after the shrine and lived there so long that the street in front of it became *She Jia Guan*, the Shrine of the She Family.

Nearly four centuries later I stood before the general's tomb and watched as two figures, dressed in the long flowing robes of the Ming and holding flowers in their hands, bowed their heads in solemn reverence. Spring can bring strong winds heavy with fine Gobi sand to Beijing. The dust-filled winds blanket the city in a stifling miasma but that day we were lucky. The skies were high and clear with the bright blue of the open steppes, and the incense from the altar rose straight and sweet. Mrs She Youzhe, a small, frail figure with a bun of untidy grey hair, began her speech, her arms held on either side by two tall students from the Beijing Arts School. 'We passed on a promise that was made by my ancestors. If I did not keep my promise, I would be unworthy of my ancestors,' she pleaded as nearby a piledriver started up, drowning out her firm voice.

A group of migrant workers stood on the balcony of their dormitory looking down at the small crowd of worshippers before the tomb. The building pressed hard up against the outer wall of the tomb and as I turned my head to look up at them, in every direction I could see giant cranes and the scaffolding of dozens of uniform, brightly coloured high-rise structures. The general's tomb, a dome of concrete behind a 6-foot-high stela, seemed much diminished amid the rows of concrete giants, a tiny island of history.

'Before dying, each generation told the next generation: "Bury me next to General Yuan." My ancestor was a soldier, She Yishi, who served the general when he won his famous battle and defeated Nurhachi in 1625. It was the only battle in which Nurhachi was ever defeated.' Nurhachi was a great warrior who founded the Manchu state north of the Great Wall, which later conquered the great Ming empire. His descendants went on to rule China and double its size and population; they became absolute monarchs of the largest empire history has seen. After his victory over Nurhachi, General Yuan wanted to press forward and take advantage of his success but was recalled and replaced. He was promoted to Minister of Defence but five years later became the victim of intrigue. The powerful eunuch Wei Zhongxian became a jealous rival and had him impeached on various false charges of secretly negotiating with Nurhachi. 'The Ming dynasty was very corrupt but people respected General Yuan because they knew he was a patriot who loved his country,' Mrs She continued. 'No other country has such examples of loyalty and patriotism. Everyone should study and learn from him.'

General Yuan came from a clan in the far south of the empire, so the offerings that lay piled up on the small altar came from distant Guangdong: bananas, mangoes and lychees. They were brought by his descendants, clansmen in Dongguan, who still revere his deeds. Their home region in the Pearl River delta is now crowded with factories churning out sneakers, toys and Christmas decorations. With a voice occasionally breaking with emotion, Mrs She repeated the story of the shrine to her audience of arts students and workers. 'Culture is very important. Our culture lies in our roots. This represents our history, our living tradition.'

The tomb had once been much bigger and more impressive, a complete shrine, with halls and statues set in a garden with a number of ancillary buildings. After 1950 the authorities built the Number 59 Middle School in the grounds but left the shrine untouched inside the schoolyard. The She family had written to Chairman Mao Zedong, appealing for his help and in 1952 he responded, ordering the mayor, Peng Zhen, to ensure that the grave and the shrine would be protected for ever. When in 1966 the Cultural Revolution broke out, the local schoolchildren became Red Guards and, obeying Chairman Mao's call to destroy 'the Four Olds', attacked the family and smashed up the shrine.

'They said we were landlords and they killed some of our relatives,' Mrs She said. The kids demolished the main temple, hammering the family graves and stela with its famous inscriptions. They even hunted for the general's head, for they believed it was made of solid gold. She and her husband were forced to live in one small building and eleven other families moved in to occupy the rest of the shrine. 'I was in hospital giving birth when it happened. When I came out, I crept out at night to see the graves but they were already destroyed. Of course, I felt very bad, but at that time who would dare say anything? Anyone could be beaten to death,' she said. The She family ended up living next to the home of one of the most violent Red Guards.

Some eighteen years later she and their unpleasant neighbours were still there when the local government of Chongwen district formally recognized the shrine as a historic relic. In theory this meant the shrine was again placed under state protection. In the 1980s the city government made plans to preserve old Beijing. During these years Mrs She went back and forth to government departments pleading for money to restore the site, but to no avail. However, she had managed to recover fragments of the smashed stones and the Yuan Clansmen Association in Hong Kong helped her repair the memorial stela.

The situation changed dramatically after 1997 when a new plan for Beijing was adopted. Secretly it called for almost the entire demolition of old Beijing and the whole area around the shrine was earmarked for redevelopment. Mrs She pulled out notebooks listing all her visits and the interviews given to the foreign and domestic press. Her neighbours mocked her as a madwoman, she said, for attempting the impossible. When the Chaoyang Jiu Ding Kaifa Gongsi, a property development company partly owned by the district government, began demolishing the neighbourhood, it saw no need to preserve the shrine at all. It did everything to force her and the other families to leave. Finally, the She family were the only ones hanging on in the middle of the construction site, with their water and electricity cut off. Against a government that brooked no opposition or dissent, and with a horrible and terrifying history of violence behind it, few Beijingers dared try to organize collective resistance. In the circumstances what Mrs She achieved was remarkable. She mobilized the Chinese and foreign media to report her story to the extent that in Hong Kong, her supporters even wrote and performed a play, *An Eternal Promise*. There was talk of a making a full-length feature film. In response the developers said nothing. 'I told them – this is our property. You do not have the right to tell us what to do. We have stayed here for five centuries through invasion and occupations by many armies,' Mrs She said.

On 20 May 2002 the developers gave notice of a final deadline. The company promised her the right to return when the building was over. The next day she had no choice but to retreat in defeat. In the circumstances, it was an honourable defeat. General Yuan's shrine would be preserved even though most of the land belonging to it was lost. The authorities never made good their promise to allow her to return and live in the shrine, but it did become a state museum. 'They told me that no one could live here because it is now a museum and there are regulations for museums. In a museum you are not allowed to prepare foods or to cook. But we lived here for seventeen generations without harming it,' she snorted.

All they now possessed after seventeen generations were some bits kept in a cardboard box which she brought out to show me. Inside were two fragments of an enamel street nameplate, one blue, the other red, on which were the three characters *She Jia Guan* – She Family Shrine.

19

The Eternal Present

A new foreign resident in Beijing used to have to apply at the Office for the Registration of Aliens, which in early 1985 lay, unmarked by any formal sign, secluded behind high walls near the Forbidden City. Like the luxuriant jungle creepers that had spread their grip over the ruins of Angkor Wat, the bureaucracy in China seemed to have multiplied and spread its tentacles into the oddest crevices of the decaying imperial city. For some reason the office was housed in a courtyard off Nanchizi, which runs just parallel to the east side of the palace, and to get there I used to cycle under an archway, gratefully leaving behind the traffic going round the dry concrete field of Tiananmen Square, and enter the shadows cast by arching elm trees. This was a cooler, more intimate world.

Vestless elderly men perched outside their houses, displaying hairless bellies; they played chess or minded small children, whose bottoms showed through split trousers, while their parents pottered about washing vegetables, throwing out wastewater or collecting briquettes of coal. Life was lived outdoors and on hot nights residents dragged their beds onto the pavement; in the afternoons many would still be dozing on the beds' steel frames. The inhabitants displayed an engaging indifference both to the neglected dynastic grandeur around them and to the bleak totalitarian monuments. Beijing was then a village where everyone behaved just as people do in any remote rural setting.

One entered the office through a door in a steel gate that was bolted shut during the two-hour lunch break. Once inside, the visitor was taken aback to find that, like the Tardis of Dr Who, there was a space that appeared much larger than anticipated. Several courtyards stretched one behind another and police officers drifted slowly between them carrying bowls of food, doing their washing or sus-pending clothes from washing lines. Sometimes one caught them squatting as they rinsed out their hair in pink-and-white enamel basins. The police officials charged with controlling the movements of foreigners evinced the same disobliging indolence. Behind the counter in one courtyard building that might once have housed a temple or a mandarin, the staff yawned and fiddled with their fans. They looked discouragingly at whoever entered with a request and then sternly barked out 'Impossible!' or '*Mei You!*' ('there isn't any').

In the 1980s it was impossible to leave the country or even get out of Beijing without first obtaining an official permit from these officials. One could not even buy a plane or train ticket without first humbly begging for their chop of official approval. If one arrived too late, the officials relished telling one that it was entirely one's own fault, but with the sort of habitual rudeness that gave no individual offence. Then one's precious document would be wrapped in a rubber band and tossed in a shabby drawer. A combination of slovenliness, tedium and fear permeated every public building the length and breadth of this vast empire. Every office had a special smell, a distillation of blocked toilet drains, dusty filing cabinets, dirty water slopped across floors, cockroach poison scattered in corners and jam jars filled with stewing green tea. For a journalist, any application also required summoning a member of the secret police from some other building where the files were stored. These officials had to give their approval and they had vague but undefined powers to make life intolerable; they could ultimately expel you, arrest your friends or imprison your contacts.

Twenty years later there was a new Office for the Registration of Aliens, housed in a vast twin office block that loomed over an elevated expressway jammed with traffic. The staff now sat in crisp uniforms staring at the latest type of digital flat-screens in an atmosphere of air-conditioned efficiency. It was undeniably an improvement on the old office and evidence of the great changes transforming China. Sometimes I would go there and feel nostalgic for the Beijing of the 1980s, which had a special charm, a flavour one found nowhere else. My job was to report on the changes in China, but troubling doubt often nagged at me. The stories I wrote omitted something vital.

Impressive though all the new buildings might be, I came to wonder if they were not another prop to create an illusion of modernity. Beijing's role as the capital was to serve as a stage for propaganda, to show what the party wished to do. It always proved very hard to get at the truth of anything, especially whether Beijingers had really embraced the changes or were just pretending, taking part in a charade.

I had arrived in search of exoticism, of girls with almond eyes and slender necks, and found a totalitarian state of spies and informers incongruously planted amidst these almost medieval slums. The two seemed deliciously mixed up. As the reforms went on and China opened up to the outside world, the ladies at the Office for the Registration of Aliens started smiling at me in a more friendly way. More often than not they were diligently studying some dog-eared English-language textbooks when I arrived. Before rummaging in a desk drawer for their chop, they would muster up as much charm as they could and start a conversation. It was confusing. They were the enemy, so how much should one reveal about one's work or life? And could one risk flirting with a policewoman earnestly learning English? And why were they learning English anyway?

The hope never quite left me that perhaps one of those tough police ladies, Miss Liu or Miss Wang, would somehow go from practising English phrases to taking me behind the propaganda façade and revealing the true China. She would volunteer to unravel some buried secrets of the Cultural Revolution or offer details of the mysterious political struggles unfolding behind the crimson walls of Zhongnanhai. But nothing like that ever happened. The Chinese seemed hopelessly trapped in their world of shabby apartments where the lifts never worked, the stairwell stank of cabbage and old bicycles cluttered the hallways. No one showed any inclination to talk except in political platitudes.

Instead, one often found oneself taking part in political theatre so absurd that it only revealed how the rulers of Beijing understood the outside world. One Monday morning, I was invited to join the commuters and take a ride on Bus Route 21 with the model conductress Li Suli. In a bid to restore public confidence in the city's crude, inefficient buses, the propaganda department of Beijing had dreamed up a scheme to convince the public, against the daily evidence of their own eyes, that Li Suli represented the future of public transport. Normally, to get off public buses requires great physical strength to push past the pack of desperate people trying to storm on board as soon as the doors open. Many people are forced to spend three or even four hours a day commuting, so the struggle to find a seat is generally waged on a take-no-prisoners basis. Our office cleaning lady once described how it took her son, burdened with a heavy bag of schoolbooks, two hours to get home from school. It took so long because he often failed to push his way on. Then he had to wait for the next bus to come along and try again. Taking a crowded bus in winter, when dark, was even more frightening. The passengers stand crammed with their neighbours in total darkness because, out of a wartime mentality, the lights go off.

The bus conductors are perched in a booth screeching abuse through their microphones, but rarely stirring to control the violent stampede of passengers. Yet here was Li Suli, a petite woman in make-up, with lacquered hair and a porcelain smile. She stood at the entrance to the bus, politely greeting each astonished passenger with a handshake as they clambered up the steps. Inside, this particular bus was like no other I had ever been on. It was spotlessly clean. Little chintzy floral curtains were tied on bows by the windows, and white doilies had been carefully folded on the back of the seats.

'Watch out. Please, be careful,' she cooed over the microphone each time the bus jerked forward. 'Take care, now,' she added in honeyed tones, solicitously offering a steadying arm to each passenger who got off. She told me she got up every day at 4 a.m. to wash the bus, and for the convenience of visitors she had memorized phrases in a dozen Chinese dialects as well as English. With me on the bus was Jiang Shan, an actress and star of several popular television soap operas. She had a distinct jutting chin and long wavy hair and it turned out that my presence was required to bear witness to Jiang Shan's repentance. 'As a young actress, I made many mistakes, suffering several setbacks in my career because all I thought about was myself,' she said in a choked-up, strangled way as the bus burrowed its way upstream against a lemming-like horde of cyclists. 'Now I realize how wrong I was,' she continued, delicately wiping away a tear that appeared in the corner of an almond eye. It turned out she was in the doghouse for selfishly refusing to perform at a concert organized by the party because the fee was too low. As the morning on the bus continued, she now declared herself to be positively inspired by Li Suli to change her thinking. 'You are truly a model for everyone to study,' she gushed. 'A model of doing true-hearted kindness for the public good.'

A few days later my photograph showing me with Li Suli and the enchanting Jiang Shan appeared prominently on the advertising hoarding on Wangfujing, the city's premier shopping street. People told me they recognized me from the newspaper and I felt oddly pleased. At last I had found my place and purpose in this strange society. Sometimes I caught myself actually beginning to enjoy the make-believe world of propaganda and then I fell to thinking that all this play-acting was like Peking Opera, an intrinsic part of Beijing's culture. Or more like a living theatre of the absurd. How many conversations did one have while attempting simple things, like asking a lift attendant when the lift was coming, sitting in a taxi with a driver who didn't want to go anywhere, calling up an official reluctant to confirm anything, including his name – all exchanges that seemed straight out of Pirandello or weighted with menacing Pinteresque pauses. Much was firmly in the *Waiting for Godot* vein of dialogue, exchanges filled with a mixture of listless boredom and humorous exchanges based on miscommunication, puns and dialects. The Chinese language is so full of similar sounds, and the dialects so many, this affords endless amusement. At other times the inhabitants of Beijing seemed to be characters cast in Brecht's *Mother Courage*, bravely surviving one calamity after another but retaining their humanity as armies come and go. Yet gruesome as life became at times, I noticed that Beijingers relished this sense of theatricality. Peking Opera, with its exaggerated gestures, no longer seemed odd but exactly fitted to this place. The 'Study Li Suli Campaign' went on for several months and then faded, to be replaced by others about selfless plumbers, street sweepers, policemen and tax collectors. Later I learned that the model conductress had stopped punching tickets and gone on to do an MBA course and then went into business. Of course the buses remained as abysmal and crowded as ever.

A visit to the Tuanhe Reform Through Labour camp in Daxing

country, a model prison, brought home Beijing's inclination to parody what you would expect from modern life. A group of journalists had been invited to see how those arrested in a campaign against the Falun Gong cult were being humanely treated and not, as elsewhere reported, beaten to death. The creation of modern prisons was a hallmark of the modernist movement and in the 1920s the newly established Ministry of Justice off Tiananmen Square included the Number 1 Model Prison to show visitors. It was quietly demolished in 2002. Behind its walls and watchtowers, which could be glimpsed from the second ring road behind the former moat, Democracy Wall activists like Wei Jingsheng, Ren Wangding or Xu Wenli spent twelve years locked up in tiny cells. After 1949 Beijing was full of prisons whose existence was sometimes revealed by streets called New Life or something similar, a reference to the new life granted to inmates. The Number 1 was just one of eighteen prisons run by the Beijing municipality where prisoners produced elevators, plumbing equipment, knitting mills, fast-food boxes and car parts.

The Tuanhe prison had 15,000 inmates who laboured in vineyards that supplied a well-known Sino-French joint venture that produced 'Dynasty' wine. I went there in the 1980s and the chief warden, a jolly man called Zhang Jingsheng, whose belly stretched out of his green uniform, showed me the prisoners working on the vines and then the barracks where they slept. He casually mentioned that he had spent six years as an inmate during the Cultural Revolution, when prisoners took charge and he and other prison guards were put to work in the same fields. 'It was for my political re-education – and I learned a great deal,' he added with a smile.

When I returned for this second visit, we were taken, after the usual introductions, to see walled parkland that looked like a holiday resort. Tame does grazed on the lawns, peacocks strutted, crying loudly, and a few rabbits hopped about. White doves fluttered here and there and from loudspeakers cleverly disguised as rocks the sound of violins wafted through the scented air. Smiling guards, who had traded olive-green uniforms for stylish black outfits with ID numbers in silver pinned on them, helpfully encouraged camera crews to film the prisoners playing tennis, croquet and basketball. Some prisoners sat on benches cheering their fellows on every time the ball dropped through the net. 'We are studying a plan to add a golf course here so the prisoners can enjoy their leisure,' beamed Zhang. 'Oh, please take as many photographs as you wish,' he repeated expansively.

Further on we saw the leisure centre, which had a large gym with weightlifting equipment, table tennis and an air-conditioned library. At each interval of the concrete slabs that formed the wall of the park, someone had recently painted the Olympic symbols for sports – cycling, diving, football and so on. Even the prisoners, it seems, were full of the Olympic spirit. Afterwards we were taken to see a class of inmates doing their political study, making a careful textual analysis of the *Legal Daily* and responding to invitations to comment. It was rather like a sleepy university seminar with students dozing at the back who reluctantly, after severe prompting by a policeman at the front, spoke up, giving their views on the importance of maintaining social order.

In a stylish two-storey visitors' meeting room at the entrance, we were introduced to some of the inmates. The room was spotless, bright and airy, and they all quietly sat there sipping tea out of Air China paper cups, chewing peanuts and steadfastly ignoring the cameras being pointed inches away from their faces. One of them, Qin Hongyi, told me how happy he was. 'We are all very happy here, even happier than on the outside,' Qin told me, explaining that he had worked as an accountant before he was caught putting up Falun Gong posters, with the distinctive wheel of life, on the famous Marco Polo Bridge outside Beijing. Like all the others, he was incarcerated without a trial. He would only be freed if he convinced his jailers that he had changed his thinking, so he duly affirmed that he no longer believed in Falun Gong but in Communism and the current 'Theory of the Three Represents', propounded by President Jiang Zemin. 'He really is a Great Thinker,' Qin said stoutly. 'I see,' I said, at a loss to know what further to ask. Then we stood up and shook hands solemnly as if we had just concluded a testing business negotiation.

'You see, we really have changed their thinking,' Zhang the warden said afterwards with an air of confidence. He had a broad, honest face and spoke with an exaggerated, stagey kind of intonation, his voice rising and falling sonorously as if he was delivering a familiar benediction. I suspected he was not really a policeman at all but an actor drafted in for the occasion. He certainly did not remember what had happened here in the Cultural Revolution, when his predecessor, another Zhang, spent years as a prisoner in his own prison camp. 'Oh,' he said, momentarily dropping his stage persona, 'I never heard of that.'

This convinced me that he was not a real warden. Beijing was, after all, just a stage where the sets changed frequently to help the audience forget what had happened in the last scene. Everyone lived brainwashed in a timeless present. Jiang Zemin's 'thoughts' would soon be forgotten, just as quickly as Mao's great 'thoughts' or the eccentric convictions of Li Hongzhi, the founder of the Falun Gong sect.

One overcast Sunday morning some five years later I was on the airport expressway driving into town before the spring festival, planning to go to B&Q, a kitchen and home supply store, and then to IKEA for sofas before meeting one of my wife's university friends for lunch at McDonald's. Beijing looked an entirely different place. On either side of the motorway marched rows of shopping malls, office towers and residential housing developments, painted in bright primary colours. Most of the old housing stock had been demolished. Big, bright advertisements showed a prosperous land of contented consumers eagerly buying shiny cars, smart houses, computers and telephones. Everyone had plunged into a brave new world financed by mortgages and consumer credit. In 1997, when IKEA opened its first shop in Beijing, in just seven days nearly a million people stampeded through the shop, sitting on furniture and trying out beds. The exhausted staff said nothing like it had happened anywhere else in the world.

The city was so changed that it was hard to find one's way, partly because there were so few landmarks. To reach the B&Q store, one left one motorway to get onto the fifth ring road and take a right-hand exit onto a slip road. After parking and paying for our goods at B&Q, I missed a turning and got lost in a forest of indistinguishable half-built residential blocks. Clusters of them stood in patches of grass and mud, separated by unfinished roads. It took hours to find my way back on to the motorway. It was all so new that if one stopped to ask for directions, nobody could help. Most people were strangers themselves, migrant workers living in slum-like shacks littered with piles of discarded rubbish.

Of course, everyone was in cars because they had to travel greater distances to work or shop, but many drivers had barely mastered the rules. Nobody paid any attention to whether they were in a fast or slow lane so the tardy drivers blocked all of them and others ended up weaving in and out. This led to accidents, long queues and endless traffic hold-ups. Twenty years earlier it had amused me that there were no traffic rules. Many things new to the Chinese remained unregulated, so, unlike the West where regulations were everywhere, donkey carts, cyclists, buses and trucks did whatever they wanted. China offered a kind of chaotic freedom, an escape from the West, and this rare example of anarchy in such a tightly regulated society was delightful, even reassuring. Now, much of Beijing is gridlocked evenings and mornings. It is hard to park or go anywhere without being watched by hundreds of surveillance cameras and fined by policeman.

'Why ever did they have to build it all like this?' I complained out loud. I began to brood on why I had ever left my London suburb to live in a tiresome copy of the West or tortured my brain to study the language. My wife said nothing, having heard it before, and pursed her lips to concentrate on the matter at hand, simply finding the name of the right bridge on the third ring road which would bring us to IKEA. 'Head for the Anhui Bridge,' she advised tersely. As usual, IKEA was packed when we arrived. We had to line up for half an hour to buy a standard lamp, and the double pull-out sofa was not there, at least not in the colour she wanted. 'Astonishing to think what an enormous choice there now is in China,' I volunteered, trying to sound helpful and upbeat. 'I mean, it wasn't so long ago you couldn't buy a decent coffee table for love or money; now half the world's furniture is made here.'

She was trying to decide whether we had time to drive into the centre of the city to a big plaza that had a broad selection of imported Italian and Spanish furniture, or drive out to one of the huge furniture markets on the outskirts where cheaper imitations were on sale. We decided to head downtown and my heart sank as we joined a stream of cars bumper to bumper along an elevated stretch of road. Then, passing the new Office for the Registration of Aliens, I glimpsed the golden roofs of the Lama Temple, which now stood in the shadow of the Office, from whose doors a steady stream of people came and went. Beijing in 2005 had 100,000 foreign residents, and growing numbers of Chinese also needed visas to go abroad for work or holidays. The sight kindled a pang of regret for that vanished city that the Emperor Qianlong had loved so much. He was born there. Across the road was the entrance to the Temple of Earth where he had performed ritual sacrifices. And as we inched forward, the sun glinted off the yellow tiles of the Temple of Confucius and the Imperial Academy, where Lao She had been tortured. Turning around, I could see workers cleaning the canal that the Emperor Yong Le had helped create to bring grain, timber and rice from the Yangtze region.

In McDonald's, my wife's friend was waiting for us with her son and husband. She was dressed plainly and had a round, pleasant face. When years ago my wife had studied modern Chinese literature in Beijing, they had shared a room together. Now we sat on plastic chairs eating cheeseburgers, French fries and drinking Coca-Cola. The city had hundreds of McDonald's and KFC outlets and my wife's tutor believed they were popular because so many people were just desperate to taste anything of Western culture. 'I like it here because it's clean and there's somewhere for the kids to play,' she remarked pleasantly. By the time I returned from the counter with more food, the talk had inevitably turned to property.

'So we bought an apartment just inside the fourth ring road. It's just a shell, really. But we rushed to get the last one. We had to queue up for several days, there was such a long queue. I thought we'd never make it. Everyone is trying to get into the property market, it was our last chance. We paid 9,000 yuan per square yard,' she said. The state had warned urban residents that the era of free housing was about to end. In the scramble for the 'last free lunch', some couples even divorced so they could legally and separately claim two apartments at the old price. In one or two cases, wives found themselves abandoned when the husband grabbed the chance to find a new and younger wife.

This couple had spent years living in a one-room apartment that can't have been more than 600 square feet. My wife kept nodding to express her admiration at her good fortune. 'Fortunately, my husband knew people who worked in the district property office, so we got an *anju* house through the backdoor.' Last year my wife's friend and her husband went to Las Vegas with a group of Chinese. 'Some of the people lost US$3 million playing blackjack,' she rattled on, with a nod in the direction of her silent husband, a round man with glasses, wearing a leather jacket. 'He was careful and just stuck to the slot machines.'

The city had once intended to maintain a social mix of rich and poor by offering low-rent subsidized *anju* housing (Comfortable Housing). Anyone forced to evacuate their old residence in the centre had been promised that once a new building was completed on the site of their old property, they could return to live there. In practice this rarely happened because even if the promise was kept, the temptation to cash in on the high prices of the new flat was too high.

'So how many square feet have you got now?' my wife asked, a little nettled by all this talk of extravagant spending. 'Eighteen hundred square feet,' was the reply. 'Oh, I know it's a lot to pay but I think it is a good investment. The prices can only go up with all these outsiders, *waidi ren*, coming in from the rest of China. You know, I heard that these business people from Wenzhou are coming here in tour groups and just driving around buying stuff because they think the prices can only go up. And then there's the Olympics of course.' At last they would finally get a proper bathroom with a bath and a flush toilet but it was still going to cost them a lot to put in the pipes and plumbing and buy all the necessary furniture, and they were applying for a mortgage. 'I want to put in one of those shiny German kitchens, all aluminium and steel,' she went on. 'Hoch and Bosch or whatever it is called.'

After we discussed the complications of getting a mortgage, she told us they were also going to get a new piano for their boy, and were going to buy one in Guangzhou. She looked over at the aforesaid boy, a round, tubby 8-year-old who was playing on the slide. 'You know, I think he's quite talented, he can already play several Bach sonatas.'

They were also thinking of visiting Hong Kong; had we heard when the Disney Park was opening? 'Now who wants an ice cream?' she said, getting up with her purse. Everybody did. 'And what happened to all your literature studies?' I asked when she came back. 'Weren't you researching something about Lao She?' 'Oh, that,' she said, her voice trailing off. 'Well. You know, there's no money in teaching, research, all that sort of thing. I had to give all that up. Besides, who cares about all those old writers any more?' She laughed. 'We just want to enjoy life, not think about all those things anymore.'

After we left the restaurant and set off in our respective cars, I said, 'Well, they seem pretty pleased with themselves. What is it exactly that they both do?'

'You know, I am not really sure,' my wife replied. 'Something in government.'

As we were going home, I began complaining again. 'China's getting to be just like everywhere else, people just talking about mortgages and new sofas.'

Back on the second ring road, the brittle January sunlight was fading. Looking out of the window, I could clearly see the Western Hills and a lone pagoda outlined against the reddening sky. 'That's the old Liao dynasty temple that Liang Sicheng discovered,' I said. 'Stop the car, I want to try and get a look this time.'

The Temple of Heavenly Tranquillity (Tianning Temple) had been one of Liang's great architectural finds. It is nearly a thousand years old, perhaps the oldest intact structure in Beijing. All that is left is a pagoda tower, the eaves floating above each other, and bronze bells hanging from each cornice, which would have tinkled in the wind. It is easily visible from the road but belongs to a factory protected by brick walls and barbed wire. Over the years I had tried to get in to see it, but somehow, from whatever side I tried, no entrance seemed to lead in. Several testy exchanges with doormen had got me nowhere and once they had even tried to detain me. My wife slowed the car down, preparing to stop, then changed her mind. 'No,' she said firmly. 'Let it go, leave it as a little mystery.'

Victor Ségalen had been correct when he predicted that modernity would produce a tiresome conformity and banality. Perhaps Beijing had always been fated to become Westernized; after the 1911 revolution it was only a matter of time before the last sanctuary of the marvellous and unknown disappeared. Like an ancient bronze ritual vessel from the Zhou dynasty, flecked with a green patina of living history, the city was destined to be sacrificed to the Gods of the Future. As we drove home in silence I looked at the new buildings. Many of them, thrown up in haste by developers in search of quick profits, seemed unlikely to last a thousand years like the Temple of Heavenly Tranquillity. This new Beijing would not survive five hundred years, as the Ming city had done, because the Gods of the Future are always demanding fresh sacrifices. The future needs to be constantly re-invented and these buildings would all be gone in twenty-five or fifty years, the names of the great men who brought them into existence lost from memory, preserved only in a closely guarded archive.

Bibliography

Abru, Hafiz, *A Persian Embassy to China: Being an Extract from Zubdatu't Tawarikh of Hafiz Abru*, trans. K. M. Maitra (New York: Paragon Book Reprint Corp., 1970; Lahore, 1934).

Acton, Harold, *Peonies and Ponies* (Hong Kong: Oxford University Press, 1941).

Aisin-Gioro, Pu Yi, *From Emperor to Citizen*, trans. W. F. Jenner (Beijing: Foreign Languages Press, 1964).

Anami, Virginia Stibbs, *Encounters with Ancient Beijing: Its Legacy in Trees, Stones and Water* (Beijing: China Intercontinental Press, 2004).

Ancient Temples in Beijing (Beijing: China Esperanto Press, 1993).

Arlington, L. C., and Lewisohn, William, *In Search of Old Peking* (Hong Kong: Oxford University Press, 1987).

Attiret, Father Jean-Denis, SJ, *A particular account of the emperor of China's gardens near Pekin: in a letter from F. Attiret, a French missionary. Now employ'd by that emperor to paint the apartments in those gardens, to his friend at Paris*, trans. Sir Harry Beaumont (London: R. Dodsley, 1752).

Ba Jin, *Random Thoughts*, trans. Geremie Barme (Hong Kong: Joint Publishing Co., 1984).

Barfield, Thomas J., *The Perilous Frontier: Nomadic Empires and China, 221 BC to AD 1757* (Boston: Blackwell Publishers, 1989).

Beijing Courtyard & Hutong Guide (Hong Kong: Naga, 1999).

Beijing Garden Administration Bureau, *Famous Ancient Trees in Beijing* (Beijing: Beijing Publishing House, 2000).

Bishop, Kevin, *China's Imperial Way* (Hong Kong: Odyssey Publications, 1997).

Blofeld, John, *City of Lingering Splendour: A Frank Account of Old Peking's Exotic Pleasures* (London: Hutchinson, 1989).

Bodde, Derk, *Peking Diary: 1948–1949. A Year of Revolution* (London: Cape, 1951).

Bramah, Ernest, *Kai Lung's Golden Hours* (Hong Kong: Oxford University Press, 1985).

Bredon, Juliet, *Peking* (London: T. Werner Laurie Ltd. 1932).

—— and Mitrophanow, Igor, *The Moon Year* (Hong Kong: Oxford University Press, 1982).

Carl, Katherine A., *With the Empress Dowager of China* (London: KPI Ltd., 1986; first published 1906).

Chan, Charis, *Imperial China*, Architectural Guides for Travellers (London: Penguin Books, 1991).

Chang, Jung, and Halliday, Jon, *Mao: The Unknown Story* (London: Jonathan Cape, 2005).

Chen Keji, *Imperial Medicaments: Medical Prescriptions for Empress Dowager Cixi and Emperor Guangxu, with Commentary* (Beijing: Foreign Languages Press, 1996).

Cheng, Nien, *Life and Death in Shanghai* (London: Grafton Books, 1987).

Ch'oe Pu's Diary: A Record of Drifting Across the Sea, trans. John Meskill (Tucson: University of Arizona Press, 1976).

Chow Tse-Tung, *The May 4th Movement: Intellectual Revolution in Modern China* (Cambridge, Mass.: Harvard University Press, 1960).

Cohn, Don J., and Zhang Jingqing, *Beijing Walks* (Hong Kong: Odyssey, 1992).

Conrads, Ulrich, *Programs and Manifestos on 20th-Century Architecture*, trans. Michael Bullock (Cambridge, Mass.: MIT Press, 1971).

Cronin, Vincent, *The Wise Man from the West: Matteo Ricci and his Mission to China* (London: The Harvill Press, 1999).

Curtis, William J. R., *Modern Architecture since 1900* (New York: Phaidon, 1982).

Danby, Hope, *The Garden of Perfect Brightness* (London: Williams and Norgate, 1950).

Dardes, John W., *Blood and History in China: The Donglin Faction and its Repression, 1620–1627* (Honolulu: University of Hawaii Press, 2002).

Dawa Norbu, *Red Star over Tibet* (New Delhi: Sterling Publishers, 1974).

Elder, Chris, *Old Peking: City of the Ruler of the World* (Hong Kong: Oxford University Press, 1997).

Fairbank, Wilma, *Liang and Lin* (Philadelphia: University of Pennsylvania Press, 1994).

Farmer, Edward L., *Early Ming Government: The Evolution of Dual Capitals* (Cambridge, Mass.: East Asian Research Center, Harvard University Press, 1976).

Fleming, Peter, *The Siege at Peking* (Hong Kong: Oxford University Press, 1983).

Fokkema, Douwe, *Report from Peking: Observations of a Western Diplomat on the Cultural Revolution* (London: C. Hurst & Company, 1970).

Gamble, Sidney D., and Burgess, John Stewart, *Peking: A Social Survey* (New York: George H. Doran Co., 1921).

Geiss, James, 'Peking under the Ming: 1368–1644', Princeton University, Ph.D. dissertation, 1979.

Goossaert, Vincent, *Dans les temples de la Chine: Histoire des cultes, vie des communautés* (Paris: Éditions Albin Michel, 2000).

Gordon, Eric, *Freedom is a Word* (New York: William Morrow & Co., 1972).

Greene, Felix, *Peking* (New York: Mayflower Books, 1978).

Grey, Anthony, *Hostage in Peking* (London: Michael Joseph, 1970).

Hibbert, Christopher, *The Dragon Wakes: China and the West, 1793–1911* (London: Penguin Books, 1970).

Hinton, William, *Hundred Day War: The Cultural Revolution at Tsinghua University* (New York and London: Monthly Review Press, 1972).

Holdsworth, May, *The Forbidden City* (Hong Kong: Oxford University Press, 1998).

—— and Courtauld, Caroline, *The Forbidden City: The Great Within* (Hong Kong: Odyssey Publications, 1995).

Hou, Helena, *Return to Peking* (Taipei: China Publishing Co., 1977).

Hu, Fu, *Tales of the Qing Court*, trans. George Meng (Hong Kong: Hai Feng Publishing Co., 1990).

Huang, Ray, *1587: A Year of No Significance. The Ming Dynasty in Decline* (New Haven and London: Yale University Press, 1980).

Johnson, Ian, *Wild Grass: Three Stories of Change in Modern China* (New York: Pantheon, 2004).

Johnson, Reginald F., *Twilight in the Forbidden City* (Oxford: Oxford University Press, 1935).

Kates, George N., *The Years that were Fat: Peking, 1933–1940* (Hong Kong: Oxford University Press, 1998).

Keown-Boyd, Henry, *The Boxer Rebellion: The Fists of Righteous Harmony. An Illustrated History of the Boxer Uprising* (London: Leo Cooper, 1991).

Kidd, David, *Peking Story* (London: John Murray, 1961).

Knapp, Ronald G., *China's Walled Cities* (Hong Kong: Oxford University Press, 2000).

Lao She, *Collected Works*, 3 vols. (Beijing: Modern Chinese Literature Library, Yilin Press, 1979).

—— *Camel Xiangzi*, trans. Shi Xiaoqing (Beijing: Foreign Languages Press, 1981).

Le Corbusier, *Towards a New Architecture*, trans. Frederick Etchwells (New York: Dover Publications, 1986).

Leys, Simon, *The Burning Forest: Essays on Chinese Culture and Politics* (New York: Henry Holt, 1986).

—— *Essais sur la chine* (Paris: Robert Laffont, 1998).

Li Zhisui, *The Private Life of Chairman Mao: The Inside Story of the Man who Made Modern China*, trans. Tai Hung-chao (London: Chatto & Windus, 1994).

Liao Jingwen, *Xu Beihong: Life of a Master Painter*, trans. Zhang Peiji (Beijing: Foreign Languages Press, 1987).

Lin Yutang, *Imperial Peking: Seven Centuries of China* (New York: Crown Publishers, 1938).

—— *Moment in Peking* (New York: Popular Library, 1967).

Loti, Pierre, *Les Derniers Jours de Pékin* (Paris: Calmann-Lévy Éditeurs, 1920).

Lu Xun, *Quanji* (Complete Works), 16 vols. (Beijing: Renmin wenxue, 1981).

Mackerras, Colin, *Peking Opera* (Hong Kong: Oxford University Press, 1997).

Marcuse, Jacques, *The Peking Papers: Leaves from the Notebook of a China Correspondent* (New York: Dutton, 1967).

Melvin, Sheila, and Jindong Cai, *Rhapsody in Red: How Western Classical Music Became Chinese* (New York: Algora Publishing and Lightning Source Inc., 2004).

Mitamura, Taisuke, *Chinese Eunuchs: The Structure of Intimate Politics*, trans. Charles A. Pomeroy (Tokyo: Tuttle Publishing, 1963).

Moser, Michael J., and Moser, Yeone Wei-chih, *Foreigners within the Gates: The Legations at Peking* (Chicago: Serindia Publications, 2006).

Mote, F. W., *Imperial China: 900–1800* (Cambridge, Mass.: Harvard University Press, 2003).

Naquin, Susan, *Peking: Temples and City Life, 1400–1900* (Berkeley: University of California Press, 2000).

Oliphant, Laurence, *Narrative of the Earl of Elgin's Mission to China and Japan in the Years 1857, 1858, and 1859* (1859).

Paludan, Ann, *The Ming Tombs* (Hong Kong: Oxford University Press, 1991).

—— *Chronicle of the Chinese Emperors: The Reign-by-Reign Record of the Rulers of Imperial China* (London: Thames and Hudson Ltd., 1998).

Peck, Graham, *Through China's Wall* (Boston: Houghton Mifflin Company, 1940).

Quennell, Peter, *A Superficial Journey through Tokyo and Peking* (Hong Kong: Oxford University Press, 1986).

Rand, Peter, *China Hands: The Adventures and Ordeals of the American Journalists who Joined Forces with the Great Chinese Revolution* (New York: Simon & Schuster, 1995).

[Ricci, Matteo], *China in the Sixteenth Century: The Journals of Matthew Ricci. 1583–1610*, trans. Louis J. Gallagher (New York: Random House, 1953).

Robinson, David M., 'Banditry and the Subversion of State Authority in China: The Capital Region during the Middle Ming Period (1450–1525)', *Journal of Social History* (Spring 2000), pp. 527–63.

Schoenhals, Michael (ed.), *China's Cultural Revolution, 1966–1969: Not a Dinner Party* (New York: M. E. Sharpe, 1992).

Scotland, Tony, *The Empty Throne. The Quest for an Imperial Heir in the People's Republic of China* (London: Penguin Books, 1994).

Seagrove, Sterling, *Dragon Lady: The Life and Legend of the Last Empress of China* (New York, Vantage Books, 1991).

Sechin Jagchid and Symons, Van Jay, *Peace, War, and Trade Along the Great Wall: Nomadic-Chinese Interaction through Two Millennia* (Bloomington: Indiana University Press, 1989).

Ségalen, Victor, *René Leys* (Paris: Gallimard, 1971).

—— *Essay on Exoticism: An Aesthetics of Diversity*, trans. Yael Rachel Schlick (Durham, NC, and London: Duke University Press, 2002).

Shi Guo, *Shi Lu Hua* (Zhengzhou: Henan People's Publishing House, 1999).

Sit, Victor F. S., *Beijing: The Nature and Planning of a Chinese Capital City* (London: John Wiley, 1995).

Spence, Jonathan D., *The Search for Modern China* (London: Hutchinson, 1990).

—— *Emperor of China: Self-Portrait of K'ang-shi* (London: Pimlico, 1992).

—— *The Gate of Heavenly Peace: The Chinese and their Revolution 1895–1980* (London: Penguin Books, 1982).

Steel, Richard A., *Through Peking's Sewer Gate: Relief of the Boxer Siege, 1900–1901* (New York: Vantage Press, 1985).

Taylor, Charles, *Reporter in Red China* (New York: Random House, 1966).

Terzani, Tiziano, *Behind the Forbidden Door: China Inside Out* (London: Allen & Unwin, 1987).

Trevor-Roper, Hugh, *Hermit of Peking: The Hidden Life of Sir Edmund Backhouse* (London: Eland Books, 1976).

Tsai, Shih-Shan Henry, *Perpetual Happiness: The Ming Emperor Yongle* (Seattle and London: University of Washington Press, 2001).

Tung, Anthony M., *Preserving the World's Great Cities: The Destruction and Renewal of the Historic Metropolis* (New York: Clarkson Potter, 2001).

Vare, Daniele, *The Maker of Heavenly Trousers* (New York: Methuen & Co., 1935).

—— *Laughing Diplomat* (London: John Murray, 1938).

—— *The Gate of Happy Sparrows* (London: Methuen & Co., 1943).

Wang Shixiang, *Beijing Pigeon Whistles* (Shenyang: Liaoning Education Press, 2004).

Wang, Y. C., *Chinese Intellectuals and the West, 1872–1949* (Chapel Hill: University of North Carolina Press, 1966).

Wang Youqin, *Victims of the Cultural Revolution: An Investigative Account of Persecution, Imprisonment and Murder* (Hong Kong: Kaifang Magazine Press, 2005).

Witke, Roxanne, *Comrade Chiang Ch'ing* (Boston: Little, Brown, & Co., 1977).

Wolfe, Tom, *From Bauhaus to Our House* (New York: Farrar, Straus, & Giroux, 1981).

Wu Liangyong, *Rehabilitating the Old City of Beijing* (Vancouver: University of British Columbia Press, 1999).

Wu Zugang, Huang Zuolin and Mei Shaowu, *Peking Opera and Mei Lanfang: A Guide to China's Traditional Theatre and the Art of its Great Master* (Beijing: New World Press, 1981).

Xiao Qian, *Chestnut and Other Stories* (Beijing: Panda Books, 1984).

Xiao Qian [Hsiao Ch'ien], *Traveller without a Map*, trans. Jeffrey C. Kinkley (London: Hutchinson, 1990).

Xu Chengbei, *Old Beijing: In the Shadow of the Imperial Throne* (Beijing: Foreign Languages Press and Jiangsu Fine Arts Publishing House, 1998).

Yang Jiang, *A Cadre School Life: Six Chapters*, trans. Geremie Barme (Hong Kong: Joint Publishing Co., 1982).

Yue Nan and Yang Shi, *The Dead Suffered Too: The Excavation of a Ming Tomb*, trans. Zhang Tingquan (Beijing: Panda Books, 1996).

Zhang Tingquan, *Chinese Imperial Cuisines and Eating Secrets* (Beijing: Panda Books, 1998).

Zhao Xinhua, *Lao Beijing Miaohui* (Beijing: Zhongguo Chengshi Chubanshe, 1999).

Chinese Language source books

Li Hui, *Hu Feng Jituan Yuanan Shimo* (Wuhan Shi: Hubei Chubanshe, 2003).

Li Hui, *Laoshe Xiaoshi Le De Taiping Hu* (Zhengzhou shi: Daxiang Chubanshe, 2000).

Lijin Longdeng, *Bada Hutong* (Zhengzhou shi: Zhongyuan Nongmin Chubanshe, 2000).

Sun Yumin, *Wo Zhe Liang Beizi* (Beijing: Huashan Wenyi Chubanshe 2003).

Wang Jun, *Chengji* (Beijing: Xinzhi Sanlian Shudian, 2004).

Wang Tongzhen, *Lao Beijing Cheng* (Beijing: Beijing Yanshan Chubanshe 1997).

Wang Youqin, *Wenge Haizhe 1966–1976* (Xianggang: Kaifang Chengshi Chubanshe 2004).

Zhang Lifang, *Beijing Wenxue De Diyu Wenhua Meili* (Beijing: Zhongguo Heping Chubanshe 1994).

Sources and Notes

Chapter 1: In Xanadu

Material for this chapter originally appeared in Jasper Becker, 'Xanadu's Glory revealed', *South China Morning Post*, 31 May 1998. Accompanying me on the trip were British journalists James Pringle and James Kynge.

Two books that discuss China's relations with nomadic cultures are: Jagchid Sechin and Van Jay Symons, *Peace, War, and Trade Along the Great Wall: Nomadic-Chinese Interaction through Two Millennia* (Bloomington: Indiana University Press, 1989), and Thomas J. Barfield, *The Perilous Frontier: Nomadic Empires and China, 221 BC to AD 1757* (Boston: Blackwell Publishers, 1989).

I am also in debt to William Lindesay, great authority on the Great Wall, from whom I learned a lot and exchanged many ideas.

1. *China in the Sixteenth Century: The Journals of Matthew Ricci. 1583–1610*, trans. Louis J. Gallagher (New York: Random House, 1953), p. 307.
2. Juliet Bredon, *Peking* (London: T. Werner Laurie Ltd., 1932), p. 369.

Chapter 2: The Emperor of Perpetual Happiness

1. Shih-Shan Henry Tsai, *Perpetual Happiness: The Ming Emperor Yongle* (Seattle and London University of Washington Press, 2001), p. 49.
2. Juliet Bredon, *Peking* (London: T. Werner Laurie Ltd., 1932).
3. Hafiz Abru, *A Persian Embassy to China: Being an Extract from Zubdatu't Tawarikh of Hafiz Abru*, trans. K. M. Maitra (New York: Paragon Book Reprint Corp., 1970; Lahore, 1934), pp. 49–50, 67, 86–7.
4. Quoted in James Geiss, 'Peking under the Ming: 1368–1644', Princeton University, Ph.D. dissertation, 1979.
5. *Ch'oe Pu's Diary: A Record of Drifting Across the Sea*, trans. John Meskill (Tucson: University of Arizona Press, 1976).

6. Quoted in Geiss, 'Peking under the Ming', p. 56.

7. Bredon, *Peking*, p. 32.

8. Xiao Qian (Hsiao Ch'ien), *Traveller without a Map*, trans. Jeffrey C. Kinkley (London: Hutchinson, 1990), p. 17.

Chapter 3: Madness in the Forbidden City

I am indebted to Shih-Shan Henry Tsai's book *Perpetual Happiness: The Ming Emperor Yongle* (Seattle and London: University of Washington Press, 2001); and to Dr Alfreda Murck for referring me to the work of Ming historian James Geiss, especially his Ph.D. thesis, 'Peking under the Ming: 1368–1644', Princeton University, 1979. More information can be found on his website (www.geissfoundation.org). Also of great use was Edward L. Farmer's research in *Early Ming Government: The Evolution of Dual Capitals* (Cambridge, Mass.: East Asian Research Center, Harvard University, 1976).

1. Lu Ben *et al.* (eds.), *Ming Taizong baoxun* (Treasure Instructions from Ming Emperor Yong Le) (1430; repr. Taipei: Academica Sinica, 1967); quoted in Tsai, *Perpetual Happiness*, p. 102.

2. Yu Jideng, *Recording Old Clichés*, juan 6: 116; Lu Ben *et al.* (eds.), *Ming Taizong baoxun*, juan 1: 17–18.

3. Tsai, *Perpetual Happiness*, p. 102.

4. Yu Jideng, *Recording Old Clichés*.

5. George N. Kates, *The Years that were Fat: Peking, 1933–1940* (Hong Kong: Oxford University Press, 1998), p. 105.

6. Ray Huang, *1587: A Year of No Significance. The Ming Dynasty in Decline* (New Haven and London: Yale University Press, 1980), p. 135.

Chapter 4: On the Wild Wall

Ray Huang's book *1587: A Year of No Significance. The Ming Dynasty in Decline* (New Haven and London: Yale University Press, 1980) gives a very readable and lucid account of this period. Another fascinating look at court politics in the late Ming is John W. Dardes, *Blood and History in China: The Donglin Faction and its Repression, 1620–1627* (Honolulu: University of Hawaii Press, 2002).

1. My account of the Mongolian bandits is based largely on the work of David M. Robinson, 'Banditry and the Subversion of State Authority in

China: The Capital Region during the Middle Ming Period (1450–1525)',
Journal of Social History (Spring 2000), pp. 527–63.
2. Documents of the Ming–Qing transition compiled by Song Yingxing.
3. Somewhat confusingly, *wan li* also sounds in Chinese like '10,000 miles'
or the '10,000-mile wall'.
4. Song Yingxing.
5. Ibid.
6. For more on the battles at the end of the Qing dynasty, one can go
to www.china-defense.com/history/1644: 1644: *Showdown at Shanhaiguan*,
peasant rebels Zhang Xianzhong and Li Zicheng; the north-east and the
enigmatic Wu Sangui; The battle of Shanhaiguan.

Chapter 5: The Ming Tombs

David M. Robinson's 'Banditry and the Subversion of State Authority in
China: The Capital Region during the Middle Ming Period (1450–1525)',
Journal of Social History (Spring 2000), was fascinating. For more on the
battles at the end of the Qing dynasty, see www.china-defense.com/history/
1644.

1. Yue Nan and Yang Shi, *The Dead Suffered Too: The Excavation of a
Ming Tomb*, trans. Zhang Tingquan (Beijing: Panda Books, 1996), p. 138.
2. Ibid, p. 156.

Chapter 6: In the Garden of Perfect Brightness

1. Norman Kutcher, 'China's Palace of Memory', *Wilson Quarterly* (Winter
2003).
2. Interview with Liang Congjie, April 2000.
3. Quoted in Hope Danby, *The Garden of Perfect Brightness* (London:
Williams and Norgate, 1950), p. 13.
4. Father Jean-Denis Attiret, SJ, *A particular account of the emperor of
China's gardens near Pekin: in a letter from F. Attiret, a French missionary.
Now employ'd by that emperor to paint the apartments in those gardens, to
his friend at Paris*, trans. Sir Harry Beaumont (London: R. Dodsley, 1752).
5. Letter to George III, 1793.
6. Quoted in Danby, *The Garden of Perfect Brightness*, pp. 199–200.
7. Donald F. Lach, *The Dictionary of the History of Ideas* (Madison: University of Wisconsin Press, 2003), vol. 1, p. 363.
8. Danby, *The Garden of Perfect Brightness*, p. 107.

9. Ibid., p. 105.

10. Laurence Oliphant, *Narrative of the Earl of Elgin's Mission to China and Japan in the Years 1857, 1858 and 1859* (1859).

Chapter 7: The Broken Bowl Tea House

1. Jung Chang and Jon Halliday, *Mao: The Unknown Story* (London: Jonathan Cape, 2005), p. 15.

2. Lu Xun, *Quanji* (Complete Works), 16 vols. (Beijing: Renmin wenxue, 1981).

3. Y. C. Wang, *Chinese Intellectuals and the West, 1872–1949* (Chapel Hill: University of North Carolina Press, 1966), pp. 394–5.

4. For a fuller account of this, see the chapter 'Death by a Thousand Cuts: The Destruction of Old Peking', in Tiziano Terzani, *Behind the Forbidden Door: China Inside Out* (London: Allen & Unwin, 1987).

5. Ron Gluckman. 'Architecture at a Juncture', *Asiaweek* (www.Gluckman.com).

6. Wu Jingshu, 'Beijing Mayor Says Preserve the Past', *China Daily*, 28 April 1986; 'Ancient Buildings Face Threat of Destruction', *China Daily*, 9 May 1985.

7. Beijing Municipal Institute of City Planning and Design, *A Brief Introduction to the Beijing Master Plan, 1990–2010*.

8. Cesar Chelala, 'Relearning Lessons of the Greeks', *Perspectives in Health*, 1/1 (June 1996).

Chapter 8: The Last Sanctuary of the Unknown and Marvellous

The writings of Ian Buruma drew my attention to Victor Ségalen's work. Two other articles were especially helpful: Yael Schlick's 'On the Persistence of a Concept: Ségalen's "René Leys" and the Death(s) of Exoticism', *Australian Journal of French Studies* (May–August 1998); and Simon Leys's 'Victor Ségalen, les tribulations d'un poète en Chine', *Le Figaro*, 3 February 2005. See also, 'Embassies of the West', *Beijing Weekend*, 6–8 March 1998.

1. Daniele Vare, *Laughing Diplomat* (London: John Murray, 1938), p. 121.

2. Hugh Trevor-Roper, *Hermit of Peking: The Hidden Life of Sir Edmund Backhouse* (London: Eland Books, 1976), p. 87.

3. Peter Fleming, *The Siege at Peking* (Hong Kong: Oxford University Press, 1983), p. 222.

4. From Pierre Loti, *Les Derniers Jours de Pékin* (Paris: Calmann-Lévy Éditeurs, 1920).

5. Chen Keji, *Imperial Medicaments: Medical Prescriptions for Empress Dowager Cixi and Emperor Guangxu, with Commentary* (Beijing: Foreign Languages Press, 1996).

6. George N. Kates, *The Years that were Fat: Peking, 1933–1940* (Hong Kong: Oxford University Press, 1998), pp. 188–9.

Chapter 9: The Last Manchus

I relied heavily on the help of writer Jia Yinghua, for his research on the last eunuch (the interview first appeared in the *South China Morning Post* article 'China's Last Eunuch', 13 July 1996) and interviews with Pu Ren and Aisin Gioro Zhao Rui. Other helpful sources were Professor Hu Zhenhua of Central Nationalities University and deputy head of the Beijing Islamic Association, and Manchu expert Professor Wang Zhonghan, also of the Central Nationalities University.

Also helpful were the following articles: David Rennie, 'China Allies to Save a Dying Dynasty', *Daily Telegraph*, 1 April 2000; Josephine Ma, 'Battle on to Save Fading Manchurian Dialect', *South China Morning Post*, 14 August 2000; and François Hauter, 'Le Frère du dernier empereur raconte ses souvenirs', *Le Figaro*.

Chapter 10: In Search of The Golden Flower

1. Xiao Qian [Hsiao Ch'ien], *Traveller without a Map*, trans. Jeffrey C. Kinkley (London: Hutchinson, 1990), p. 177.

2. David Kidd, *Peking Story* (London: John Murray, 1961), pp. 135–9.

3. Jacques Marcuse, *The Peking Papers: Leaves from the Notebook of a China Correspondent* (New York: Dutton, 1967), p. 21.

4. Lin Yutang, *Imperial Peking: Seven Centuries of China* (New York: Crown Publishers 1938), pp. 158–61.

5. John Blofeld, *City of Lingering Splendour: A Frank Account of Old Peking's Exotic Pleasures* (London: Hutchinson, 1989), p. 62.

6. Information can be found at www.yutopian.com

7. Graham Peck, *Through China's Wall* (Boston: Houghton Mifflin Company, 1940), pp. 336–7.

Chapter 11: Mao and Beijing

1. Derk Bodde, *Peking Diary: 1948–1949. A Year of Revolution* (London: Cape, 1951), p. 82.

2. Peter Rand, *China Hands: The Adventures and Ordeals of the American Journalists who Joined Forces with the Great Chinese Revolution* (New York: Simon & Schuster, 1995), pp. 281–3.

3. Bodde, *Peking Diary*, pp. 79, 81.

4. Ibid., p. 101.

5. David Kidd, *Peking Story* (London: John Murray, 1961), pp. 145, 148–9.

6. F. W. Mote, *Imperial China: 900–1800* (Cambridge, Mass.: Harvard University Press, 2003), p. 576.

7. Jacques Marcuse, *The Peking Papers: Leaves from the Notebook of a China Correspondent* (New York: Dutton, 1967), p. 21.

8. Wang Youqin, now a senior lecturer at the University of Chicago, was a student in 1966 at Beijing Normal University's Girls School. She has established a website at www.chinese-memorial.org which provides details and translations of her research into the Cultural Revolution, including the article 'Student Attacks Against Teachers: The Revolution of 1966'. She has since published *Victims of the Cultural Revolution: An Investigative Account of Persecution, Imprisonment and Murder* (Hong Kong: Kaifang Magazine Press, 2005).

9. Song Yongyi, a librarian at Dickinson College, Carlisle, Pennysylvania, provided much material for this chapter. He has collected many Red Guard publications for his own book on the Cultural Revolution, from which this letter is quoted. The Chinese government detained Song for three years, for gathering Red Guard materials, and released him only after a public outcry in the United States.

10. Eric Gordon, *Freedom is a Word* (New York: William Morrow & Co., 1972), p. 69.

11. Xiao Qian [Hsiao Ch'ien], *Traveller without a Map*, trans. Jeffrey C. Kinkley (London: Hutchinson, 1990), pp. 236–9.

12. Quoted in Michael Schoenhals (ed.), *China's Cultural Revolution, 1966–1969: Not a Dinner Party* (New York: M. E. Sharpe, 1992), p. 17.

13. Quoted by Paul Majendie, 'Upper Lip Stayed Stiff as Embassy Stormed', Reuters, 6 January 2005.

14. Douwe Fokkema, *Report from Peking: Observations of a Western Diplomat on the Cultural Revolution* (London: C. Hurst and Company, 1970), p. 37.

15. Interviews with Beijing civil defence officials in 2002.

Chapter 12: History in Stone

1. William Hinton, *Hundred Day War: The Cultural Revolution at Tsinghua University* (New York and London: Monthly Review Press, 1972).
2. Frederick W. Mote, 'A Millennium of Chinese Urban History: Form, Time, and Space Concepts in Soochow', *Rice University Studies*, 59/4 (1974), p. 53; Ann Paludan, *The Ming Tombs* (Hong Kong: Oxford University Press), 1991, p. 16.
3. Quoted in Simon Leys, *Essais sur la chine* (Paris: Robert Laffont, 1998), p. 744.
4. Wilma Fairbank, *Liang and Lin* (Philadelphia: University of Pennsylvania Press, 1994), pp. 65–72.
5. Ibid., p. 162.
6. A detailed account of Liang's struggle is covered in Wang Jun's book, *Cheng Ji Yu Ling* (Beijing: Xinzhi Sanlian Shudian, 2004). See also, 'Liang Sicheng: Striving to Preserve Old Beijing', *China Daily*, 27 November 1986.
7. For this section, I am grateful to the research of Song Yongyi, Dr Wang Youqin and others.
8. Fairbank, *Liang and Lin*, pp. 176–90. I interviewed Zhu Lin in August 2001 and March 2005.

Chapter 13: The Strange Death of Lao She

For the account of Lao She's last days I relied on the research by the scholar Fu Guangmin, and also the assistance of Shu Yi and Dr Henry Y. H. Zhao of SOAS, University of London.

1. Peter Rand, *China Hands: The Adventures and Ordeals of the American Journalists who Joined Forces with the Great Chinese Revolution* (New York: Simon & Schuster, 1995), p. 137.
2. Xiao Qian [Hsiao Ch'ien], *Traveller without a Map*, trans. Jeffrey C. Kinkley (London: Hutchinson, 1990), pp. 56–8.
3. Lao She, *Camel Xiangzi*, trans. Shi Xiaoqing (Beijing: Foreign Languages Press, 1981).
4. Fan Jun, 'The Literary Journey of Lao She', in *Collected Works* (Beijing: Modern Chinese Literature Library, Yilin Press, 1979), vol. 3, p. 454.
5. Quoted in Rand, *China Hands*, p. 281.
6. Yang Jiang, *A Cadre School Life: Six Chapters*, trans. Geremie Barme (Hong Kong: Joint Publishing Co., 1982), p. 89.

Chapter 14: The Red Maid's Tale

Ghaffar Pourazar provided invaluable help throughout the years in under-standing Peking Opera. See also, Jasper Becker, 'Singing to Deaf Ears', *South China Morning Post*, 26 January 1997.

1. *The Vocal Art of Chinese Beijing Opera*, 30 pieces of digital audio CD with a Chinese–English book (Beijing: Culture & Art Audio-Video Publishing House, 1998).
2. Roxanne Witke, *Comrade Chiang Ch'ing* (Boston: Little, Brown, & Co., 1977), pp. 327, 386.

Chapter 15: The Last Playboy of Beijing

For information in this section, I am also grateful to the American dealer Robert Ellsworth, Dr Alfreda Murck, Professor Qin Dashu of the Department of Archaeology, Beijing University, the Chinese archaeologist Liu Qingzhu and Beijing antiques dealer Dick Wang.

1. Wang Shixiang, *Beijing Pigeon Whistles* (Shenyang: Liaoning Education Press, 2004).
2. Daniele Vare, *Laughing Diplomat* (London: John Murray, 1938), pp. 110–11.
3. Interview with Ma Chengyuan, Shanghai, May 2001.
4. Interview with Shenyang officials, May 2001.
5. Interview with Swiss researcher. He provided much of the information on Tibet but has asked to remain anonymous.
6. Dawa Norbu, in *Red Star over Tibet* (New Delhi: Sterling Publishers, 1974), described how the Commission of Cultural Relics always arrived before the Red Guards.
7. Charles Taylor, *Reporter in Red China* (New York: Random House, 1966), p. 351.
8. I am indebted to the research on Shi Lu by Xenia Tetmayer von Przerwa, who showed me her thesis on Shi Lu: 'Socialist Themes in Post-1949 Chinese Ink Painting' (University of London, 2001). I also received the cooperation of Shi Lu's son, Shi Guo, who wrote a biography, *Shi Lu Hua* (Zhengzhou: Henan People's Publishing House, 1999).
9. This information comes from an article in the Chinese press, including a piece by Menren, 'The Decade of Cultural Relics Fell Low in China', pub-lished in *Cultural Relics Magazine* (April 2001).

10. See also Richard Hornik, 'Reclaiming Red Guard Booty: A Program for Giving Back Seized Books and Artworks', *Time Magazine*, 16 September 1985.

11. 'Chinese Experts Demand Return of Cultural Relics', *People's Daily*, 22 January 2003; and 'China Plans to Recover Million "Looted" Relics From Across the World', Reuters, 22 May 2005.

Chapter 16: The Protectress of Flowers

I am very grateful for the help of French scholar Marianne Bujuard and especially the work and advice of Professor Susan Naquin and the research of Professor Kristofer Schipper, including his paper 'Liturgical Structures of Ancient Beijing'. L'École Pratique des Hautes Études, Université de Leyde, was also invaluable.

The following articles and books were also useful: Liu Zongren, 'Abolished Grand Temple Fairs Make a Big Come Back', *China Daily*, 15 March 1987; *Ancient Temples in Beijing* (Beijing: China Esperanto Press, 1993); and Zhao Xinhua, *Lao Beijing Miaohui* (Beijing: Zhongguo Chengshi Chubanshe, 1999).

1. *Guan* is the term for a Taoist temple.

Chapter 17: Radiant City of the Future

1. Douwe Fokkema, *Report from Peking: Observations of a Western Diplomat on the Cultural Revolution* (London: C. Hurst and Company, 1970), pp. 18, 46.

2. For this research I am grateful to Song Yongyi, Dr Wang Youqin and others.

3. 'Beijing's New Mayor a Man of the People', *People's Daily*, 21 January 2003.

4. Xinhua news agency, 28 March 2004. '500,000 to be Moved in Bid to Quell Sandstorms', *China Daily*, 12 March 2005; Xinhua, 'Beijing City Government Told to Shift to Suburbs', 12 March 2005.

5. www.china.org.cn; Xinhua, 'Injury Insurance for Construction Workers', 5 November 2005; Tang Min, 'Unpaid Debts Hamper Construction', *China Daily*, 31 March 2003.

6. Interview with a Chinese official who refused to be named.

7. In 2003 the Beijing Municipal Bureau of Environmental Protection said the city would try to reduce the amount of suspended particles from 150

micrograms per cubic metre to 100 micrograms by 2008. The authorities said the construction sites covered 114 million square yards in Beijing and were the major cause of air pollution. Liu Li, 'Beijing to Tackle Particle Pollution', *China Daily*, 4 March 2003.

8. Oliver August, 'Beijing Signs up Son of Hitler's Architect', *The Times*, 14 February 2003.

9. Mark O'Neill, 'Andreu's "Egg" on the Line', *South China Morning Post*, 7 August 2000; 'To Build or Not to Build', *South China Morning Post*, 21 September 2000; 'Bubble Opera House Project "too expensive"', *South China Morning Post*, 3 September 1999; 'National Theatre or National Joke?' *South China Morning Post*, 31 March 2000.

10. Paul Andreu, 'Defiant Design', *South China Morning Post*, 10 July 2000.

11. Interview with Zhang Dali in 2005.

12. 'Old Beijing: the Director of UNESCO Office Beijing has Met the Beijing Municipality', UNESCO press release, April 2003.

13. Interview with Ole Scheeren in April 2005.

14. 'CCTV to Get New Home: Kool Enough for Beijing?' *China Daily*, 2 March 2004.

15. Speech at press conference, 28 March 2002 (see www.beijing-2008.org).

16. 'Woodhead Competes for Beijing Olympic Hotel', 20 December 2002, www.infolink.com.au; 'Beijing Gives Nod to U.S. Urban Designer for Vision of New City Center – Chinese Commissioned International Design Firms to Create Scheme for a New Beijing Central Business District', Johnson Fain Partners, Business Wire, 19 April 2001, Los Angeles.

17. Ron Gluckman, 'I. M. Pei', August 2001 (www.gluckman.com).

18. Xinhua, 'City Planning Blamed for Beijing's Extreme Weather', 6 September 2004.

Chapter 18: Destroy!

1. I am grateful for the help and research of Dmitri Napara.
2. Ian Johnson, *Wild Grass: Three Stories of Change in Modern China* (New York: Pantheon, 2004).

Index

Academy of Engineering 293
Academy of Science 293
Acton, Harold 200
   Peonies and Ponies 200
actresses 220, 222, 227, 233,
   317–18
   see also Jiang Qing; Peking Opera
Adams, John: *Nixon in China*
   (opera) 234–5
Afghanistan 296
Africa 36
Ahmad the Saracen 22
Ai Qing 282–3
Ai Weiwei (son of Ai Qing) 282–3,
   295
Aisin Gioro clan 120–21, 127, 128,
   134, 137
   see also Manchu dynasty/empire
Albazinian community 301, 302,
   304
All-China Daoist Federation 263
All-China National Association of
   Literati against Japanese
   Aggression 204, 207
All-China Writers' Association 212
almanacs *see* calendars/almanacs
Alsop, Joseph 181
Altan Khan 36
Altar of the Sun 257–8

America 70, 212, 278
   Beijing, liberation of, 1945 205
   Beijing Legation 114–15
   China and 163, 164, 224
   Lao She in 205
   Liang Sicheng in 189, 276
   museum collections 239, 240–41
Amur (Black Dragon) River 128,
   180, 301–2
amusements/pastimes 151–2, 158,
   166–7, 191, 237, 238, 258–9,
   269
   karaoke 149, 159, 160
   see also cultural life/traditions
ancestral worship 23, 73–4, 75, 76,
   135, 260, 309, 310–11
Andreu, Paul 234, 293–5, 296, 299
Anti-Japanese War of Resistance
   158–9
antiques trade/markets 236, 239,
   240–42, 243–52
   imitations/fakes 252
archaeological excavations 25–6,
   76, 238
   in Xanadu 31–2
architectural history 185, 188–9
architecture *see* buildings/
   architecture; individual
   architects

archives/manuscripts 112, 113,
119–22, 123, 133, 134, 213,
214–15
Communist Party 216
destruction of 119–20, 215
Ming dynasty 214
personal files 213–14, 215, 229
Qing dynasty 214–15
armaments/warfare 18–19, 22, 64
armies
Manchu 68, 128, 129, 130
Ming 34, 35, 36, 65–6, 68
Mongol 18–19, 21–2, 35, 36, 65
see also People's Liberation Army
art/art collections 13, 21, 104, 132,
134, 236, 237, 240–42, 253–4
animals in art 241
art as propaganda 245–7
Communist leaders as collectors
249, 253–4
dispersal of 239, 240–42, 243–53
European/American collectors
92–3, 239, 240
graffiti art 295–6
imperial art collection 158,
239–40
modern 282–3, 295–6
pen and ink 242, 247
performance art 282
social realism in art 246–7
Zen Buddhism influence on
241–2
see also cultural life/traditions;
museums/museum collections
art dealers 242, 245, 250, 251, 252
art history 238, 242, 282
Ove Arup Engineering 294
Associated Press 165
Association to Protect the Country
98, 102
Association of Small Peoples and

Ethnic Groups of the North
(modern Russia) 20
astrology see geomancy
astronomy 16, 30, 118, 154, 305
Attiret, Father 85–6
auctions 253, 254
see also antiques trade/markets
Avenue of Eternal Peace (Chang'an
Jie) 169–70, 292

Ba Jin 201, 202, 216, 217
Babaoshan crematorium 135–6,
212
Backhouse, Sir Edmund 110–11,
112–13, 119, 126
Annals and Memoirs of the Court
of Peking 113
China under the Empress
Dowager 112
The Diary of His Excellency
Ching-san 112
Bada Hutong see brothels
Badaling 26, 27, 70
Baikal, Lake 25
bandits 65–6, 67–9, 90
Bank of China headquarters 298
Bauhaus design school 277–8, 296
bazaars see markets/bazaars
Beijing
as Beiping (Northern Peace) 37,
157
business/financial districts 288,
297
as capital city 6, 15, 17, 35, 39,
191–2; under Mao 165, 278
Chaoyang district 288, 297
Chongwen district 312
city gates 169, 182, 192; see also
individual gates
Hepingli district 23
history 1–2, 4–5, 6–11, 15–24,

33, 34, 36, 37–44, 156–7; *see also individual dynasties/ emperors*
as Khanbalik 16
Manchu quarter (Tartar City) 17, 128, 129
as military headquarters 6, 7, 16, 35, 37, 39, 43, 65
as Peiping 205
as religious centre 6, 12, 16, 18, 22–3, 49, 256–60, 262–5, 269; *see also individual religions*
as a ruin 33; rebuilding 33, 34, 35, 37–44
Tianqiao district 152
as a walled city 17, 23, 37, 42–3, 182, 191, 192
Xicheng (western) district 39, 288
Xuanwu district 304, 307
Xuanwumen district 39
Beijing City God temple 257
Beijing City Master Plan, 1991–2010 106
Beijing City Planning Commission 190–91
Beijing Performing Arts School 220, 225–6, 231, 234
see also Peking Opera
Beijing Union Medical Hospital 278
Beijing University 2–3, 92, 108, 151, 162, 172, 173, 174, 194, 200, 203–4, 278
Beijing Writers' Association 212
Beixin Book Company 202
Belgian Legation 124, 125
Bell Temple fair 268–9
Bell Tower 46, 169, 187
Belvedere Palace 86
Benoît, Father 93–4, 253
Bian Zhongyun 173, 174

Bing Xin 217
Bixia (Jade Maiden of Divine Immortality) 266, 267
Black Dragon River *see* Amur River
Bland, J. O. P. 112
Blofeld, John 153
    Peking: City of Lingering Splendour 222
Bloody August, 1966 173–5, 176
Bloomsbury Group 197, 200
Blue Shirt youth organization 158
Bo Xilai (son of Bo Yibo) 194, 284
Bo Yibo 194, 284
Bodde, Derk 163, 164, 166
Bodleian Library, Oxford 112
Boerschmann, Ernst 185
Bourgeois, Father 93
Boxer rebellion, 1900 75, 89–90, 91, 98, 115–18, 154, 178
    effects of 113, 115, 119, 123, 130, 154
    Empress Dowager (Cixi) and 98, 116–18, 140, 154, 272
Boxers (Society of Righteous Fists) 98, 117, 228, 272
Bramah, Ernest 110
Brecht, Bertolt 11, 224–5, 226
    The Good Woman of Sichuan 225
    The Measures Taken 225
Bredon, Juliet: *Peking* 26–7, 42
bribery *see* corruption/bribery
British Museum 241
brothels 148–50, 152–6, 159–61, 181, 210, 221–2
    Communist Party purging of 149–50, 152, 159
    numbers of 152
Buck, Pearl 110
A Bucket of Manure (play) 227

Buddhism 18, 49, 142, 226
  eunuchs as Buddhists 54, 58–9,
    145
  living Buddhas 262–3
  Tantric 262
  Tibetan 262–3
  Zen 242
Buddhist temples 189
Building Height Zoning Act 105–6,
    283, 292, 294
building methods/materials 185–8,
    192, 193, 278
  Ming dynasty 186–7
  modern 285–6
  Qing dynasty 187
  Sung dynasty 185
buildings/architecture 156, 185–7
  chai demolition signs 301, 302–3
  conservation of 6, 12, 102–8,
    190–93, 194–5, 279, 296–7,
    306–8, 309, 310, 311–13
  courtyard houses 2, 8, 103, 104,
    105, 106, 107–8, 162, 293
  entrance halls 107–8
  as engineering projects 280, 281,
    283, 284, 285–6, 294–5, 297
  hutongs (streets) 8, 22, 40–41,
    106, 126
  Liang Sicheng on 185, 188–9
  modernization/destruction of
    1–9, 13, 22, 23, 102–8, 151,
    168–71, 188–9, 192–3,
    276–300, 306–8, 315–26
  'nail households' 305
  pailou 196
  as social engineering 276–7, 285
  Soviet designed 168, 278–9, 280
  standardization of 280, 281
  town plans/layouts 30, 187,
    191–2, 193, 285–7, 291–2,
    312–13

watertowns 12
  see also housing shortages;
    individual buildings/architects
Bureau of Returning Looted Goods
    249
burial *see* death/burial
Bush, George (Sr), in China 249
businesses *see* trades/businesses

Cai Er, General (Yunnan warlord)
    156
Cai Jinhua (the Golden Flower)
    154–5, 222, 228
Cai Shen (God of Wealth) 260–61
Cai Yuanpei 108
calendars/almanacs 47, 260, 261,
    262, 267–8
  Wannian Li 305
  calligraphy 21, 75, 81, 134
  see also languages/orthographies
Cambodia 7, 126
Camel caravans 19, 25
Canton (Guangzhou) 87, 200
Cao Ming 211, 212, 218
Cao Wulin 157, 201
Cao Yu 217
Capital Architectural Commission
    105
Carter, Howard 76
Castiglione, Giuseppe (Lang Shi-
    nong) 93, 308, 309
castration 144
  see also eunuchs
censorship 13, 55, 202
Central Academy of Arts 245–6
Ceramics *see* porcelain/ceramics
Ch'oe P'u 38–9
Chagadai Khan 22
chai (demolition) signs 301, 302–3
  see also modernization
Chan sect *see* Zen Buddhism

Chang Yuchun, General 306
Changchun 139, 163, 165
Changzhen, Ming Emperor 72
Chaoyang Park 157
Chen Boda 249
Chen Chen: 'To the Hall of
   Heavenly Enlightenment' 51–2
Chen Xitong 105, 106–7, 160, 231,
   282, 283, 284
Chen Yi, Marshal 104
Chen You, Ming General 43
Chen Zhanxiang 192, 193
Cheng Yanqiu 223
Chiang Kai-shek 157–8, 159, 164,
   207
children 130, 131, 268–9, 279
   one-child policy 134
China
   European image of 92–3,
      109–13, 119, 125, 163, 200,
      205, 224
   European influence on 93–4, 109,
      113, 185, 197; see also
      missionaries
   as a nation 22
   as People's Republic of China 83,
      101–2, 132–4, 151–2, 157–9,
      165
   Western authors writing on 109,
      110–13, 124–5, 126; see also
      individual authors
China Cultural Relics Recovery
   Programme 253
Chinese Central Television
   headquarters 297
China Environmental News 279
Chinese empire 26–7
Chinese flag, design of 190, 191
Chinese Forestry Research Institute 80
Chinese Institute of Theoretical
   Physics 272

Chinese League of Nations
   Association 201
Chirac, Jacques, in China 293
Chongqing (Chunking) 159, 189,
   204
Chongzhen, Ming Emperor 198,
   309–10
Christianity 115, 117
   Russian Orthodox 114, 301, 302,
      304
   see also churches; missionaries
Christies auction house 243
Chu Yu-lin, David 107
churches 114, 124, 202, 269
   see also Christianity
Civil servants 34, 38, 50, 53–4,
   56–7, 67, 100, 314–15, 316
   see also public administration
Cixi (Yehonola), Qing Empress
   Dowager 50, 88, 98, 104,
      121–2, 152, 198, 250
   Edmund Backhouse on 112, 113
   Boxer rebellion and 98, 116–18,
      140, 154, 272
   character 111, 219, 221
   death/burial 73, 135
   opera, love of 219, 221
   power/influence 89–91, 97,
      118–19, 122, 123, 156
   Pu Yi and 138
climatic conditions 39, 81
   pollution 2, 39, 62, 71, 279,
      289–90, 299, 310
Clinton, Bill, in China 233–4
clothes/textiles 38–9, 47, 77–9,
   151, 208, 262
   dragon robes 77
   as indication of rank 54
   Manchu 128, 129
   standardization of design 281
   women's 86, 151

Coleridge, Samuel Taylor: *Kubla Khan* 25, 30, 31, 32
colours, significance of 48, 187
communes/community living 170–71, 277, 279–80
Communist Mansions 171, 280
communications 27, 121, 151, 170, 289
see also transportation
Communist Party 4, 9–11, 12, 13, 63, 102, 103, 104, 136, 157
archives/records 216
'Cleanse the Ranks' movement 178, 229
cultural life, attitude to 226–8, 232, 243–6
economic programme 285–6
founding of 202
history, their official version of 83, 86, 205
housing allocated to members of 280–81
'Let One Hundred Flowers Bloom' campaign 207, 209
opposition to 202–3, 208
political ideals 167–8, 204, 292
public morality, commitment to 149–50, 152, 159
purges 207, 208, 209–10; Anti-Rightist 167–8, 208, 212, 243
religious life/festivals: eradication of 256, 257–8; support for 267–8
support for 164–5, 166; membership numbers 291–2
works of art, destruction of 243–6
see also Cultural Revolution; political issues; Red Guards
Communist Youth League 83, 194, 202, 284

concubines 86, 118, 151, 153, 154, 198, 308–9
Confucius 100, 196, 238
Confucius, Temple of 82, 163, 196, 197, 248, 262
examinations held by 196–7
Confucianism 6, 7, 49, 52, 74, 82, 101, 113, 197, 198
political reform and 96–8, 99, 100
corruption/bribery 4, 5, 42, 55–6, 91, 283, 307
court life 38, 39, 41, 43, 45–6, 47–50, 51–3, 85–6, 112, 118
archival records of 119–22, 123
eunuchs *see* eunuchs
politics and 54–6
as pro-Western 113
see also individual emperors/ empresses
courtesans 222, 228
see also brothels/prostitutes
courtyard houses 2, 8, 103, 104, 105, 106, 107–8, 162, 293
see also buildings/architecture
crafts 187–8,
furniture-making 6, 236–7, 243, 252, 254
toy-making 130–32
Creation Society 202
Crematoria *see* Babaoshan crematorium
Crescent Moon Society 183, 201–2, 208, 213
crime/punishment 9–10, 37–8, 55, 56, 146, 273
corruption/bribery 4, 5, 42, 55–6, 91, 283, 307
executions 96, 97–8, 118, 166, 309–10
labour camps 141, 166, 179, 243, 303

prisons 318–21

secret police 49, 104, 111, 121, 160, 167, 271, 273, 315

Crook, Carl 4

cultural life/traditions 6, 7–8, 11, 12, 129, 151, 185, 209

amusements/pastimes 149, 151–2, 158, 159, 160, 166–7, 191, 237, 238, 258–9, 269

art see art/art collections

attacks on 78, 100–101, 102, 172–9, 226–8; in Cultural Revolution 167–8, 172–9, 184, 193, 197–213, 217–18, 228–31, 247–9

barbarian customs 19; Mongol 38–9

for children 130, 131

Communist Party attitude to 226–8, 231, 243–6

crafts 6, 187–8, 130–32, 236–7, 243, 252, 254

literature 81, 197–218, 264

music/dance see music/dance; Peking Opera

theatre see theatre

Cultural Relics Bureau 242, 245, 248, 250, 251, 253, 307

Cultural Revolution, 1966–76 4, 5–6, 12–13, 63, 126, 134, 136, 141, 145, 193–4, 215

as anti-intellectual 167–8, 172–9, 184, 193, 197–213, 217–18, 228–31, 247–9

Anti-Rightist Movement 167–8, 208, 212, 243

atrocities during 166–8, 173–6, 178–9, 183, 184, 194, 197–8, 209, 211, 212, 228–30, 236, 247–8, 309

Beijing during 125–6, 162–7, 169

'Cleanse the Ranks' movement 178, 229

destruction during: of monuments 75, 92; of museum collections 78–9, 179, 236, 248–9

development/growth 101, 162–7

ending of 103, 306

Four Olds campaign 78, 176, 243, 285, 312

Great Leap Forward 168, 170–71; famine during see famine

Legation Quarter during 125–6, 169

Red Guards see Red Guards

'struggle' sessions 184, 198, 209, 216, 229, 248

student participation 172–9, 194; see also Red Guards

see also Mao Zedong

Dalai Lama 244–5, 262

Danby, Hope 91–2, 94

The Garden of Perfect Brightness 90

dance see music/dance

Daoguang, Emperor 87, 94, 132

Daoism 49, 53, 226, 263–5, 269

Quanzhen Sect 263

Righteous Sect 263–4, 266

Datong garrison 35, 64, 65

de Beauvoir, Simone 126

death/burial 26–7

Babaoshan crematorium 135–6, 212

commercial cemeteries 135, 136

funeral rituals 73, 74–5, 135, 146

Hua Long Imperial Cemetery 134

Ming tombs 17, 42, 44, 71–9

of Mongol khans 32, 72

Qing tombs 73, 134–5, 136

death/burial – *cont.*
 suicide 198, 208, 229–30, 234, 254
defence issues 64–5, 66–7, 68, 91, 111
 see also armies; Great Wall
democracy movements 9, 10–11, 13, 55, 106, 151–2, 319
 see also internal conflict; political issues
Democracy Wall, Xidan 11, 55, 319
Deng Tuo 104
Deng Rong (daughter of Deng Xiaoping) 194, 284–5
Deng Xiaoping 10, 55, 75, 231, 270, 271, 284, 286
 death 270, 286
 economic reforms 250
Dengshikou 41, 43
Deshengmen Gate 103, 188
Detheve, Doctor 123
Di Wang Miao temple 74
Diaoyutai, Lake 21
dissent *see* democracy movements
Ditan Park 52–3, 82, 181
Ditan Temple (Temple of the Earth) 269
divorce *see* marriage/divorce
doctors *see* medicine
dogs, as pets 166–7
Dongan Gate 43
Dongbei 128
 see also Manchuria
Dongbian Gate 43
Dongdan airfield 163, 169
Dongsi mosque 43
Dongyue Miao (Zhengyi Daoist temple) 263–5
Dorgon, Manchu General 72–3
dragon motifs, significance of 107

dragons 261–2
Dream of the Chamber 209
Dream of the Red Mountain 104
drink *see* food/drink
drought 290–91
 see also water supplies
Drum Tower 45, 46, 169, 187
Drunken Beauty (opera) 232
Du Zhonglian 301, 302, 303
Duan Kang (high consort of Pu Yi) 144
Duan Qirui 156–7
Dubinin, Viktor *see* Du Zhonglian
Dunhuang 242

earthquakes 182
East Asian Art Museum, Berlin 241
East Asian Art Museum, Stockholm 241
Eastern Peak Temple, Mount Tai (Daoist) 263–4
economic crisis, 1997 285
Einstein, Albert 257
Eisenstein, Sergei 224
Elgin, James Bruce, 8th Earl (Lord Elgin) 88–9, 90, 94, 299
Ellsworth, Robert 250
Empress Dowager *see* Cixi
Empson, William 51, 200
England
 Beijing Legation 114, 123, 125, 178–9
 English residents in Beijing 109, 110–11, 314–15, 322
 trade delegation to China 24, 69, 87, 121
 Yuanming Yuan, burning of 83, 89, 90
Enlightenment (newspaper) 101
ethnic/minority groups 132, 133, 134, 303–4

see also individual groups
eunuchs 1, 4, 36, 51, 65, 97, 113, 187, 306, 311
  castration 144
  characteristics 57–8, 142–4
  as corrupt 56
  numbers of 54, 56, 57, 76
  palace duties 24, 45, 46, 54, 56, 57–8, 67, 80, 91, 122–3, 138, 141–5
  as 'palace rats' 57
  as a political group 54, 56, 57, 65
  power/influence 54, 56–60, 65, 104
  Pu Yi's expulsion of 144–5
  surviving in modern China 142–6
  temples/monasteries endowed by 58–9
environmental issues 299
  see also pollution
Evenk people 20
executions 96, 97–8, 118, 166, 309–10
  see also crime/punishment

Fahai Temple 58–9
Fairbank, Wilma 190
  Liang and Lin . . . 188
Falun Gong sect 271–2, 273, 275, 319, 320, 321
family
  ancestral worship 23, 73–4, 75, 76, 135, 260, 309, 310–11
  children 130, 131, 268–9, 279; one-child policy 134
  importance of 260–61
famine, 1958–62 79, 82, 140, 168, 171, 172, 210, 227, 244, 270, 280
Fan Jun 204
fatalism 133, 203

Fayuan Si temple 21
female impersonators (*dan*) 219, 222–4, 227, 232; *see also* Peking Opera
Feng Xiaonian 307
Feng Xuefeng 207
Feng Yuxiang 91, 145
Fengxian (Little Fenxian) 155–6
festivals/rituals 21, 52–3, 131, 134, 137, 258–62, 264–9, 309
  see also religious life
film industry 220, 224, 228
First World War, 1914–18 101, 111, 157, 277
Fleming, Peter: *The Siege at Peking* 113, 117–18
the 'floating world' 222
Fokkema, Douwe 180
folk religions 131, 257, 265–7
  see also festivals/rituals
food/drink 27–8, 32, 39, 40, 41, 46, 121–2, 269, 274, 304, 305
  Manchu 129
  market gardens 41
  moon cakes 132
  rationing 163
  rice 24, 40
  see also famine
Forbidden City 7, 8, 21, 23, 42, 44, 45–60, 68, 85, 103, 105–6, 118, 191, 183
  as administrative centre 45–6, 47–9, 53–4
  art collection 158, 239–40
  audiences given in 45, 46, 53
  design/layout 46–7, 187, 188
  First History Archives 120, 134
  foreigners admitted to 75
  Hall of Supreme Harmony (Taihe Dian) 46, 47, 48
  living quarters 51–2

Forbidden City – *cont.*
  as the Palace Museum 120, 147,
    179
  as the Purple City 48
  Sea of Flagstones (Haimen) 46,
    47
  size 49–50
  as World Heritage Site 283, 296
foreign currency 250
foreign occupations 113, 115, 119,
    123, 130, 154, 156–7, 163–4,
    165–6, 239
  Japanese, 1937 120, 126, 137–8,
    158–9, 203–4, 205, 241
  Manchu, 1644 68, 72, 85, 129
foreign relations 87–90, 97, 102,
    113–18, 126
  Opium Wars 16, 84, 87–8, 97,
    114, 117
  see also Legation Quarter
foreign residents, regulation of
    314–15, 322–3
foreign travel, by the Chinese 253,
    323
Forster, E. M. 200
fortune telling 267
  see also geomancy
Foster, Lord Norman 294, 298
France 88–90
  Beijing Legation 114, 123–4,
    125, 126
  China and 239–40
  French residents in Beijing
    109–10, 123
  Paris 276–7, 293
Freeman-Mitford, Algernon 89
Freer, Charles Lang 240
Friendship Stores 245, 249
Fu Zuoyi, Nationalist General 163,
    164
funerals *see* death/burial

furniture/furniture-making 6
  Ming dynasty 237, 243, 250,
    252, 253, 254

Gang of Four 220, 271
  see also Jiang Qing
gardens/parks 80–86, 88, 89–95
  trees 71, 80, 81–2, 94–5, 163
  see also individual gardens/parks
Gate of Heavenly Peace
    (Tiananmen) 12, 46–7, 55,
    169
Genghis Khan 21–2, 25–6, 28, 36,
    263, 269
  ancestral temple to 31–2
geomancy 36, 72, 122, 267
George III 87
Germany 101, 118, 154
  Beijing Legation 124, 125, 272
  Berlin 277–8, 297
Ghaffar Pourazar 225–6, 231, 232,
    233–4
Gobelin tapestries 239–40
Golden Water Canal 46
Gong, Prince (brother of Xianfeng)
    88, 89, 97, 104
Gordon, Eric 175
Gorky, Maxim 201
graffiti art 295–6
Grand Canal 1, 2, 16, 21, 23–4, 36,
    40, 288, 291
  barge traffic 24, 36, 130
  Tonghui He extension 23
Grand National Theatre 234, 291,
    293, 294, 295, 299
  see also theatre
Great Hall of the People 278, 290
Great Khan's Palace 15, 16
Great Leap Forward, 1958–62 168,
    170–71, 193, 210, 227, 243,
    270, 279, 286

Lin Xu 96, 97–8, 99, 100
Lin Yutang 152–3, 159
Lin Zexu 87
literature/authors 197–218
    artistic freedom/repression
        206–7, 210–13
    Chinese translations of Western
        authors 200, 202
    left-wing 201, 202
    poetry 81, 201, 247, 283
    Wen Chang, God of Literature
        264
    women writers 217
    see also cultural life; individual
        authors
Literature Research Institute 209
Liu Guangdi 96, 97–8, 99, 100
Liu Meide 173
Liu Qi 284, 286, 297–8
Liu Qin 65
Liu Shaoqi, President 171, 172, 174
Liuli Chang antique market 239,
    240, 252
local government 34, 35
    see also public administration
Longfu Temple 43
Loti, Pierre 109, 115–16, 123
Lu Ling 218
Lu Xiaoman 201
Lu Xun 100–101, 108, 176, 202,
    217
Lu Xun Arts Academy, Yan'an
    226–7
Lu Zhong 58
Luo Zhenyu 119–20

Ma, Empress (wife of Zhu
    Yuanzhang) 35
Ma Chengyuan 236, 237, 242,
    254
    in Tibet 244

Ma family 305–7, 308
Macartney, George, 1st Earl 24, 69,
    87, 121
Madagascar 36
Malraux, André 133
Manchu army 68, 128, 129, 130
Manchu bannermen 128, 129, 130,
    135, 201, 302
Manchu dynasty/empire 6, 7, 17,
    18, 20, 24, 34, 66–7, 85, 86,
    118, 262
    Aisin Gioro clan 120–21, 127,
        128, 134, 137
    Beijing, invasion of, 1644 68, 72,
        85, 129
    China, impact on 128–9
    decline 137–47
    genealogy 120–21, 124
    as Jurchens 22, 66
    numbers of 128, 34
    Russia and 301–2
    see also Qing dynasty/empire
Manchu language 128, 129, 132
Manchuguo (Japanese puppet state)
    137–8, 139
Manchuria 69, 118, 128, 133
    Chinese population 139
    as Dongbei 128
    Japan and 139, 157; occupation
        of, 1932 69
    labour camps 41, 166, 243
    Russia and 138, 139, 140
Manchurian language 128, 129
Manchurian nationalism 138–9
mandarins 54–5, 57, 87, 91, 144
    as Confucians 54
    see also political groups
Mao: The Unknown Story 166
Mao Zedong 7, 8, 12, 34, 43, 104,
    162–82, 210–11, 311–12
    in Beijing 112, 162–8, 278

Mao Zedong – *cont.*
  'bombard the headquarters'
    proclamation 174
  character 162–3, 168
  criticism of 79, 171–2, 227
  death 11, 55, 103, 182, 220, 231
  as an icon 268
  as a librarian 151, 162
  literary works 209–10
  marriage *see* Jiang Qing
  mausoleum 12, 79, 182, 290
  political ideals 102, 133, 166,
    177
  public appearances 165
  Western reactions to 125–6
Marco Polo 15–16, 22, 23–4, 28,
    30, 64
  Travels 22, 305
Marco Polo Bridge 158, 320
Marcuse, Jacques 169
  The Peking Papers 151, 242
markets/bazaars 40–42, 43, 46, 91,
    98, 131, 164, 264
  imperial (make-believe) 85–6
  Lantern Bazaar 41–2, 43
marriage/divorce 151
Marx, Karl 63, 162, 177, 225
May Fourth Movement, 1919 101,
    108, 157, 199, 201
medicine 8, 82–3, 121, 123, 146
  hospitals 269, 270, 305
  qigong based 269–70, 275
Mei Lanfung 223, 224, 227, 228,
    232, 234
de Mendoza, Juan Gonzalez: *The
    great and mighty kingdom of
    China* 53
Meng Xuenong 286, 296
mental asylums 247–8
Meridian (Wumen) Gate 46–7, 52,
    54, 55, 98, 310

Metropolitan Museum of Art, New
    York 240
Miaofeng Shan pilgrimage centre
    265–7, 273–4
millenarianism 33–4, 87
Ming army 34, 35, 36, 68
  ethnic Mongols in 65–6
Ming dynasty/empire (Han Chinese)
    2, 6, 8, 17–18, 24, 25, 33–5,
    36, 68–9, 75–6, 152, 165
  archives/records 214
  building methods/materials
    186–7
  decline 42, 54, 59–60, 63, 120
  furniture from 237, 243, 250,
    252, 253, 254
  see also individual Ming emperors
Ming tombs 17, 42, 44, 71–9
  construction 73
  destruction/restoration 71, 72–3
  grave goods 77
  tomb robbers 76
missionaries 75, 114
  Boxer massacre of 117
  Catholic/Jesuit *see* Jesuit
    missionaries
Miyun Reservoir 170, 290
modernization 5–6, 8–13, 125,
    127, 150, 151, 238–9, 257–8,
    265, 309, 315–26
  American 278
  of buildings/architecture *see*
    buildings/architecture
  chai (demolition) signs 301,
    302–3
  of cultural life 78, 100–101, 102;
    during Cultural Revolution
    167–8, 171, 17–9, 184, 193,
    197–211, 217–18, 228–31
  environmental problems caused
    by 299

European 276–8
of Legation Quarter 113–14
resistance to 6, 13, 81, 82,
    106–7, 287, 288, 289, 295–6,
    298–9, 302–3, 312–13
as social engineering 276–7,
    279–80
tree-planting schemes 81, 82,
    287
monasteries *see* temples/monasteries
Mongol army 18–19, 21–2, 35, 36,
    65
Mongol khans 32, 72, 262, 305
    see also individual khans
Mongolia 25, 26, 27–8, 66, 139
Mongolian nationalism 29
Mongols 6, 7, 16, 17, 21–3, 25–6,
    59, 64–5, 302
    campaigns against 35, 36, 37
    customs/language 38–9
    as nomads 30, 31
    rebellions against 33–4
    as Tartars 16–17
The Monkey King 226
de Montauban, General Charles 90
Montesquieu, Charles-Louis de
    Secondat 113
Monument to the People's Heroes
    191
Morrison, Dr George Ernest 11
mortality rate 299
mosques 304, 306, 307, 308, 309
    see also Muslims
Mote, Professor Frederick W. 185
Mu Xin: 'On the Reactionary
    Thought of the Play Sai
    Junhua' 228–9
Museé Cernuschi, Paris 241
Museé National des Arts Asiatiques-
    Guimet, Paris 241
Museum of Chinese Art 239–40

Museum of Modern Chinese
    Literature 103, 216–18
Museum of Revolutionary History
    246, 278
museums/museum collections 12,
    59, 78, 119–20, 244, 265
    in America 239, 240–41
    during Cultural Revolution 78–9,
        179, 236
    Tibetan art in Chinese museums
        244, 265
    see also art/art collections
music/dance 59, 151, 169, 259
    Communist Party attitude to
        226–7
    opera 79, 144, 171, 219, 220–21,
        223–4, 227, 228, 230, 231,
        233; *see also* Peking Opera
    Yangge planting song 164
    see also cultural life
musical instruments 238, 254, 259
Muslims 16, 36, 43, 86, 304–9
    Hui community 304
    mosques 304, 306, 307, 308,
        309
    as Saracens 22, 305
Mussolini, Benito 277

Nanjing 17, 24, 34, 35, 38, 55, 69,
    73, 157
    as Nationalist centre 157, 158,
        159, 165, 200
    as Taiping capital 87
Nanjing, Treaty of, 1842 87–8
Nankou Pass 21, 25, 26–7
Nanquin, Professor Susan 267
    Peking Temples and City Life . . .
        256–7
Nanting (Southern) Church 114
National Art Gallery 282
National Sports Commission 271

Nationalist Party (KMT) 12–13,
    104, 120, 133, 158–9, 162
  Beijing, liberation by, 1945 205
  censorship by 202
  Communist defeat of, 1948–9
    162–7
Nationalist Party Propaganda
    Committee 207
Nelson, William Rockhill 240
New Life Movement 158
New Year festival 260–61, 267
Nguyen An 47
Nie Rongzhen, Marshal 104
Nie Yuanzi 172
Nien Cheng: *Life and Death in
    Shanghai* 249
Nieuhof, Johan 37
night soil 163
Nixon, Richard, in China 70, 230
  Nixon in China (opera) 234–5
nomadic peoples 17, 18–20
  Mongols as 30, 31
nuclear warfare 180–81, 270–71
numbers, significance of 187
Nurhachi, Manchu leader 66, 311

Office for Metropolitan
    Architecture (OMA) 297
Ogodei Khan 22
Olympic Games 1936 277–8
Olympic Games 2008 8, 288–90,
    292, 294, 295, 297–8, 301
one-child policy 134
opera 79, 144, 171, 219, 224, 227,
    228, 230
  Communist Party attitudes to
    227, 231
  plots 220–21, 223–4
  training for 220, 223
  travelling companies 221
  Yue 233

  see also Peking Opera
opera dynasties 221–2
opium 87, 152, 167, 222
Opium Wars 16, 84, 87–8, 97, 114,
    117
Ortega y Gasset, José 177
Otani, Count 238

palaces (*wangfu*) 8, 37, 93, 103,
    104, 107, 118
  see also individual palaces
Panchen Lama 262
parades, political 168–70
paranormal powers 255, 256,
    269–75
Parkes, Harry 88
parliamentary assemblies 151, 152,
    291
Peck, Graham 158–9
peddlers 131
Pei, I. M. 105, 293, 298
Pei, Li Chung (son of I. M. Pei) 298
Pei, Lien (son of I. M. Pei) 298
Peking, Treaty of, 1901 118
Peking Opera 6, 57, 172, 198, 206,
    219, 220, 221, 222, 231–2
  acting styles 224–6, 233
  Communist Party attitude to 227
  in Cultural Revolution 197,
    228–31
  English translations of their plays
    200
  history 221–2, 228
  Jiang Qing and 220, 224, 227–31
  males in female roles (*dan*) 219,
    222–4, 227, 232, 234
  as a propaganda tool 227–8
  reputation 224, 230–31
  training for 220, 225–6, 228,
    230, 234
  see also opera

Pelliot, Paul 238
Peng Dehuai, Marshal 168, 172, 227
Peng Zhen 166, 169, 170, 171, 172, 311–12
People's Liberation Army (PLA) 10–11, 32, 157, 158–9, 162, 179
  8th Route Army 163, 164
  eight points of discipline 164
  hospitals run by 269, 270
  Zhang Baosen and 255, 272
Percival, Sir David 241
Perry, Commodore Matthew 97
Persia 36, 37, 64
Philadelphia Museum of Art 239
pigeons 237, 238
pigtails, significance of 86
Pingyao, Shanxi province 12, 13, 251
pleasure houses *see* brothels
poetry 81, 201, 247, 283
  see also individual authors; literature/authors
Poland 278
political freedom 151–2
political groups
  eunuchs as 54, 56, 57, 65
  mandarins 54–5, 57, 87, 91, 144
  May Fourth Movement, 1919 101, 108, 157, 199, 201
  students as 101, 157, 158, 164, 166, 203–4; in Cultural Revolution 172–9, 194
  see also Communist Party
political issues 7, 9–11, 166
  Boxer rebellion, 1900 *see* Boxer rebellion
  at court 54–6
  Cultural Revolution *see* Cultural Revolution

democracy movements 9, 10–11, 13, 55, 106, 151–2, 319
  Marxism 63, 162, 177, 225
  Mongolian nationalism 29
  reform movements 96–102, 117, 156, 185
  sexual behaviour and 159–61
pollution 279, 287, 299
  atmospheric 2, 39, 62, 71, 279, 289–90, 299, 310
  see also environmental issues
Poly Investments Holdings Ltd 253
population displacement/migration 4–5, 9, 12, 138–9, 287, 291
population levels 6, 39, 53
porcelain/ceramics 40, 239, 241, 249, 252
Potala Palace, Lhasa 244, 245, 248
poverty/the poor 8, 9, 38, 67, 287–8
  death by starvation 42; *see also* famine
  living conditions 99
power supplies 170, 289
press/publishing 152, 164–5
Pringle, James 25, 28–9, 30
prisons 318–21
  see also crime/punishment
propaganda
  art as 245–7
  film as 155
  theatre as 225, 227–8
prostitutes *see* brothels/prostitutes
PTW Australia (architects) 294
Pu Jie (brother of Pu Yi) 128, 137–8
Pu Pingbo 209
Pu Ren (brother of Pu Yi) 127–8, 133, 137–8, 147

Pu Yi, Henry, Qing Emperor
     118–19, 127, 128, 130, 134–8,
     144–5, 146, 147, 239, 240–41
   abdication 138, 139
   death/burial 134–5, 136
   From Emperor to Citizen 137,
     138, 140, 206
   Japan and 139
   marriage 136–7; *see also* Li
     Shuxian
   possible homosexuality 137,
     138
   as a prisoner 139, 140, 145
Pu Ziwei 132, 133, 134
Pu Zong 132, 133
public administration 45–6, 47–9,
     53–4, 114, 115, 314–15
   archival records of 119–22, 123
   civil servants 34, 38, 50, 53–4,
     56–7, 67, 100, 314–15, 316
   examinations in 196–7
   local government 32, 35
   memorials to the emperor 54–6,
     96–7, 121
   under Communism 291–2
punishment *see* crime/punishment
purple (colour), significance of 48,
     187

Qi Baishi 241
Qian Xuesen, Professor 270
Qian Zhongshu 208–10
   Fortress Besieged (*Wei Cheng*)
     208
   Guan Zhu Bian 209
Qianlong, Emperor 1–2, 69, 80–81,
     121, 156, 197, 221, 262, 310
   European art, interest in 93–4
   his Fragrant Concubine (Xiang
     Fei) 86, 198, 308–9
   gardens, love of 85, 86, 87, 94–5

   Jesuit missionaries and 92, 93–4,
     308, 309
   his tomb 135
Qiantang River 23
qigong techniques/sects 269–70,
     271, 272, 273–4, 275
Qin, Duke of 114
Qin Gui, Song prime minister 21
Qin Shi Huangdi, first Emperor of
     all China 63–4, 69, 238
Qing dynasty/empire 18, 45, 46, 50,
     51, 69, 80, 86–7, 133, 152,
     156, 262
   archives/records 214–15
   building methods/materials 187
   decline 117–18, 119, 222
   reform proposals for 96–8
   see also individual Qing rulers;
     Manchu dynasty/empire
Qing Ming festival 134, 137
Qing tombs 73, 134–5, 136
Qingdao *see* Shandong province
Qinghua University 3, 10, 92,
     163–4, 270, 271, 278, 284
   architecture department 184, 189,
     193–4, 293
   in Cultural Revolution 172–3,
     177–8, 179, 183, 184, 193–4
   founding of 193
Qiu Bai 202
Qiu Chuji (the Perfect Man) (Daoist
     abbot) 263

Raggi, Marchese Salvago 124
railways 24, 25, 43, 138–9, 279,
     290
   see also transportation
Raise the Red Lantern (opera) 230
Rashid Al-Din 30
Red Detachment of Women (play)
     230

Red Guards 5, 52, 78, 79, 92, 136,
    145, 172–81, 183, 211, 212,
    228, 312
  100 days war 177–8, 184, 185,
    194, 284
  April Fourteenth Faction 178,
    184, 194, 284
  as Communist Party officials 194,
    284
  factionalism among 177–8, 236
  Jinggangshan Regiment 177–8,
    194, 284
  in Legation Quarter 125–6
  origins of 172–3
  in Tibet 245
  see also Cultural Revolution
The Red Maid (opera) 223–4, 231
Red Turbans (millenarian sect)
    33–4
reform movements 96–102, 117,
    156, 185
  see also Cultural Revolution;
    democracy movements;
    political issues
religious life 6, 12, 48, 49, 50,
    256–60, 262–5
  ancestral worship 23, 73–4, 75,
    76, 135, 260, 309
  Buddhism 18, 49, 54, 58–9, 142,
    145, 226, 262–3; Tantric 262;
    Zen 241–2
  Christianity 114, 115, 124, 127,
    202, 269; Russian Orthodox
    114, 301, 302, 304
  Communist support for 267–8;
    for recognised faiths 269
  Daoism 49, 53, 226, 263–5, 266,
    269
  eradication of, under Mao 256,
    257–8
  folk religions 131, 257, 265–7

Mao as a religious icon 268
  missionaries see missionaries
  Muslims 16, 36, 43, 86, 304–9
  paranormal powers 255, 256,
    269–75
  qigong sects 269–70, 271, 272,
    273–4
  temple/monasteries see temples/
    monasteries
  see also festivals/rituals
Ren Ti Ke medicine 269
Ren Wangding 319
Ren Yansheng 194, 285
Ricci, Matteo 24, 39, 75, 114
  'Complete Map of the World'
    240
rice 24, 40
Rickshaw Boy (film) 205–6
rituals see festivals/rituals
Rong Lu, Manchu prince 108,
    113
Rousseau, Jean Jacques 113
Ruan An 187
Russia 16–17, 18, 86, 133, 224
  China and 301–2
  Cossacks in Manchu China 301,
    302
  Magadan 20
  Manchuria and 138–9, 140
  Moscow 25, 277
  trade routes to 25
  see also Soviet Union
Russian literature/authors 201, 202
Russian Orthodox Church 114,
    301, 302, 304

Sackler, Dr Arthur M. 240
salt monopoly 16, 260
Samarkand 36
Saracens 22, 305
  see also Muslims

SARS epidemic 286
satellite towns 5, 11, 287
Scheeren, Ole 297
School of Oriental and African
     Studies (SOAS), London
     199–200
School of Peasant Painters 248
the seasons 261–2
Second World War, 1939–45 190,
     278
secret police 49, 104, 111, 121,
     160, 167, 271, 273, 315
     see also crime/punishment
Ségalen, Victor 109–10, 111, 112,
     123, 124, 125, 126, 185, 325
     Essays on Exoticism 112, 125
     René Leys 111–12, 126
sexual behaviour 51–2, 53, 113,
     122–3, 222
     brothels see brothels/prostitutes
     homosexuality 113, 137, 138,
     222
     politics and 159–61
Shang Di (the Supreme Deity) 48
Shang dynasty 238
Shang Xiaoyun 223
Shangdong province, German
     colonies in 101, 157
Shangdu (Xanadu) 16, 25–6, 27,
     29–32
     archaeological excavations 31–2
     sack of, 1368 32
     see also Khublai Khan
Shanghai 104, 155, 158, 159, 165,
     200, 201, 294
     film industry 220, 222, 228
Shanghai Museum 236, 237, 249,
     254
     Zhuang Gallery of Ming furniture
     237, 254
Shanghai Stock Market 288

Shanhaiguan garrison 68
Shanxi 189
Shaoxing 100
She Yishi 311
She Youzhe, Mrs 309, 310, 311–13
Shen Congwen 202, 208
Shenyang 120
Shenzhen Stock Market 288
Shi Lu 246–8
     Down with Feudalism (painting)
     246–7
     Shifting to Fight in North Shaanxi
     (painting) 246, 247
Shu Guo (son of Shi Lu) 248
Shu Yi (son of Lao She) 96, 98, 99,
     100, 101, 102, 103–4, 107,
     108, 193, 212, 216–17, 296
Sickman, Lawrence 59, 241
siege warfare 18–19, 22, 64
Sihanouk, Prince 126
Silk Route 19, 25
Sirén, Osvald 185, 238
slave labour 37–8
Snow, Edgar 162, 200, 203–4
Snow, Helen (Mrs Edgar Snow) 200
social engineering 276–7, 285
Society of Righteous Fists see
     Boxers
Society for the Study of Marxism
     162
Song Binbin 174
Song dynasty 18, 19–22, 35, 185
Sotheby's auction house 253
Soviet Union 69–70
     China and 166, 168–9, 180
     see also Russia
Speer, Albert (senior) 277–8, 292
Speer, Albert (junior) 292
Squiers, Herbert 239
Stanislavsky (Konstantin Alekseyev)
     225, 226

Stars group of modern architects
282
Staunton, George 69
Steele, Arch 205
Stein, Sir Aurel 238
stock markets 288
'struggle' sessions 184, 198, 209,
216, 229, 248
see also Cultural Revolution
students 10, 55, 101, 102, 133
as a political force 101, 157, 158,
164, 166, 203–4; in Cultural
Revolution 172–9, 194
see also universities
the succession 51, 54, 118–19,
139–41
Suharto, Thojib 285
suicide 198, 208, 229–30, 234, 254
see also death/burial
Summer Palace 1, 2, 21, 97, 281
see also Yuanming Yuan
Sun, Madame 6, 219, 220, 223,
227, 229–32, 234
Sun Guoliang 175
Sun Tianying 135
Sun Yaoting (the last eunuch)
142–6
Sun Yat-sen, Doctor, President of
Chinese Republic 69, 110, 158,
222
the supernatural/superstition see
paranormal powers

Tai Miao (Temple of the Ancestors)
23, 73–4
Taichang, Ming Emperor 74
Taiping Hu, Lake 198, 211–12
Taipings (millenarian sect) 87
Taiwan 97
Tamerlane 36
Tan dynasty 19

Tan Sitong 96, 97–100, 108
Verses from the Misty Room
98–9
Tang dynasty wall paintings 242
Tang Qilang 129–32
Tang Song 282
Tantric Buddhism 262
Tartars see Mongols
taxation 19, 34, 36, 46, 56, 130
criticism of 55, 63
Taylor, Charles: Reporter in Red
China 246
Temple, Sir William 95
temple musicians 59
temples/monasteries 18, 22–3, 49,
104, 142, 188, 189, 256–7,
269
endowed by eunuchs 58–9, 145
Tibetan 244, 245
see also Christianity; individual
buildings
textiles see clothes/textiles
Thailand 197
theatre 220, 221, 222, 230, 232–4
actresses 220, 222, 227
acting styles 224–5, 226, 233
as a propaganda tool 225, 227–8
see also cultural life; Grand
National Theatre; Peking
Opera
Tian Han 229, 234
Tiananmen Democracy Movement
9, 10–11, 282–3
Tiananmen Square 12, 13, 15, 40,
54, 101, 115, 164, 191, 273,
299
rebuilding under Mao 168–9,
278–9
Red Guard rallies 173–4
Tianjin 24, 132, 133, 290
Tianjin, Treaty of, 1858 88

Tianning (Heavenly Tranquillity) Temple 18, 163, 189, 262, 309, 325
Tianqi, Emperor 4, 53, 56, 74
Tianqiao Theatre 230
Tibetan Buddhism 262–3
Tibetan culture 243–4
  Chinese destruction of 244, 249; protests against 244–5
Tibetan monasteries 244, 245
Tibetans 19, 26
The Times 111
Toghon Timur, Mongol Yuan Emperor 32
Tolui Khan 22
tomb robbers 250, 251
  see also death/burial
Tongxian (Tongzhou) 21, 23, 287
Tongzhi, Emperor 90–91, 152
tourism 12, 13, 152, 233–4, 267
town plans/layouts 30, 187, 191–2, 193, 285–7, 291–2, 312–13
  see also buildings/architecture
toys/toy-making 130–32
trade/trade routes 15, 16, 18, 21, 22, 27, 87–8
  Beijing as trade centre 24–5
  camel caravans 19, 25
  Canton as foreign trade centre 87
  in Chinese art 92–3
  customs tariffs 114
  English trade delegation 24, 69, 87
  Grand Canal 21, 23–4, 36, 40, 130, 288, 291
  naval exploration of 36
  Silk Route 19, 25
  warehouses 24, 130
trade guilds (*huiguan*) 259, 266
trades/businesses 39–40, 130–32, 151–2

traditions *see* cultural life/traditions
transportation 67, 170, 192–3
  by bus 316–18
  by camel 19, 25
  by car 321–2
  railways 24, 25, 43, 138–9, 279
  by water 21, 23–4, 36, 40, 130, 288, 291
  see also communications
trees 71, 80, 81, 94–5, 163
  afforestation projects 81, 82, 287
  importance of 80, 81–2
  qi attributes 81, 82
  see also gardens/parks
tribute payments 16, 18, 19–20, 24, 36, 66, 239–40
Tsai, Henry 35, 49
Tun, Prince 140
Turkestan 86

Uighurs 19, 86
UNESCO 84, 196
United Nations 190, 205, 276
United Press International (UPI) 164–5
United States *see* America
universities 10, 21, 55, 125, 133, 152, 179, 200
  see also Beijing University; Qinghua University
urban development/planning 9, 67, 105–6, 190–91
  see also modernization

Vairochana (the transcendent Buddha) 262
Vare, Daniele 109, 112, 124–5
  Laughing Diplomat 239–40
Verbiest, Ferdinand 75
Versailles, Treaty of, 1919 101, 157

Victoria and Albert Museum, London: T. T. Tsui Gallery of Chinese Art 241
Vietnam 6, 7, 47, 117, 197
Voltaire (François Marie Arouet) 63, 113
von Le Coq, Albert 238
von Schall, Adam 75, 121
von Waldersee, Field Marshal Count 154, 155

Wade, Thomas 88
Wan Li, Emperor 1, 53, 72, 74, 75, 171
    as an administrator 54, 55–6
    death 56; his tomb 71, 73, 76–7, 78–9, 208
    family 54, 56, 77
    Great Wall and 63, 66–7
Wang Baosen 160
Wang Hongcheng 270
Wang Qishan 286
Wang Rong, Empress (wife of Pu Yi) 144
Wang Shixiang 6, 237–8, 241, 242–3, 248
    art collection 237, 242, 245
    Classical Chinese Furniture . . . 237, 242
    imprisonment 242–3
    Ming furniture collection 237, 243, 250, 252, 254
Wang Ying 206, 212
Wang Youqin, Mrs 174–5
Wang Yumin 232–3, 234
Wang Zhen 59
Wang Zhi 65
Wanshou (Longevity) Temple 1, 216
warfare see armaments/warfare
Warner, Langdon 240–41

water supplies 21, 170, 279, 290–91, 299
    drought 290–91
    irrigation systems 41
watertowns 12
Wei Changsheng 202
Wei Jingshen 319
Wei Shen (Protectress of Flowers) 266
Wei Zhongxian 56, 311
Wen Chang (God of Literature) 264
Wen Hanjiang 175
Weng Tonghe 240
Wenyu River 279
White Cloud Temple (Bai Yun Guan) (Daoist) 263
White Pagoda Temple 262
Wilhelm II, Kaiser 154
wine-making 319
Witke, Roxane 228, 230
women 117, 266, 267
    as actresses 220, 222, 227, 233; see also Jiang Qing
    as concubines 86, 118, 151, 153, 154, 198, 308–9
    as courtesans 152, 154–5, 222, 228
    eunuchs and 144
    foot-binding 85, 151
    in harems 138
    as prostitutes/hostesses see brothels
    role of 220
    see also female impersonators
women writers 217
women's clothes 86, 151
women's education 152
Woodhead International (architects) 298
World Trade Organization 288
Wu Bing 282

Wu Han 75–6, 79, 165, 168, 172, 212, 222
  Hai Rui Dismissed from Office (Hai RuiBa Guan) 171–2, 227–8
Wu Liangyong, Professor 194, 293, 294
Wu Sangui, General 68, 69
Wu Shaozu 271
Wu Xian temple 131
Wu Zetian, Tang Empress 220, 229, 231
Wutai Shan Buddhist temple, Shanxi 189

Xanadu *see* Shangdu
Xi'an 19
Xi Yiangyuan 232
Xia dynasty 26
Xia Nai, Professor 76, 78
Xia Yan 222, 228–9, 234
Xianfeng, Emperor 88, 90, 219
Xiang Fei (Jipar Han) (the Fragrant Concubine) 86, 198, 308–9
Xianyang 64
Xiao Lu 282
Xiao Qian 149, 176, 200, 217
  Traveller without a Map 43, 175–6, 201–2
Xiao Rui-ji, Khitan Empress 20
Xiaoduan, Empress (wife of Wan Li) 54, 77, 78
Xiaojing (wife of Wan Li) 77–8
Xie Chensheng 253
Xinlong Temple 145
Xizhimen Gate 192, 266
Xu Da, General 34–5
Xu Daoning 241
Xu Wenli 319
Xu Xiangqian, Marshal 104
Xu Zhimou 201

Xu family 40
Xun Huisheng 172, 212, 219, 223–4, 227, 228, 229, 234

Yan'an 220, 226–7, 246
Yan Jisi 104
Yan Xin 270
Yang Fang 159
Yang Jiang (wife of Qian Zhongshu) 208–9
Yang Jisheng 99
Yang Memorial Temple 99–100
Yang Rui 96, 97–8, 99, 100
Yang Shangkun, Marshal 104
Yang Shenxiu 96, 97–8, 99, 100
Yang Yiqing, Ming General 65
Yangtze River/valley 16, 23, 24, 33–4, 35, 40, 64, 290, 291
Yangzhou 16
Yao family 40
Ye Jianying, Marshal 271
Yeh-Hei-tieh-erh (Muslim architect) 305
Yehonala (concubine to Xianfeng) *see* Cixi, Empress Dowager
Yellow City (Huang Cheng) 128
Yellow River 19, 20, 23, 24, 290
Yellow Temple 88
Ye-lu-chu-cai 31
Ying Ruocheng 208
Yingzong, Emperor 58, 59, 65
Yong He Gong (Lama Temple) 263
Yong Le (Zhu Di), Emperor (The Razor) 17, 33–44, 188, 306
  as an administrator 45–6, 47–9, 50–51, 54, 57
  Beijing, rebuilding of 33, 34, 35, 37–44
  death 36–7, 38; his tomb 71, 73, 76
  family 34–5; his purge of 35

Great Wall and 63, 64–5
personal appearance 33, 35
as a soldier 34–5, 36, 51
Yong Zheng, Emperor 263
Yongdin River 128
Yu Qiuli 104
Yu Yan (Little Jui) (father of Jin
    Hengkai) 140, 141
Yuan Chonghuan, General 66,
    309–10, 311–12, 313
Yuan dynasty (Mongol) 15, 23, 26,
    32, 41
Yuan Shikai, General 97, 120, 156
Yuanming Yuan (Garden of Perfect
    Brightness) 82, 84–6, 88,
    89–95, 182, 253, 308
    artists colony 282
    fountains 93–4, 253
    Jesuit missionaries at 113
    Porcelain Pagoda 91
    sacking of 83, 89, 90, 116–17,
    239; restoration following 90,
    91
    water clock 94
    as World Heritage Site 84
Yue Fei, Song General 21
Yue Opera 233

Zai Tao, Prince (uncle of Pu Yi) 144
Zen Buddhism 242
Zhang Baosen (The Master) 255–6,
    271, 272–5
Zhang Dali 295–6
Zhang Daqian 241–2
Zhang Fusen 194, 284
Zhang Futing 99
Zhang Jingsheng 319, 320–21
Zhang Liusun (Daoist Master)
    263–4, 269
Zhang Xianzhong 67, 68–9

Zhang Xueliang (son of Zhang
    Zuolin) (the Young Marshal)
    157, 200
Zhang Zuolin 157, 202
Zhangjiakou see Kalgan
Zhangzong, Jin Emperor 21
Zhao Qichang 76
Zhao Ziyang 9, 12, 274
Zhao family 4–5, 6
Zheng, Lady (mistress of Wan Li)
    54, 76, 77
Zheng He, Admiral 36, 306
Zheng Yici Theatre 232–4
Zheng Xiangliang 270
Zhengde, Emperor 53, 71–2
Zhengzhou 229, 230
Zhenzong, Song Emperor 18
Zhi Yin (propaganda film) 155
Zhihua (Wisdom Attained) Temple
    59, 201
Zhongnanhia gardens 165, 174,
    198, 273, 308
Zhongshan Park 82, 175
Zhou dynasty 240
Zhou Enlai 133, 184, 190, 204,
    206, 207, 210, 227, 249
Zhou Zuoren (brother of Lu Xun)
    202
Zhu Biao see Jianwen, Emperor
Zhu De 164
Zhu Di see Yong Le, Emperor
Zhu Lin (second wife of Liang
    Sicheng) 184, 185, 194–5
Zhu Rongji 285
Zhu Yuanzhang, (Hong Wu) (father
    of Yong Le) (The Pig) 33–4,
    55–6, 57, 75–6, 165, 168
    character 168, 246
    The Grand Monitions 34
Zhuang family 237